It's volume 28! Thanks for picking it up! My
family's cat passed away. For 21 years, it watched
over the Horikoshi household. This is the first
time I've really felt what it's like to have a hole
open up in my heart. Thank you for
everything, Maru-chan.

KOHEI HORIKOSHI

MY HERO ACADEMIA

28

SHONEN JUMP Manga Edition

STORY & ART KOHEI HORIKOSHI

TRANSLATION & ENGLISH ADAPTATION **Caleb Cook**
TOUCH-UP ART & LETTERING **John Hunt**
DESIGNER **Julian [JR] Robinson**
SHONEN JUMP SERIES EDITOR **John Bae**
GRAPHIC NOVEL EDITOR **Mike Montesa**

BOKU NO HERO ACADEMIA © 2014 by Kohei Horikoshi
All rights reserved.
First published in Japan in 2014 by SHUEISHA Inc., Tokyo.
English translation rights arranged by SHUEISHA Inc.

The stories, characters and incidents mentioned in this publication are entirely fictional.

Printed in the U.S.A.

Published by VIZ Media, LLC
P.O. Box 77010
San Francisco, CA 94107

10 9 8 7 6 5 4 3 2 1
First printing, June 2021

PARENTAL ADVISORY
MY HERO ACADEMIA is rated T for Teen
and is recommended for ages 13 and up.
This volume contains fantasy violence.

MY HERO ACADEMIA vol.28

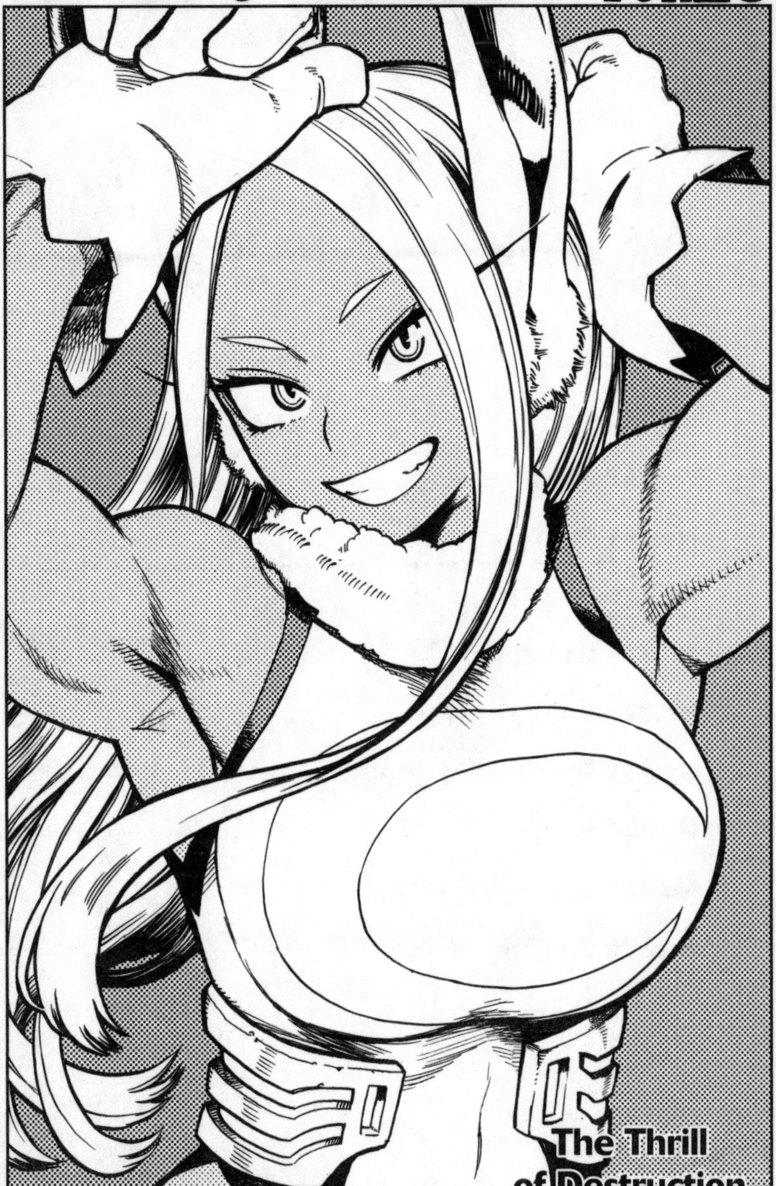
The Thrill
of Destruction

KOHEI HORIKOSHI

Vol. 28

MY HERO ACADEMIA

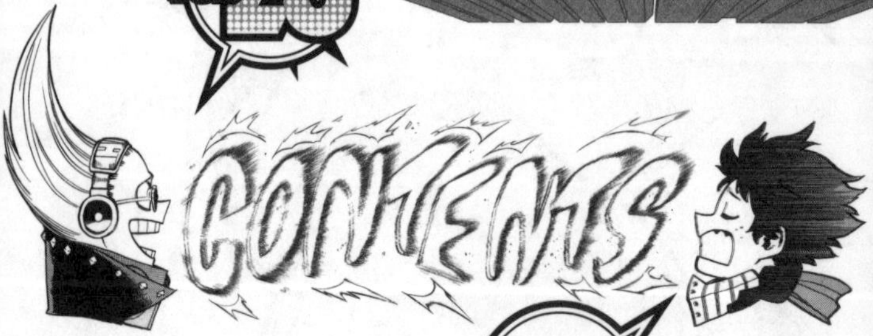
CONTENTS

The Thrill of Destruction

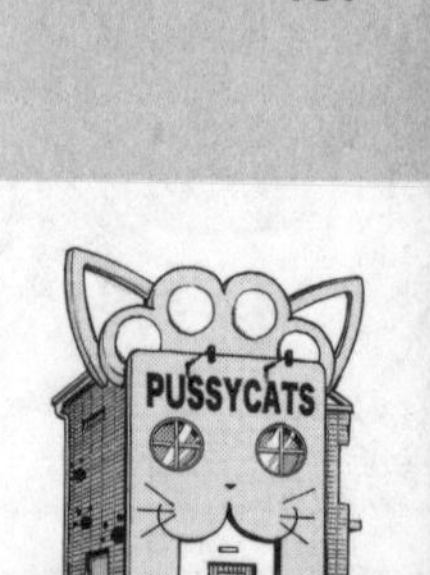
PUSSYCATS

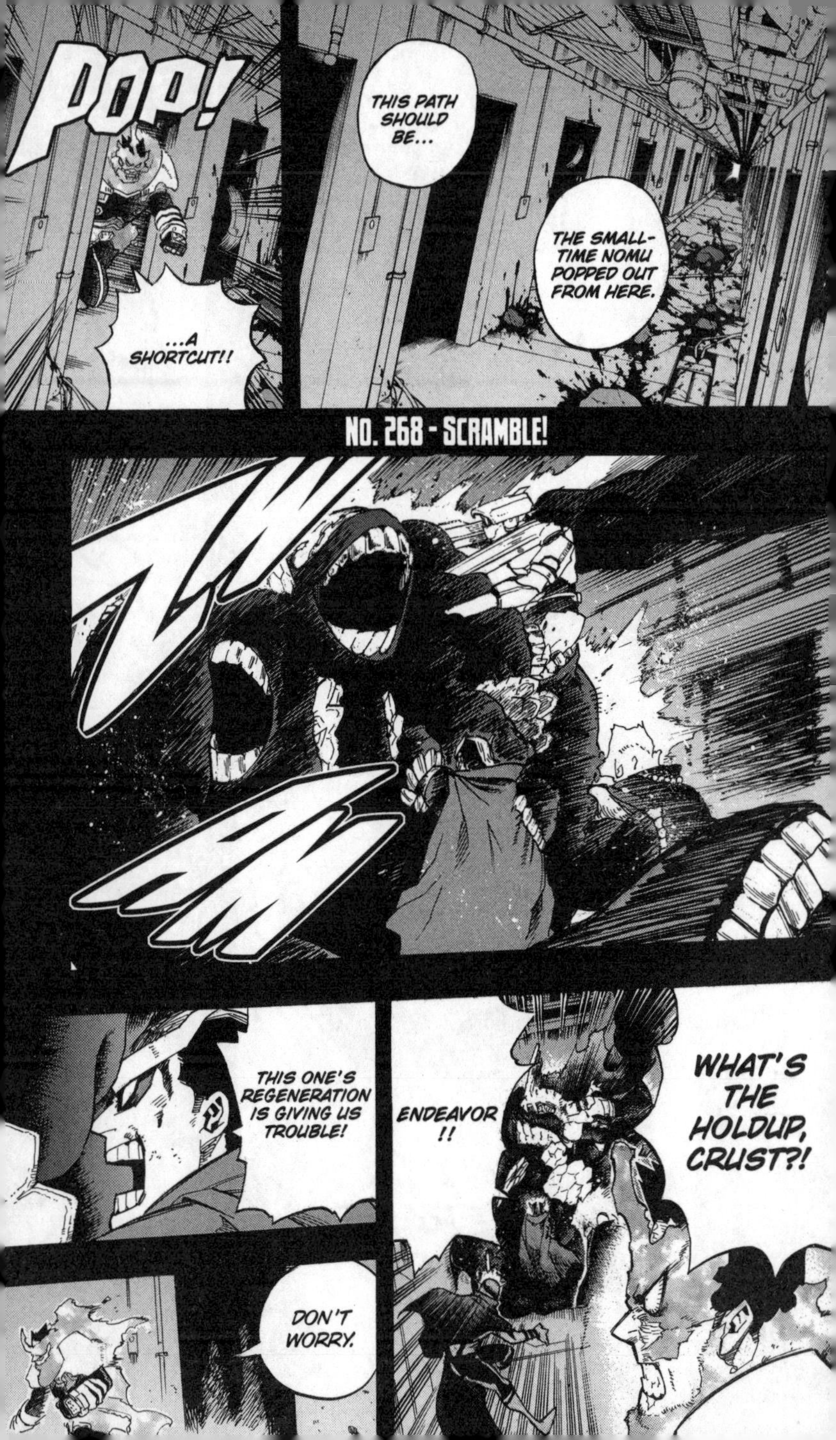
THIS PATH SHOULD BE...
THE SMALL-TIME NOMU POPPED OUT FROM HERE.
POP!
...A SHORTCUT!!
No. 268 - SCRAMBLE!
WHAT'S THE HOLDUP, CRUST?!
ENDEAVOR !!
THIS ONE'S REGENERATION IS GIVING US TROUBLE!
DON'T WORRY.

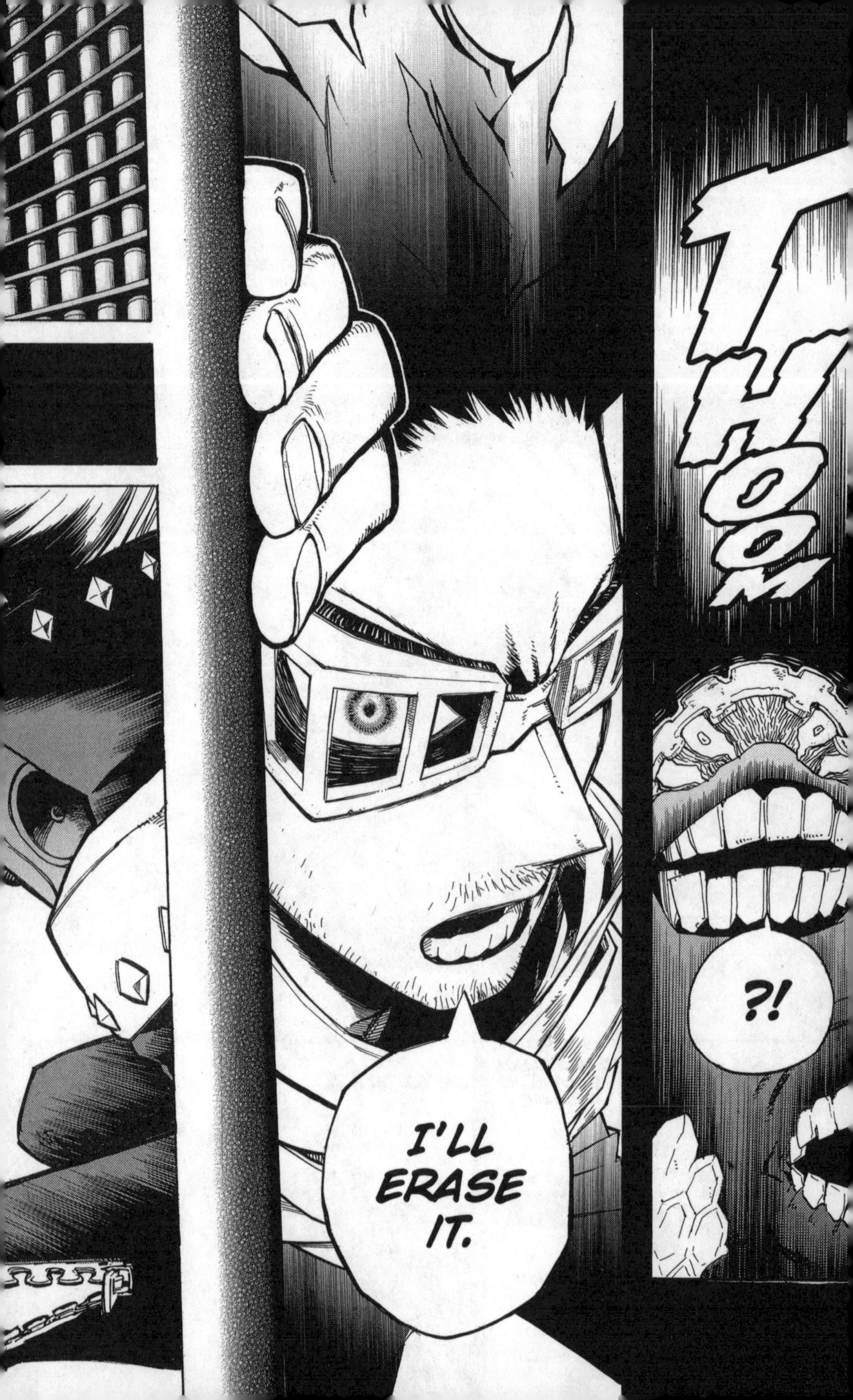
THOOM
?!
I'LL ERASE IT.

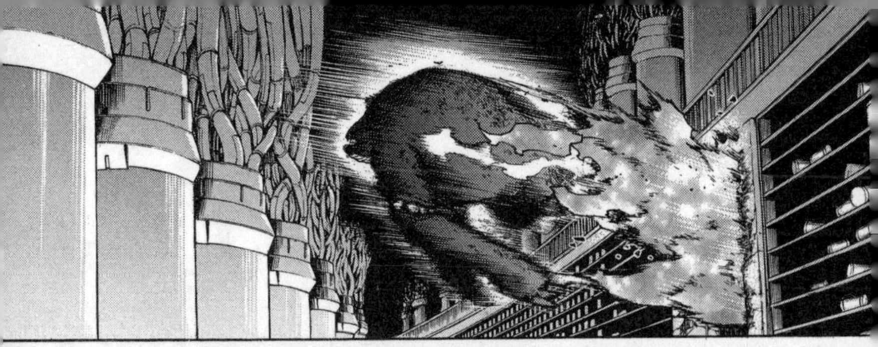

No. 268 - Scramble!

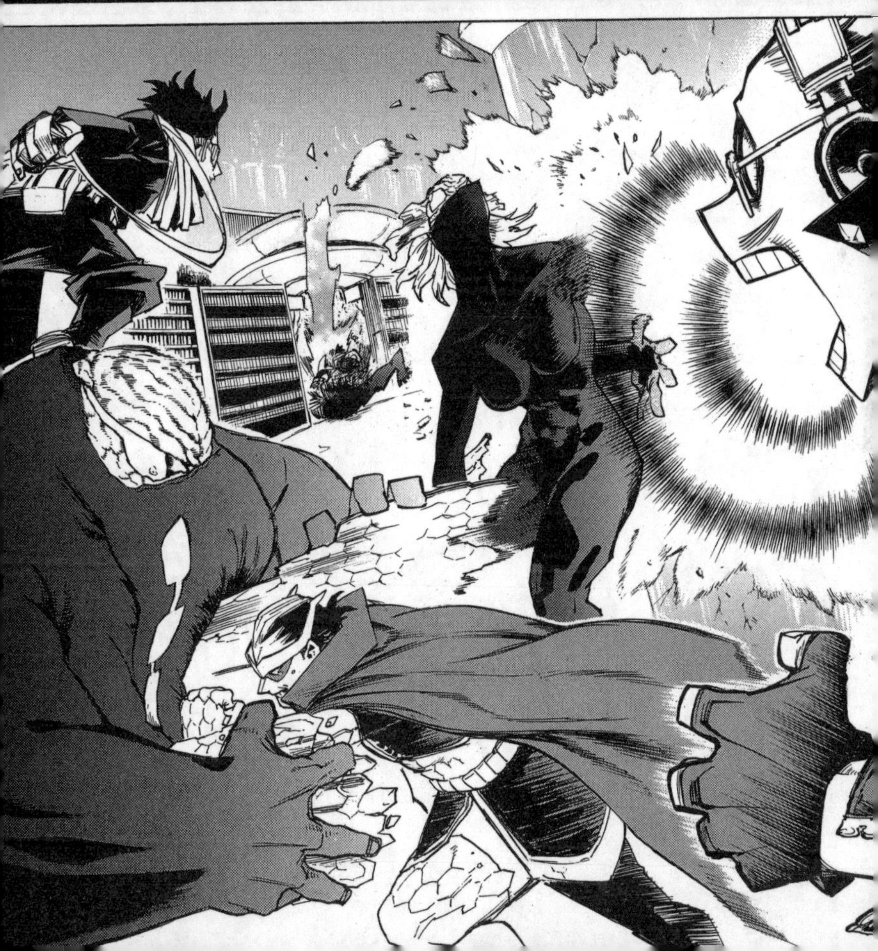

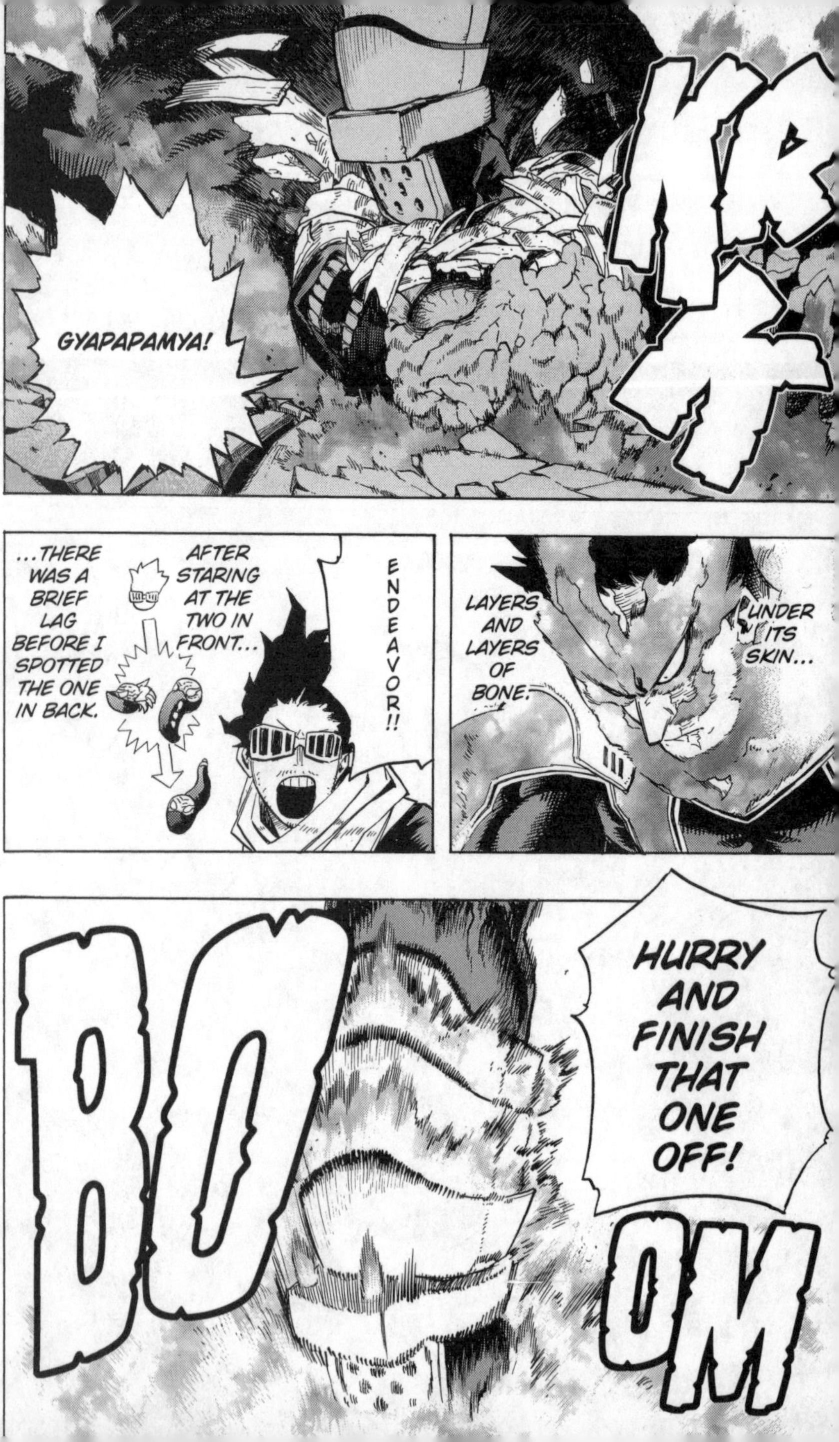
GYAPAPAMYA!
UNDER ITS SKIN...
LAYERS AND LAYERS OF BONE.
ENDEAVOR!!
AFTER STARING AT THE TWO IN FRONT...
...THERE WAS A BRIEF LAG BEFORE I SPOTTED THE ONE IN BACK.
HURRY AND FINISH THAT ONE OFF!
BOOM

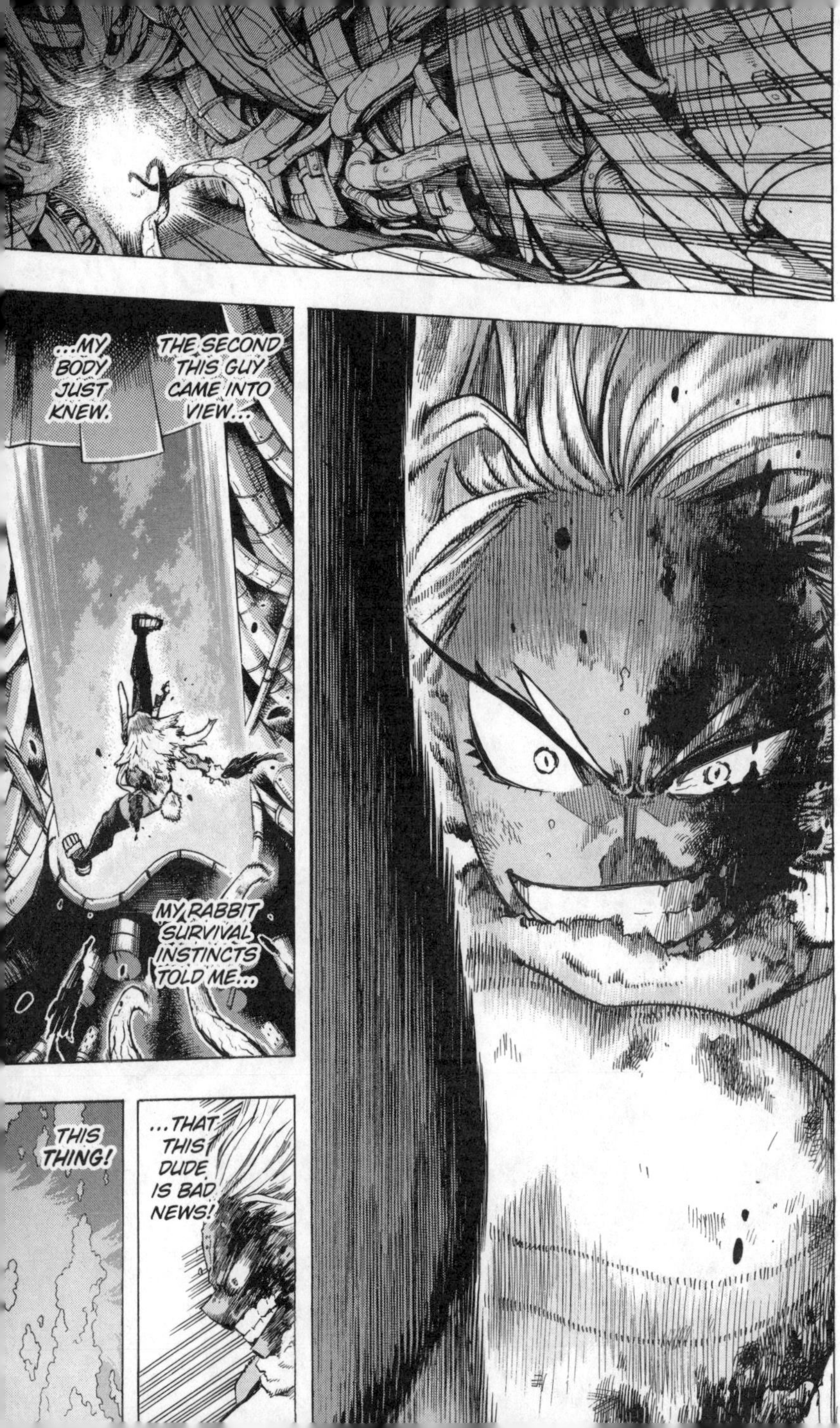
THE SECOND THIS GUY CAME INTO VIEW...
...MY BODY JUST KNEW.
MY RABBIT SURVIVAL INSTINCTS TOLD ME...
...THAT THIS DUDE IS BAD NEWS!
THIS THING!

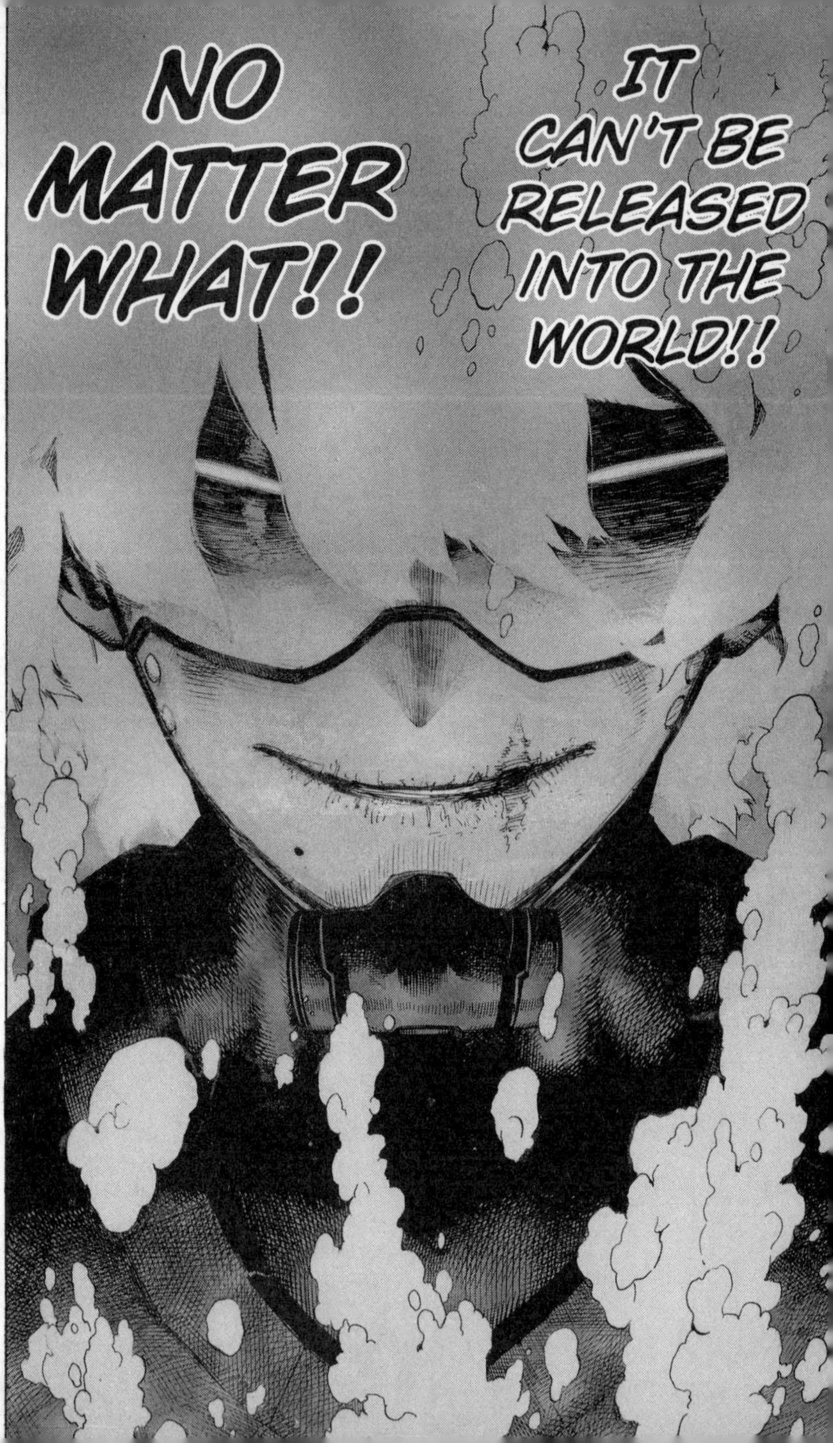
IT CAN'T BE RELEASED INTO THE WORLD!!
NO MATTER WHAT!!

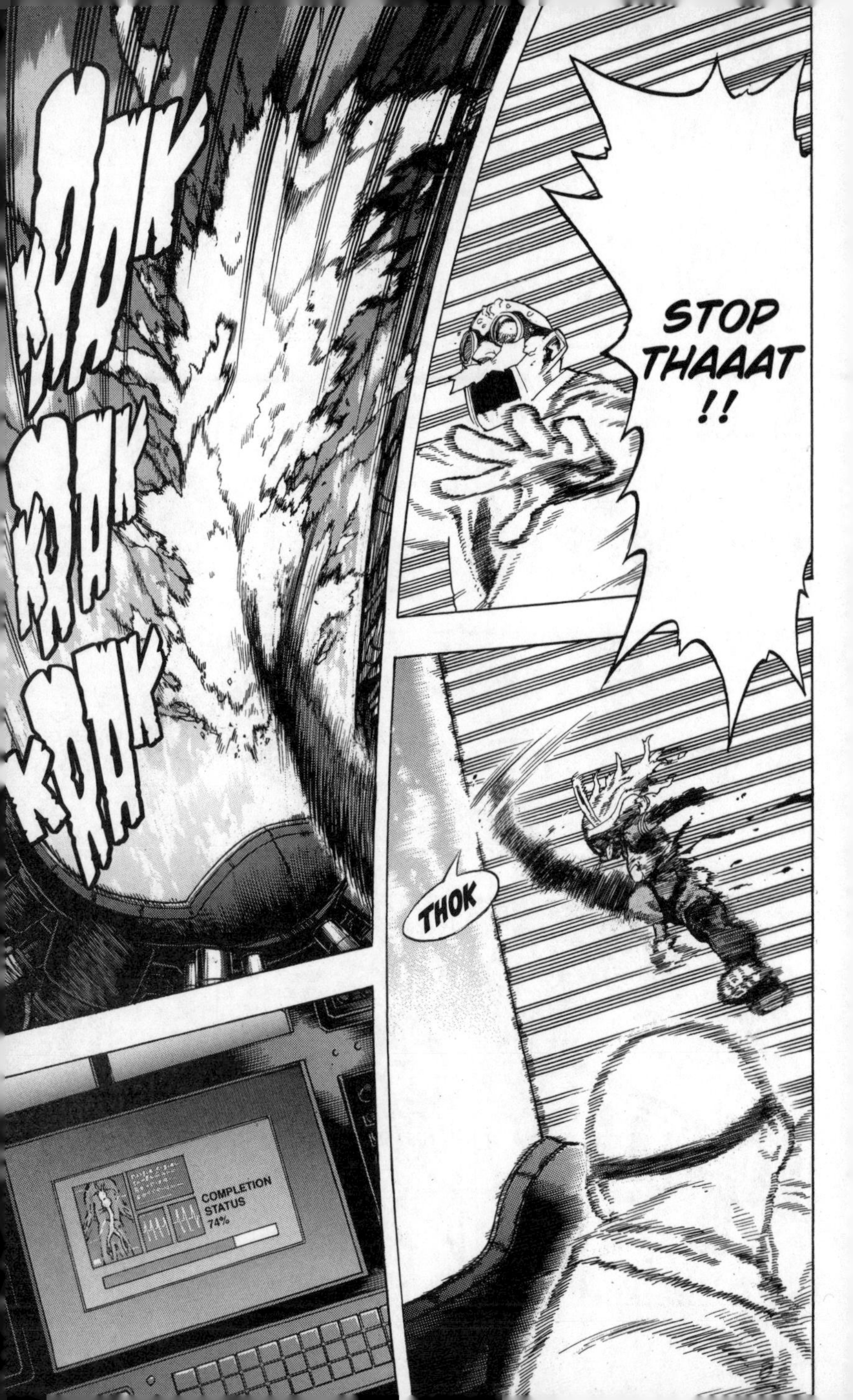
STOP THAAAT !!
THOK
KRAK
KRAK
KRAK
COMPLETION STATUS 74%

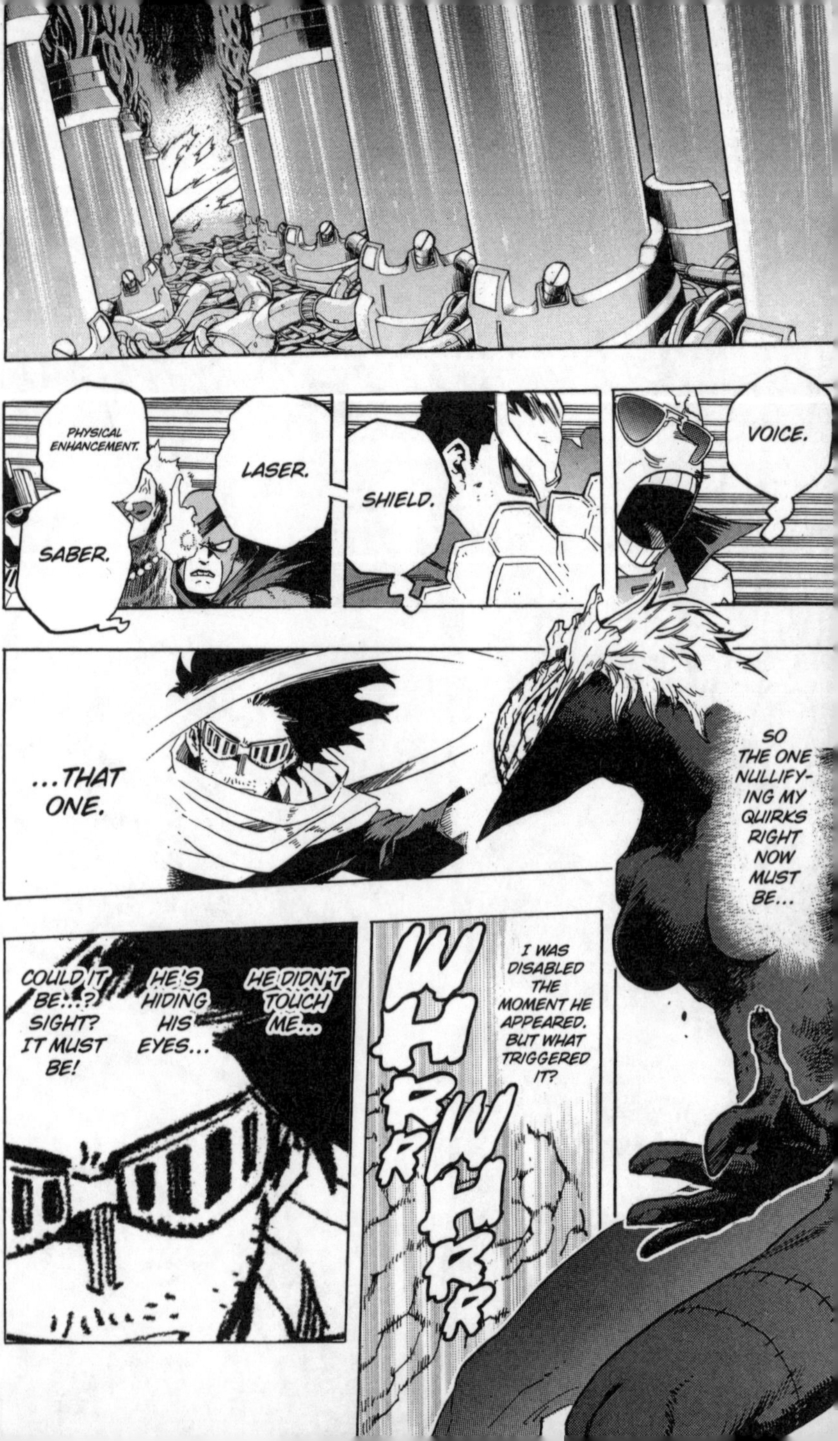
VOICE.
SHIELD.
LASER.
PHYSICAL ENHANCEMENT.
SABER.
SO THE ONE NULLIFYING MY QUIRKS RIGHT NOW MUST BE...
...THAT ONE.
I WAS DISABLED THE MOMENT HE APPEARED. BUT WHAT TRIGGERED IT?
WHRR
WHRR
HE DIDN'T TOUCH ME...
HE'S HIDING HIS EYES...
COULD IT BE...? SIGHT? IT MUST BE!

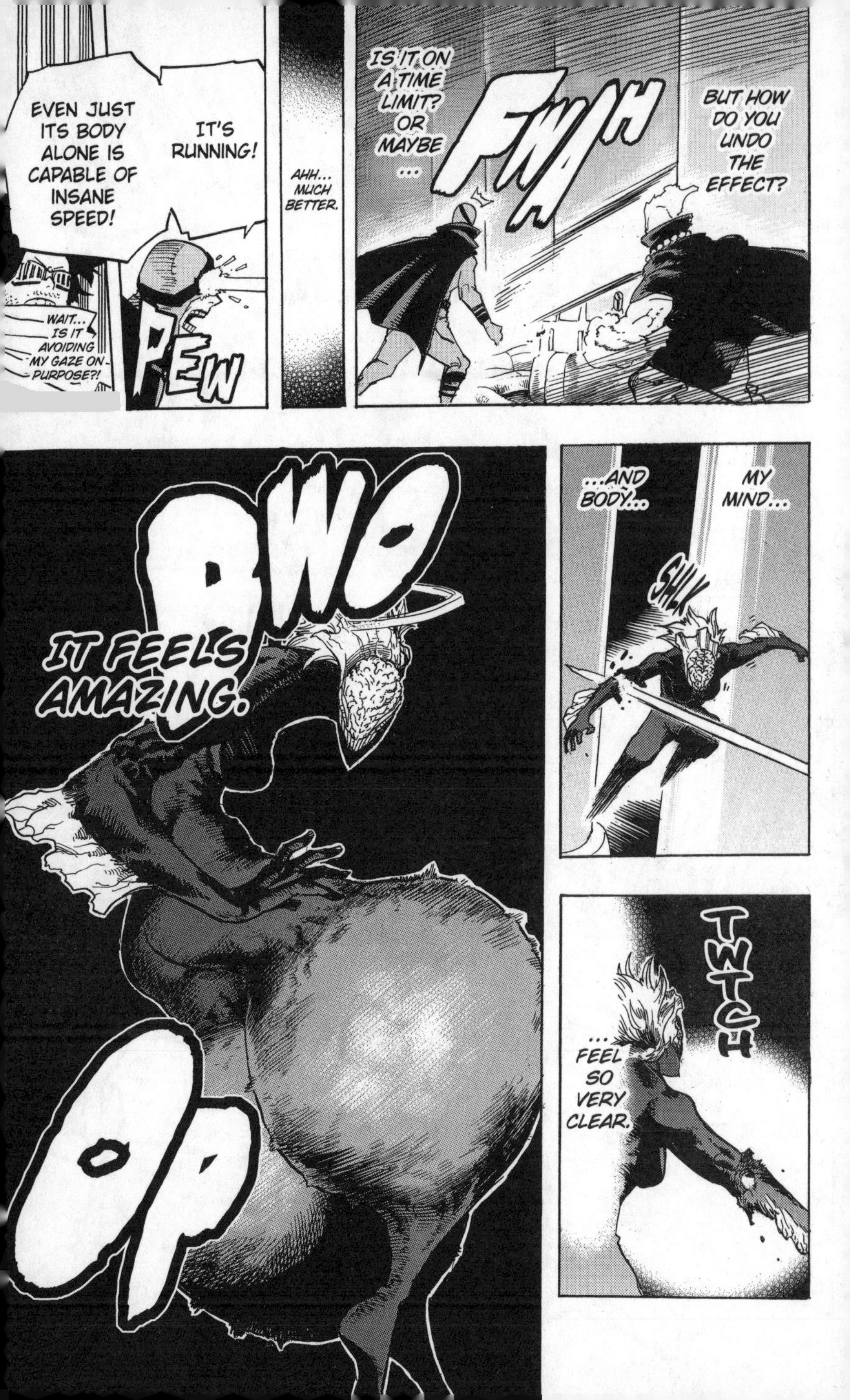
IS IT ON A TIME LIMIT? OR MAYBE ...
FWAH
BUT HOW DO YOU UNDO THE EFFECT?
AHH... MUCH BETTER.
IT'S RUNNING!
EVEN JUST ITS BODY ALONE IS CAPABLE OF INSANE SPEED!
PEW
WAIT... IS IT AVOIDING MY GAZE ON PURPOSE?!
MY MIND...
...AND BODY...
SHLK
TWITCH
...FEEL SO VERY CLEAR.
BWO
OP
IT FEELS AMAZING.

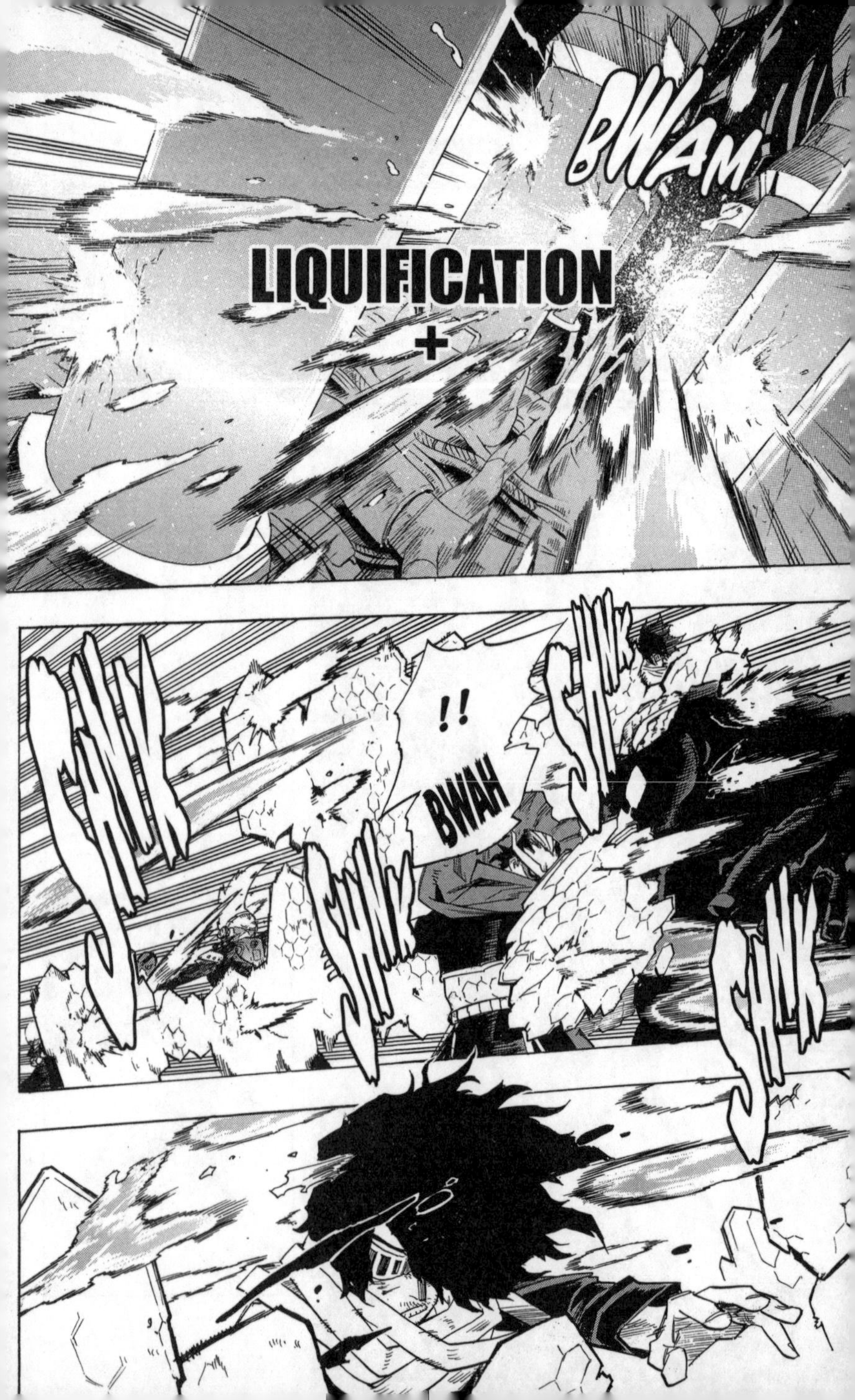
BWAM
LIQUIFICATION
+
SHINK
!!
BWAH
SHINK
SHINK
SHINK

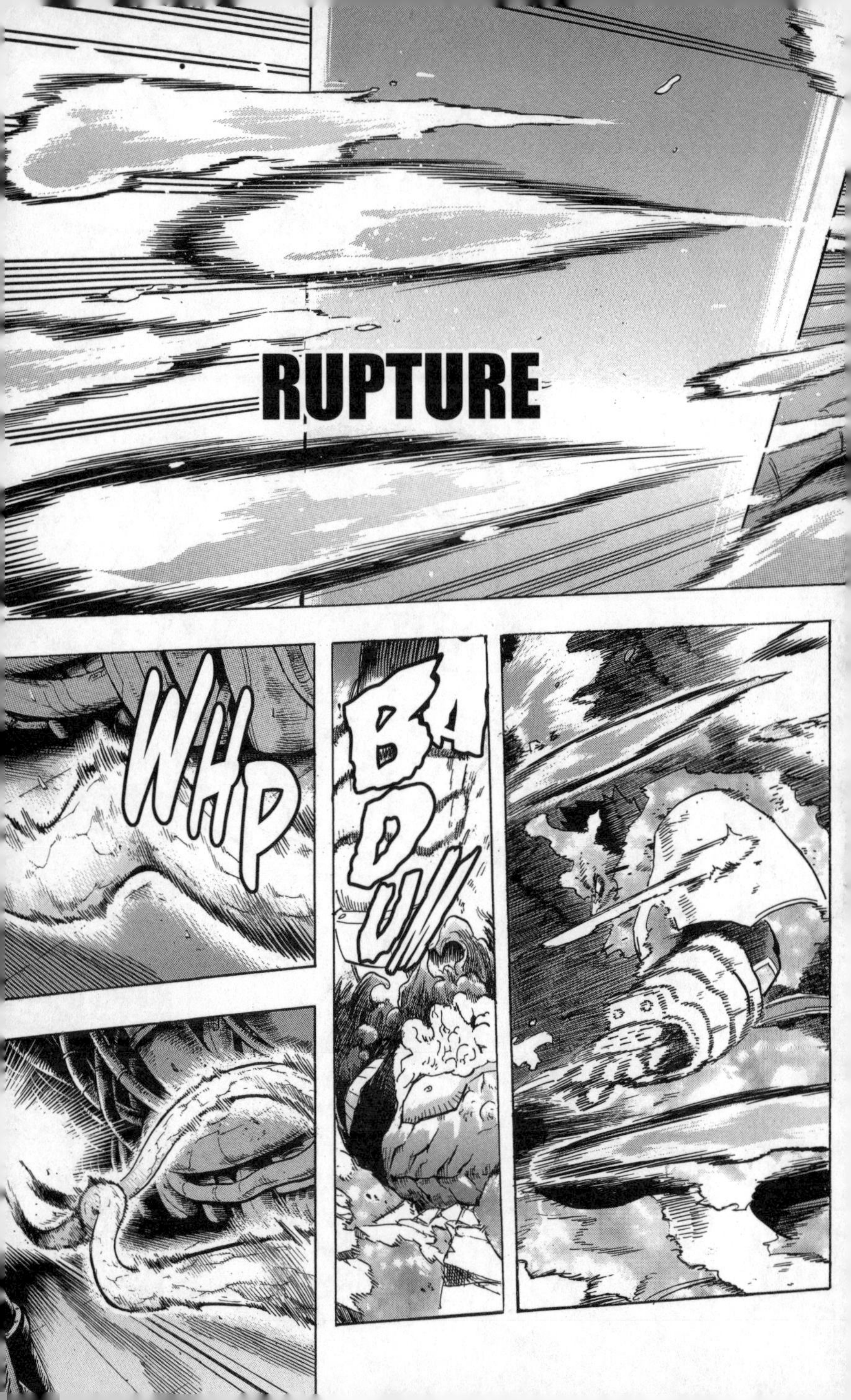
RUPTURE
BA
DU
WHIP

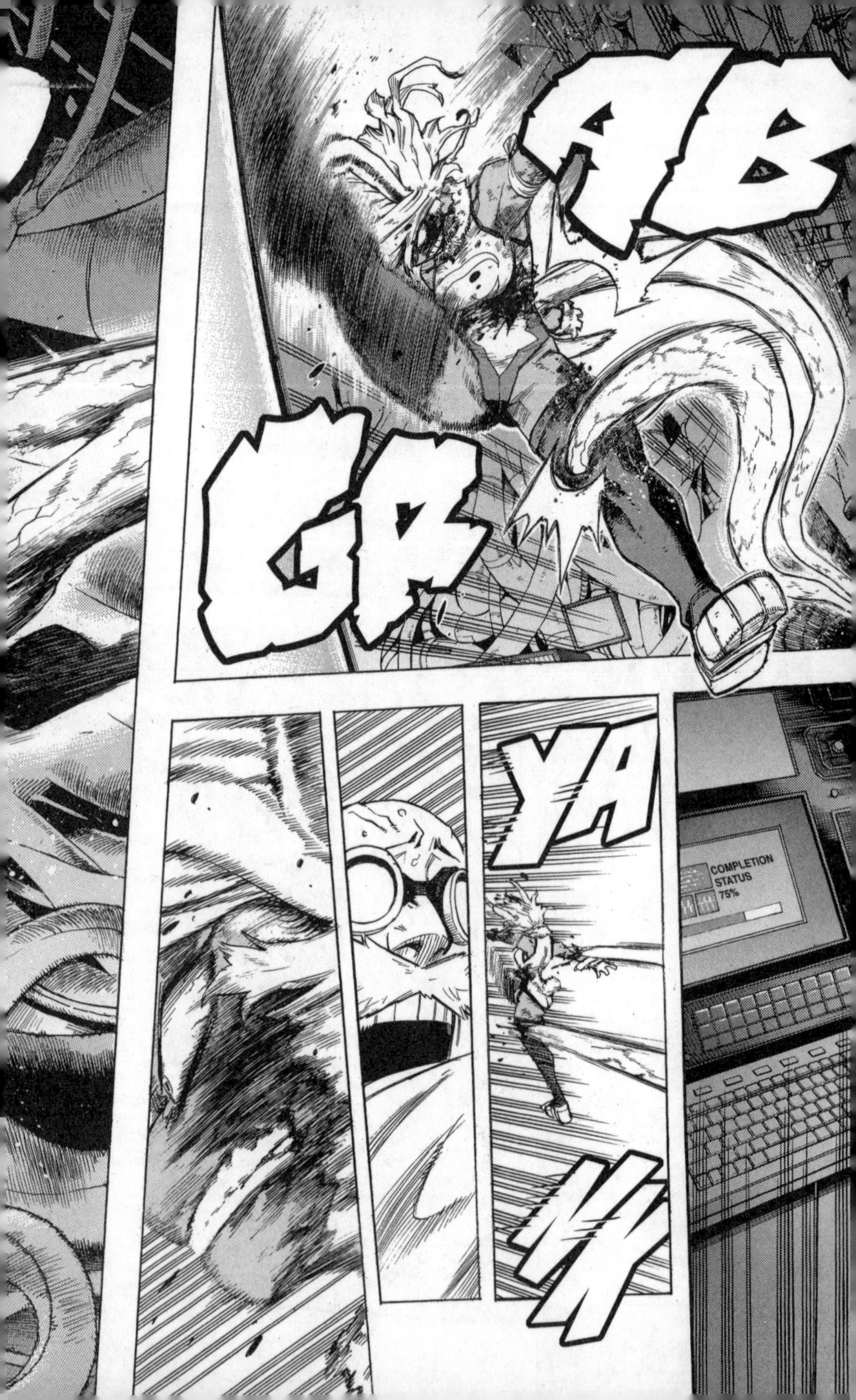
GRAB
COMPLETION
STATUS
75%
YANK

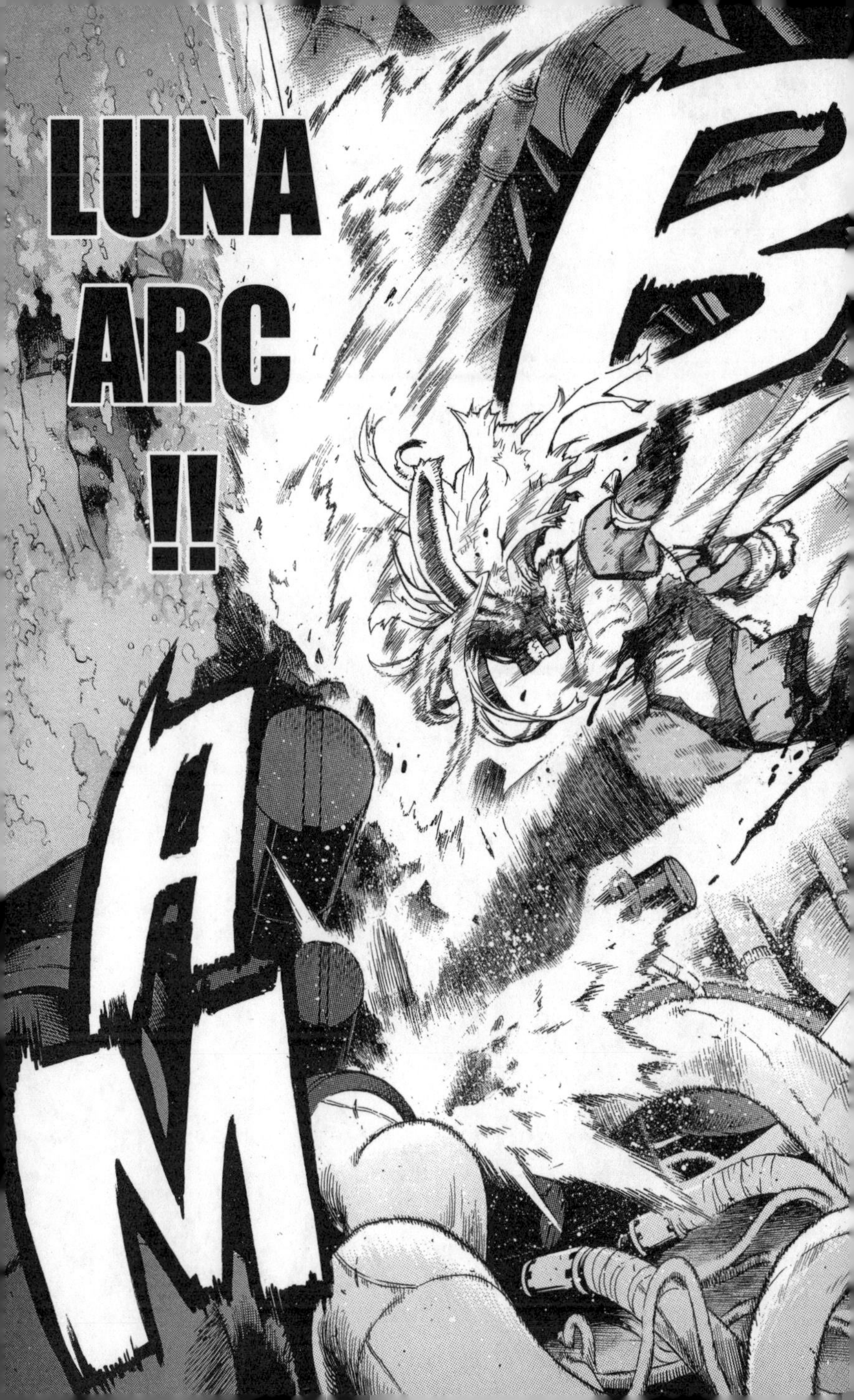
LUNA ARC!!

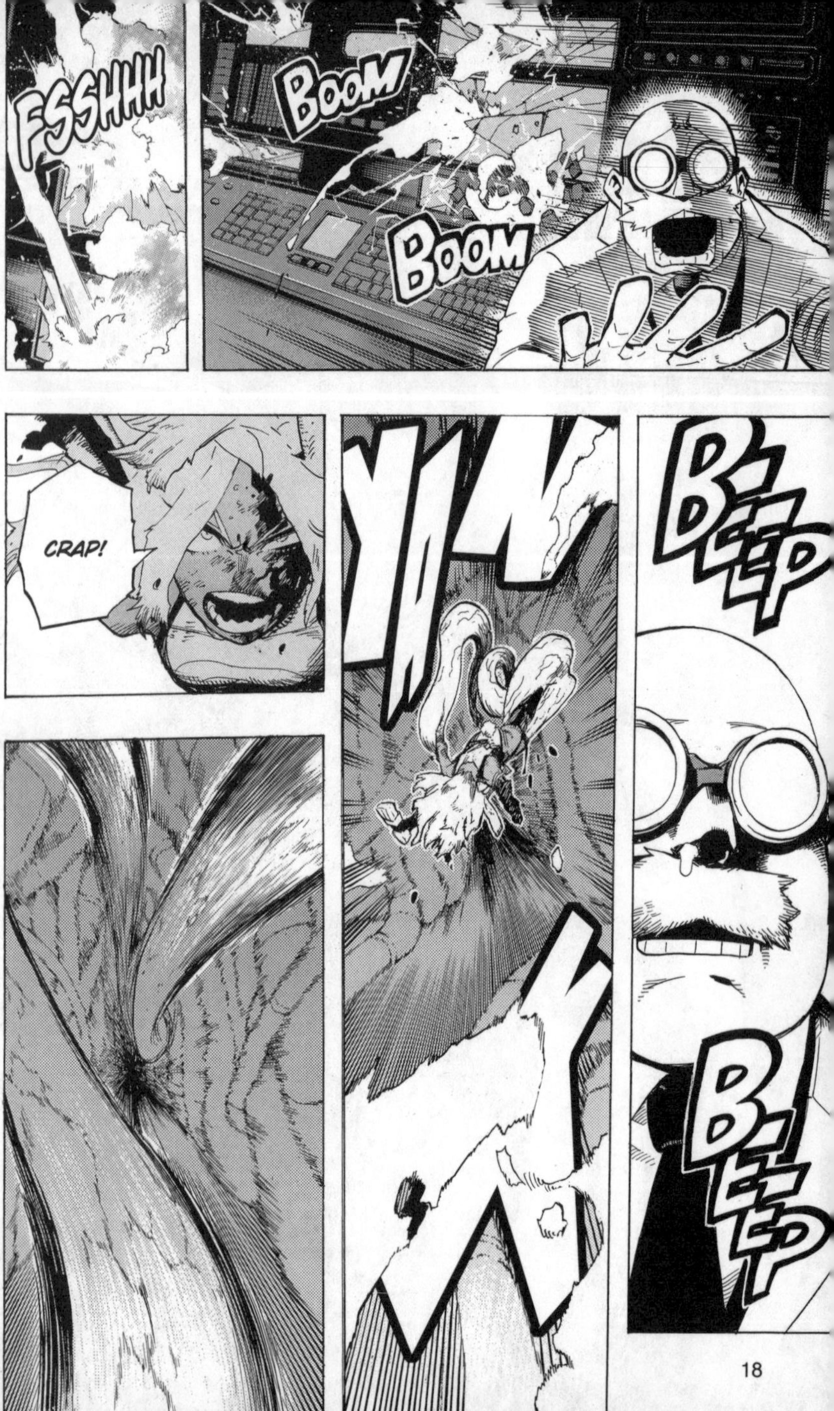
BOOM
BOOM
FSSHHH
BEEP
BEEP
CRAP!

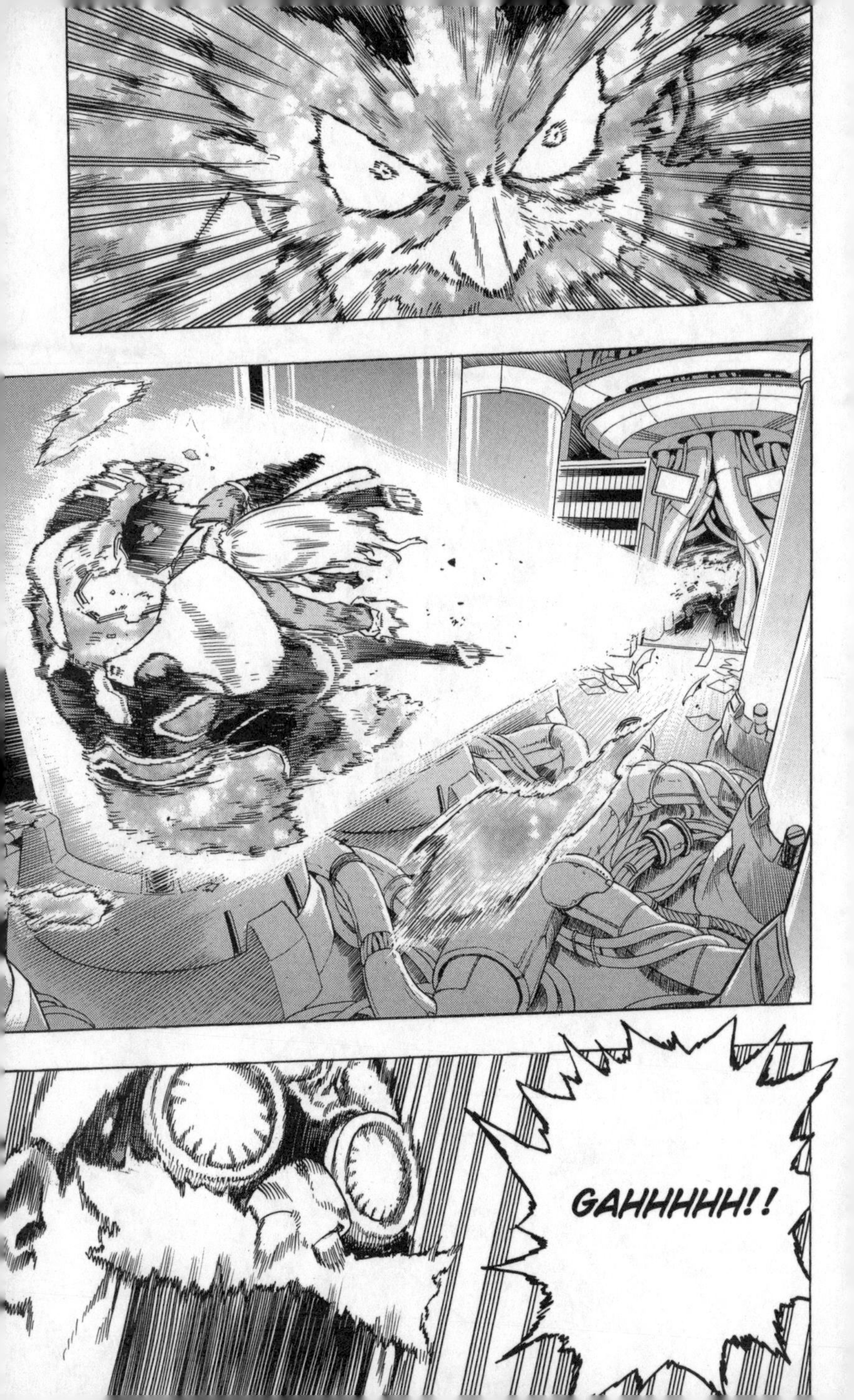
GAHHHHH!!

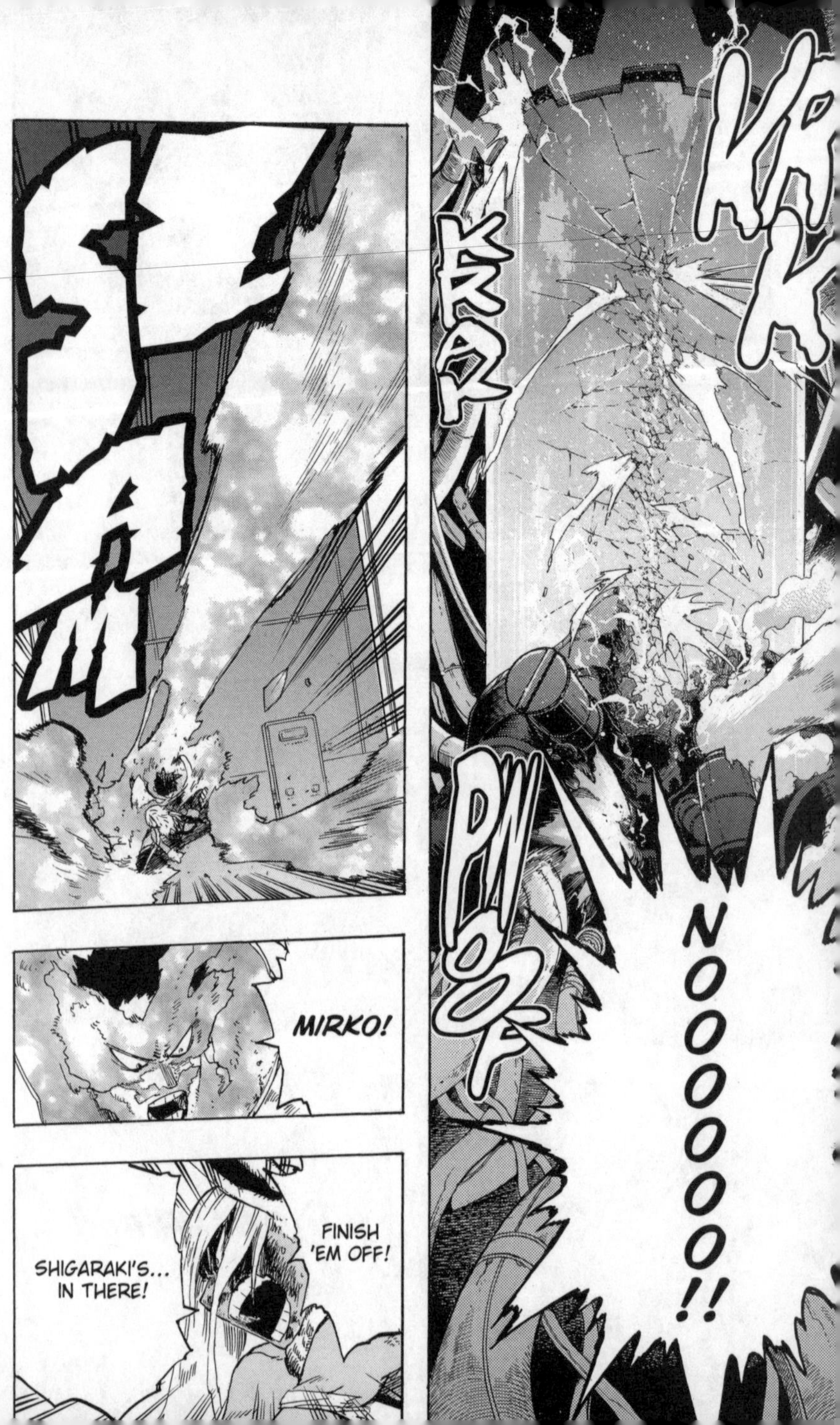
KRAK
PWOOF
NOOOOOOOO!!
SLAM
MIRKO!
FINISH 'EM OFF!
SHIGARAKI'S... IN THERE!

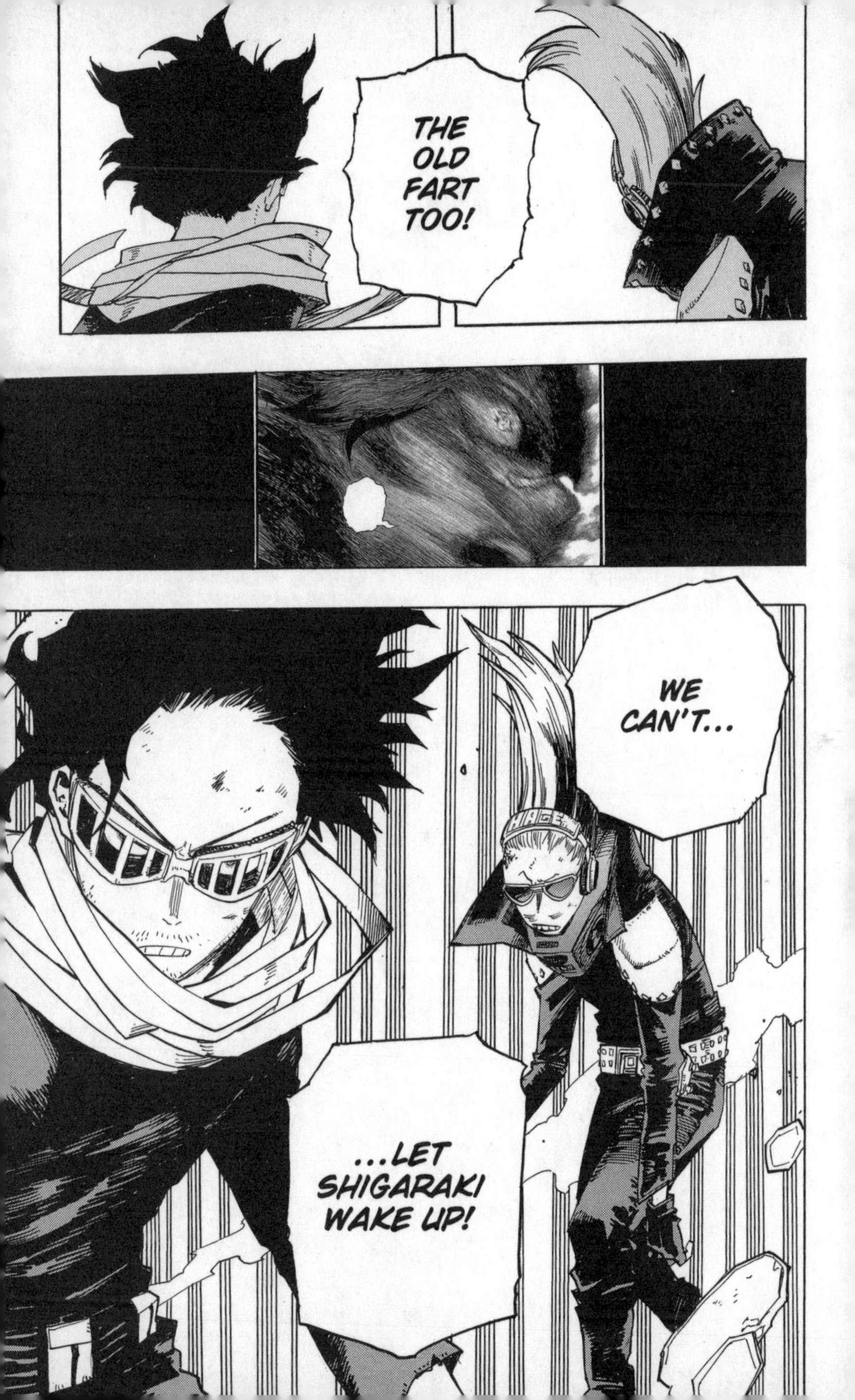
THE OLD FART TOO!
WE CAN'T...
...LET SHIGARAKI WAKE UP!

THE COVER ART

When I showed my family the cover of this volume, they all said, "Aizawa looks like Deku there." Maybe Aizawa really is Deku, huh? Too spooky.

What it actually is, is Aizawa being lit up by Deku's sheer luminescence.

MHA sure has a lot of primarily red covers. Whatever, it's fine.

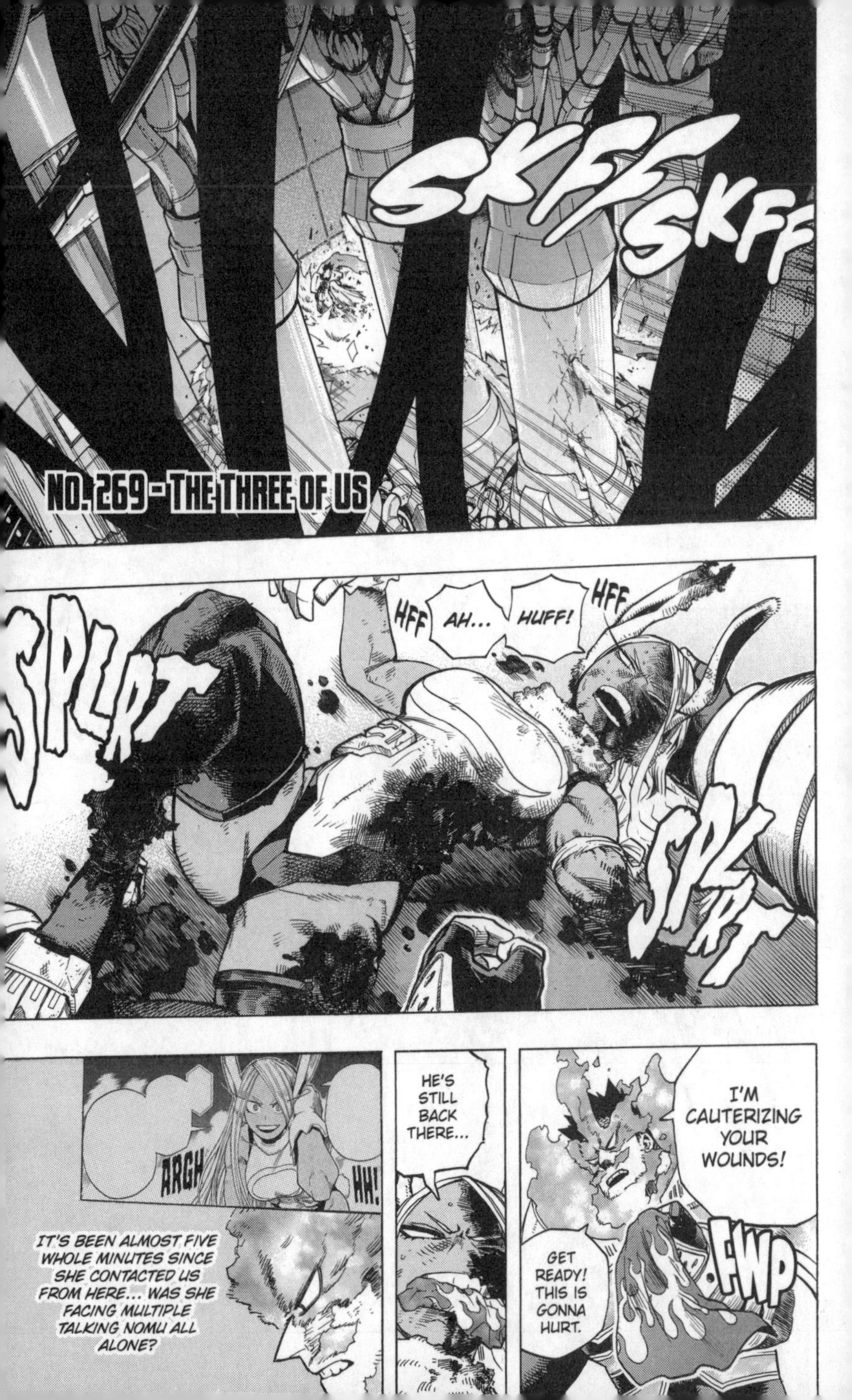
SKFF
SKFF
NO. 269 - THE THREE OF US
SPLRT
HFF
HUFF!
AH...
HFF
SPLRT
I'M CAUTERIZING YOUR WOUNDS!
GET READY! THIS IS GONNA HURT.
FWP
HE'S STILL BACK THERE...
ARGH
HH!
IT'S BEEN ALMOST FIVE WHOLE MINUTES SINCE SHE CONTACTED US FROM HERE... WAS SHE FACING MULTIPLE TALKING NOMU ALL ALONE?

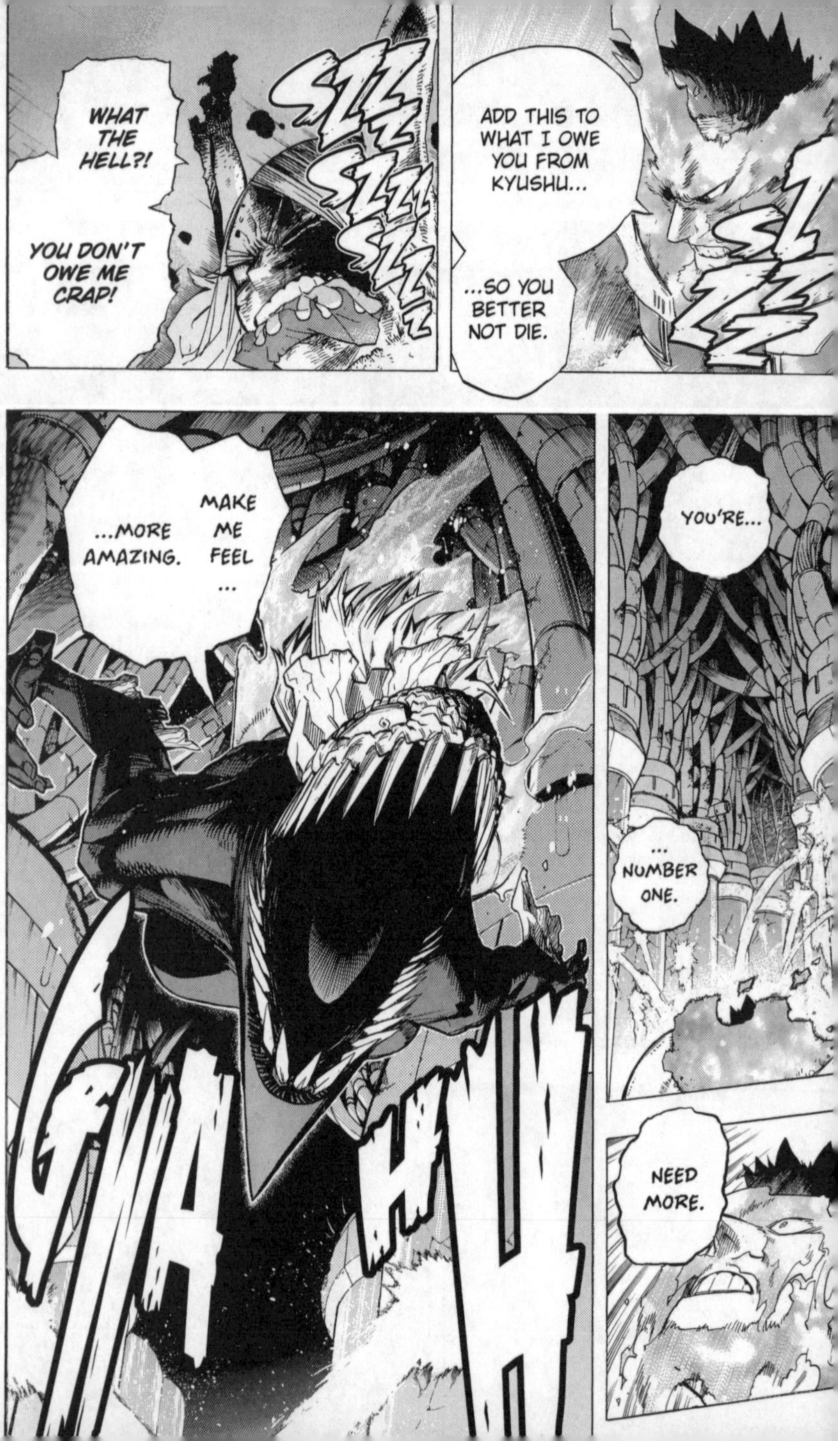

ADD THIS TO WHAT I OWE YOU FROM KYUSHU...
...SO YOU BETTER NOT DIE.
SIZZZ
WHAT THE HELL?!
SIZZZ SIZZZ SIZZZ
YOU DON'T OWE ME CRAP!
YOU'RE...
...NUMBER ONE.
NEED MORE.
MAKE ME FEEL ...
...MORE AMAZING.

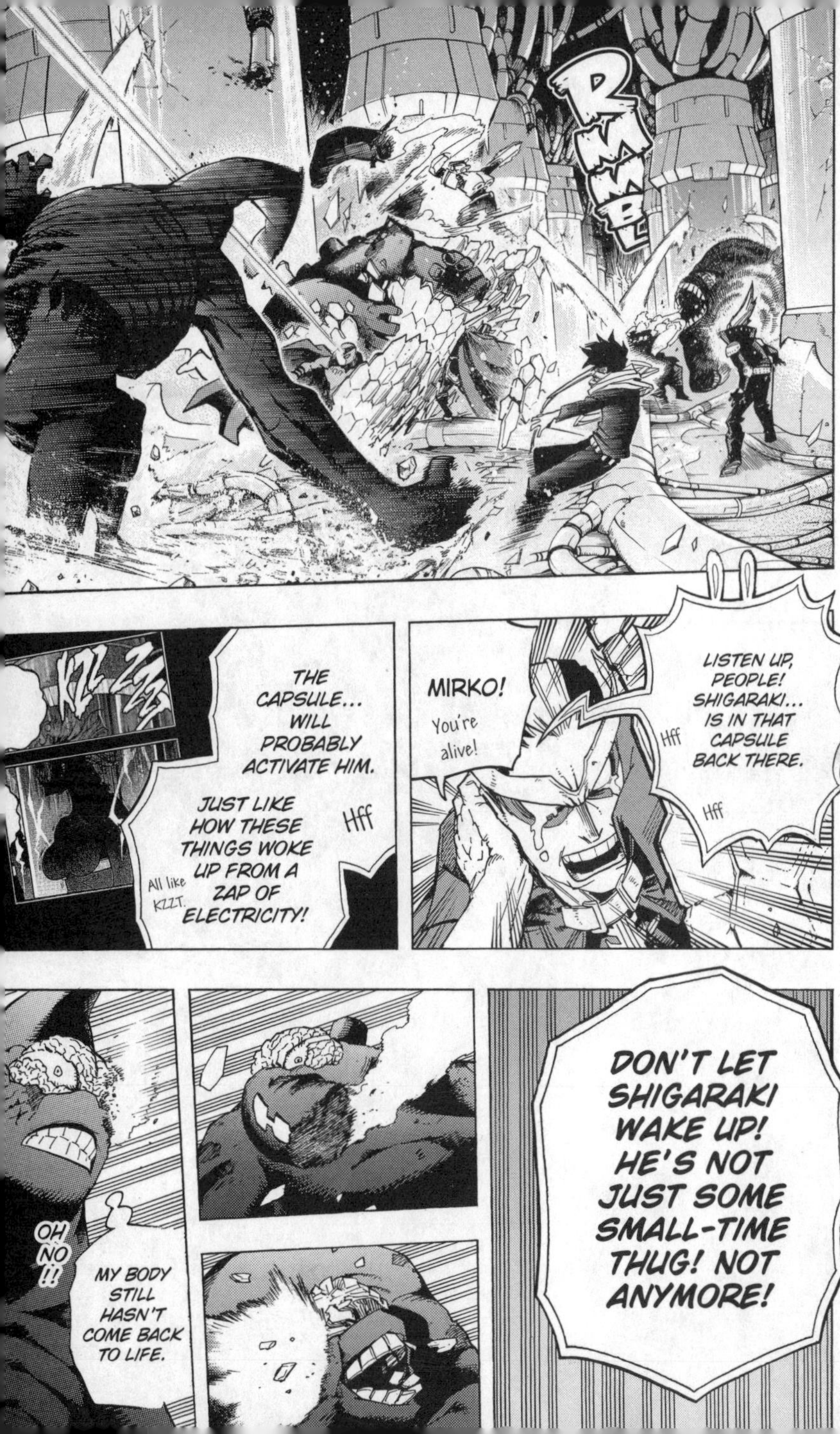
RMMBL
LISTEN UP, PEOPLE! SHIGARAKI... IS IN THAT CAPSULE BACK THERE.
Hff
Hff
MIRKO!
You're alive!
THE CAPSULE... WILL PROBABLY ACTIVATE HIM.
Hff
JUST LIKE HOW THESE THINGS WOKE UP FROM A ZAP OF ELECTRICITY!
All like KZZT.
KZZ ZZZ
DON'T LET SHIGARAKI WAKE UP! HE'S NOT JUST SOME SMALL-TIME THUG! NOT ANYMORE!
OH NO!!
MY BODY STILL HASN'T COME BACK TO LIFE.

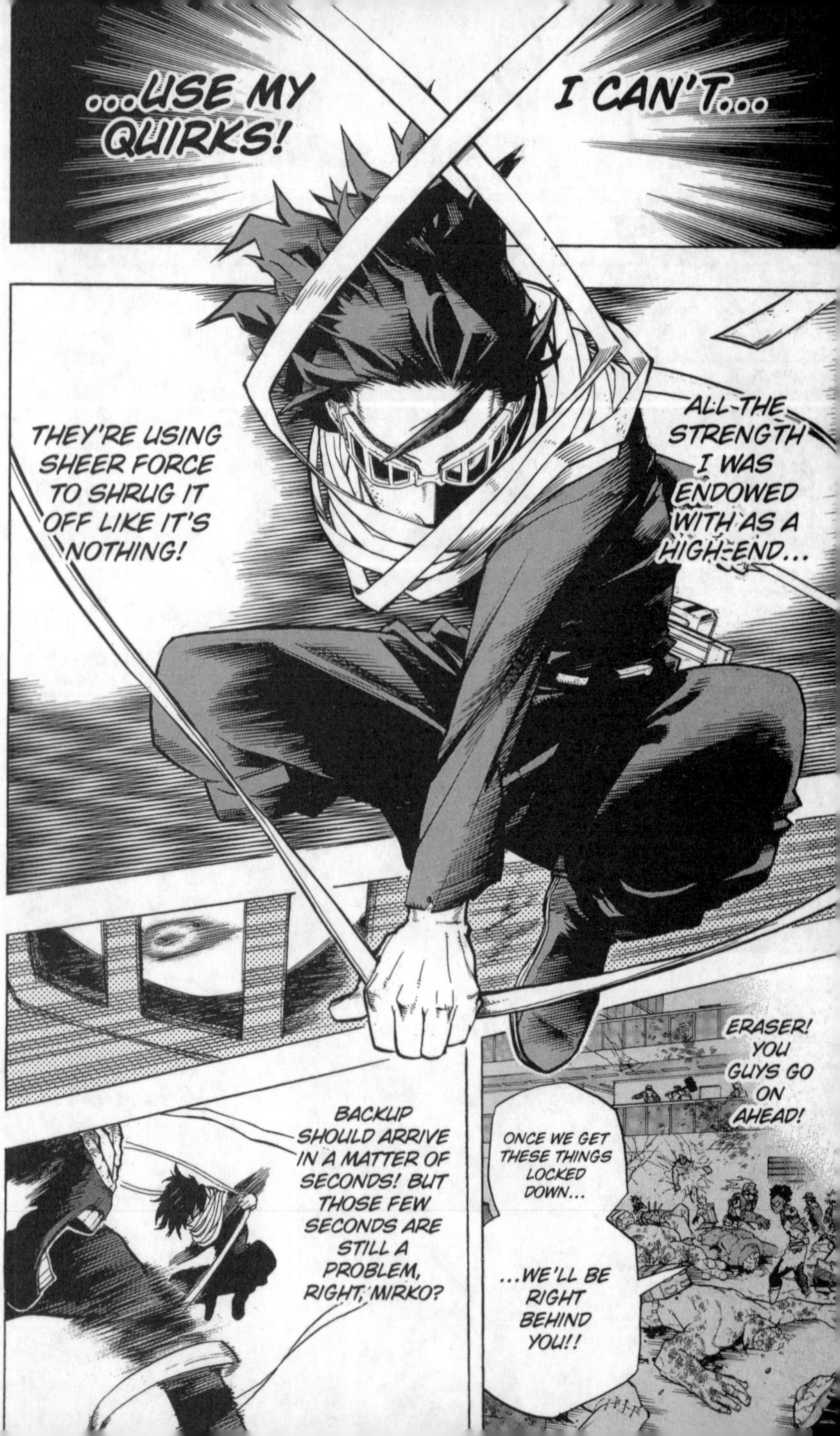
I CAN'T...
...USE MY QUIRKS!
ALL-THE STRENGTH I WAS ENDOWED WITH AS A HIGH-END...
THEY'RE USING SHEER FORCE TO SHRUG IT OFF LIKE IT'S NOTHING!
ERASER! YOU GUYS GO ON AHEAD!
ONCE WE GET THESE THINGS LOCKED DOWN...
...WE'LL BE RIGHT BEHIND YOU!!
BACKUP SHOULD ARRIVE IN A MATTER OF SECONDS! BUT THOSE FEW SECONDS ARE STILL A PROBLEM, RIGHT, MIRKO?

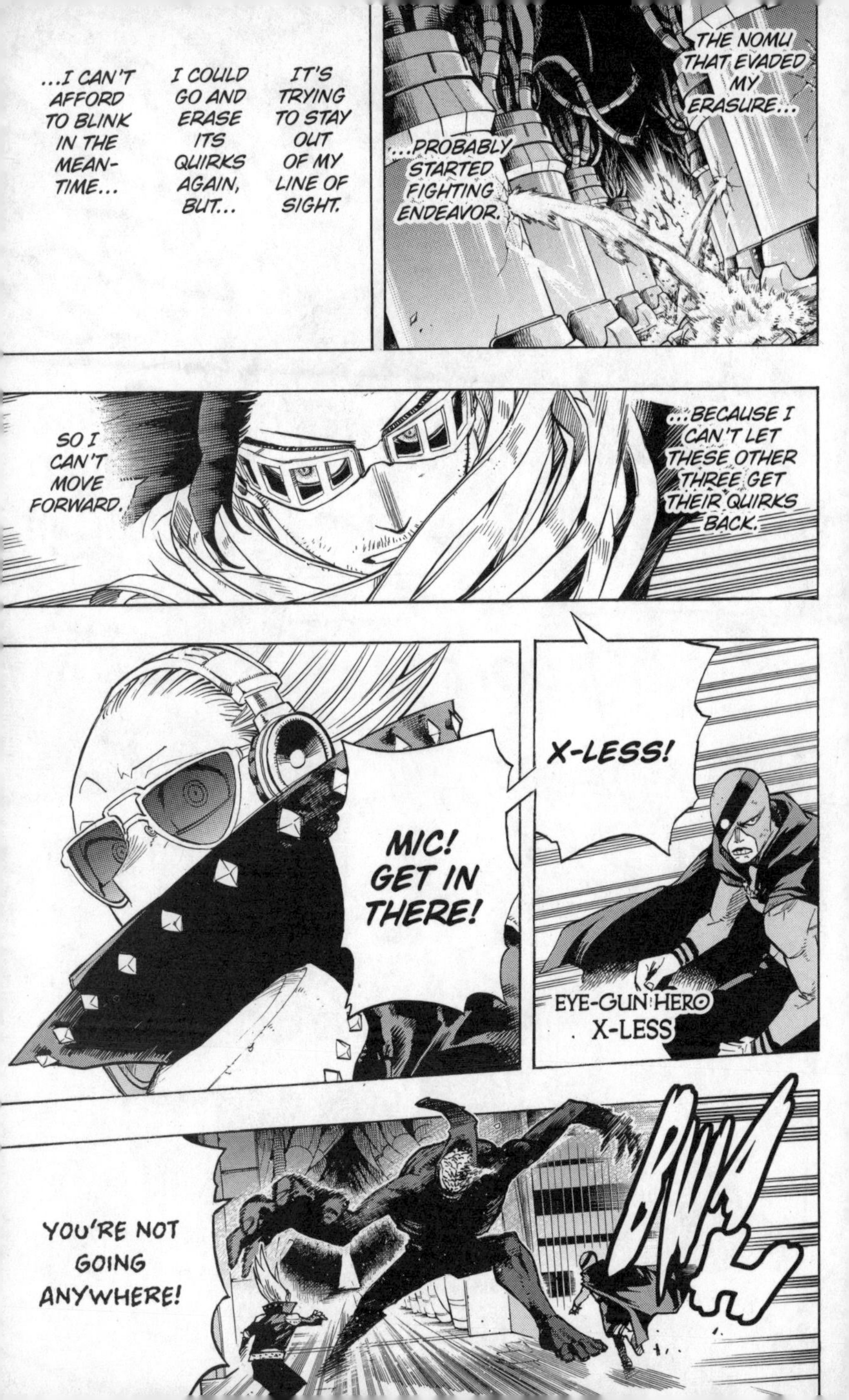
THE NOMU THAT EVADED MY ERASURE...
...PROBABLY STARTED FIGHTING ENDEAVOR.
IT'S TRYING TO STAY OUT OF MY LINE OF SIGHT.
I COULD GO AND ERASE ITS QUIRKS AGAIN, BUT...
...I CAN'T AFFORD TO BLINK IN THE MEANTIME...
...BECAUSE I CAN'T LET THESE OTHER THREE GET THEIR QUIRKS BACK.
SO I CAN'T MOVE FORWARD.
X-LESS!
EYE-GUN HERO X-LESS
MIC! GET IN THERE!
YOU'RE NOT GOING ANYWHERE!

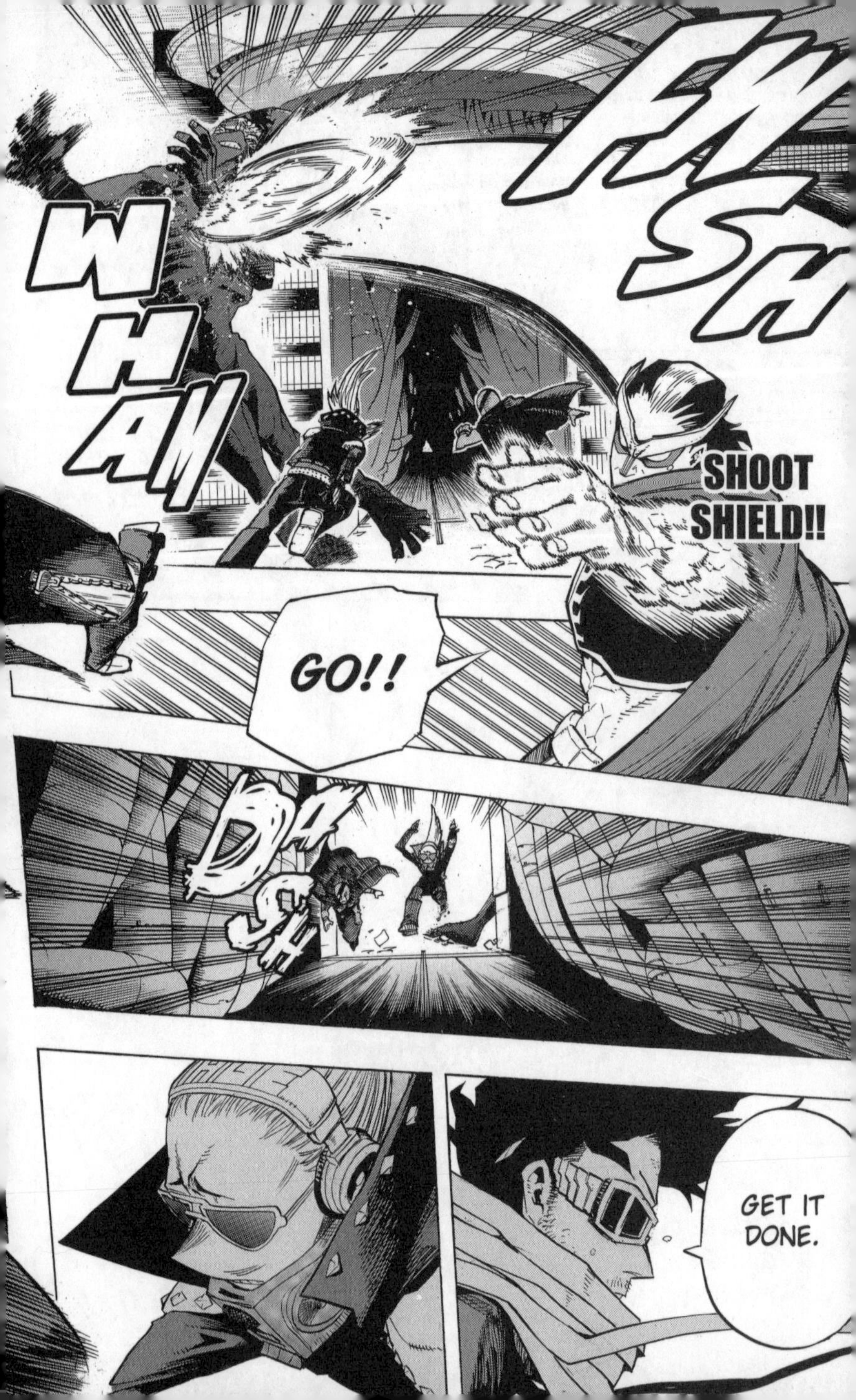
SHOOT SHIELD!!
WHAM
GO!!
DASH
GET IT DONE.

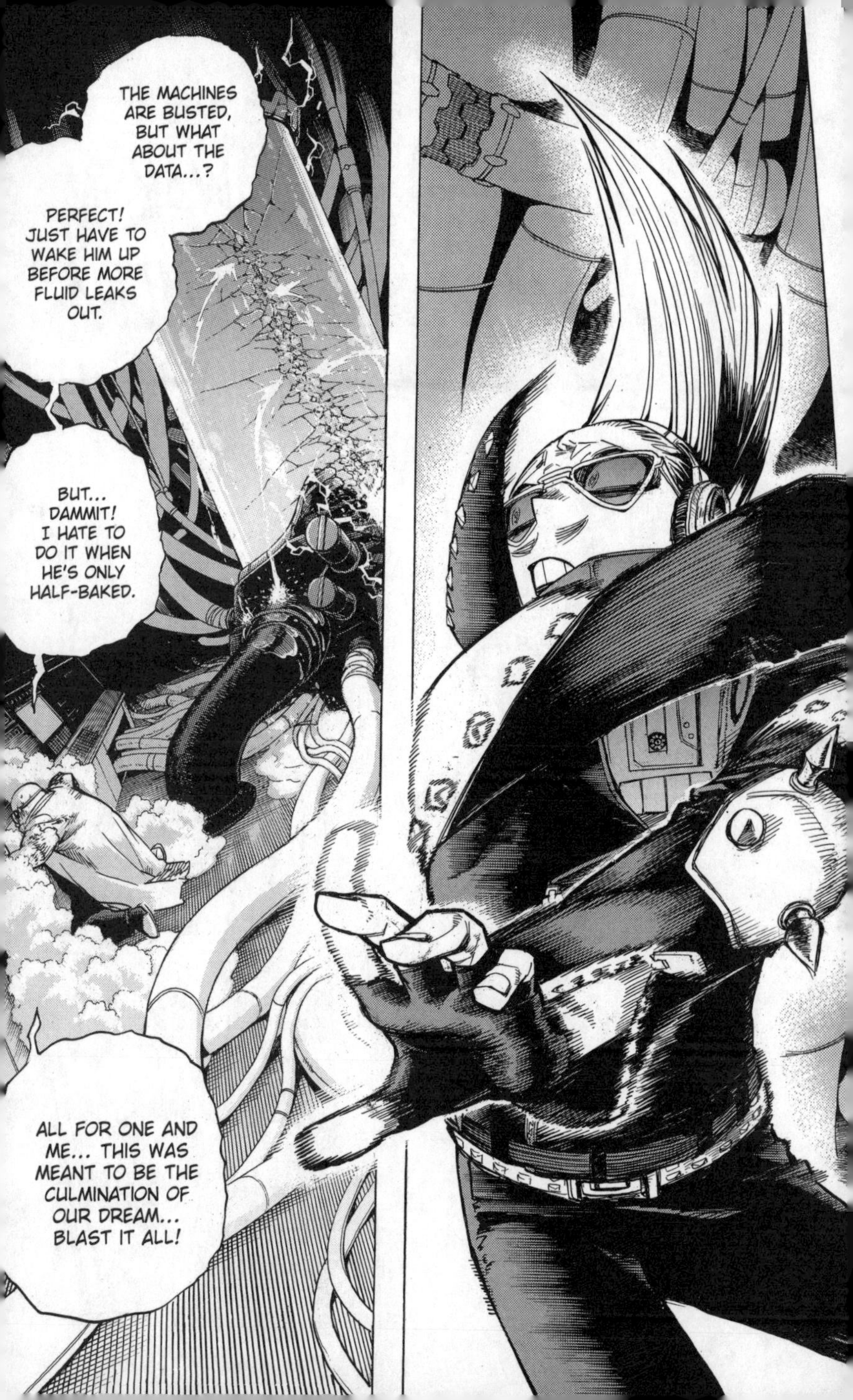
THE MACHINES ARE BUSTED, BUT WHAT ABOUT THE DATA...?
PERFECT! JUST HAVE TO WAKE HIM UP BEFORE MORE FLUID LEAKS OUT.
BUT... DAMMIT! I HATE TO DO IT WHEN HE'S ONLY HALF-BAKED.
ALL FOR ONE AND ME... THIS WAS MEANT TO BE THE CULMINATION OF OUR DREAM... BLAST IT ALL!

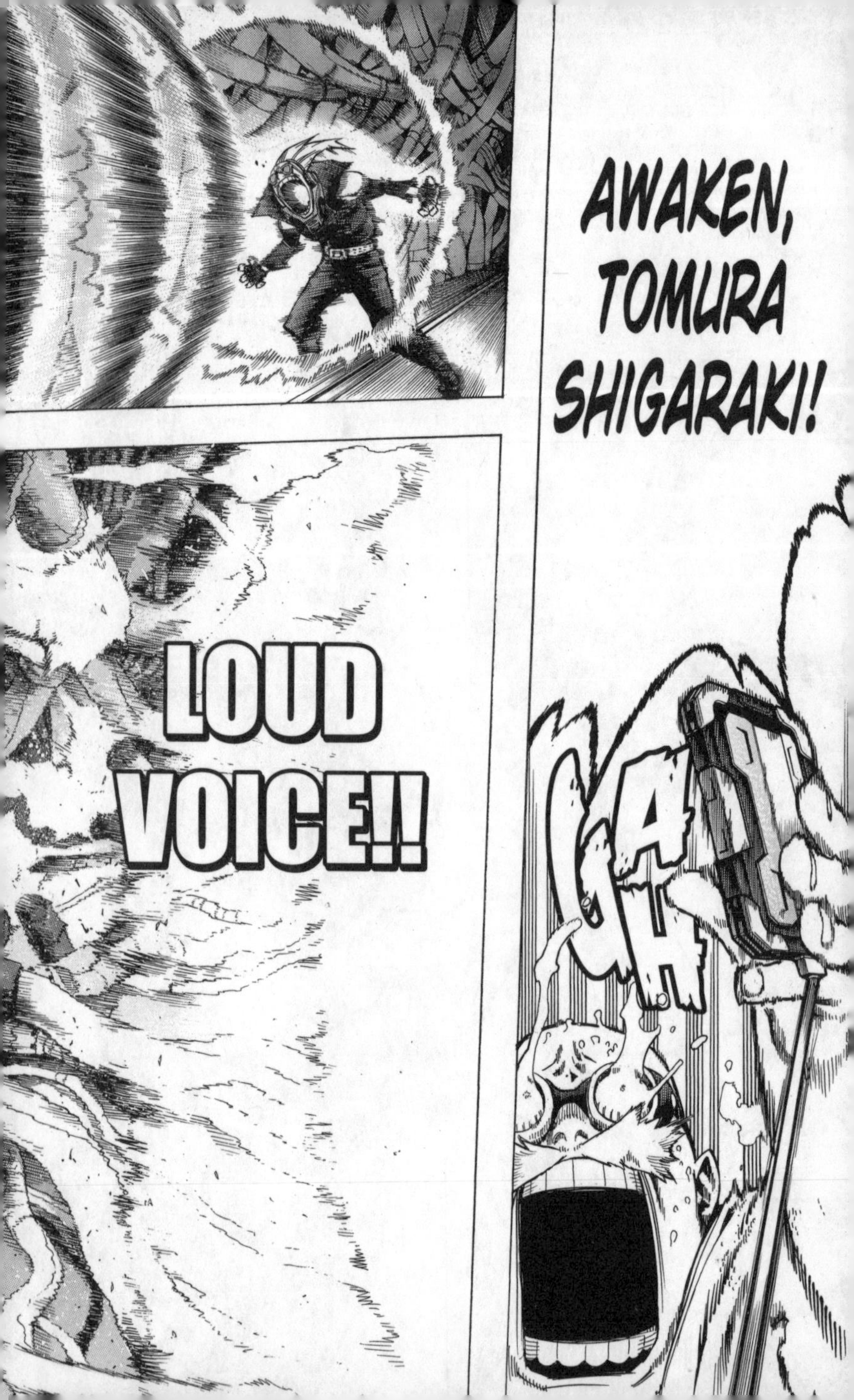
AWAKEN, TOMURA SHIGARAKI!
GA
LOUD VOICE!!

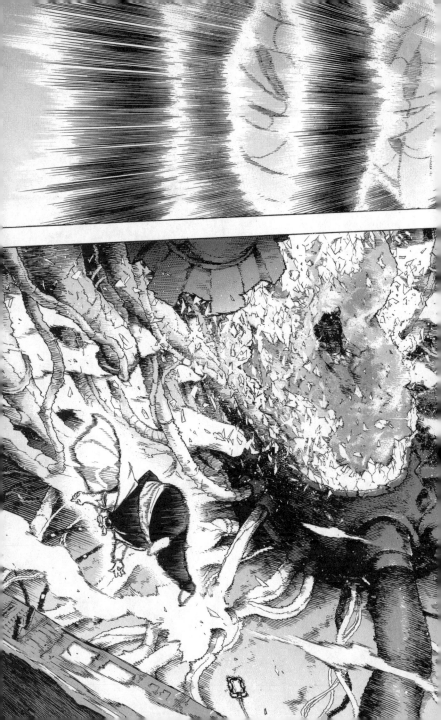

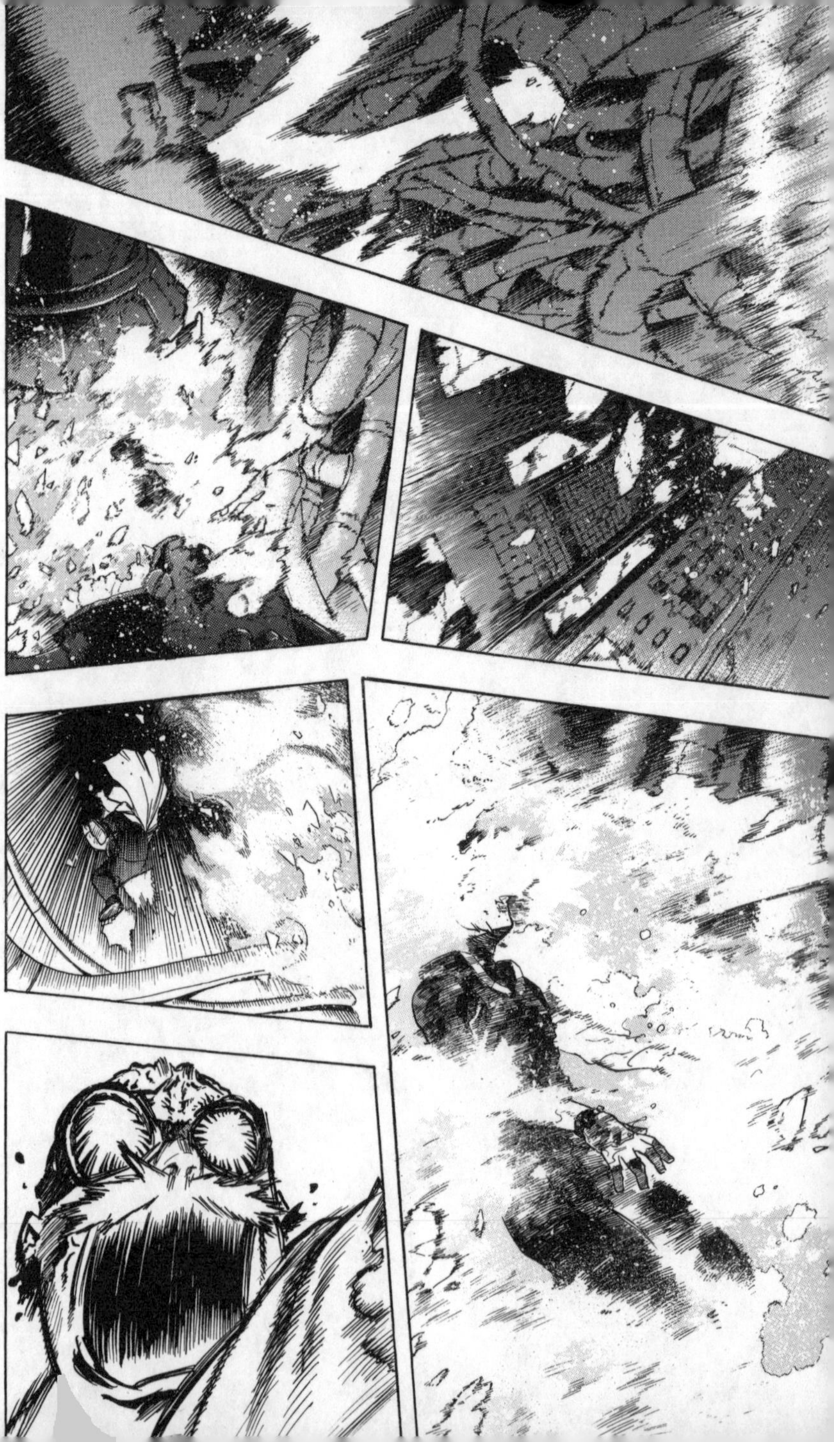

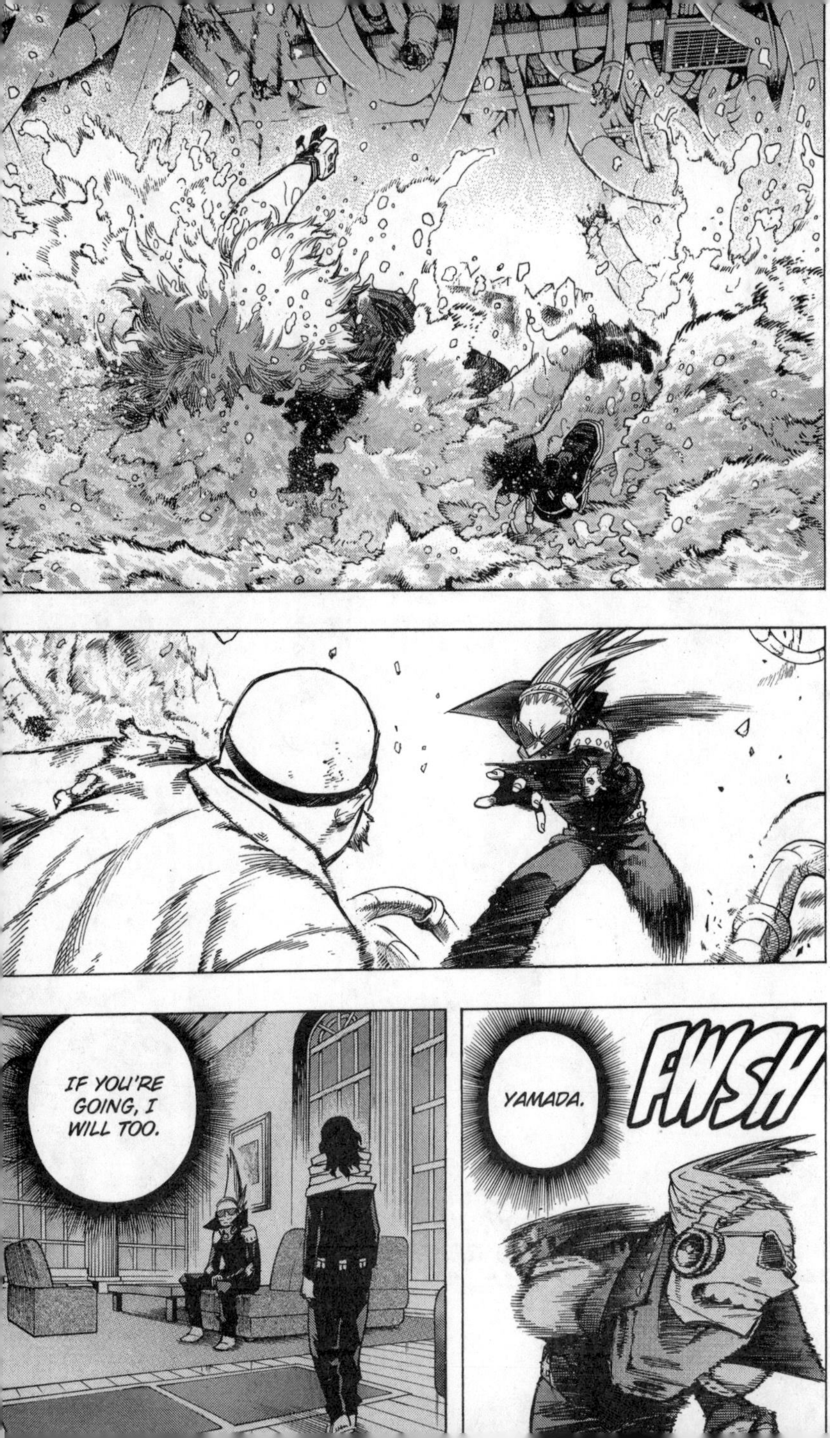
FWSH
YAMADA.
IF YOU'RE GOING, I WILL TOO.

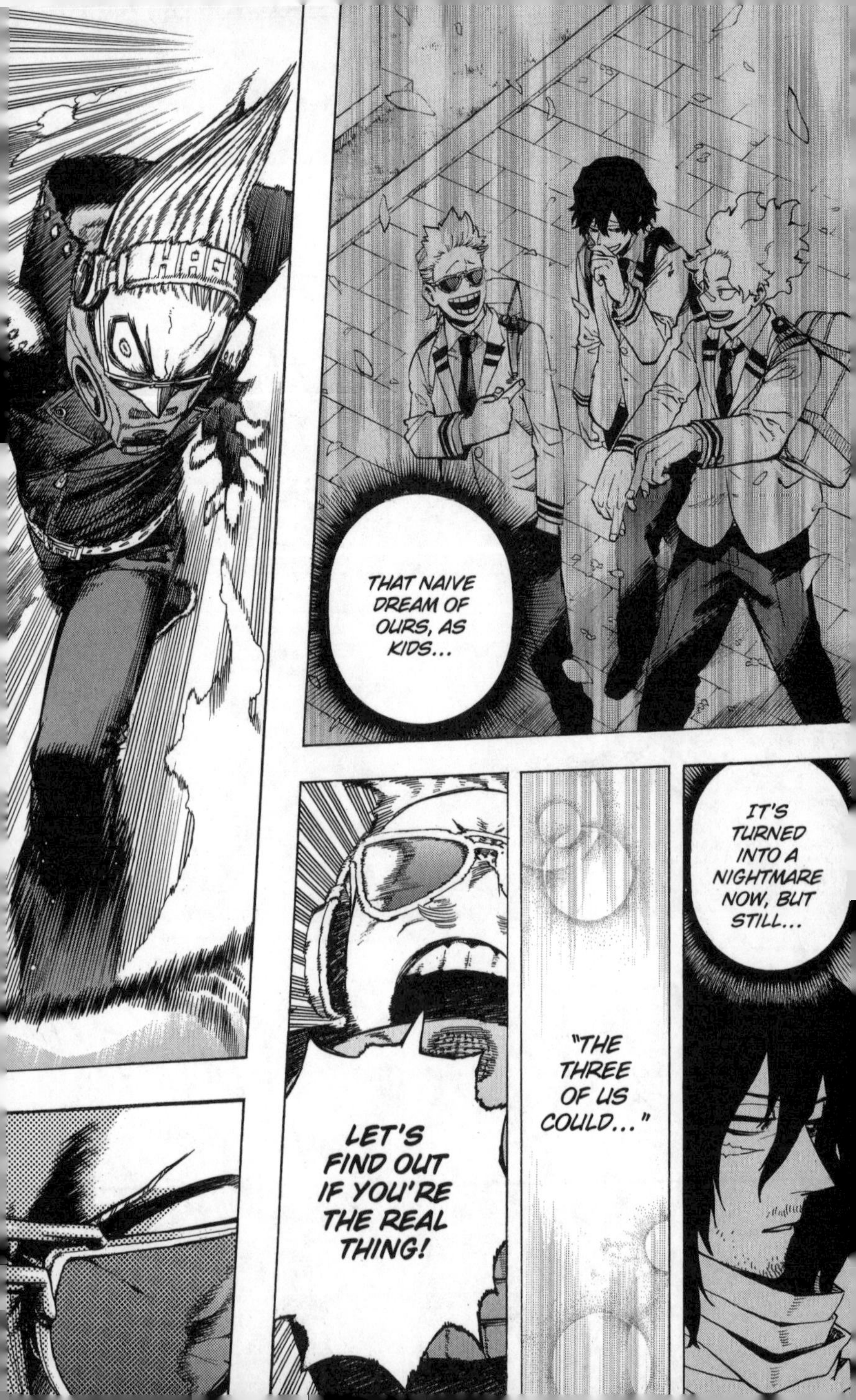
THAT NAIVE DREAM OF OURS, AS KIDS...
IT'S TURNED INTO A NIGHTMARE NOW, BUT STILL...
"THE THREE OF US COULD..."
LET'S FIND OUT IF YOU'RE THE REAL THING!

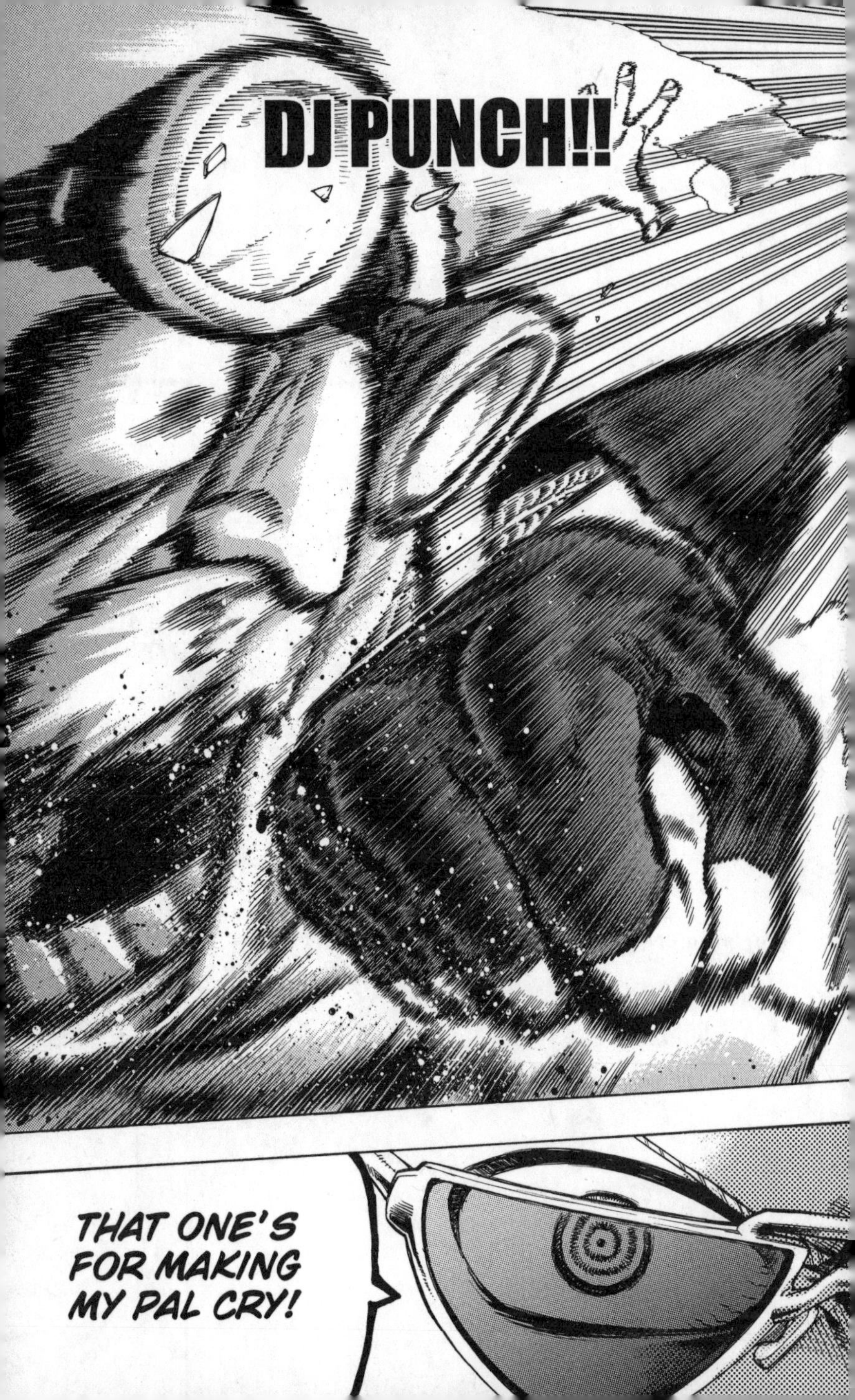
DJ PUNCH!!
THAT ONE'S FOR MAKING MY PAL CRY!

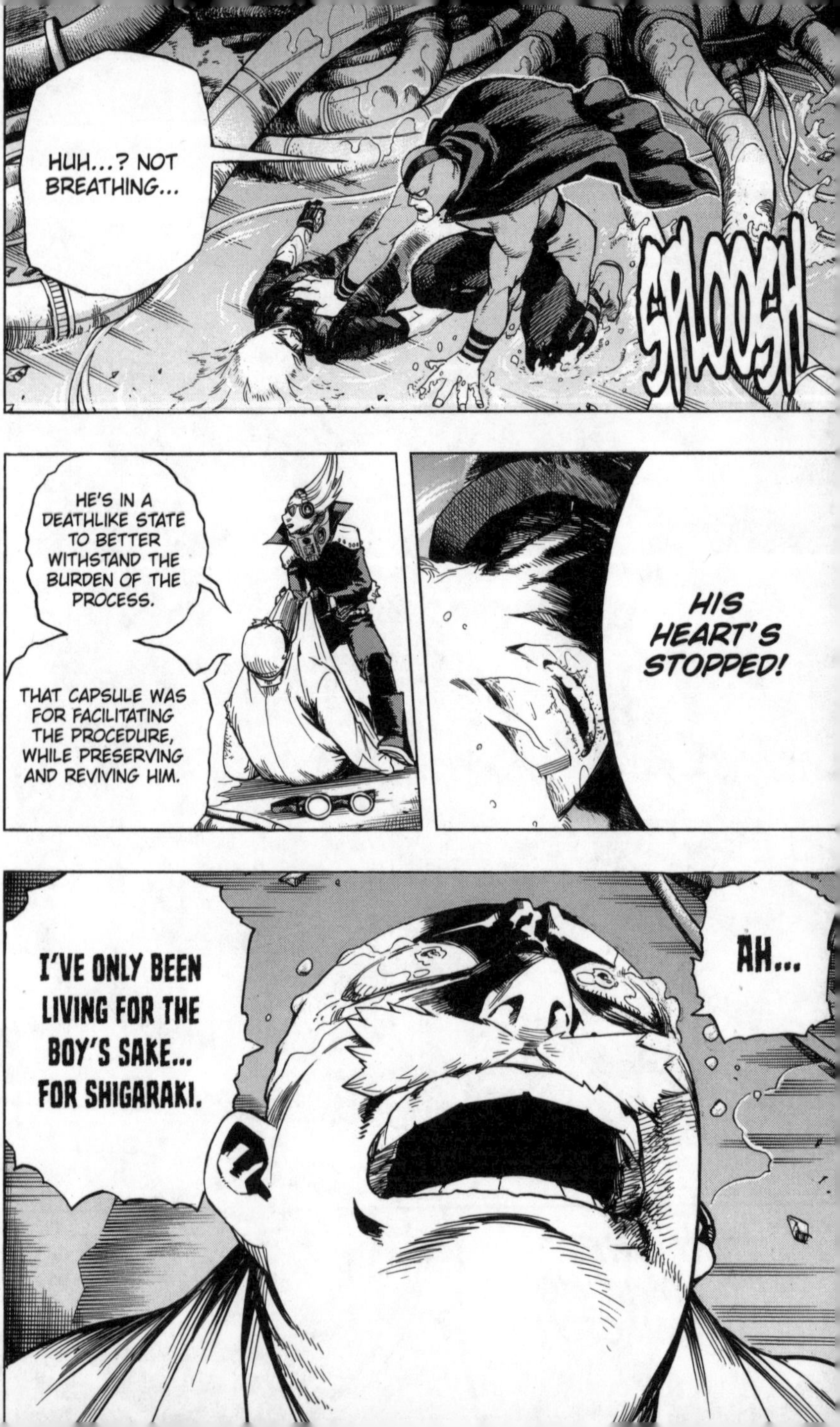
SPLOOSH
HUH...? NOT BREATHING...
HIS HEART'S STOPPED!
HE'S IN A DEATHLIKE STATE TO BETTER WITHSTAND THE BURDEN OF THE PROCESS.
THAT CAPSULE WAS FOR FACILITATING THE PROCEDURE, WHILE PRESERVING AND REVIVING HIM.
AH...
I'VE ONLY BEEN LIVING FOR THE BOY'S SAKE... FOR SHIGARAKI.

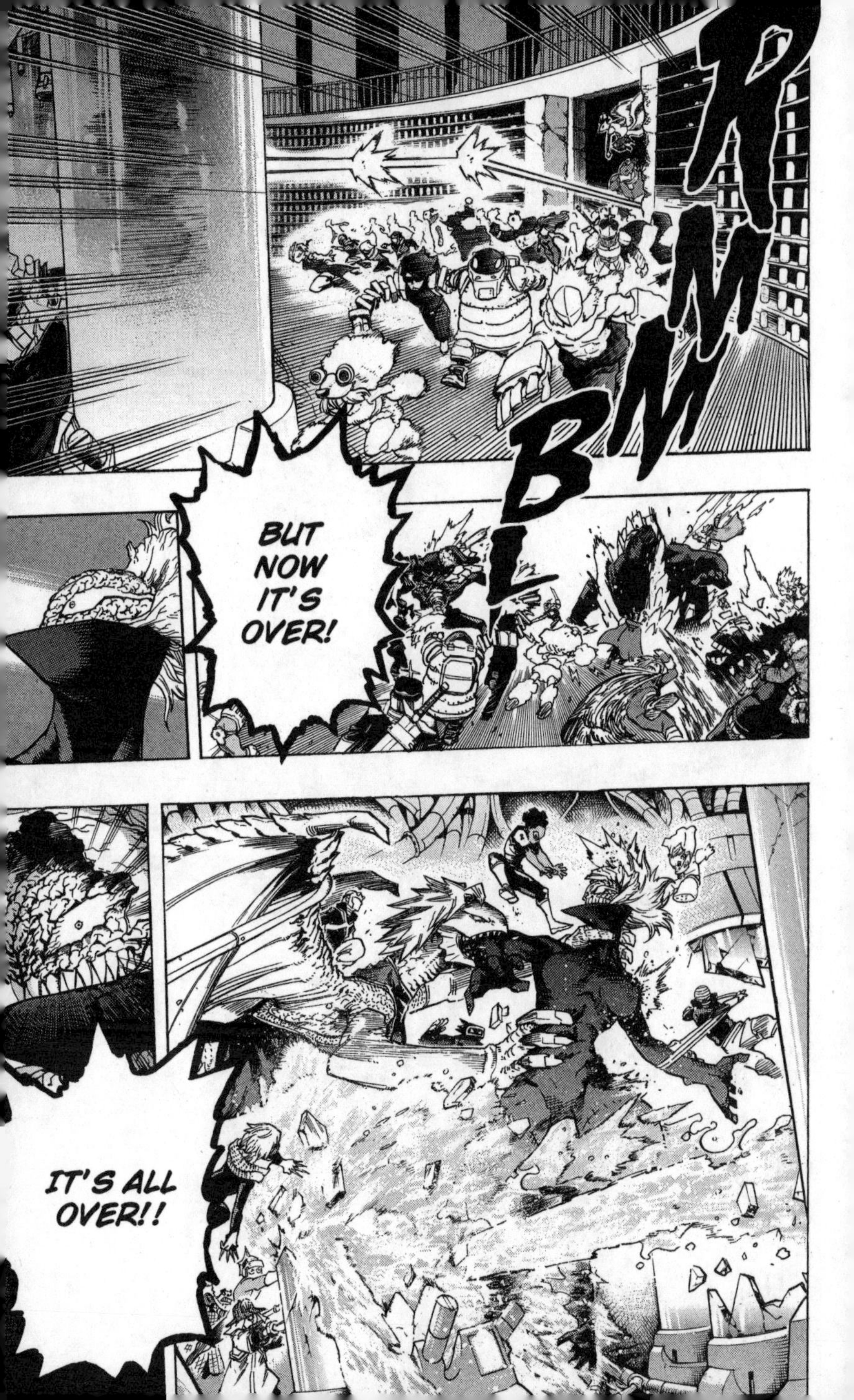
KRMM
BUT NOW IT'S OVER!
BLAM
IT'S ALL OVER!!

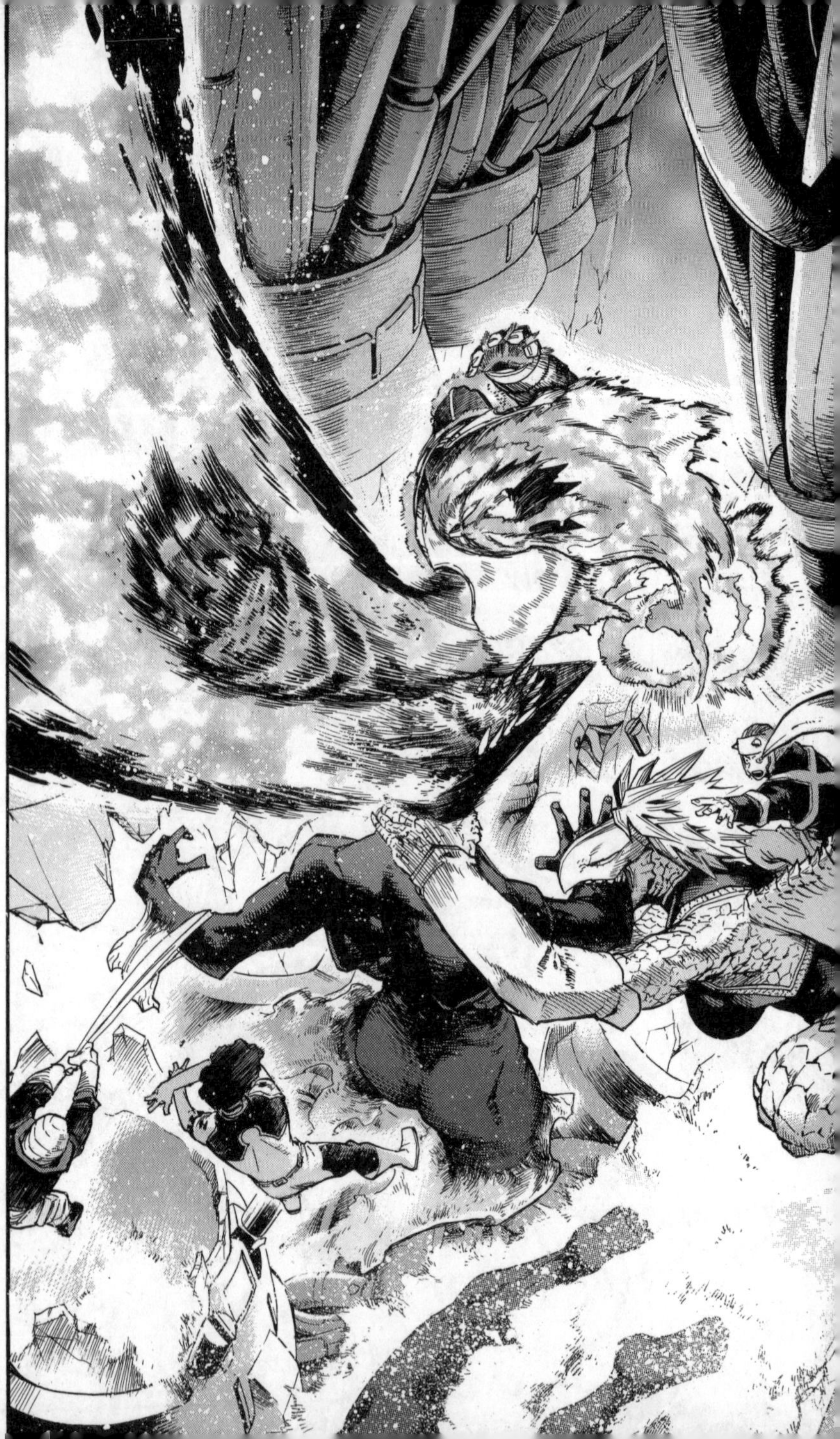

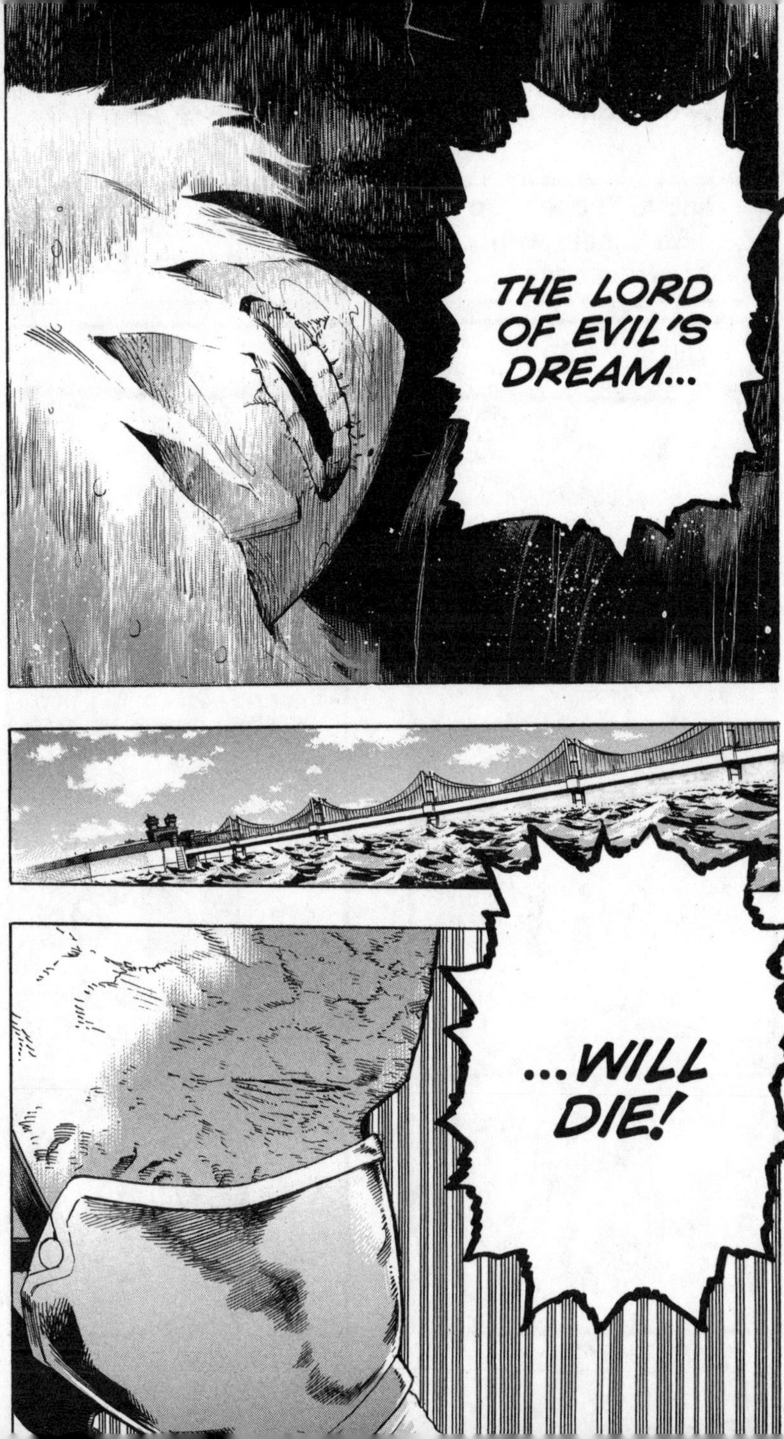
THE LORD OF EVIL'S DREAM...
...WILL DIE!

SIDE STORIES

I missed the chance to include these in a volume closer to when they ran in *Shonen Jump*.

Messed-Up Mentor and Pupil

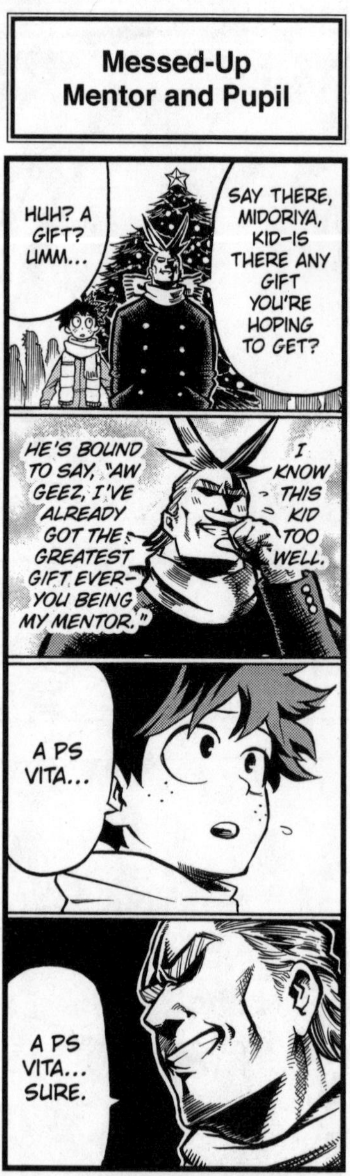
SAY THERE, MIDORIYA, KID—IS THERE ANY GIFT YOU'RE HOPING TO GET?
HUH? A GIFT? UMM...
I KNOW THIS KID TOO WELL.
HE'S BOUND TO SAY, "AW GEEZ, I'VE ALREADY GOT THE GREATEST GIFT EVER—YOU BEING MY MENTOR."
A PS VITA...
A PS VITA... SURE.

(WEEKLY SHONEN JUMP 2016, ISSUE 3/4)

Imbue Those Carp Streamers with Messages

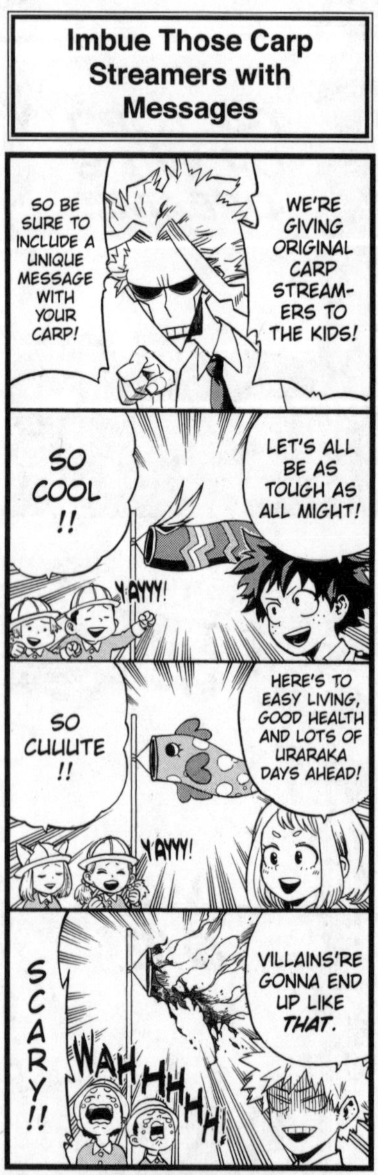
WE'RE GIVING ORIGINAL CARP STREAMERS TO THE KIDS!
SO BE SURE TO INCLUDE A UNIQUE MESSAGE WITH YOUR CARP!
LET'S ALL BE AS TOUGH AS ALL MIGHT!
SO COOL !!
YAYYY!
HERE'S TO EASY LIVING, GOOD HEALTH AND LOTS OF URARAKA DAYS AHEAD!
SO CUUUTE !!
YAYYY!
VILLAINS'RE GONNA END UP LIKE *THAT*.
SCARY!!
WAHHHHHH!

(WEEKLY SHONEN JUMP 2017, ISSUE 21/22)

No. 270 - Inheritance

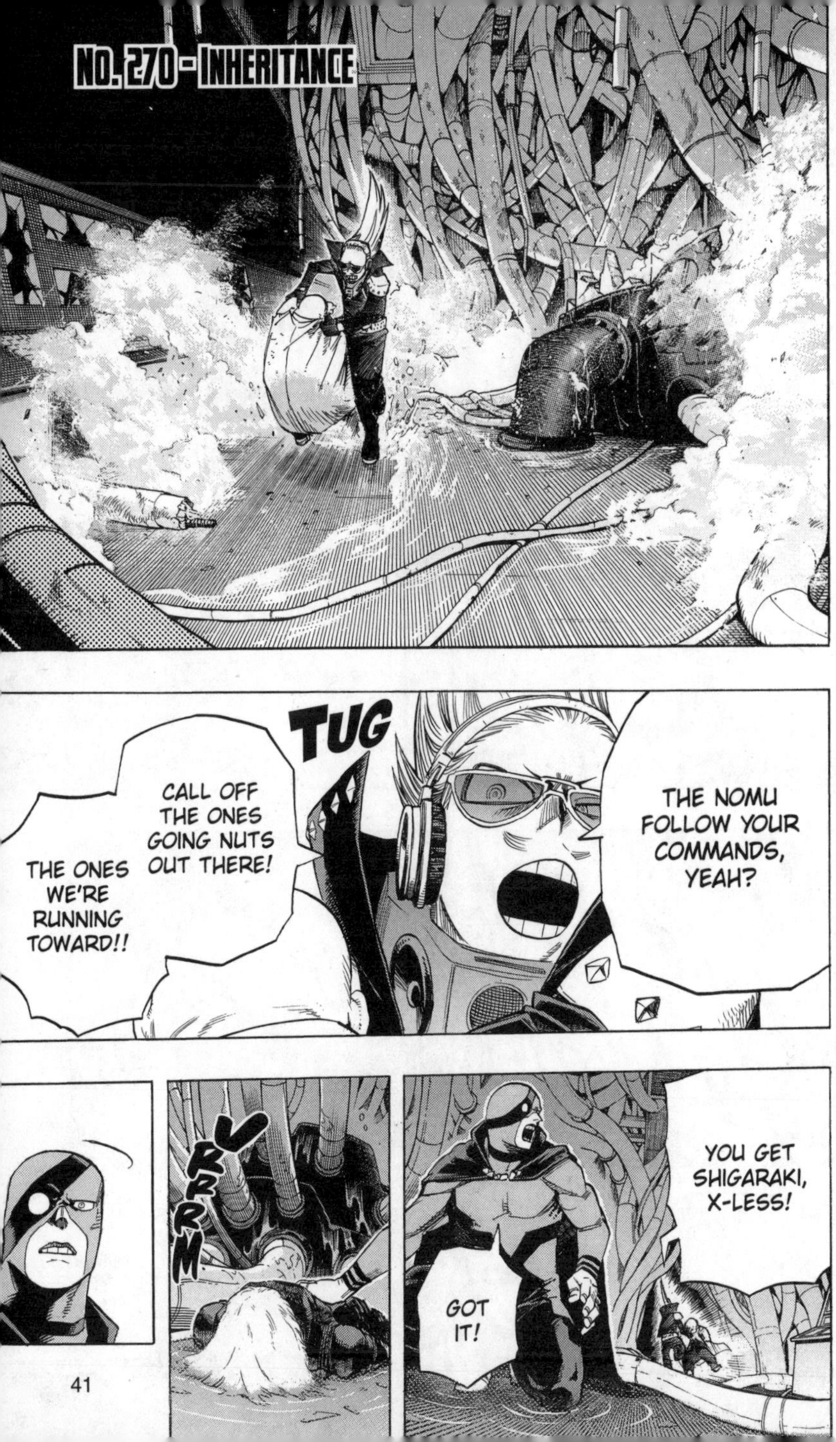
THE NOMU FOLLOW YOUR COMMANDS, YEAH?
TUG
CALL OFF THE ONES GOING NUTS OUT THERE!
THE ONES WE'RE RUNNING TOWARD!!
YOU GET SHIGARAKI, X-LESS!
GOT IT!
VRRRM

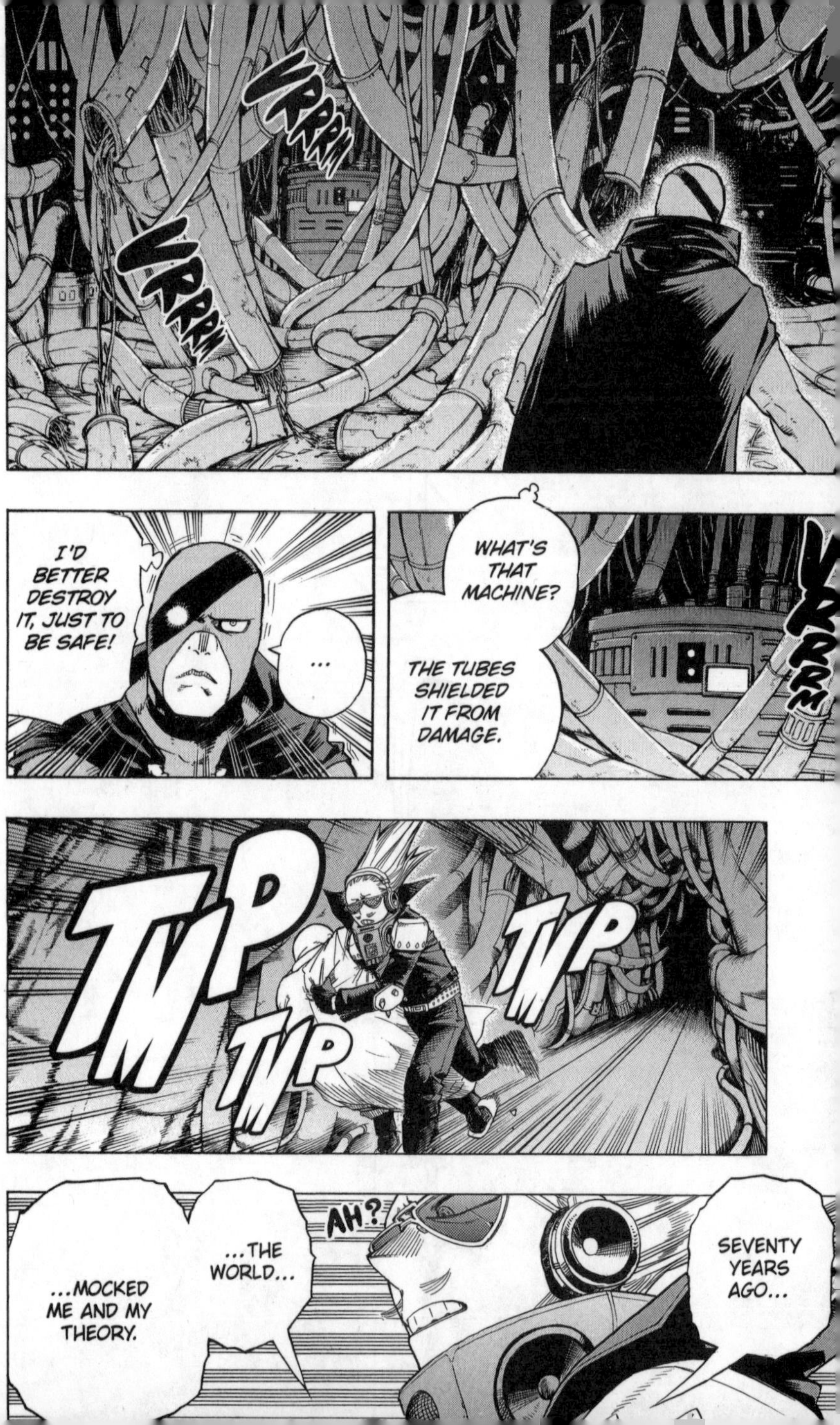
VRRRM
VRRRM
WHAT'S THAT MACHINE?
THE TUBES SHIELDED IT FROM DAMAGE.
VRRRM
...
I'D BETTER DESTROY IT, JUST TO BE SAFE!
TMP
TMP
TMP
SEVENTY YEARS AGO...
AH?
...THE WORLD...
...MOCKED ME AND MY THEORY.

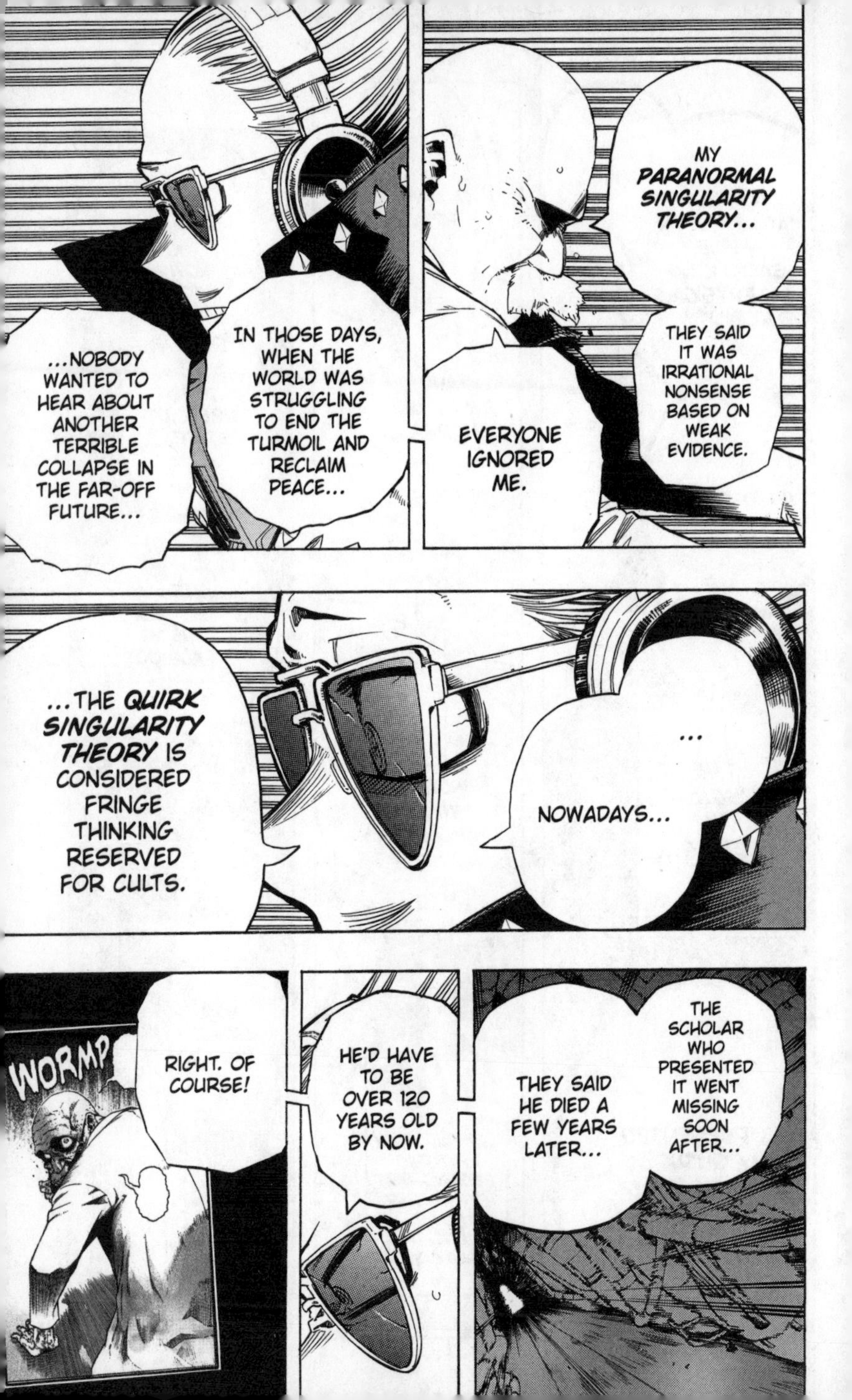

MY PARANORMAL SINGULARITY THEORY...
THEY SAID IT WAS IRRATIONAL NONSENSE BASED ON WEAK EVIDENCE.
EVERYONE IGNORED ME.
IN THOSE DAYS, WHEN THE WORLD WAS STRUGGLING TO END THE TURMOIL AND RECLAIM PEACE...
...NOBODY WANTED TO HEAR ABOUT ANOTHER TERRIBLE COLLAPSE IN THE FAR-OFF FUTURE...
...
NOWADAYS...
...THE QUIRK SINGULARITY THEORY IS CONSIDERED FRINGE THINKING RESERVED FOR CULTS.
THE SCHOLAR WHO PRESENTED IT WENT MISSING SOON AFTER...
THEY SAID HE DIED A FEW YEARS LATER...
HE'D HAVE TO BE OVER 120 YEARS OLD BY NOW.
RIGHT. OF COURSE!
WORMP

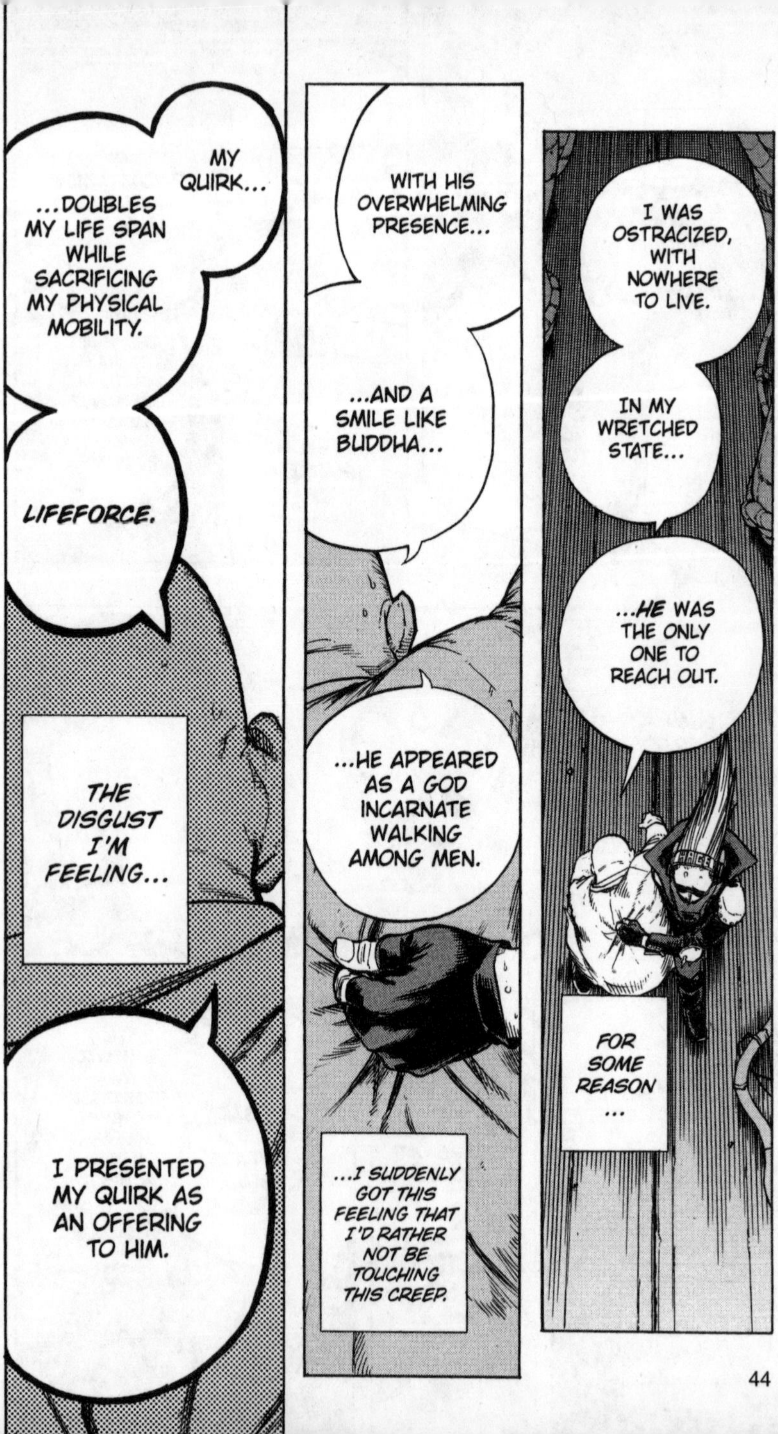
I WAS OSTRACIZED, WITH NOWHERE TO LIVE.
IN MY WRETCHED STATE...
...HE WAS THE ONLY ONE TO REACH OUT.
FOR SOME REASON ...
WITH HIS OVERWHELMING PRESENCE...
...AND A SMILE LIKE BUDDHA...
...HE APPEARED AS A GOD INCARNATE WALKING AMONG MEN.
...I SUDDENLY GOT THIS FEELING THAT I'D RATHER NOT BE TOUCHING THIS CREEP.
MY QUIRK...
...DOUBLES MY LIFE SPAN WHILE SACRIFICING MY PHYSICAL MOBILITY.
LIFEFORCE.
THE DISGUST I'M FEELING...
I PRESENTED MY QUIRK AS AN OFFERING TO HIM.

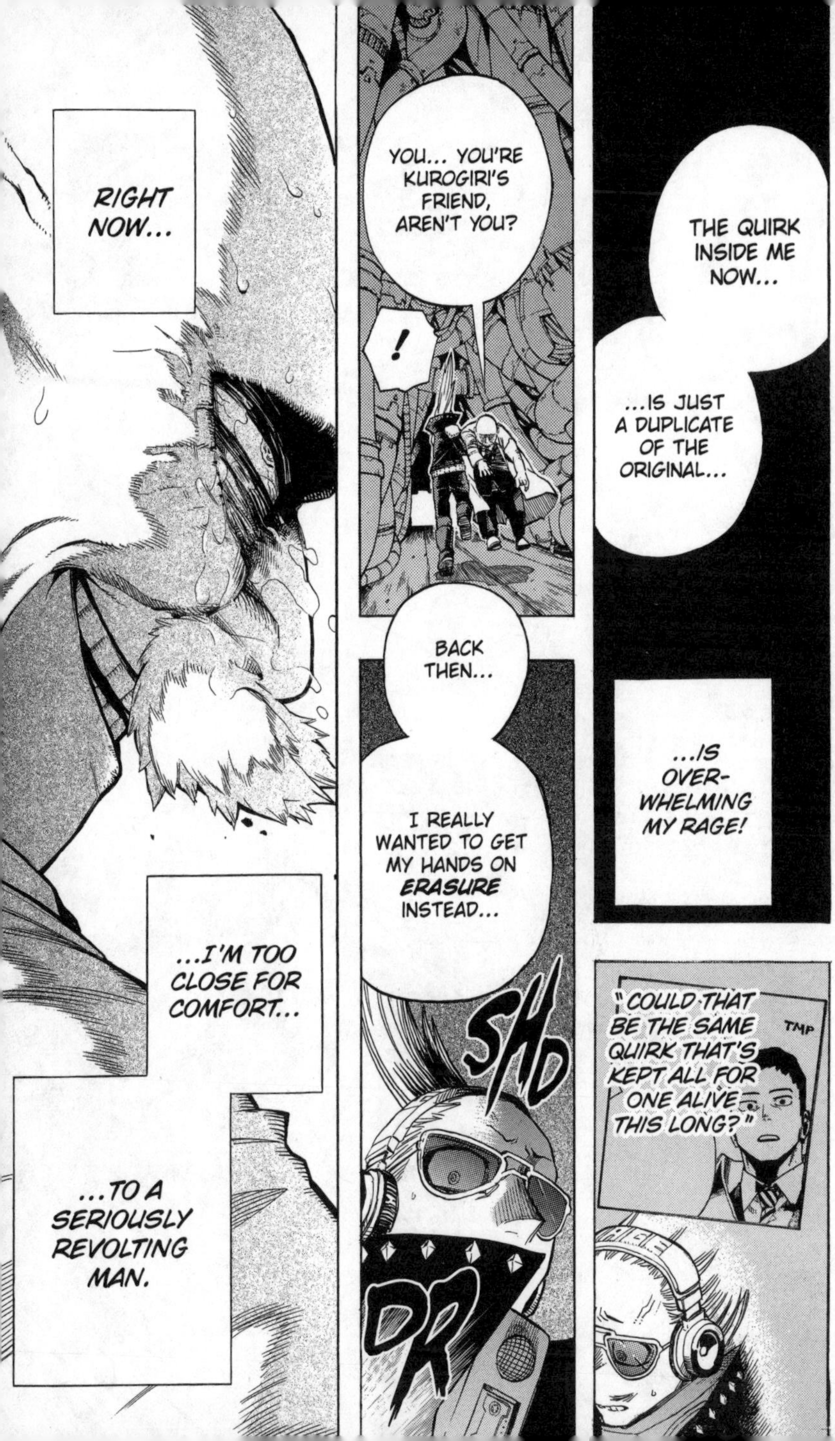
THE QUIRK INSIDE ME NOW...
...IS JUST A DUPLICATE OF THE ORIGINAL...
...IS OVER-WHELMING MY RAGE!
"COULD THAT BE THE SAME QUIRK THAT'S KEPT ALL FOR ONE ALIVE THIS LONG?"
TMP
YOU... YOU'RE KUROGIRI'S FRIEND, AREN'T YOU?
!
BACK THEN...
I REALLY WANTED TO GET MY HANDS ON ERASURE INSTEAD...
SHD
DR
RIGHT NOW...
...I'M TOO CLOSE FOR COMFORT...
...TO A SERIOUSLY REVOLTING MAN.

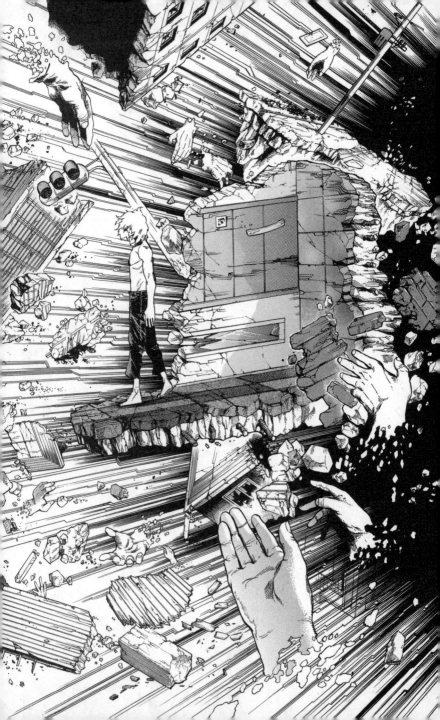

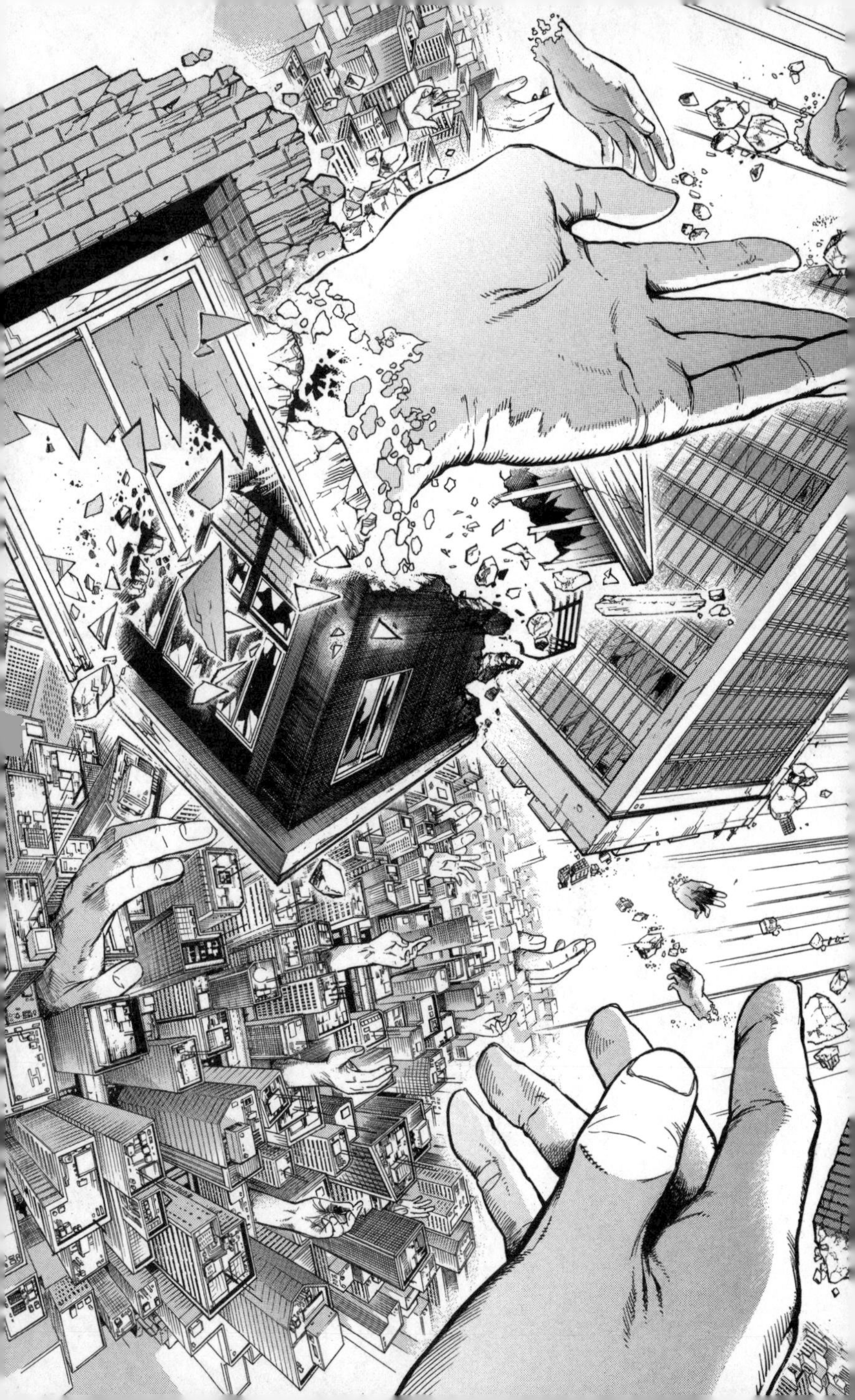

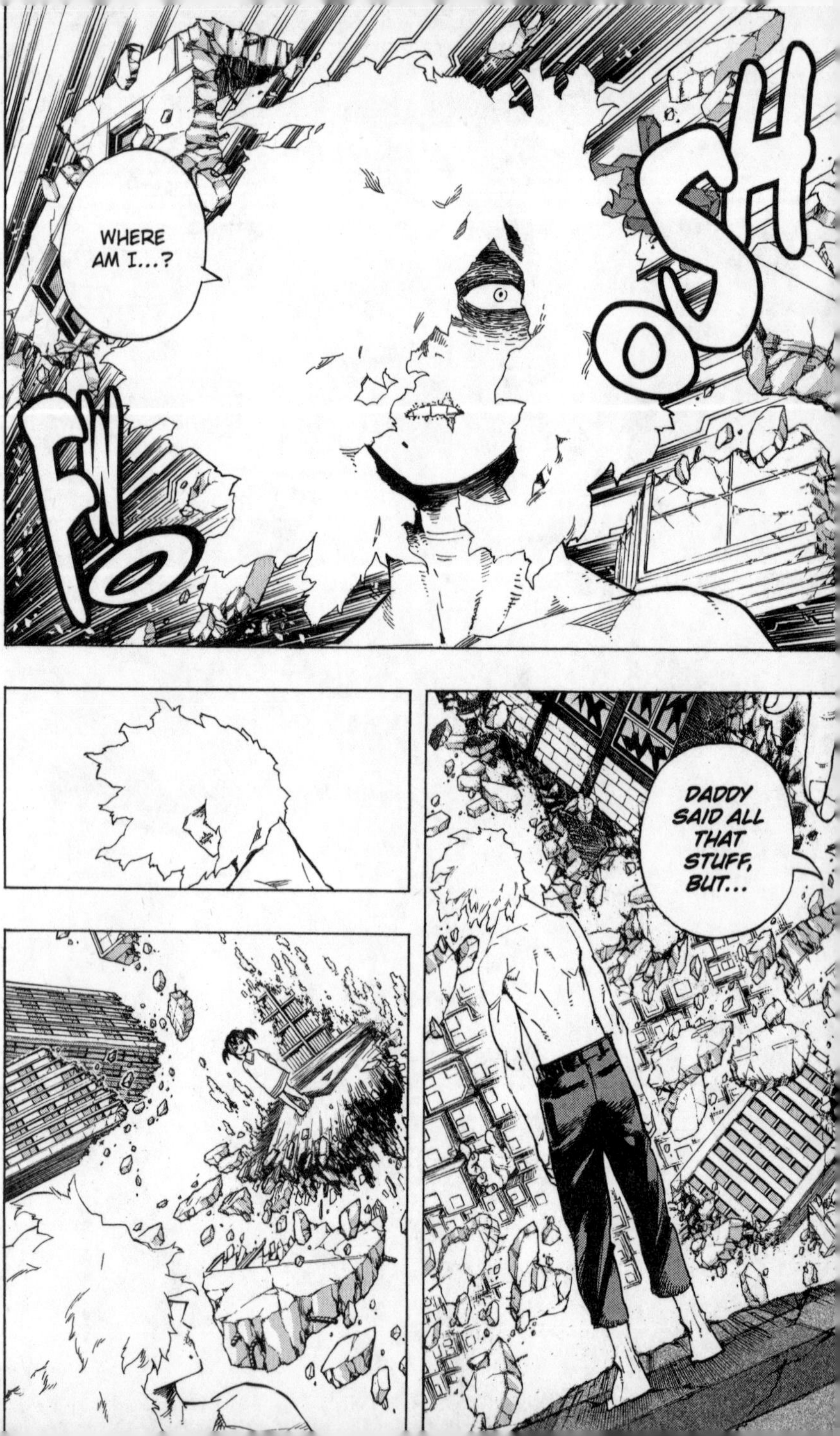
WHERE AM I...?
FWOOSH
DADDY SAID ALL THAT STUFF, BUT...

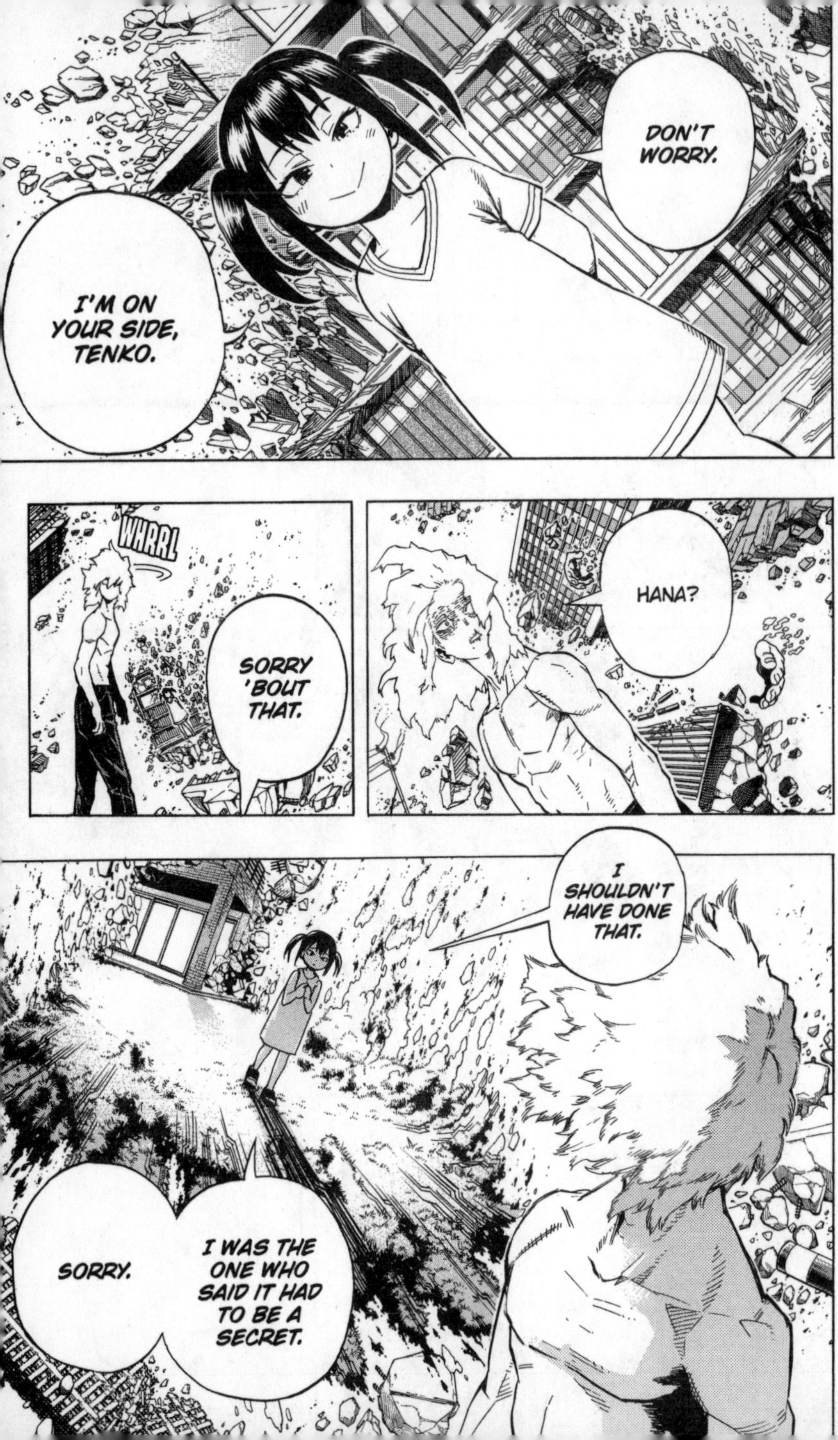
DON'T WORRY.
I'M ON YOUR SIDE, TENKO.
HANA?
WHRRL
SORRY 'BOUT THAT.
I SHOULDN'T HAVE DONE THAT.
I WAS THE ONE WHO SAID IT HAD TO BE A SECRET.
SORRY.

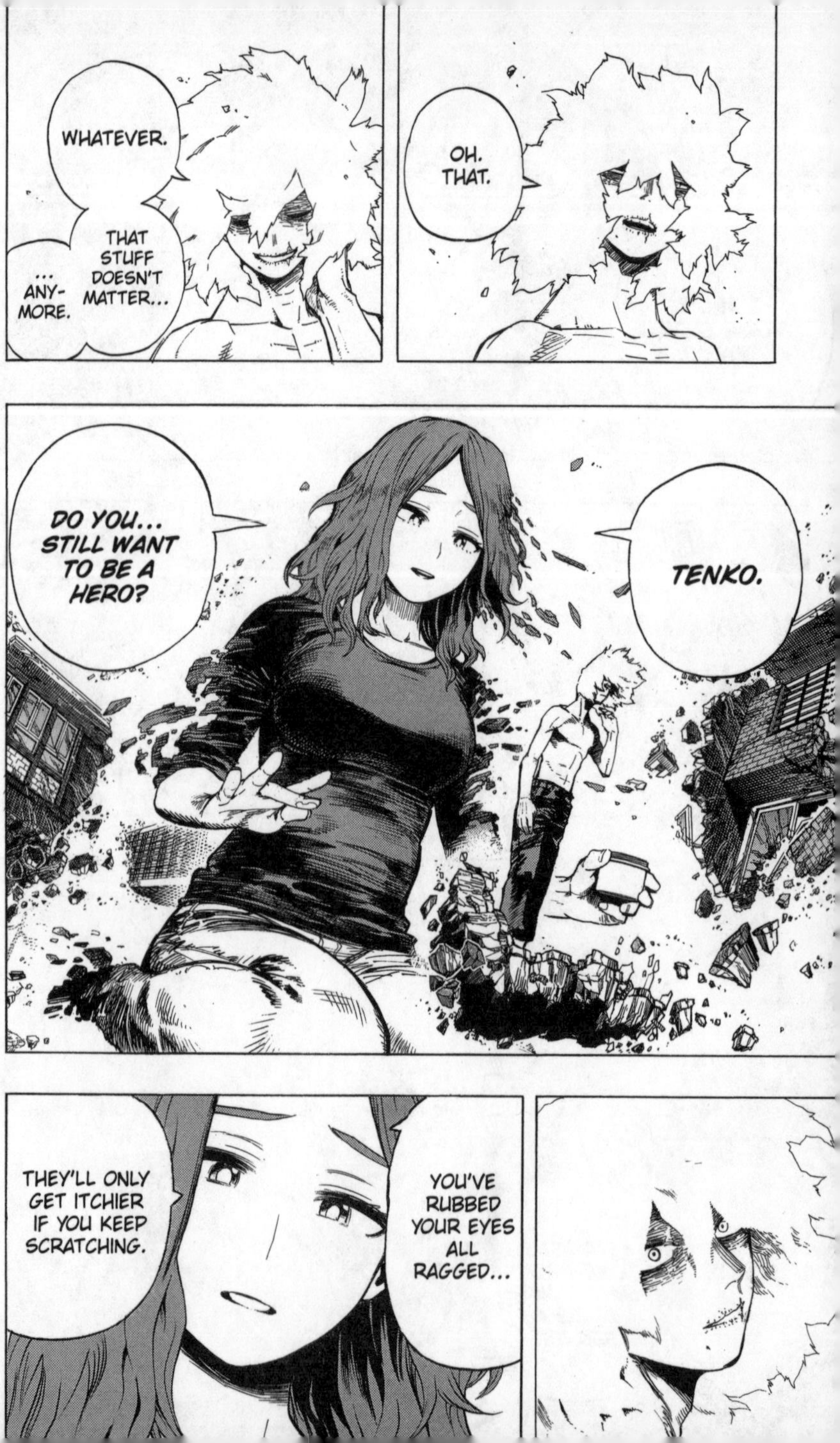
OH. THAT.
WHATEVER.
THAT STUFF DOESN'T MATTER...
... ANYMORE.
TENKO.
DO YOU... STILL WANT TO BE A HERO?
YOU'VE RUBBED YOUR EYES ALL RAGGED...
THEY'LL ONLY GET ITCHIER IF YOU KEEP SCRATCHING.

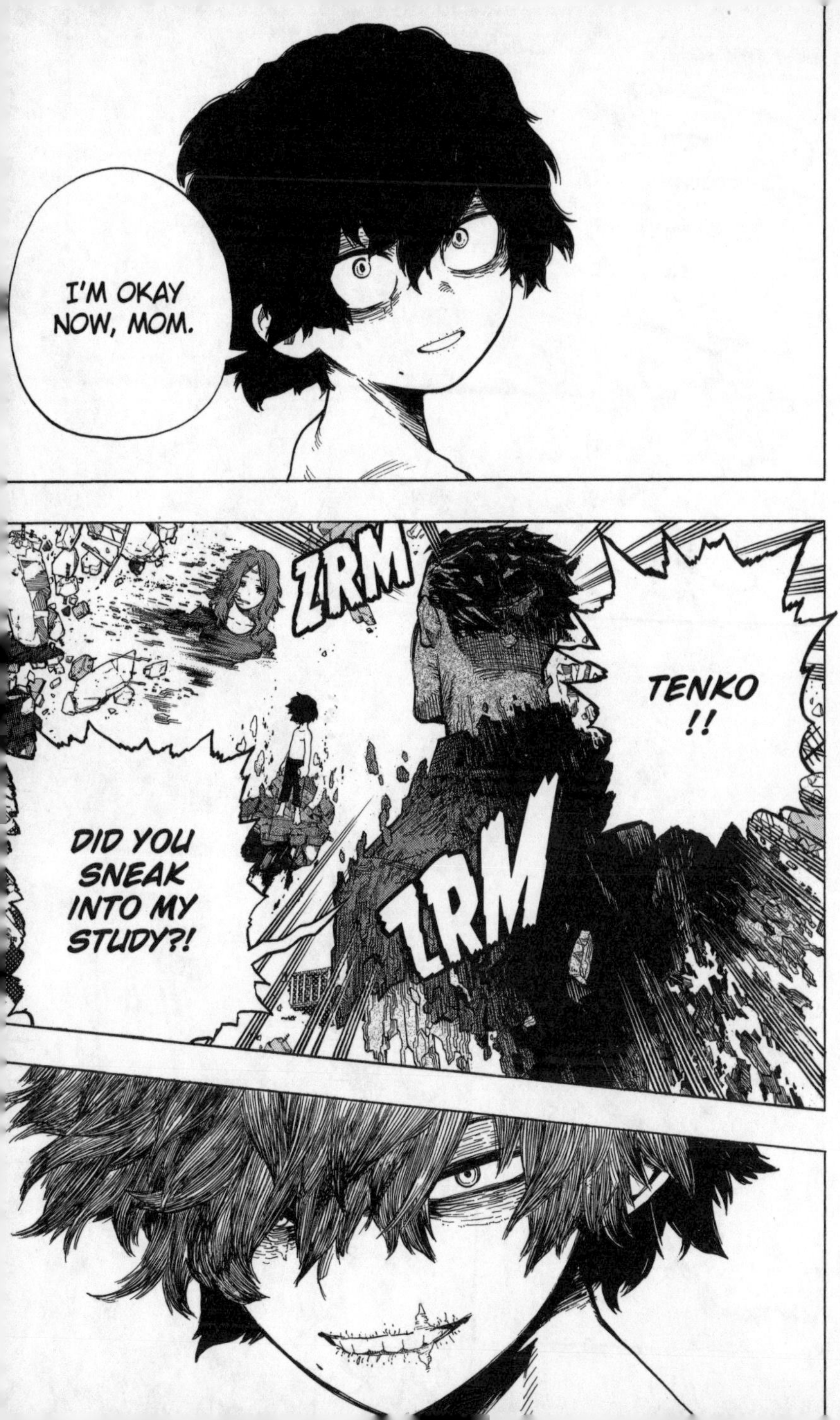
I'M OKAY NOW, MOM.
TENKO !!
ZRM
ZRM
DID YOU SNEAK INTO MY STUDY?!

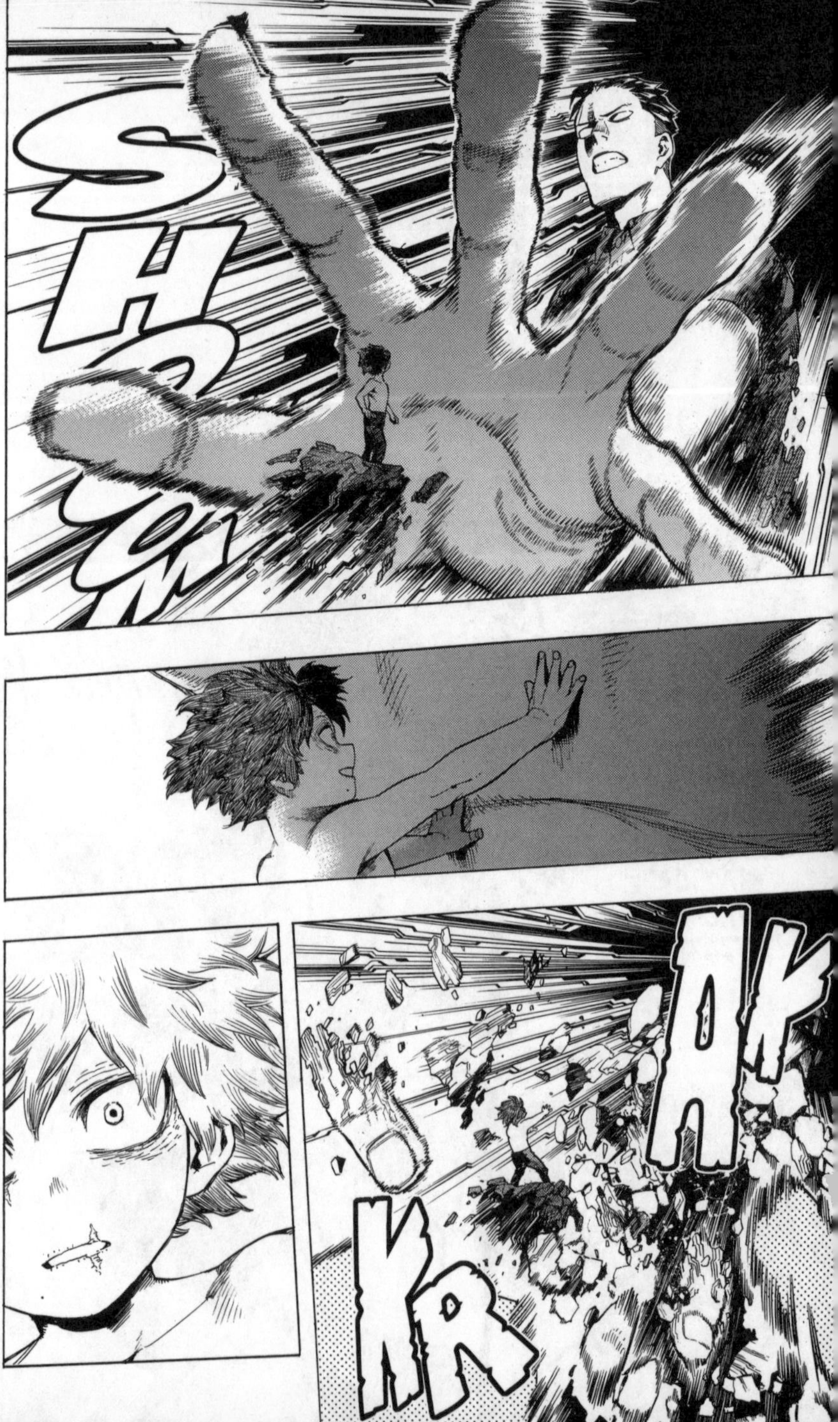
SHOOM
KRAK

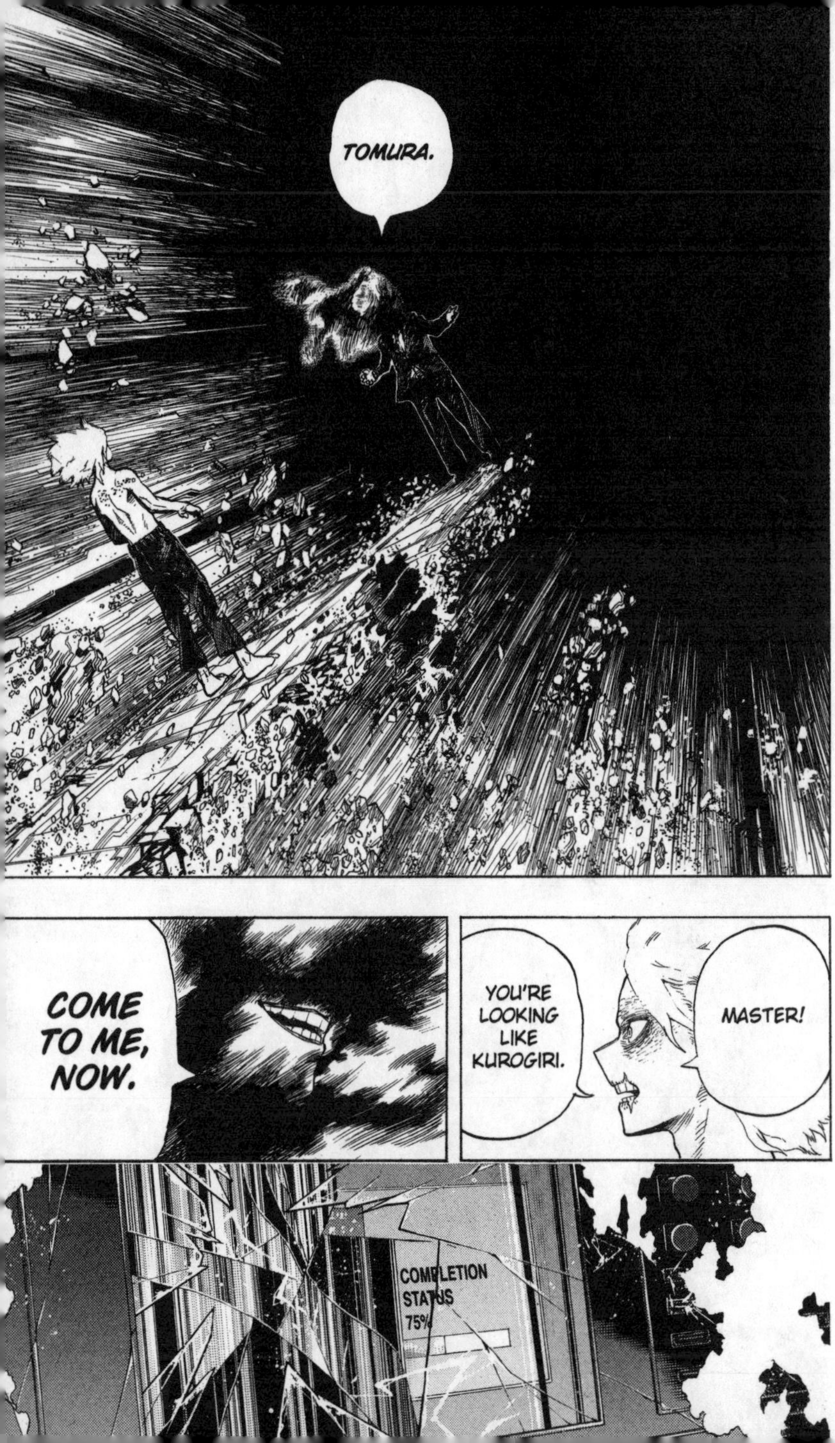
TOMURA.
MASTER!
YOU'RE LOOKING LIKE KUROGIRI.
COME TO ME, NOW.
COMPLETION STATUS 75%

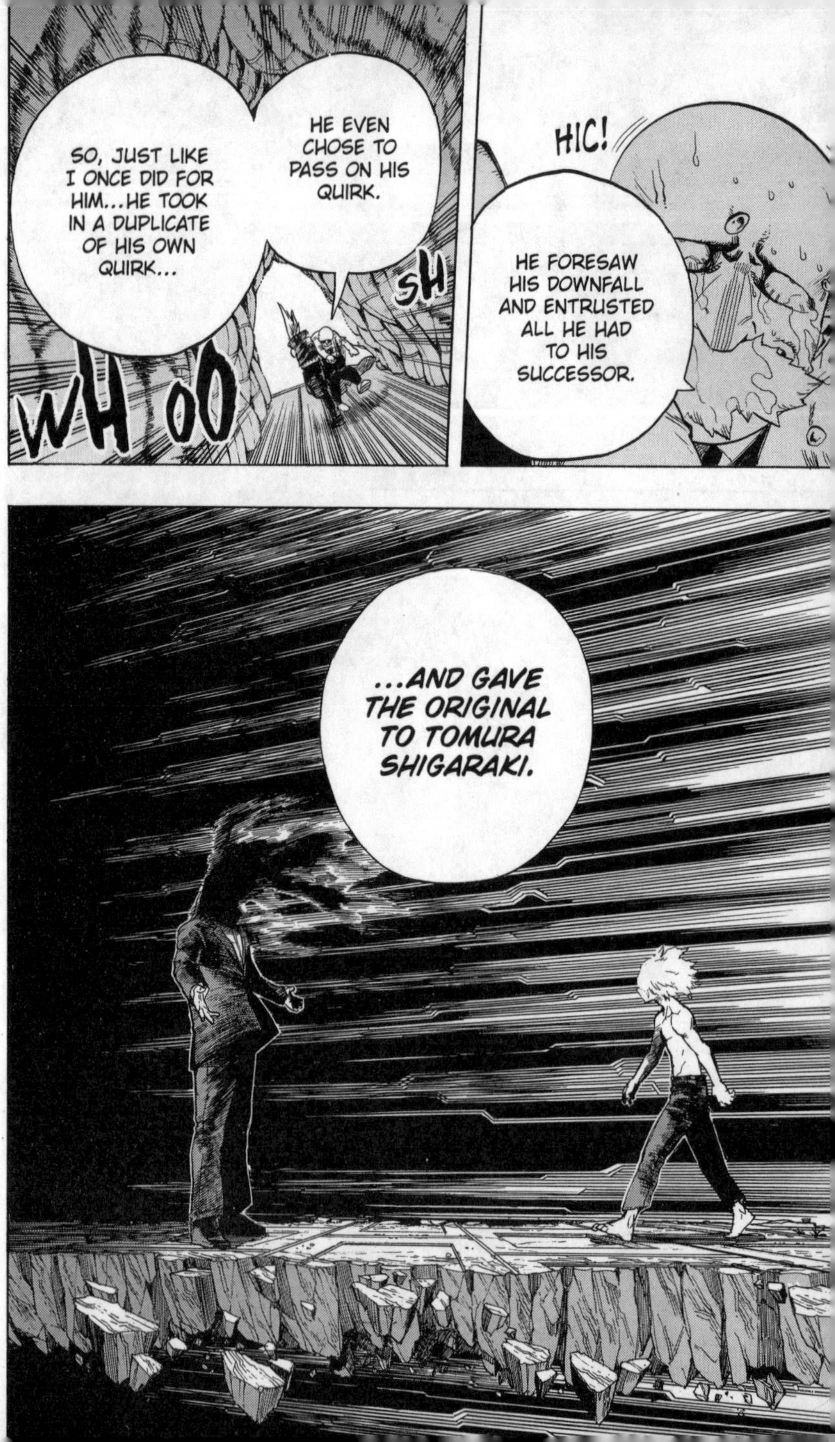
HIC!
HE FORESAW HIS DOWNFALL AND ENTRUSTED ALL HE HAD TO HIS SUCCESSOR.
HE EVEN CHOSE TO PASS ON HIS QUIRK.
SO, JUST LIKE I ONCE DID FOR HIM...HE TOOK IN A DUPLICATE OF HIS OWN QUIRK...
SH
WHOO
...AND GAVE THE ORIGINAL TO TOMURA SHIGARAKI.

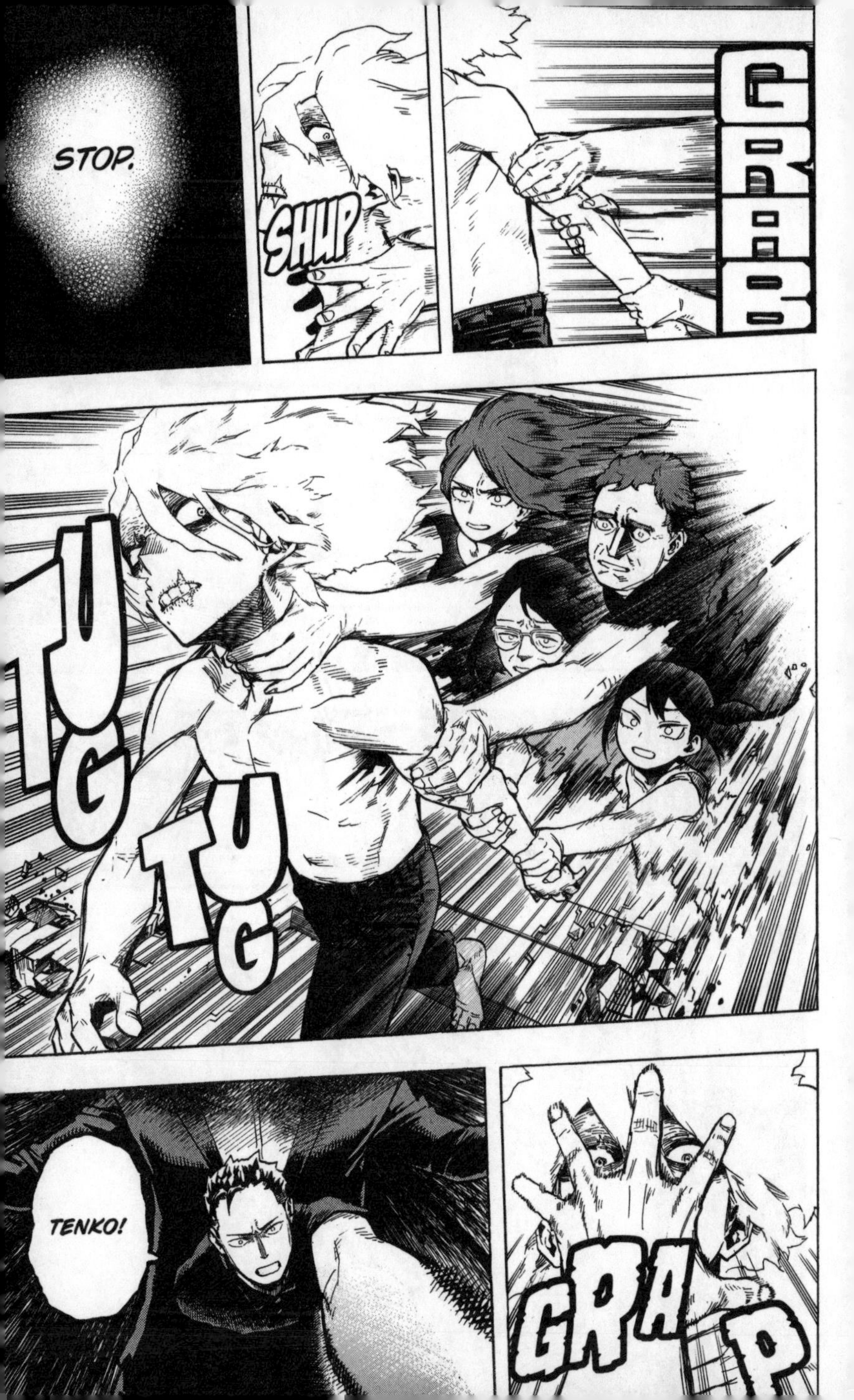
GRAB
SHUP
STOP.
TUG
TUG
GRAP
TENKO!

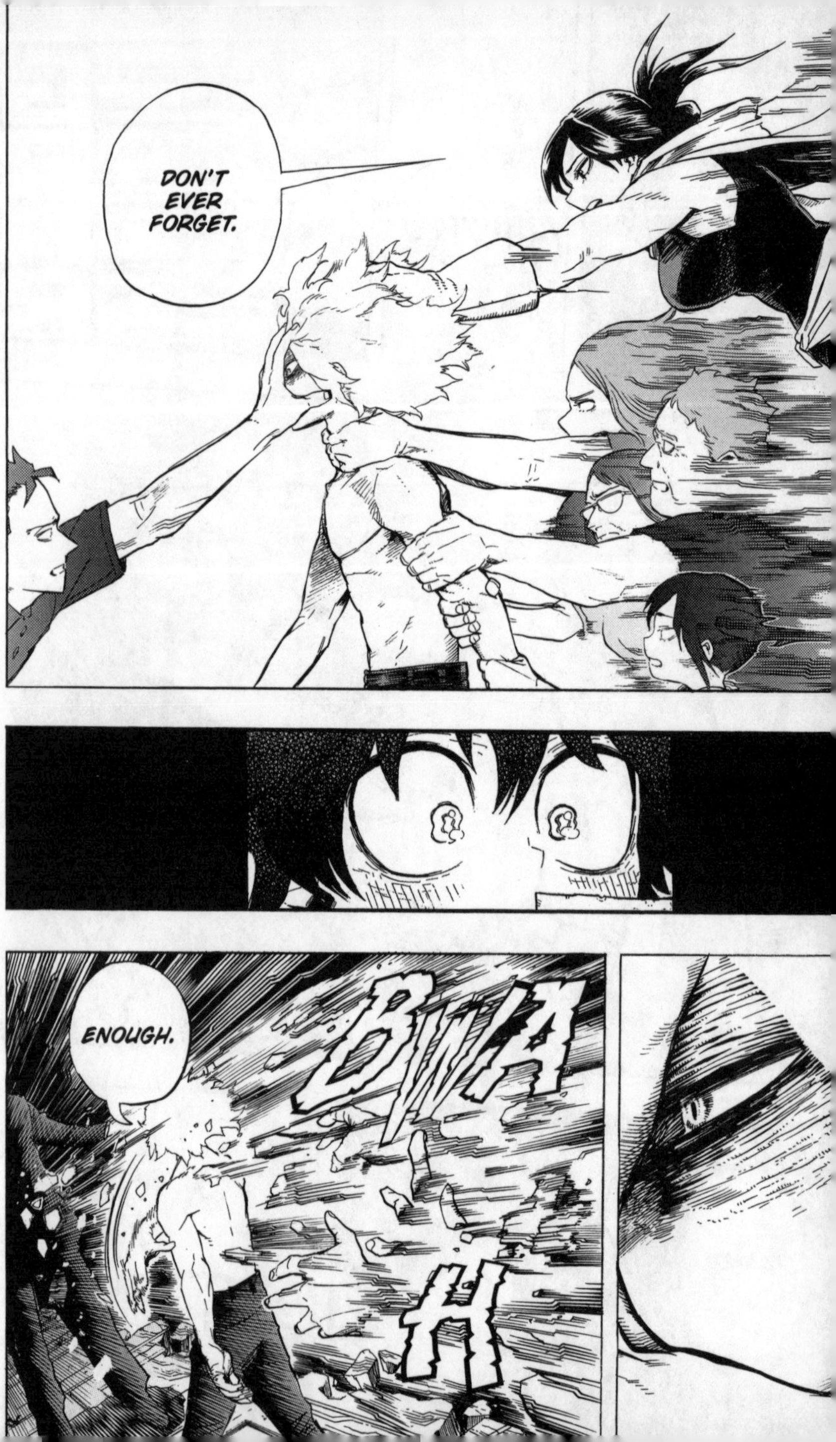
DON'T EVER FORGET.
ENOUGH.
BWAH

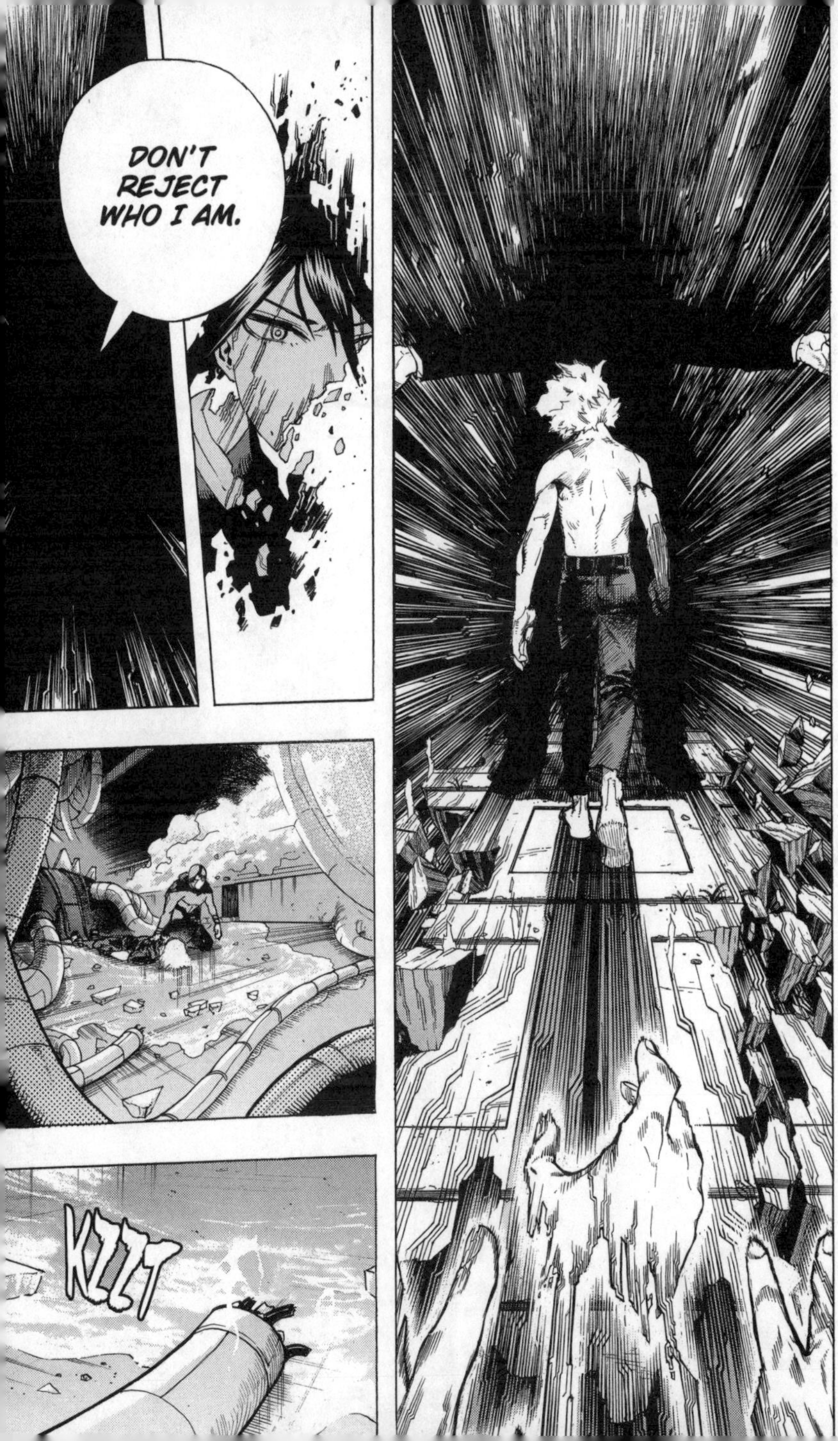
DON'T REJECT WHO I AM.
KZZT

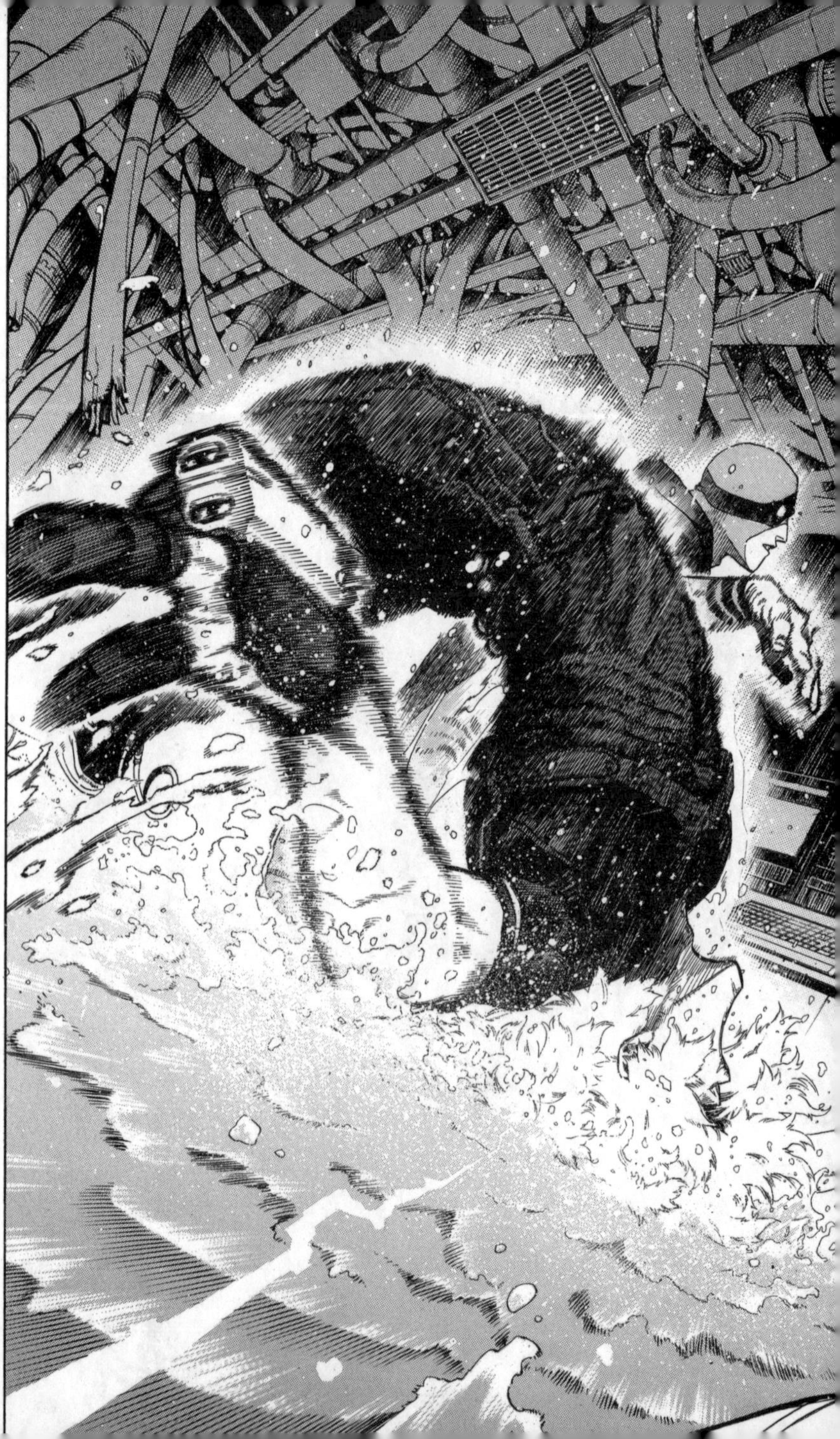

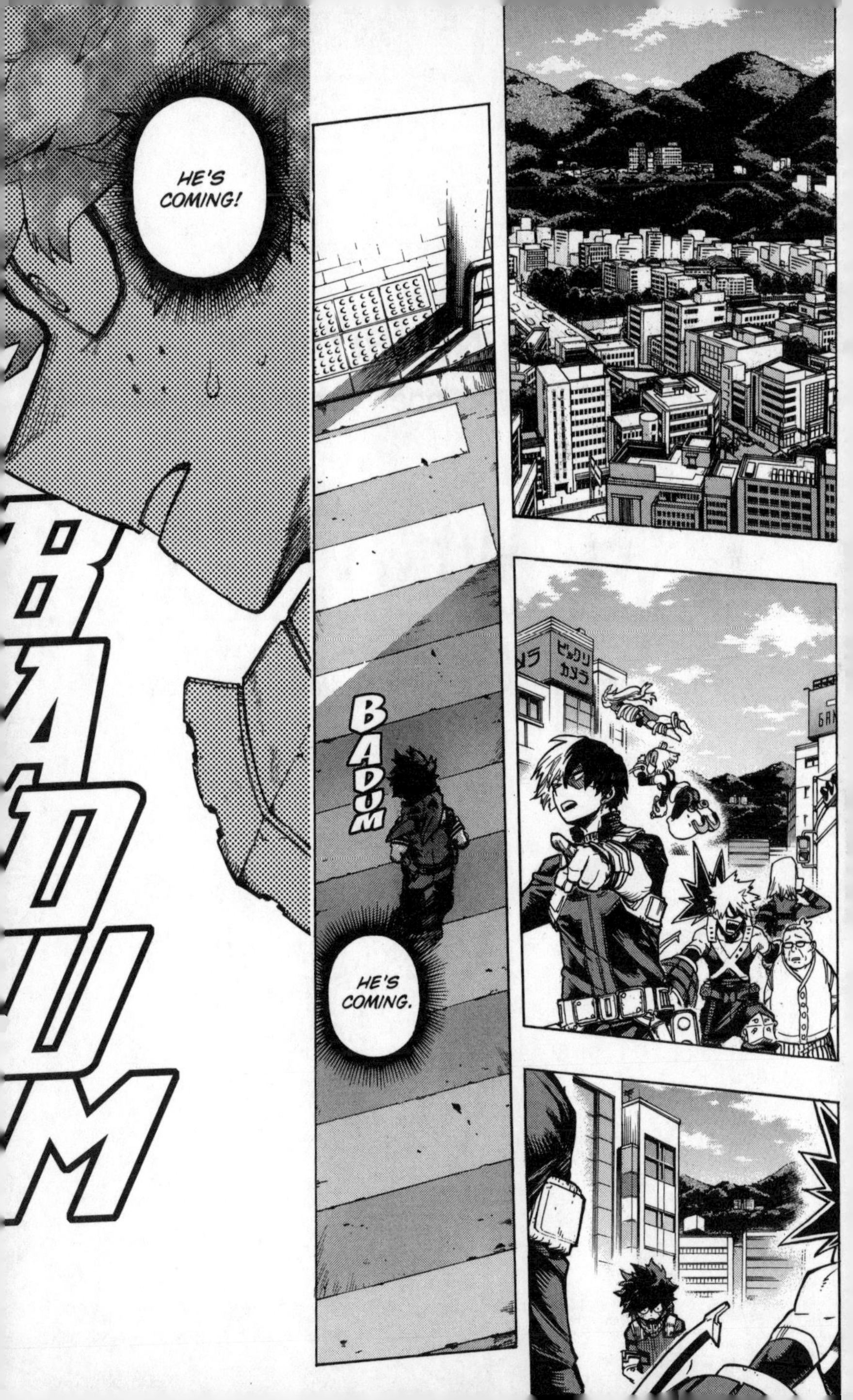
BADUM
HE'S COMING.
HE'S COMING!
BADUM

NO. 270 – INHERITANCE
A chapter that was oddly fun to draw.

THE WHAT-IF

What if Mon the dog's paws had also survived?

This is our time.

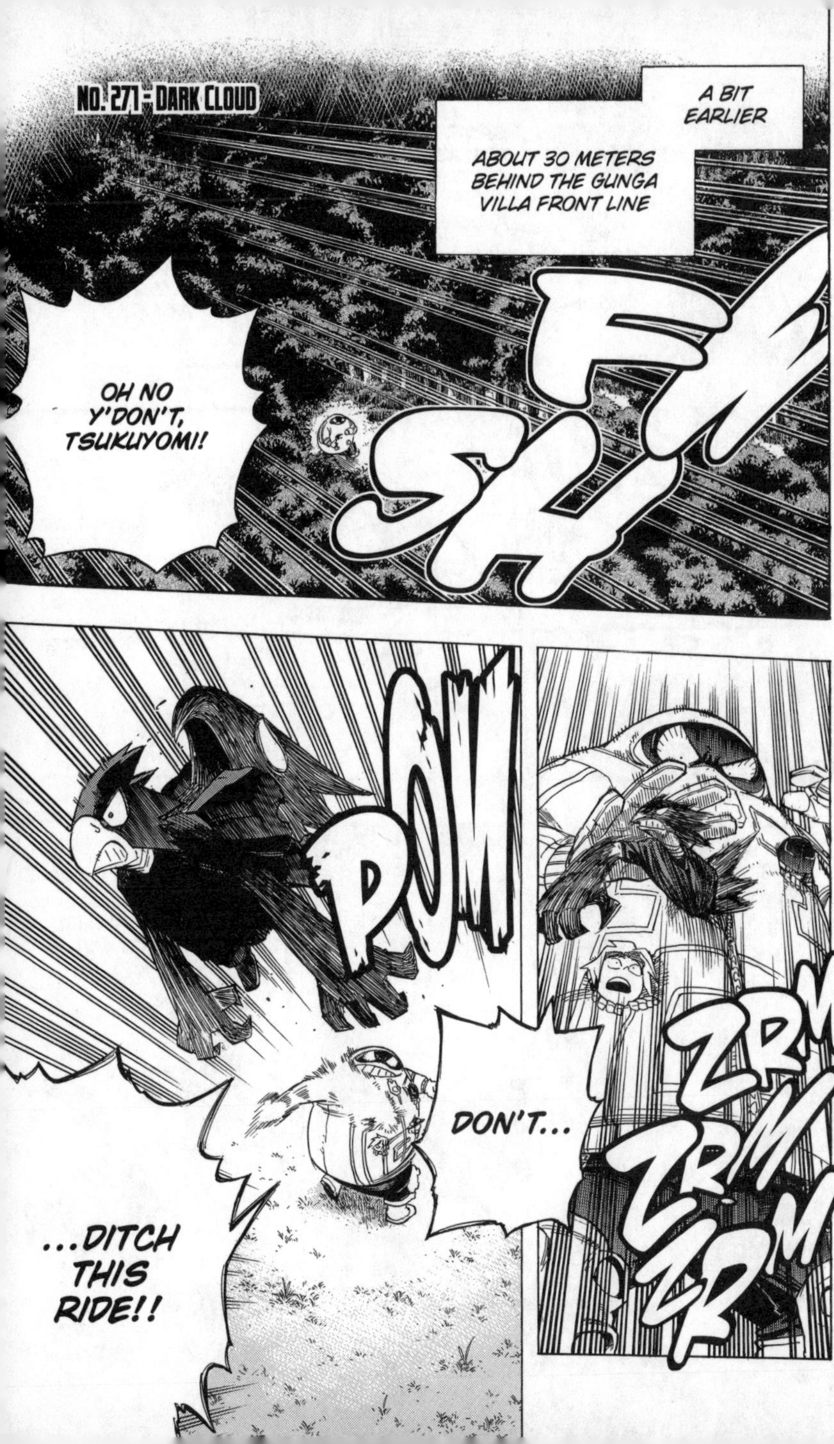
No. 271: Dark Cloud
A BIT EARLIER
ABOUT 30 METERS BEHIND THE GUNGA VILLA FRONT LINE
FWSH
OH NO Y'DON'T, TSUKUYOMI!
ZRM
ZRM
ZRM
ZRM
POM
DON'T...
...DITCH THIS RIDE!!

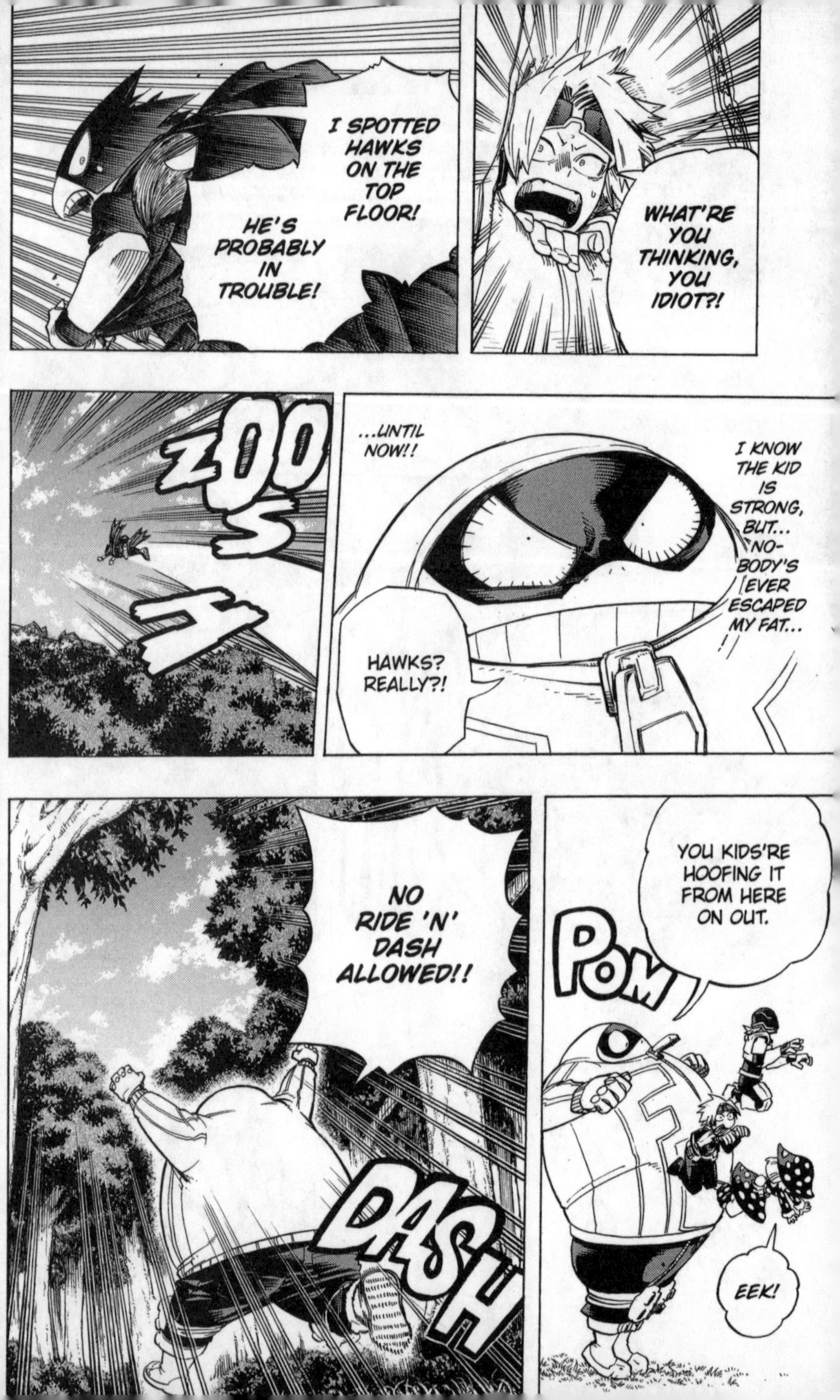
WHAT'RE YOU THINKING, YOU IDIOT?!
I SPOTTED HAWKS ON THE TOP FLOOR!
HE'S PROBABLY IN TROUBLE!
I KNOW THE KID IS STRONG, BUT... NOBODY'S EVER ESCAPED MY FAT...
...UNTIL NOW!!
HAWKS? REALLY?!
ZOOSH
YOU KIDS'RE HOOFING IT FROM HERE ON OUT.
POM
EEK!
NO RIDE 'N' DASH ALLOWED!!
DASH

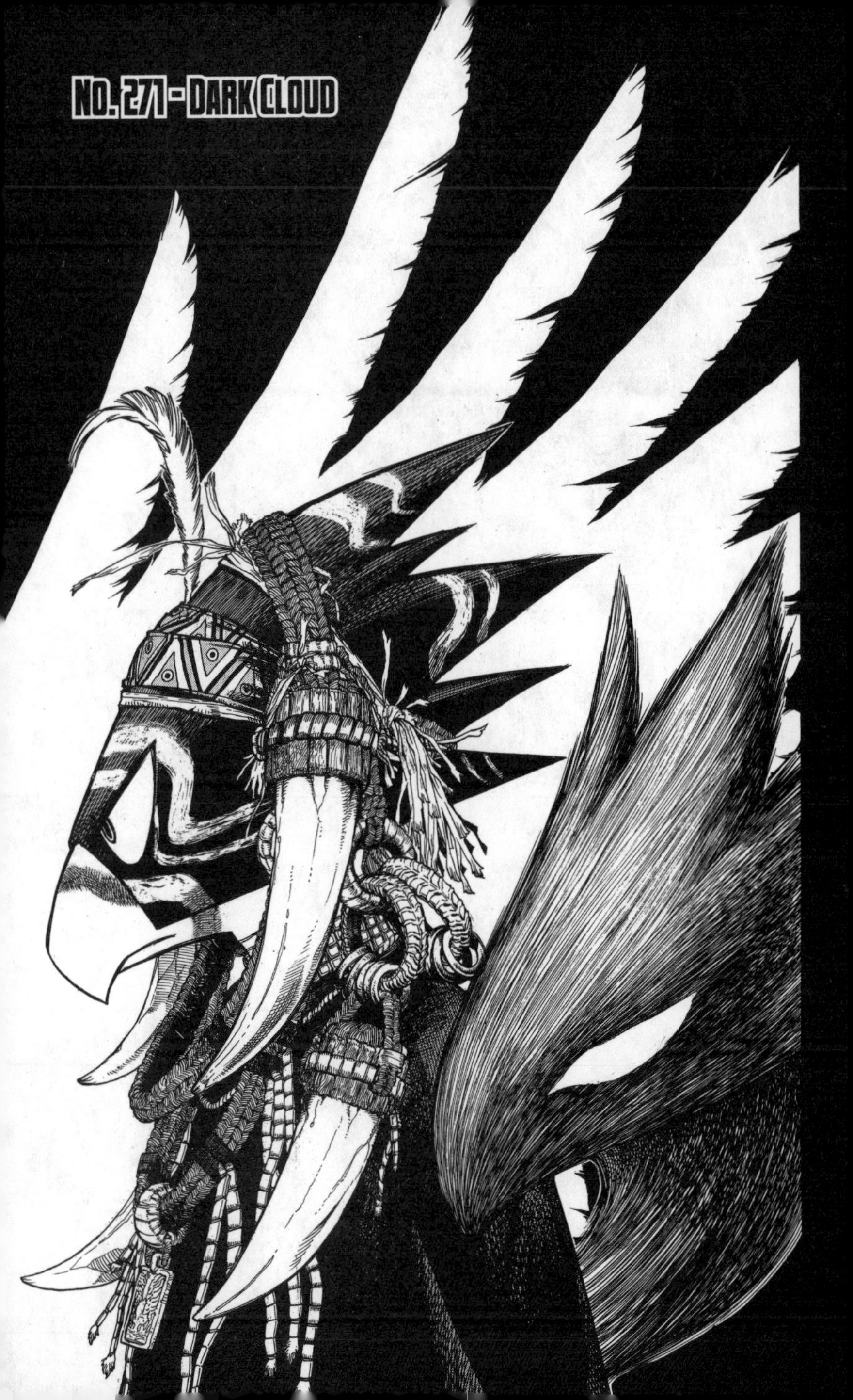
No. 271 - Dark Cloud

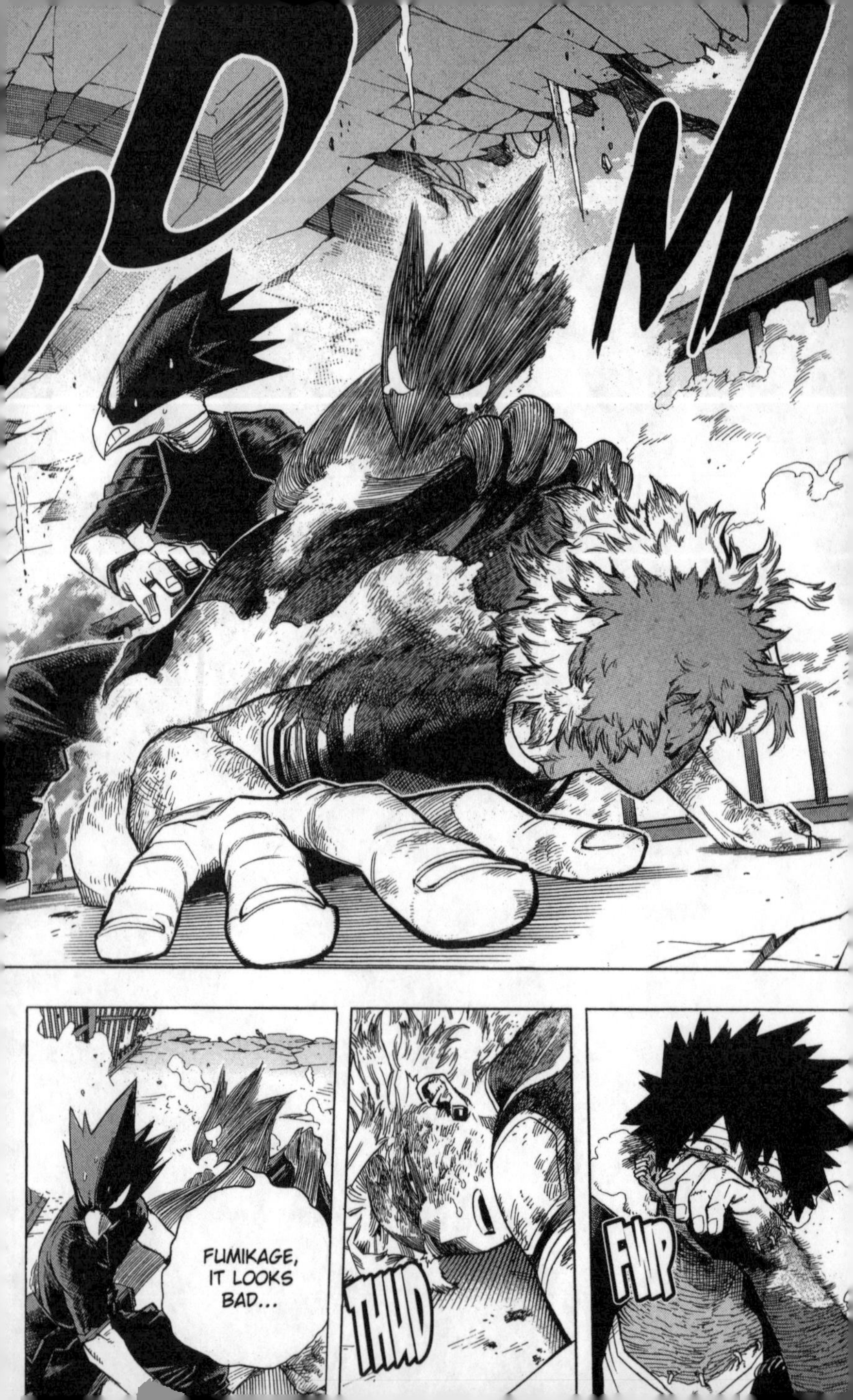
FWIP
THUD
FUMIKAGE, IT LOOKS BAD...

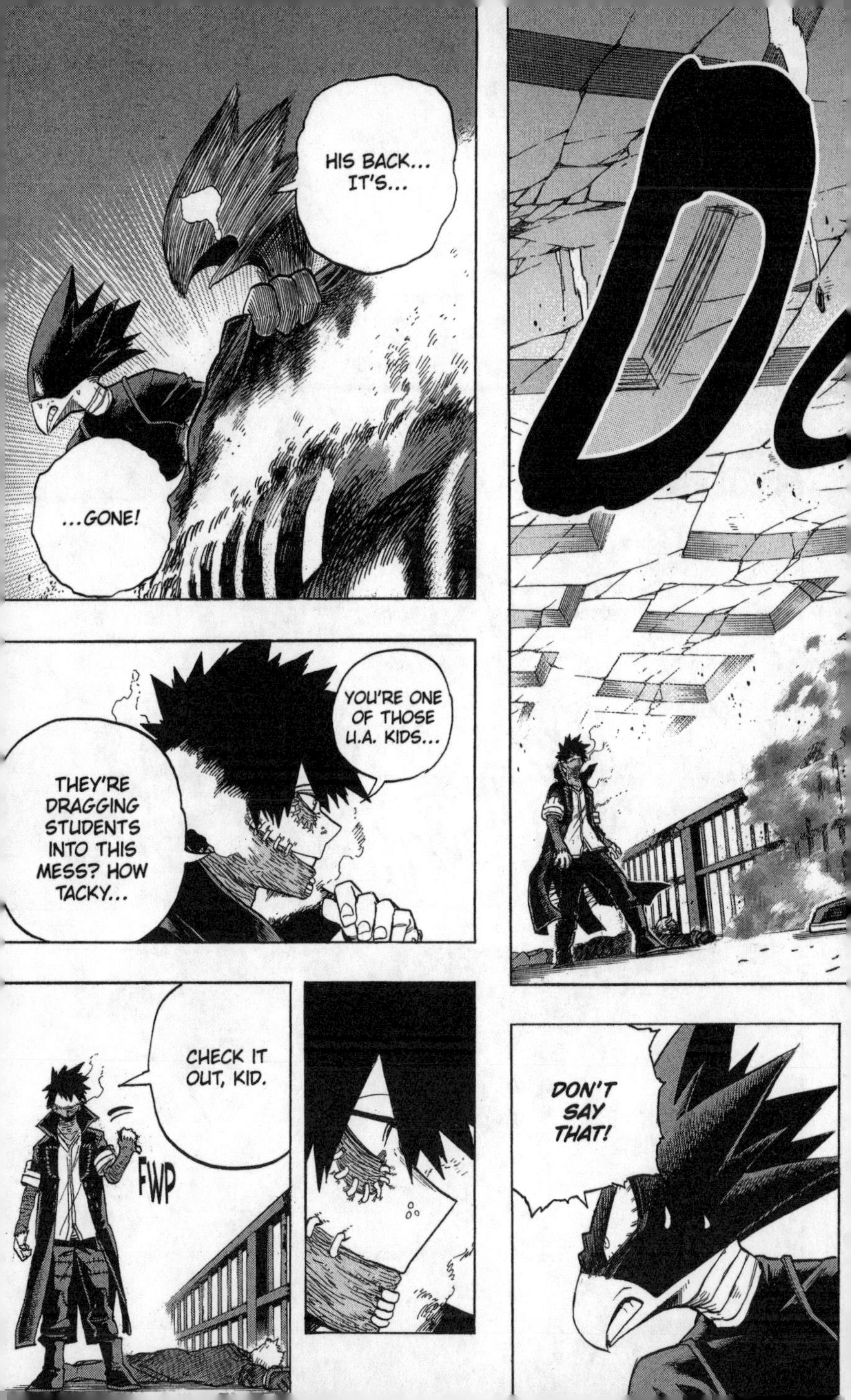
HIS BACK... IT'S...
...GONE!
YOU'RE ONE OF THOSE U.A. KIDS...
THEY'RE DRAGGING STUDENTS INTO THIS MESS? HOW TACKY...
DON'T SAY THAT!
CHECK IT OUT, KID.
FWP

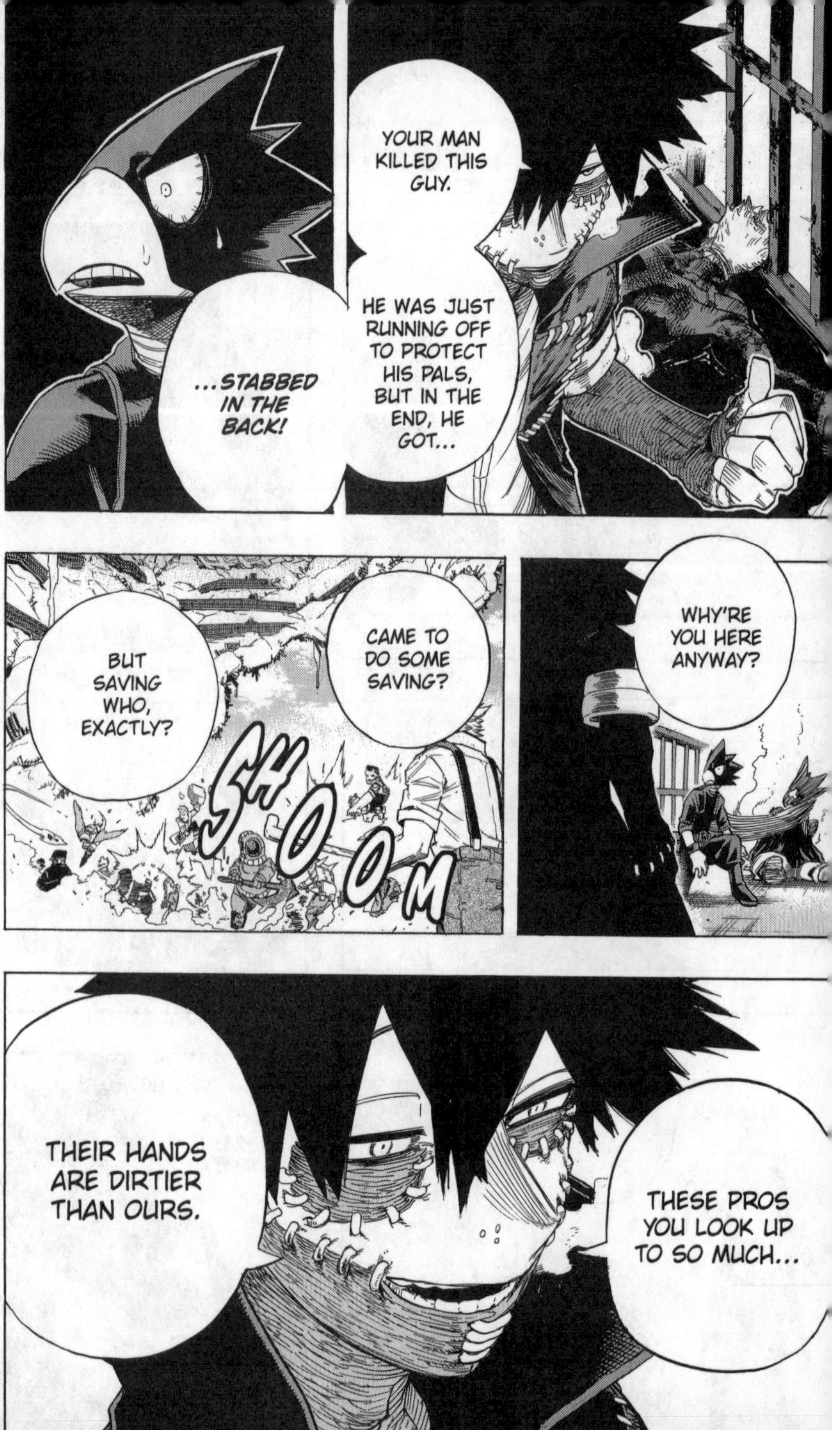
YOUR MAN KILLED THIS GUY.
HE WAS JUST RUNNING OFF TO PROTECT HIS PALS, BUT IN THE END, HE GOT...
...STABBED IN THE BACK!
WHY'RE YOU HERE ANYWAY?
CAME TO DO SOME SAVING?
BUT SAVING WHO, EXACTLY?
SHOOOM
THESE PROS YOU LOOK UP TO SO MUCH...
THEIR HANDS ARE DIRTIER THAN OURS.

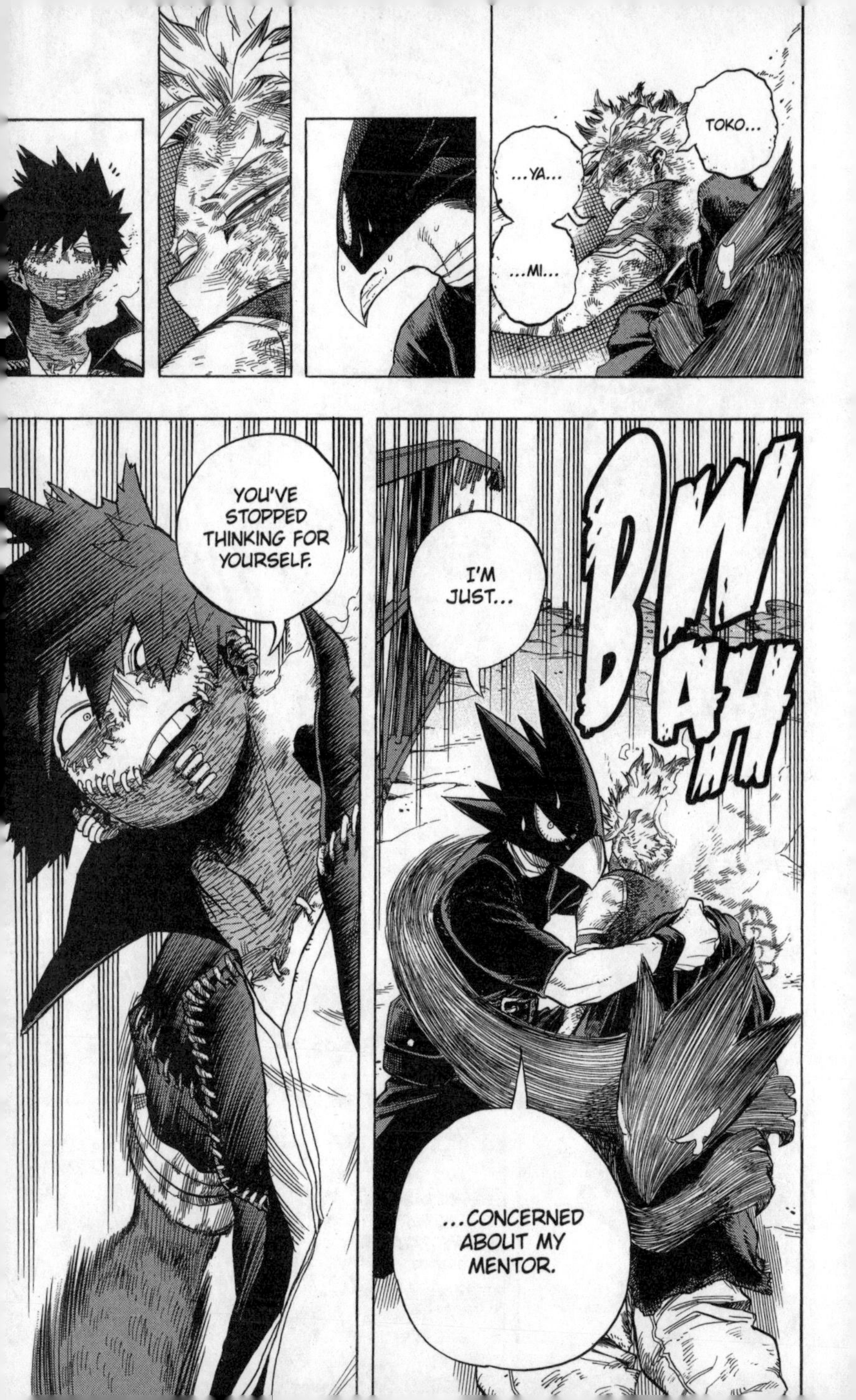
TOKO...
...YA...
...MI...
BWAH
I'M JUST...
...CONCERNED ABOUT MY MENTOR.
YOU'VE STOPPED THINKING FOR YOURSELF.

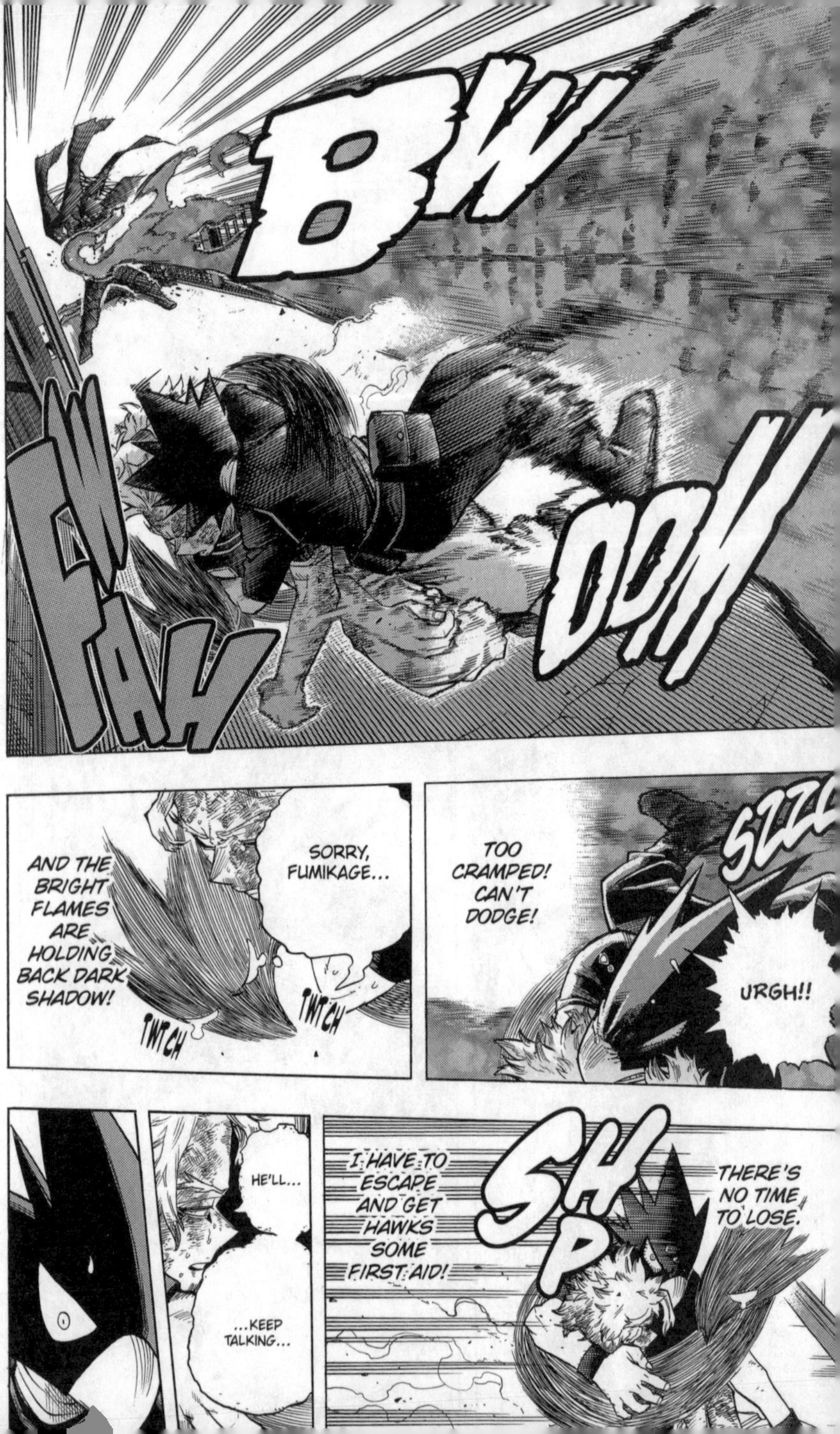
BW
SZZZ
TOO CRAMPED! CAN'T DODGE!
URGH!!
SORRY, FUMIKAGE...
AND THE BRIGHT FLAMES ARE HOLDING BACK DARK SHADOW!
TWITCH
TWITCH
THERE'S NO TIME TO LOSE.
SHP
I HAVE TO ESCAPE AND GET HAWKS SOME FIRST AID!
HE'LL...
...KEEP TALKING...

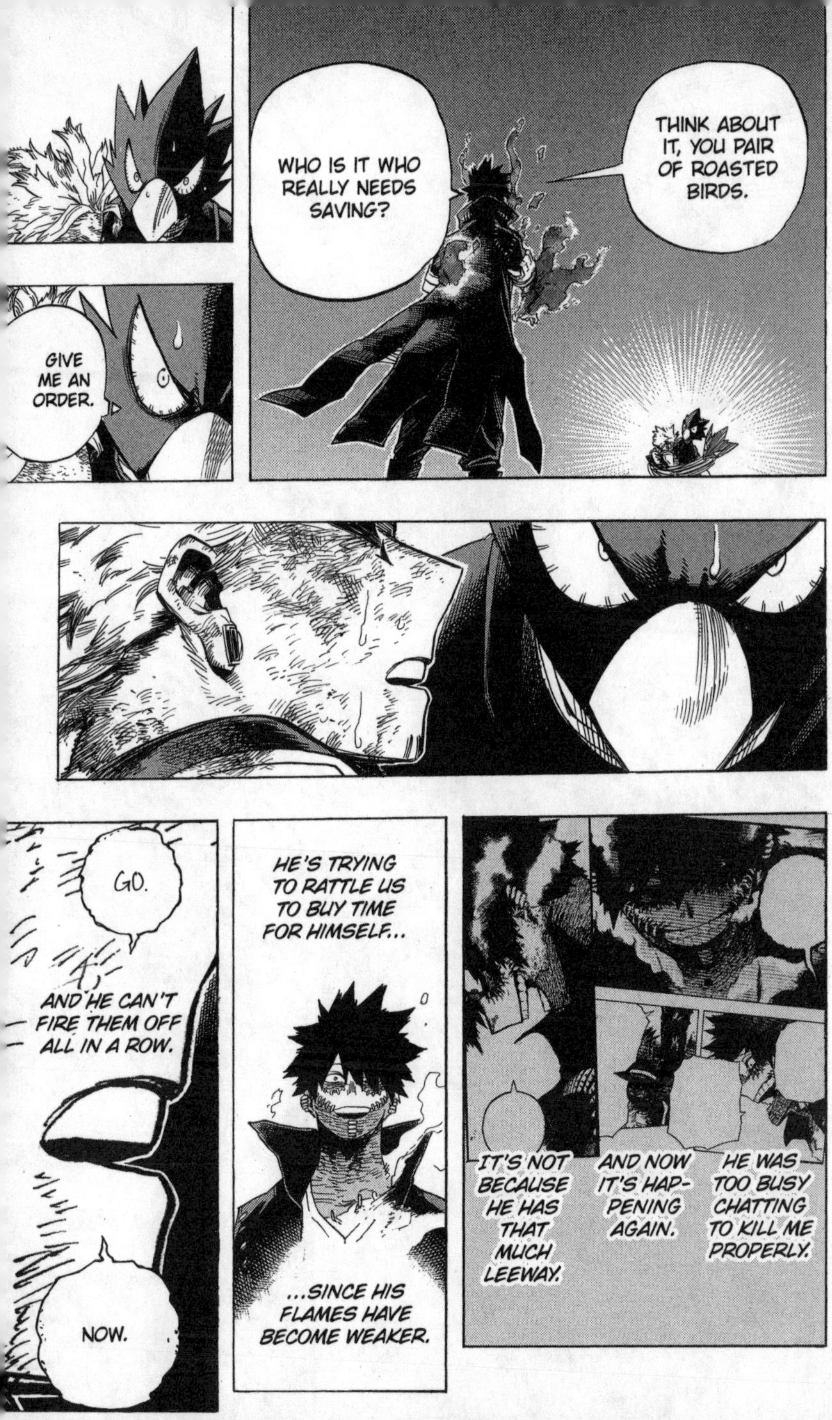
THINK ABOUT IT, YOU PAIR OF ROASTED BIRDS.
WHO IS IT WHO REALLY NEEDS SAVING?
GIVE ME AN ORDER.
HE WAS TOO BUSY CHATTING TO KILL ME PROPERLY.
AND NOW IT'S HAPPENING AGAIN.
IT'S NOT BECAUSE HE HAS THAT MUCH LEEWAY.
HE'S TRYING TO RATTLE US TO BUY TIME FOR HIMSELF...
...SINCE HIS FLAMES HAVE BECOME WEAKER.
GO.
AND HE CAN'T FIRE THEM OFF ALL IN A ROW.
NOW.

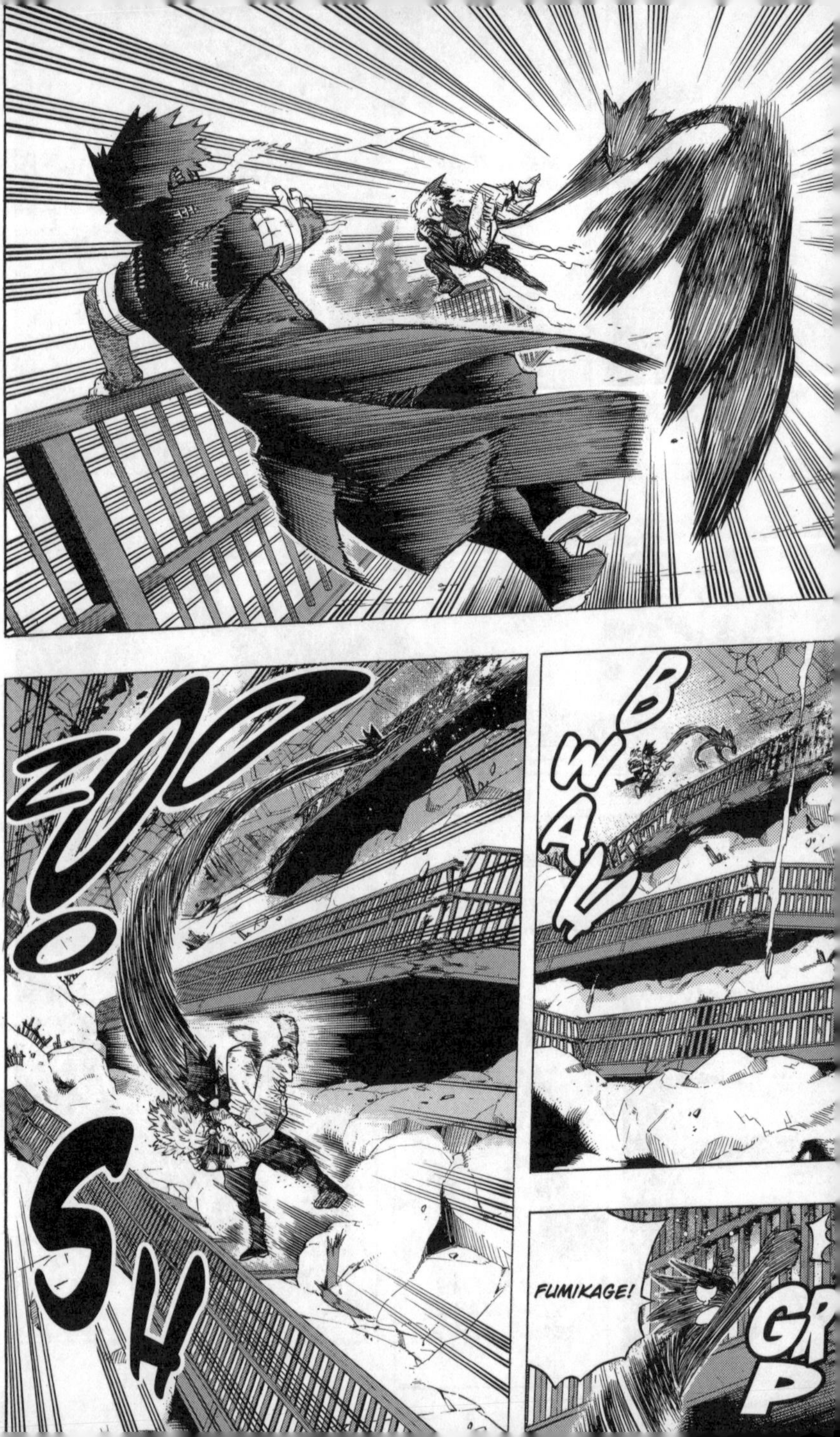
BWAM
FUMIKAGE!
!
GRP
SH

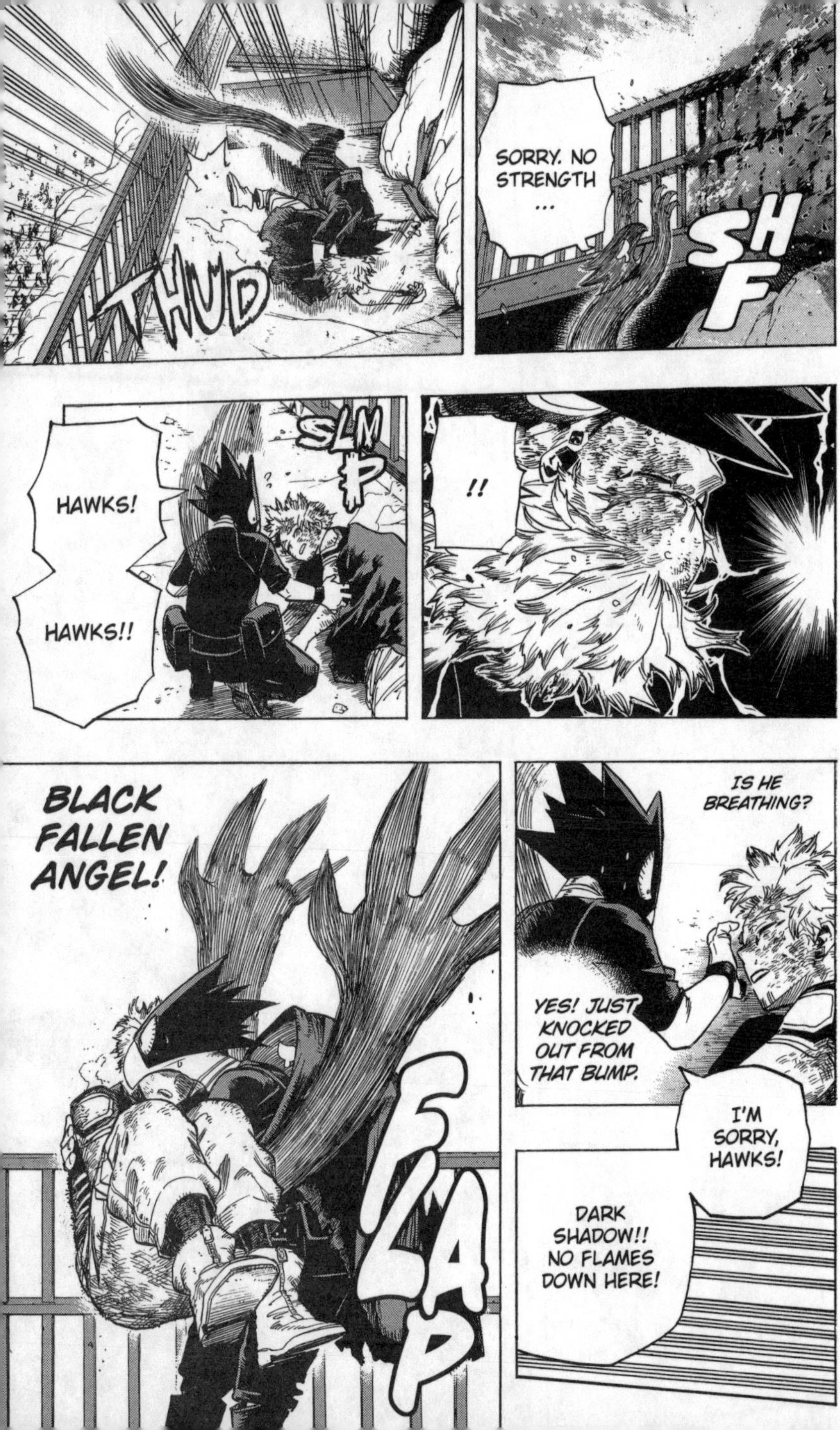

SORRY. NO STRENGTH ...
SHF
THUD
!!
SLMP
HAWKS!
HAWKS!!
IS HE BREATHING?
YES! JUST KNOCKED OUT FROM THAT BUMP.
I'M SORRY, HAWKS!
DARK SHADOW!! NO FLAMES DOWN HERE!
BLACK FALLEN ANGEL!
FLAP

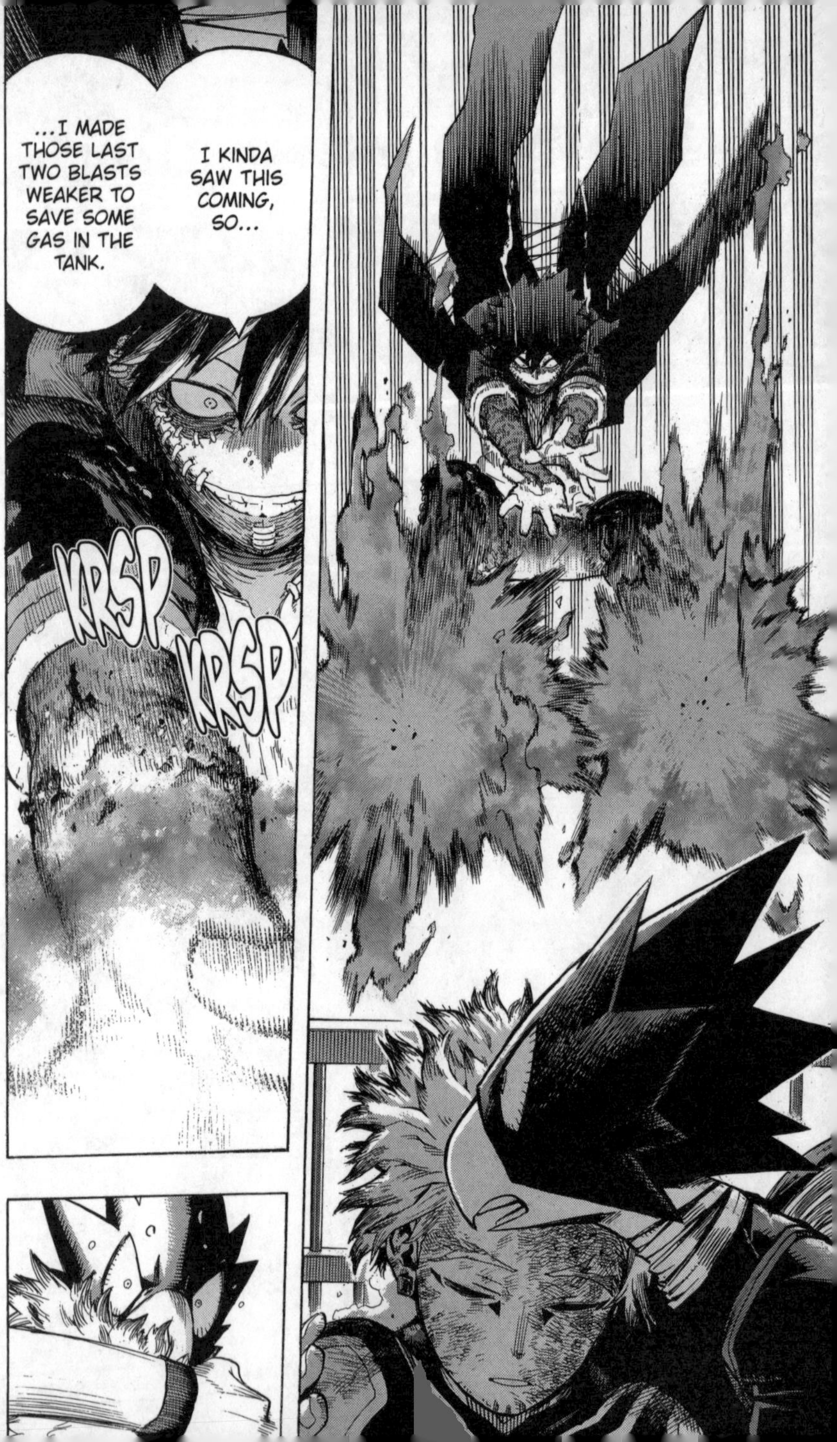
I KINDA SAW THIS COMING, SO...
...I MADE THOSE LAST TWO BLASTS WEAKER TO SAVE SOME GAS IN THE TANK.
KRSP
KRSP

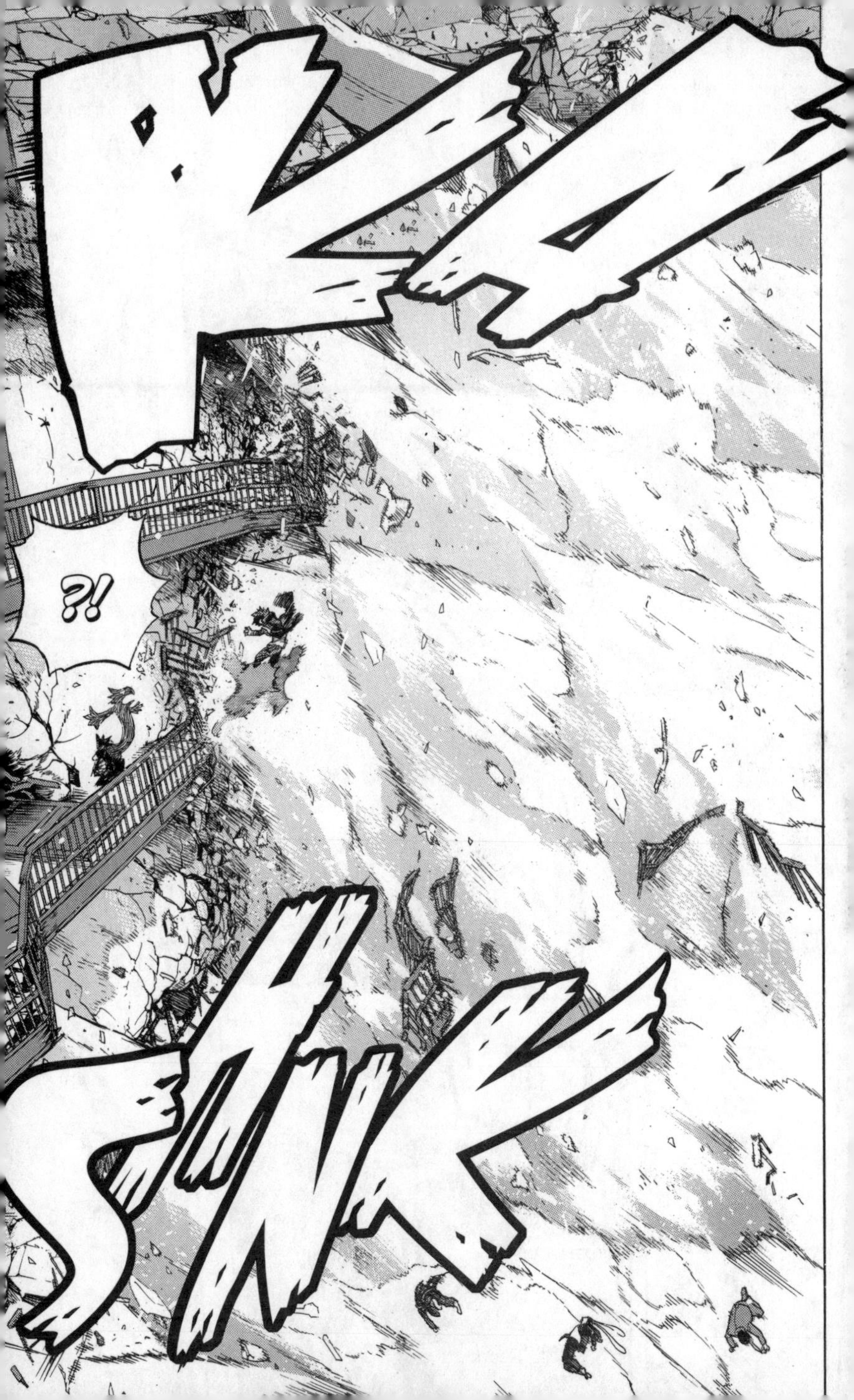
?!

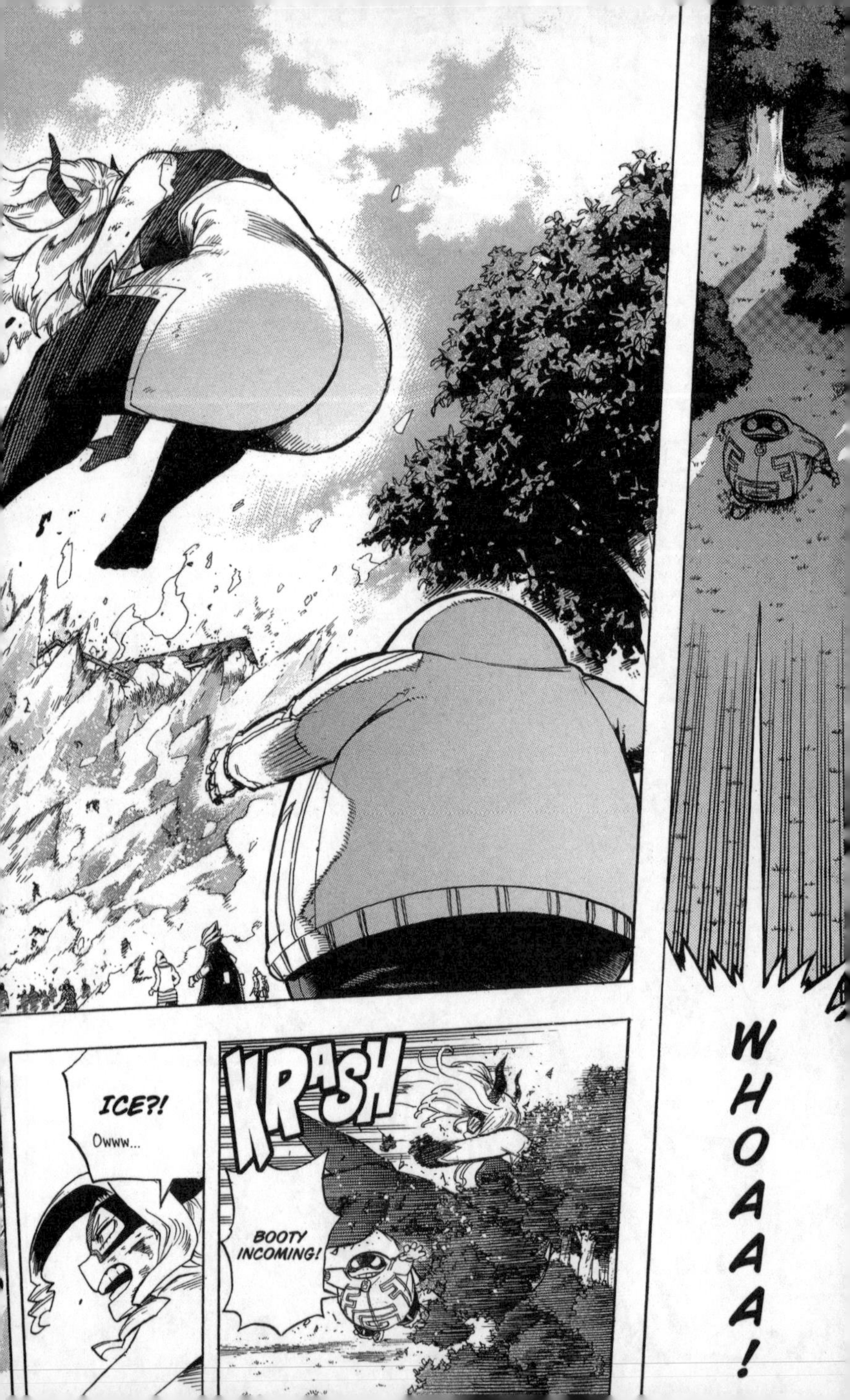
WHOAAAA!
KRASH
BOOTY INCOMING!
ICE?!
Owww...

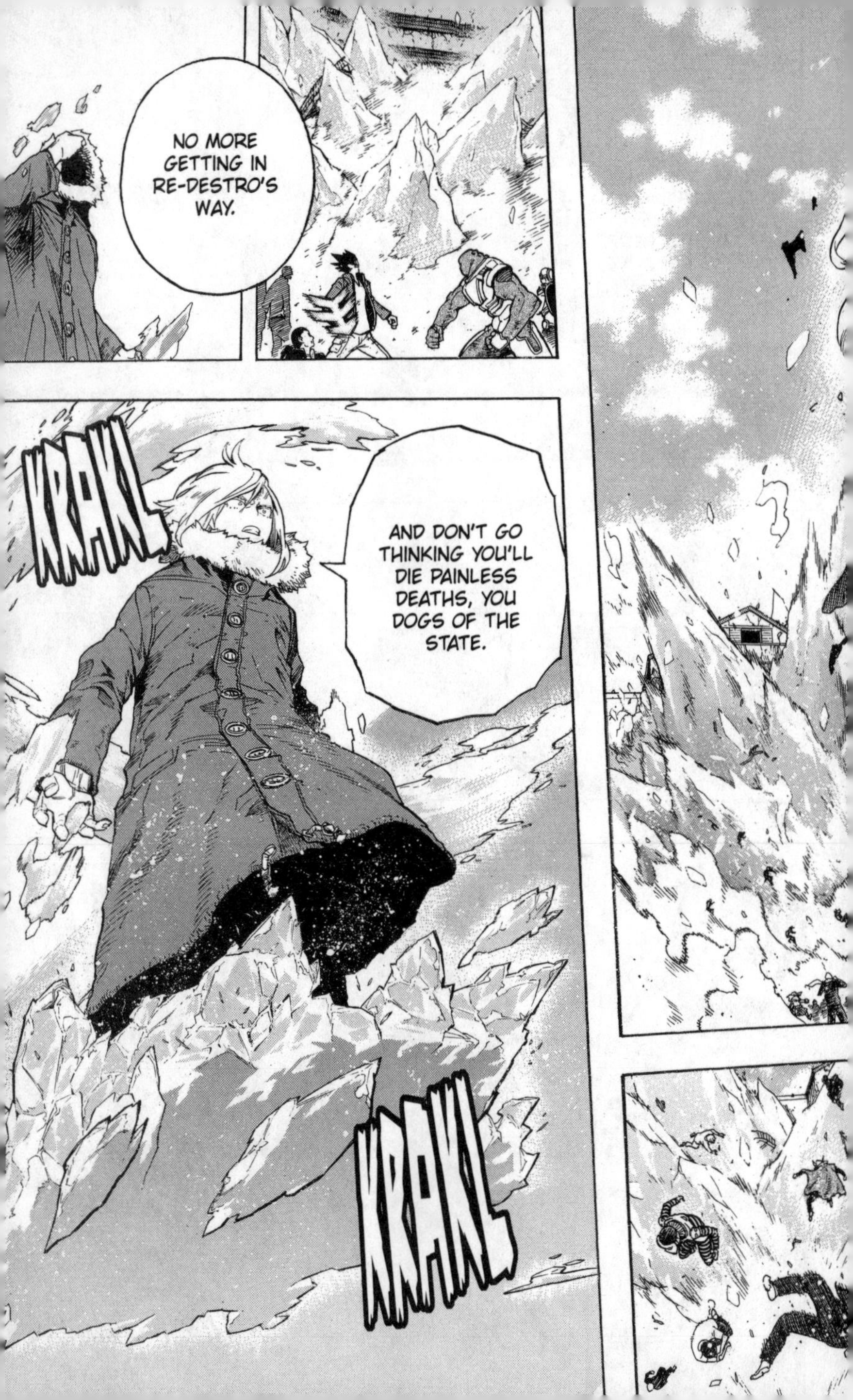
NO MORE GETTING IN RE-DESTRO'S WAY.
AND DON'T GO THINKING YOU'LL DIE PAINLESS DEATHS, YOU DOGS OF THE STATE.
KRAK!
KRAK!

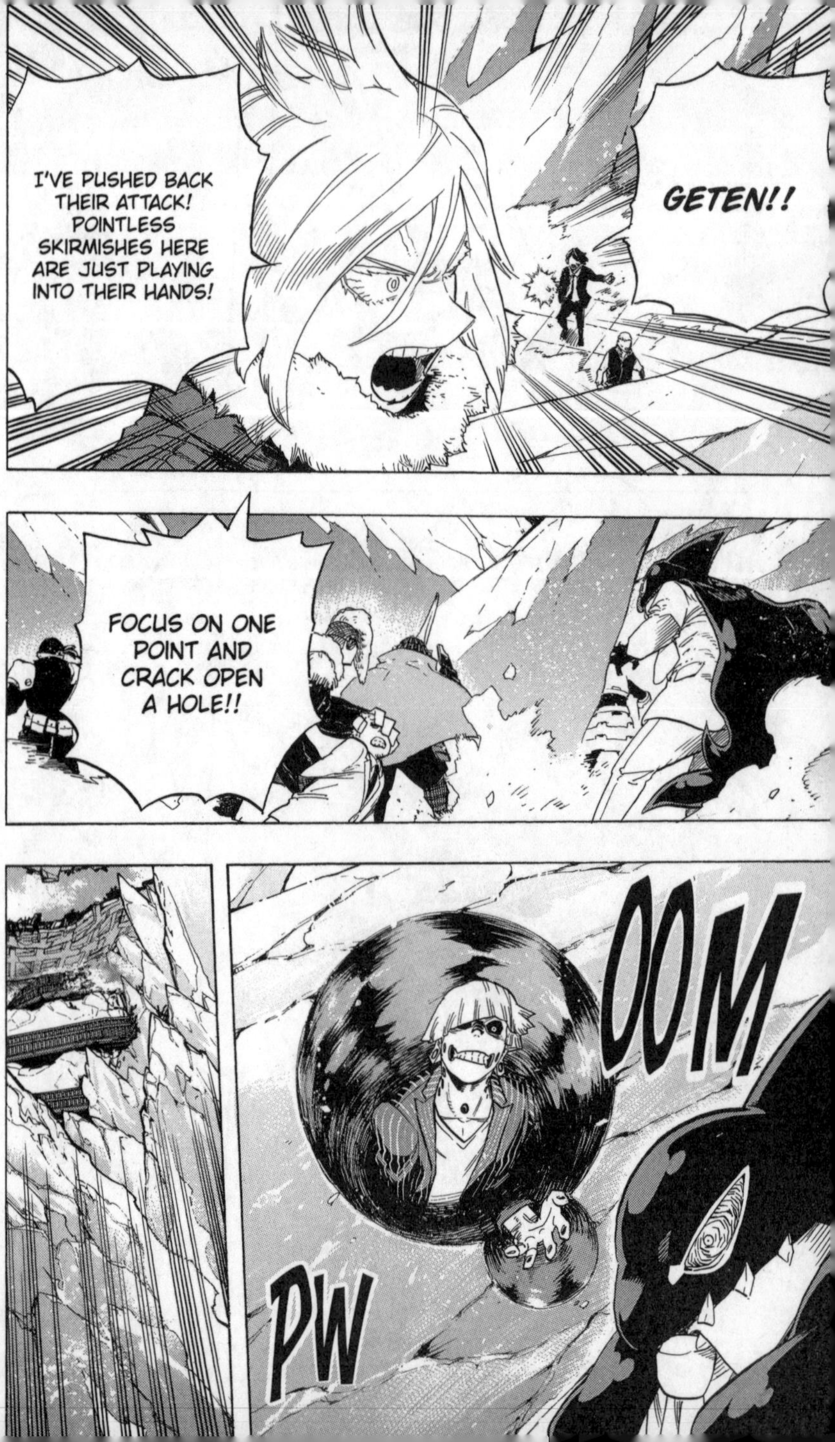
GETEN!!
I'VE PUSHED BACK THEIR ATTACK! POINTLESS SKIRMISHES HERE ARE JUST PLAYING INTO THEIR HANDS!
FOCUS ON ONE POINT AND CRACK OPEN A HOLE!!
OOM
PW

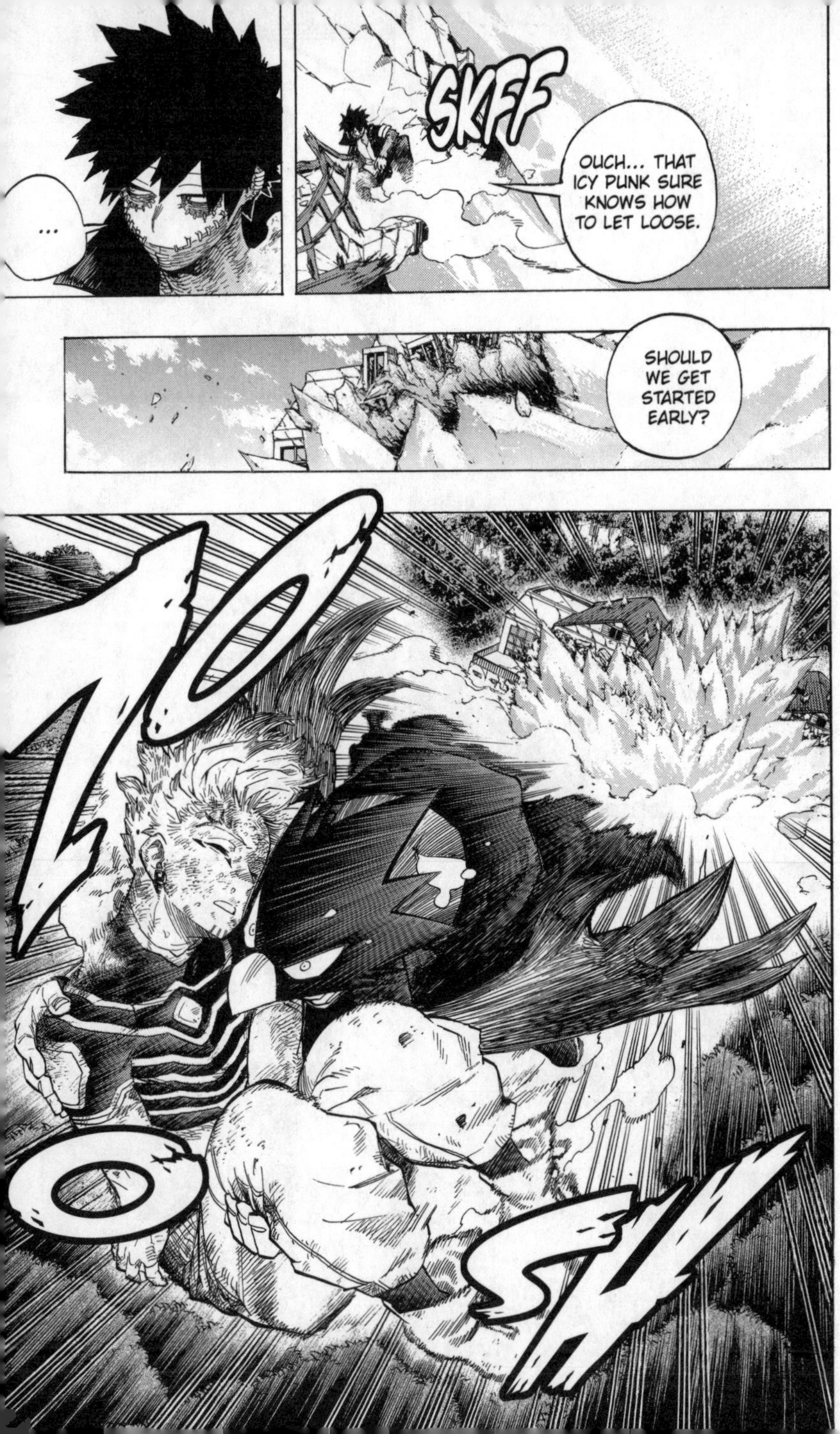
SKFF
OUCH... THAT ICY PUNK SURE KNOWS HOW TO LET LOOSE.
...
SHOULD WE GET STARTED EARLY?
ZOOSH

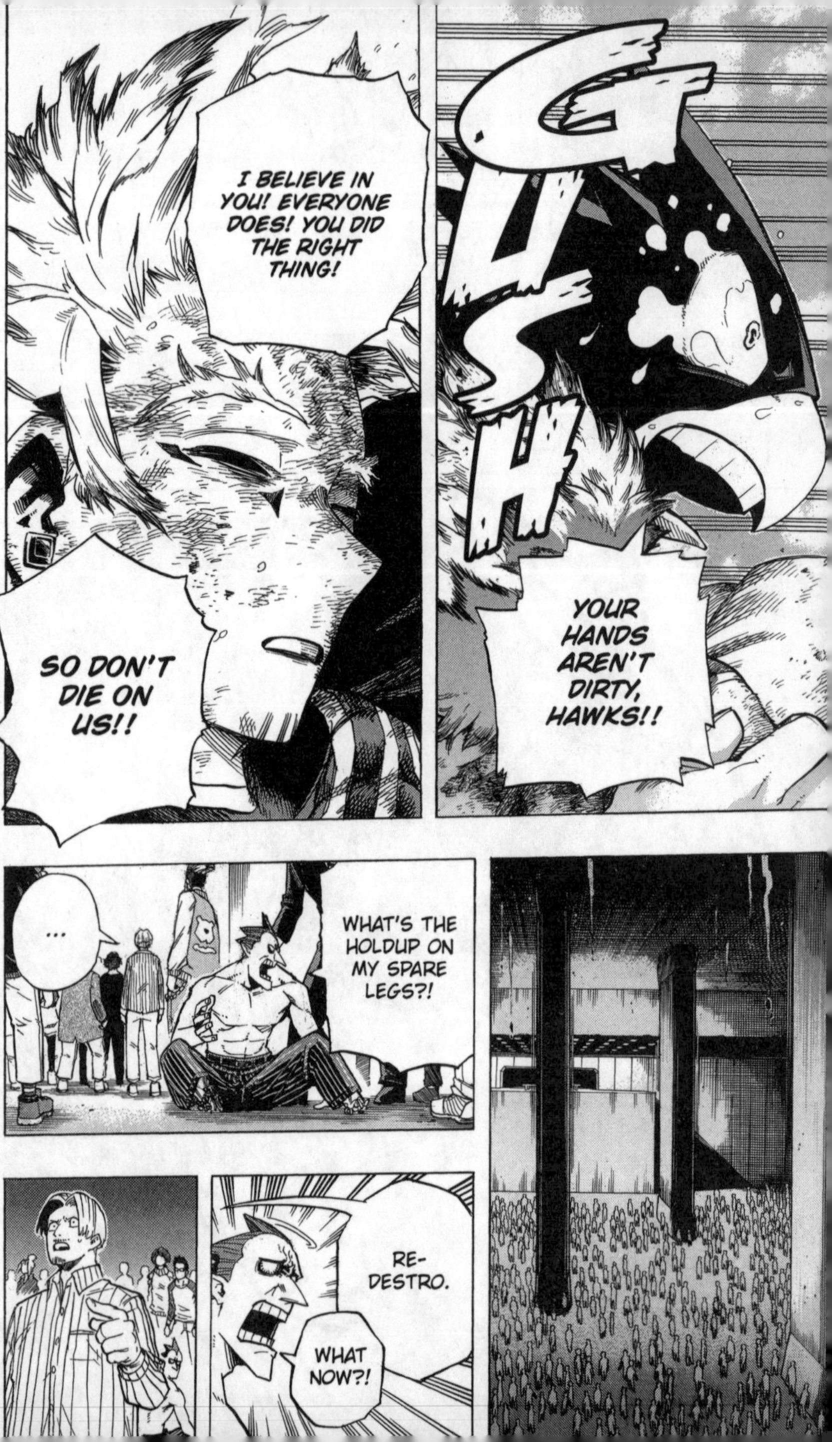
GASH
YOUR HANDS AREN'T DIRTY, HAWKS!!
I BELIEVE IN YOU! EVERYONE DOES! YOU DID THE RIGHT THING!
SO DON'T DIE ON US!!
WHAT'S THE HOLDUP ON MY SPARE LEGS?!
...
RE-DESTRO.
WHAT NOW?!

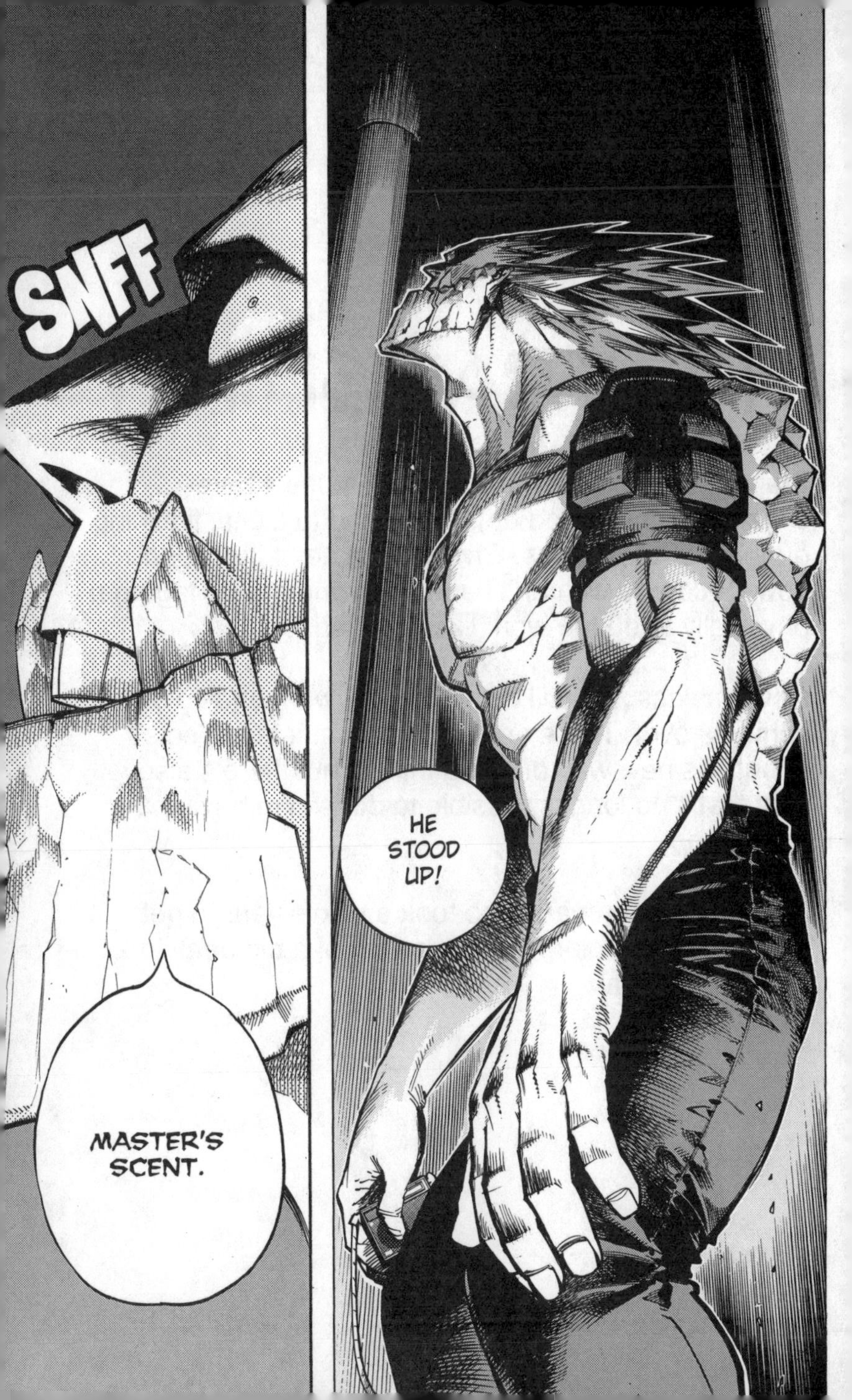
HE STOOD UP!
SNFF
MASTER'S SCENT.

THE TRANSITION

Starting with the previous page (the one where Gigantomachia stood up), I switched to digital finishing during the art process. Given the state of the world now, of course we can't have everyone gather together physically to do the work like we used to…

Nevertheless, I'm still doing the line work analog style, same as ever. There are some convenient aspects about this new way of doing things, but there's also stuff that's no longer possible to do, so I'm having a hard time.

As an analog human (who took a whole year to get used to digital coloring), this is kind of a big deal, in a not-so-great way.

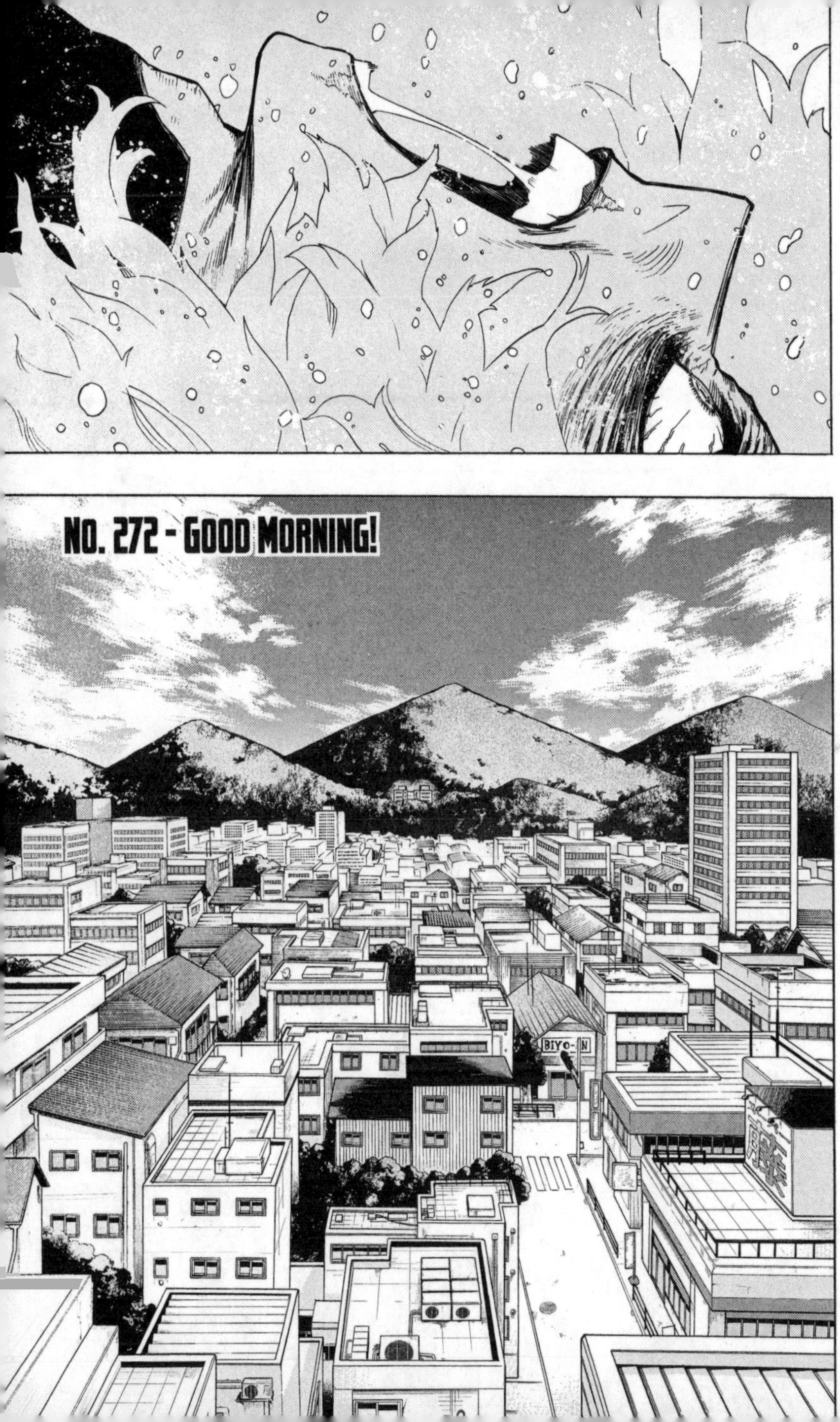
No. 272 - Good Morning!
BIYO-IN

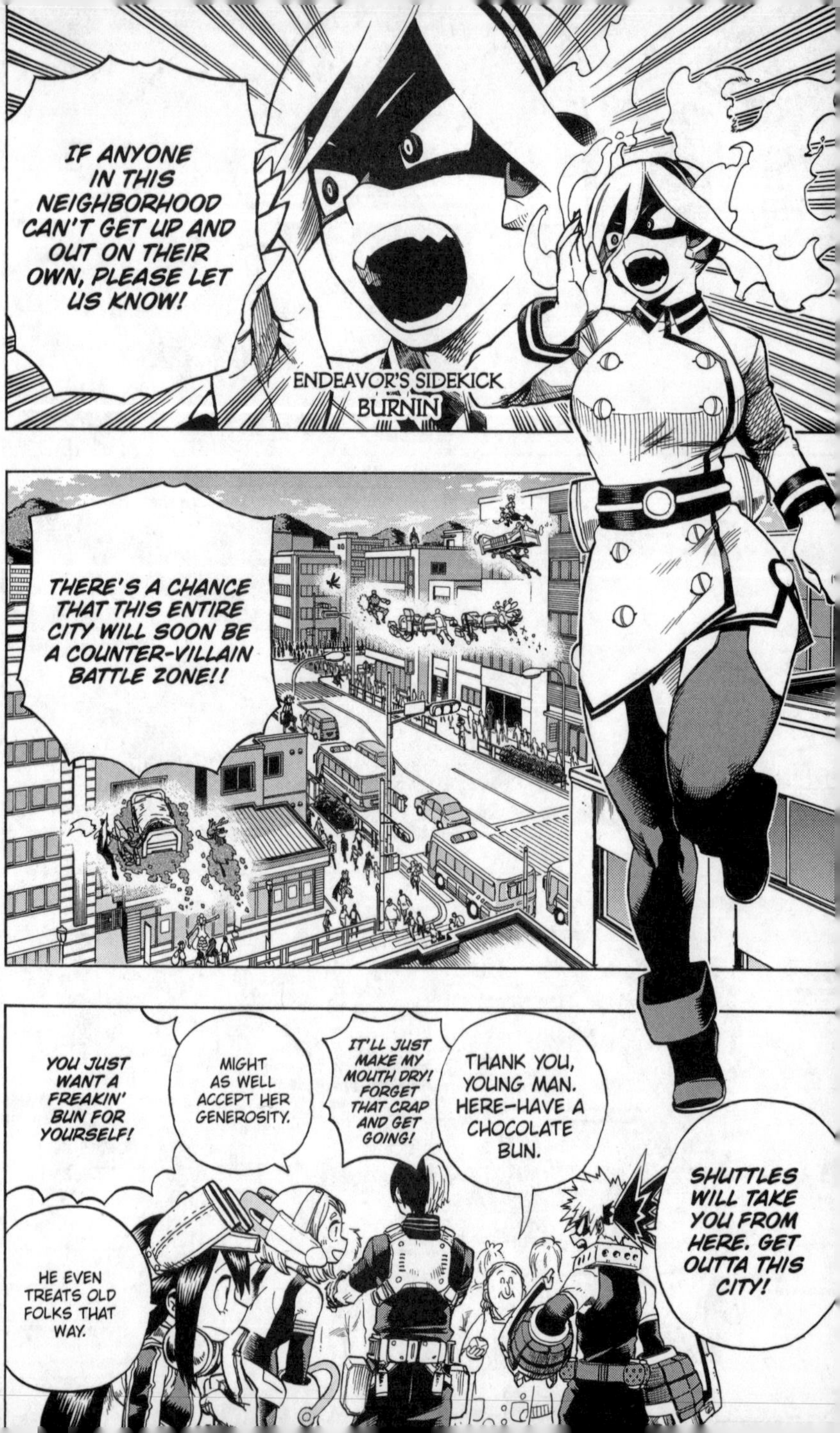
IF ANYONE IN THIS NEIGHBORHOOD CAN'T GET UP AND OUT ON THEIR OWN, PLEASE LET US KNOW!
ENDEAVOR'S SIDEKICK BURNIN
THERE'S A CHANCE THAT THIS ENTIRE CITY WILL SOON BE A COUNTER-VILLAIN BATTLE ZONE!!
SHUTTLES WILL TAKE YOU FROM HERE. GET OUTTA THIS CITY!
THANK YOU, YOUNG MAN. HERE—HAVE A CHOCOLATE BUN.
IT'LL JUST MAKE MY MOUTH DRY! FORGET THAT CRAP AND GET GOING!
MIGHT AS WELL ACCEPT HER GENEROSITY.
YOU JUST WANT A FREAKIN' BUN FOR YOURSELF!
HE EVEN TREATS OLD FOLKS THAT WAY.

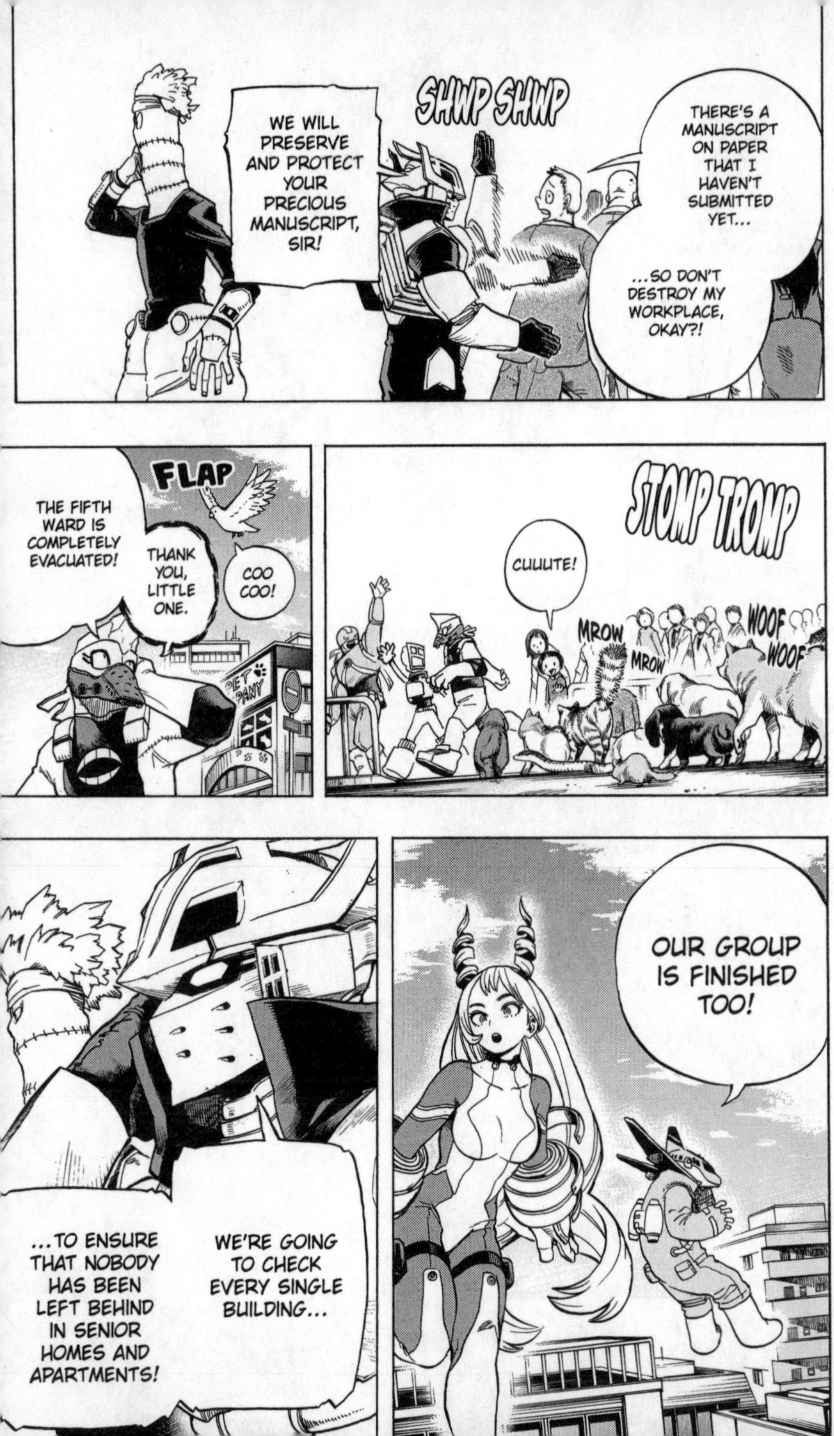
THERE'S A MANUSCRIPT ON PAPER THAT I HAVEN'T SUBMITTED YET...
...SO DON'T DESTROY MY WORKPLACE, OKAY?!
SHWP SHWP
WE WILL PRESERVE AND PROTECT YOUR PRECIOUS MANUSCRIPT, SIR!
STOMP TROMP
CUUUTE!
WOOF
WOOF
MROW
MROW
FLAP
THE FIFTH WARD IS COMPLETELY EVACUATED!
THANK YOU, LITTLE ONE.
COO COO!
PET
PANY
OUR GROUP IS FINISHED TOO!
WE'RE GOING TO CHECK EVERY SINGLE BUILDING...
...TO ENSURE THAT NOBODY HAS BEEN LEFT BEHIND IN SENIOR HOMES AND APARTMENTS!

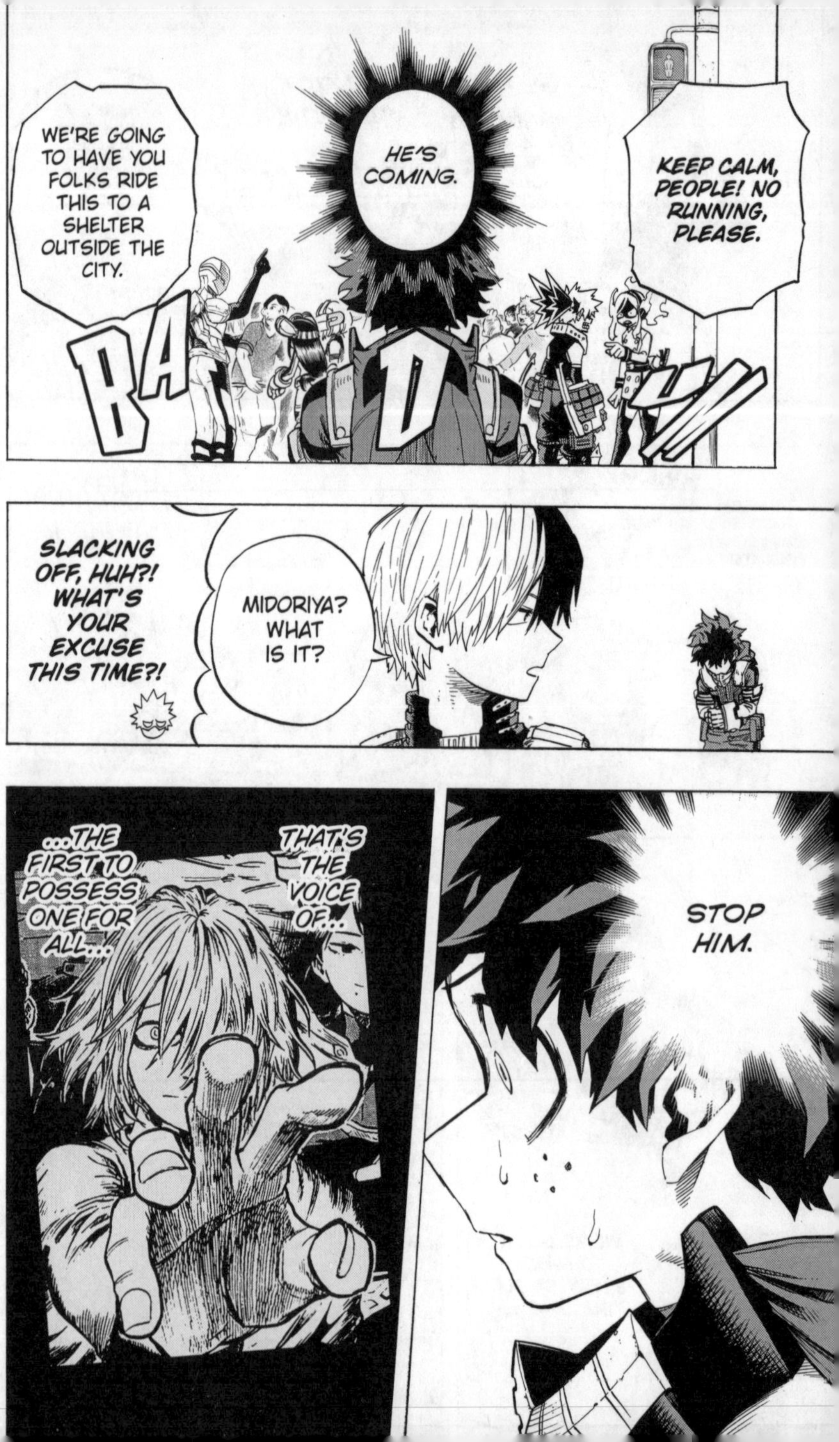
KEEP CALM, PEOPLE! NO RUNNING, PLEASE.
HE'S COMING.
WE'RE GOING TO HAVE YOU FOLKS RIDE THIS TO A SHELTER OUTSIDE THE CITY.
MIDORIYA? WHAT IS IT?
SLACKING OFF, HUH?! WHAT'S YOUR EXCUSE THIS TIME?!
STOP HIM.
THAT'S THE VOICE OF...
...THE FIRST TO POSSESS ONE FOR ALL...

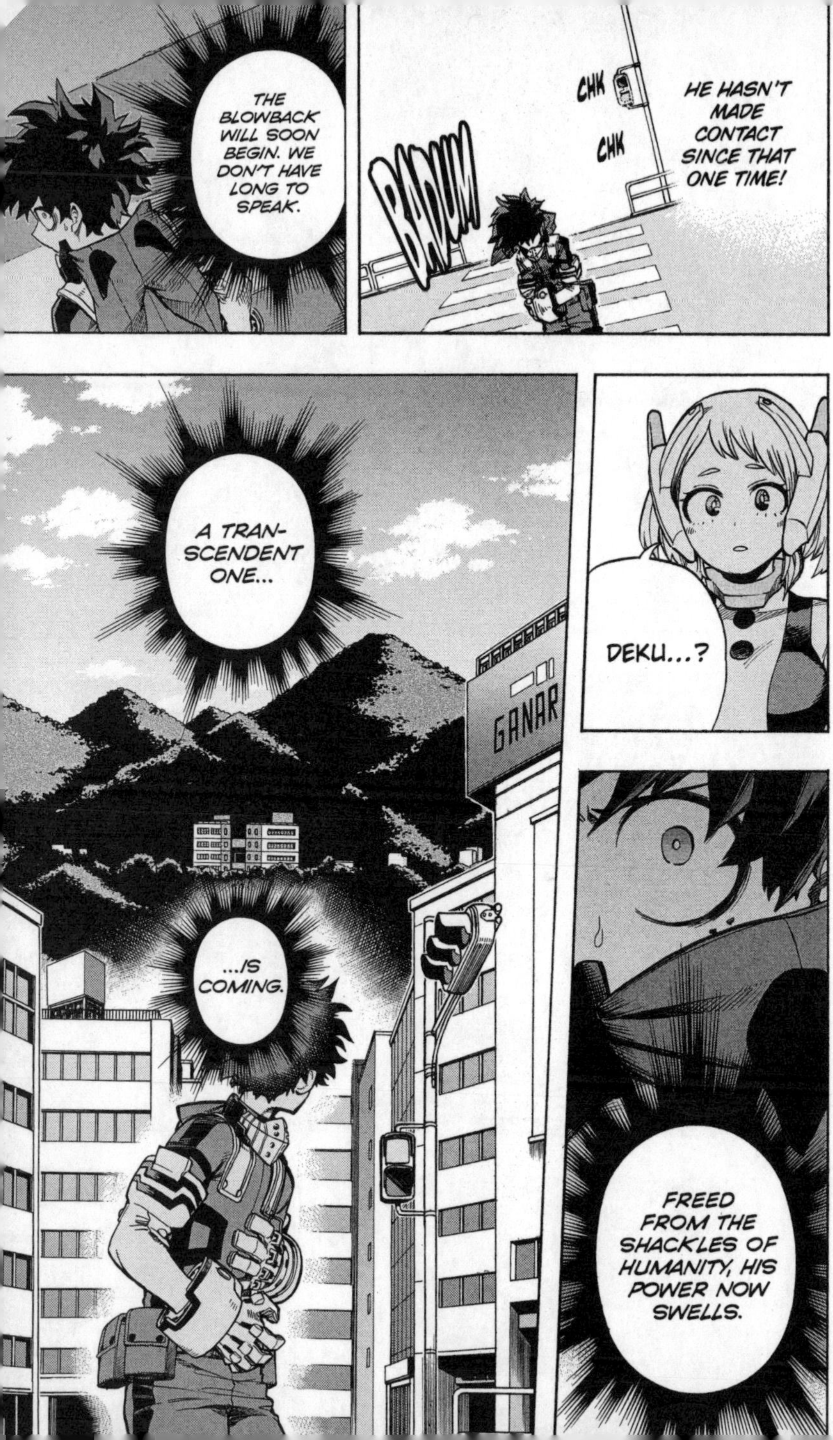
HE HASN'T MADE CONTACT SINCE THAT ONE TIME!
CHK
CHK
BADUM
THE BLOWBACK WILL SOON BEGIN. WE DON'T HAVE LONG TO SPEAK.
DEKU...?
FREED FROM THE SHACKLES OF HUMANITY, HIS POWER NOW SWELLS.
A TRAN-SCENDENT ONE...
GANAR
...IS COMING.

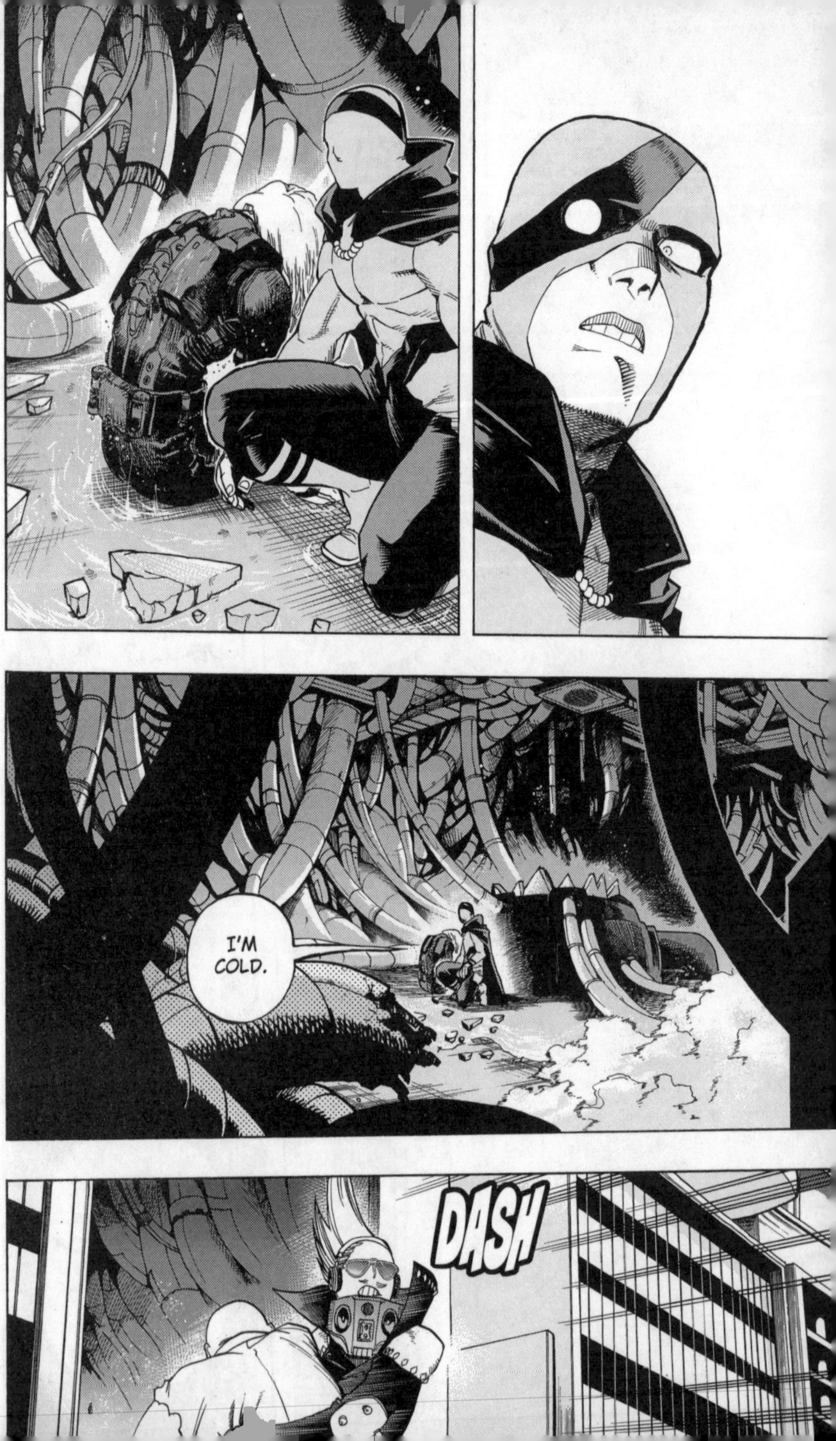

I'M COLD.
DASH

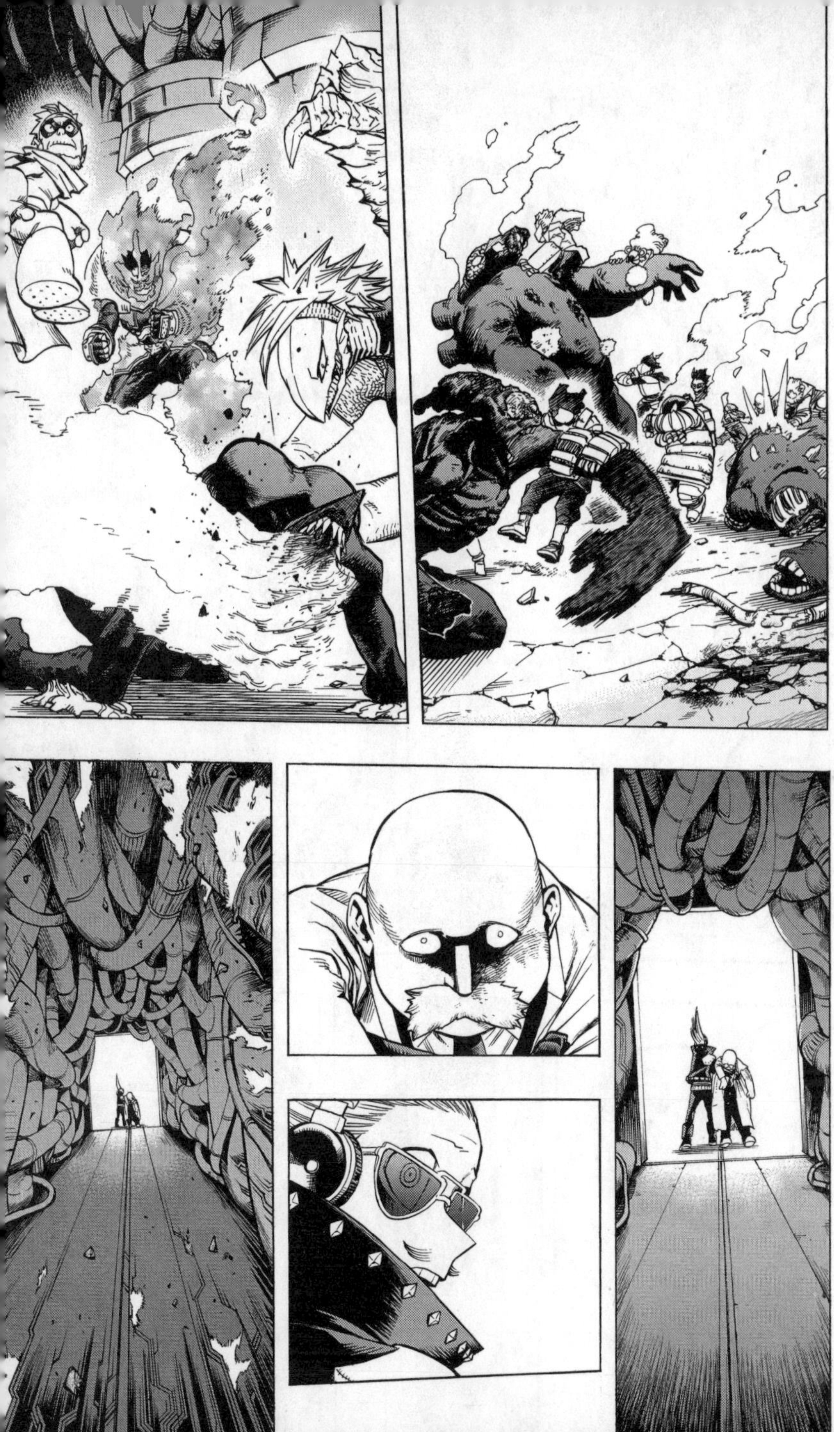

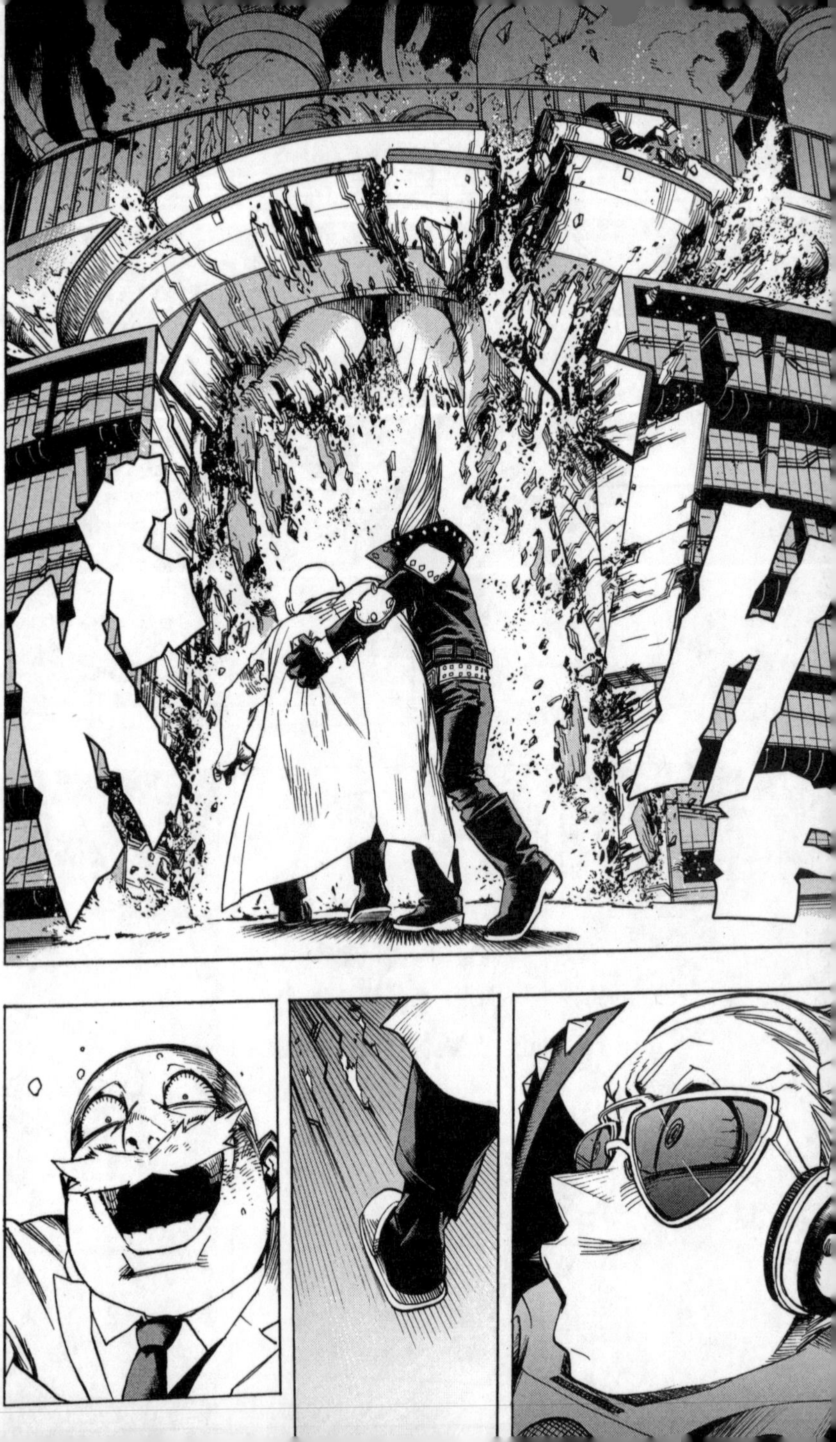

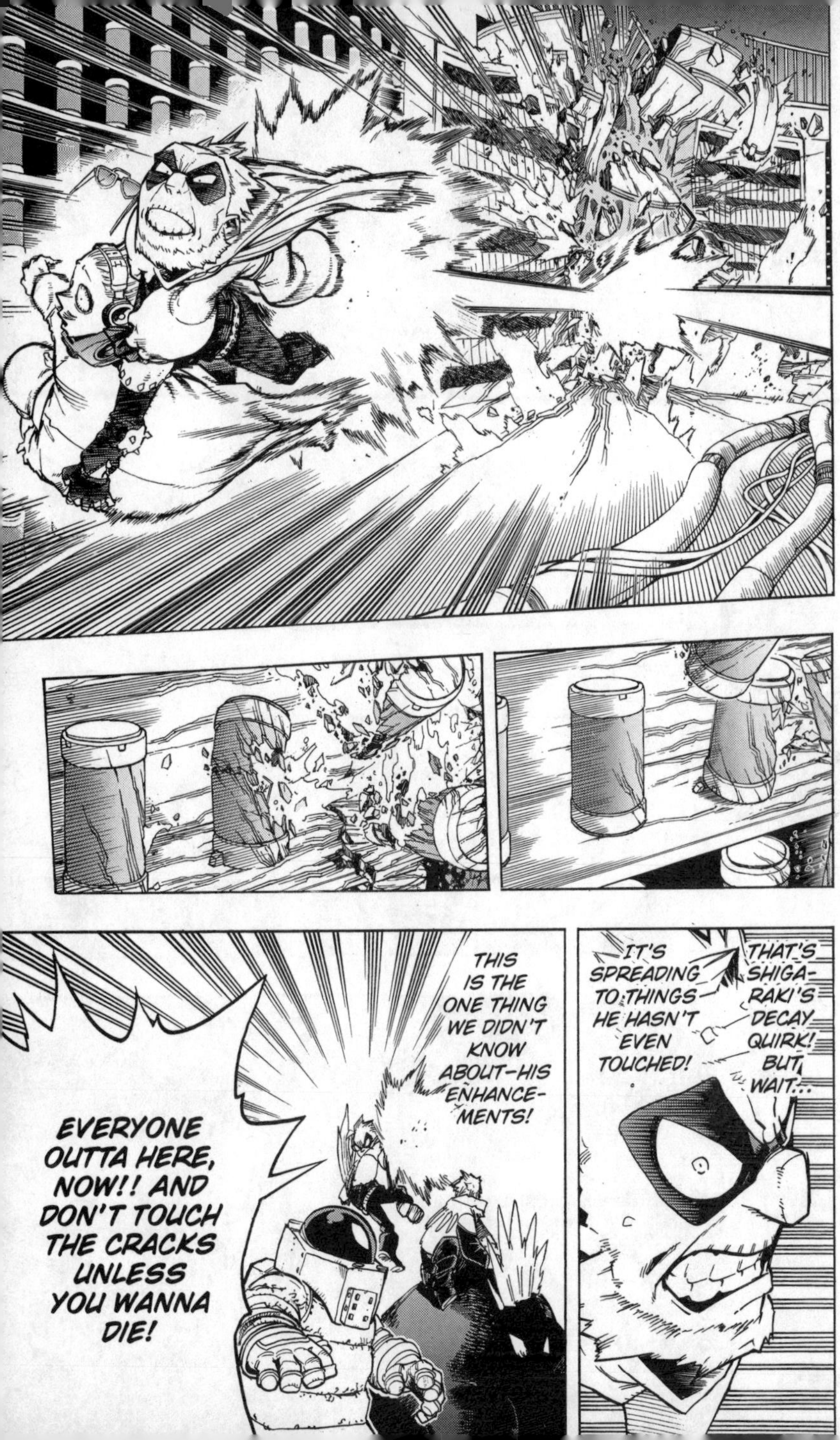
THAT'S SHIGARAKI'S DECAY QUIRK! BUT WAIT...
IT'S SPREADING TO THINGS HE HASN'T EVEN TOUCHED!
THIS IS THE ONE THING WE DIDN'T KNOW ABOUT—HIS ENHANCEMENTS!
EVERYONE OUTTA HERE, NOW!! AND DON'T TOUCH THE CRACKS UNLESS YOU WANNA DIE!

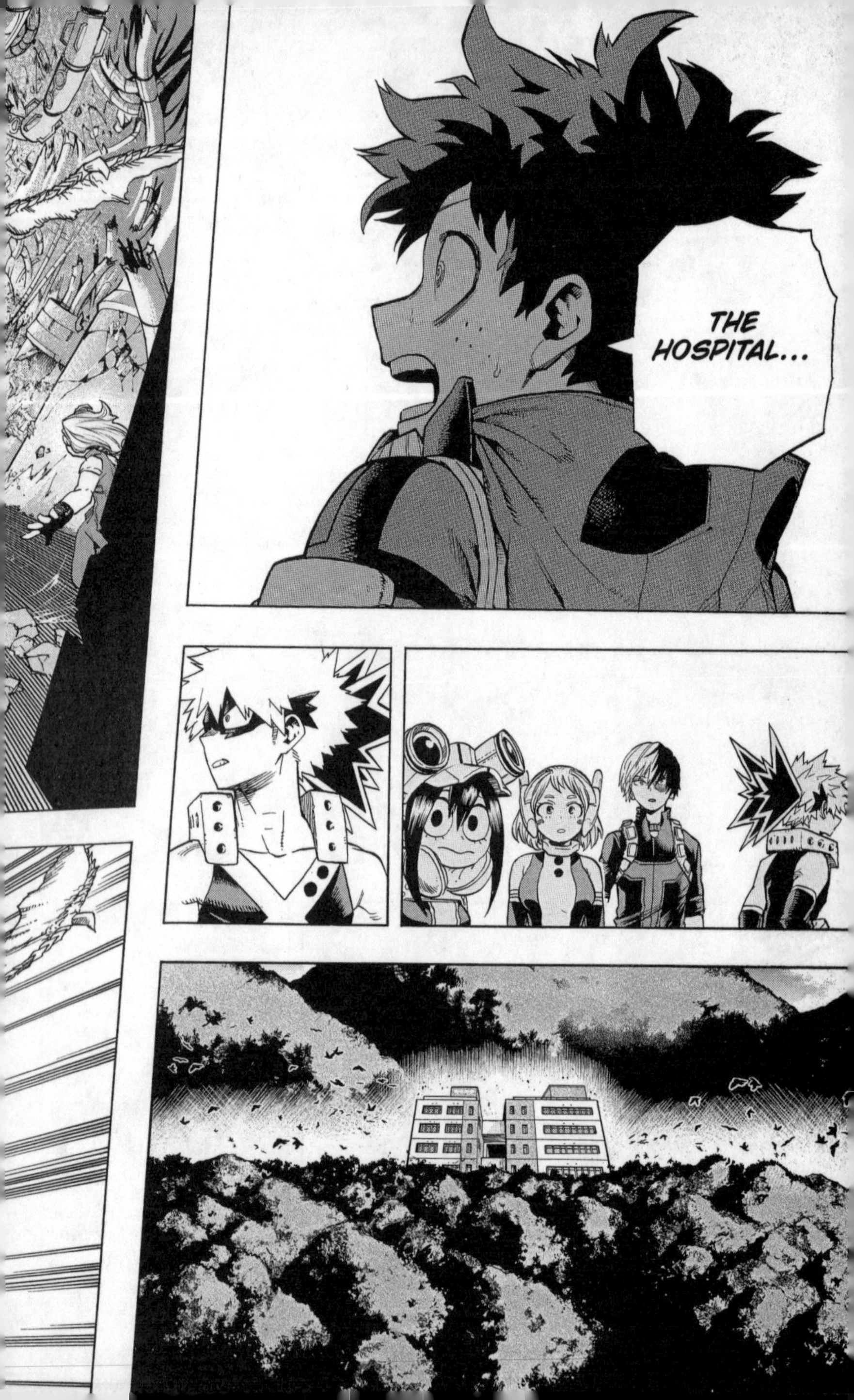
THE HOSPITAL...

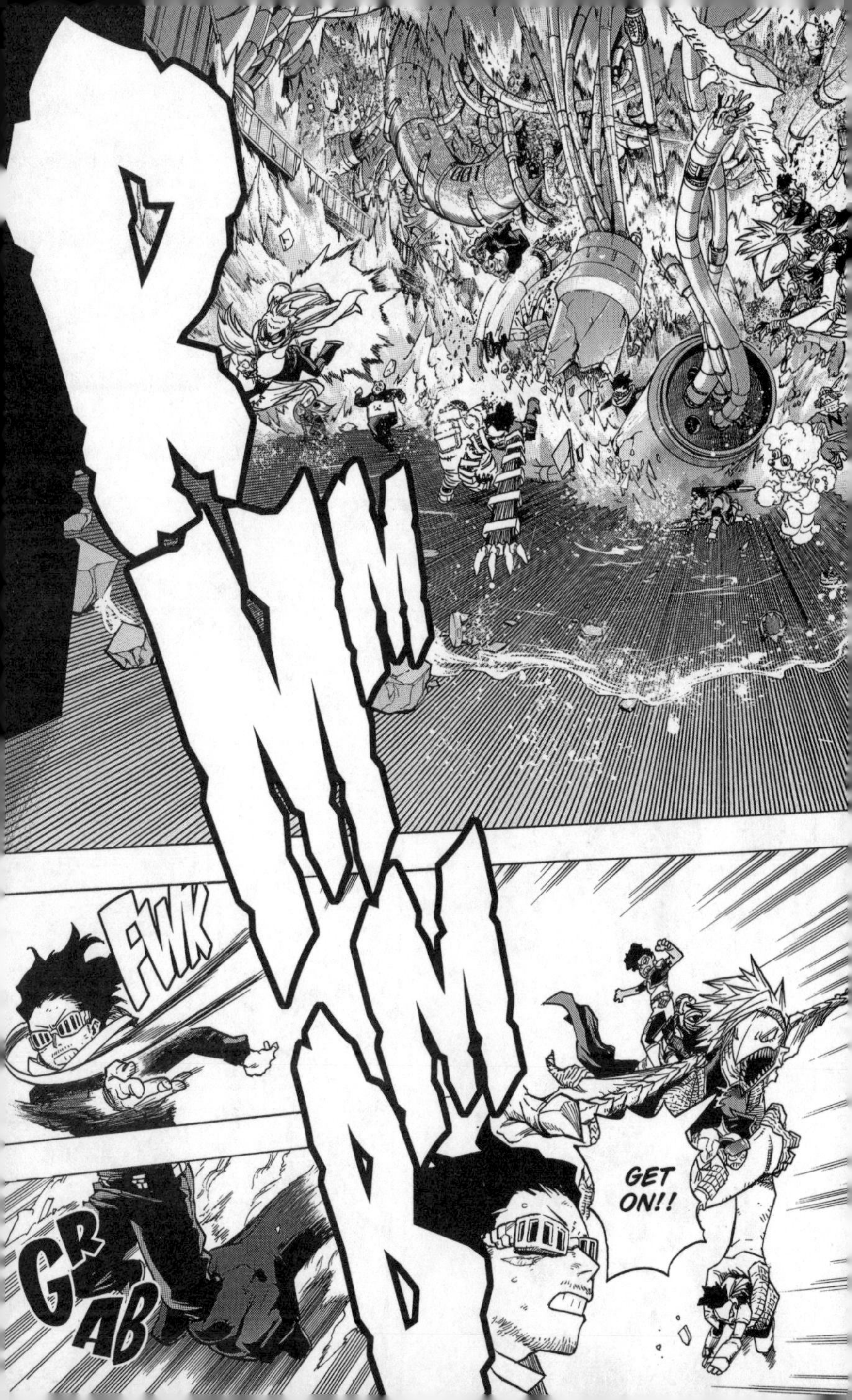

GET ON!!
FWK
GRAB

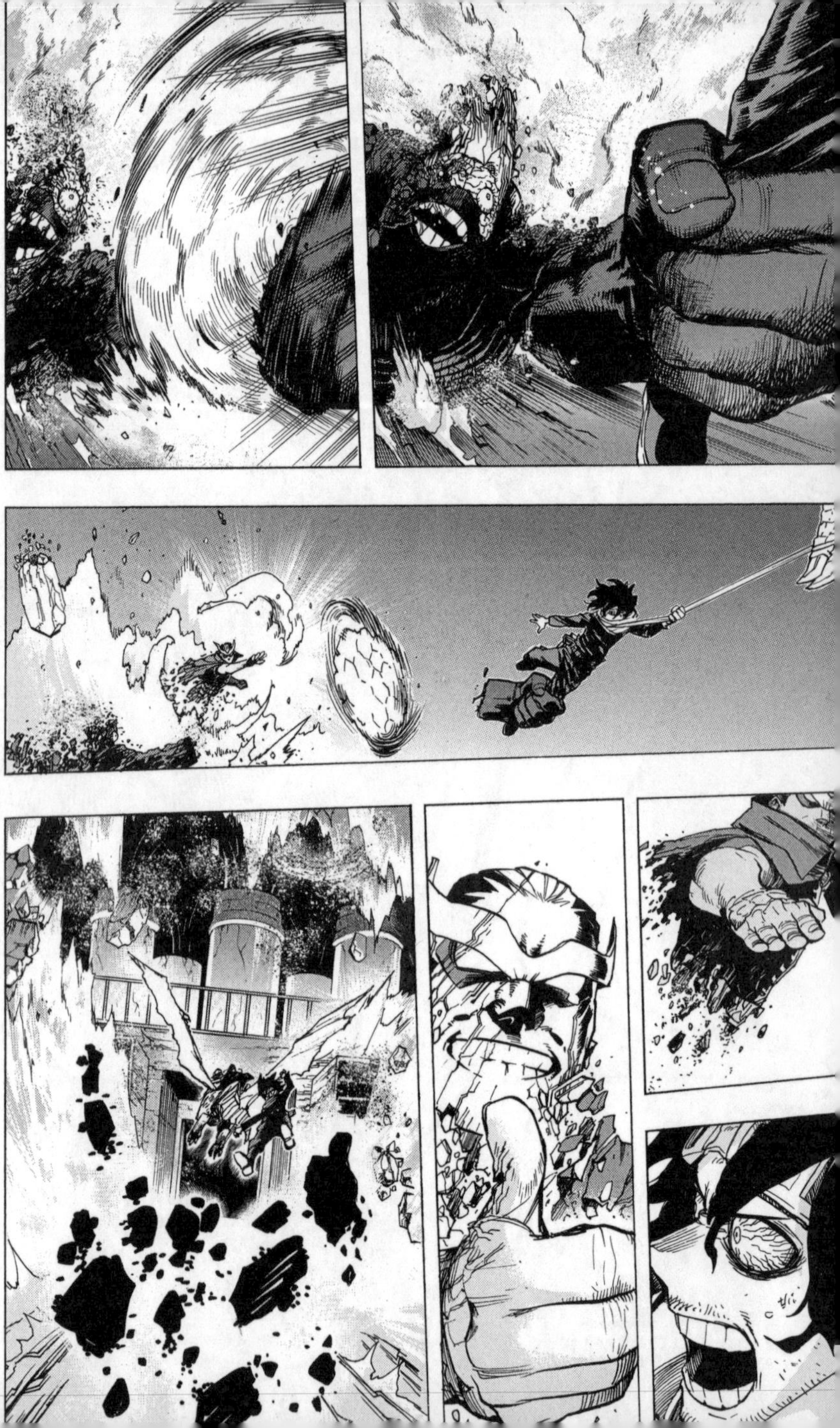

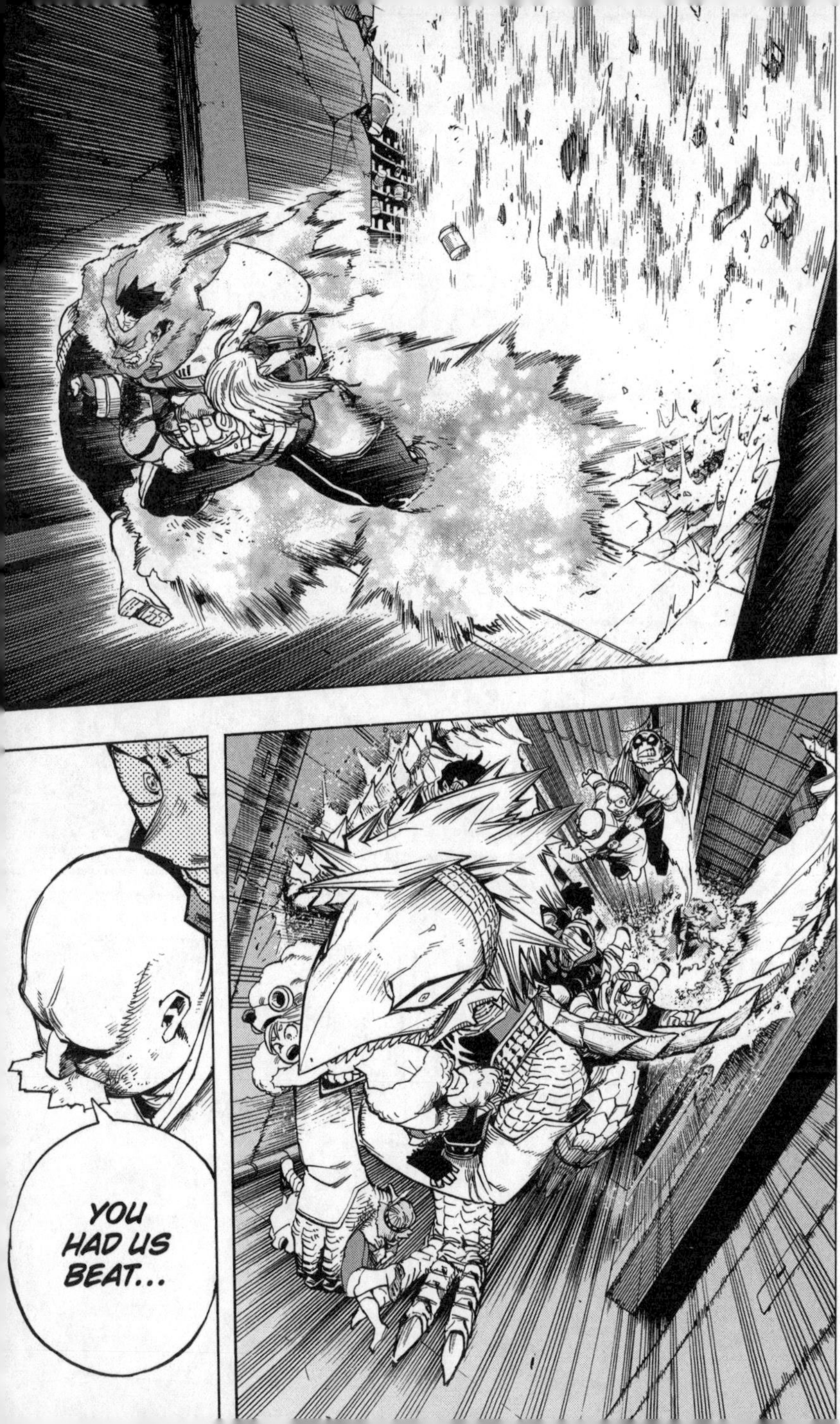
YOU HAD US BEAT...

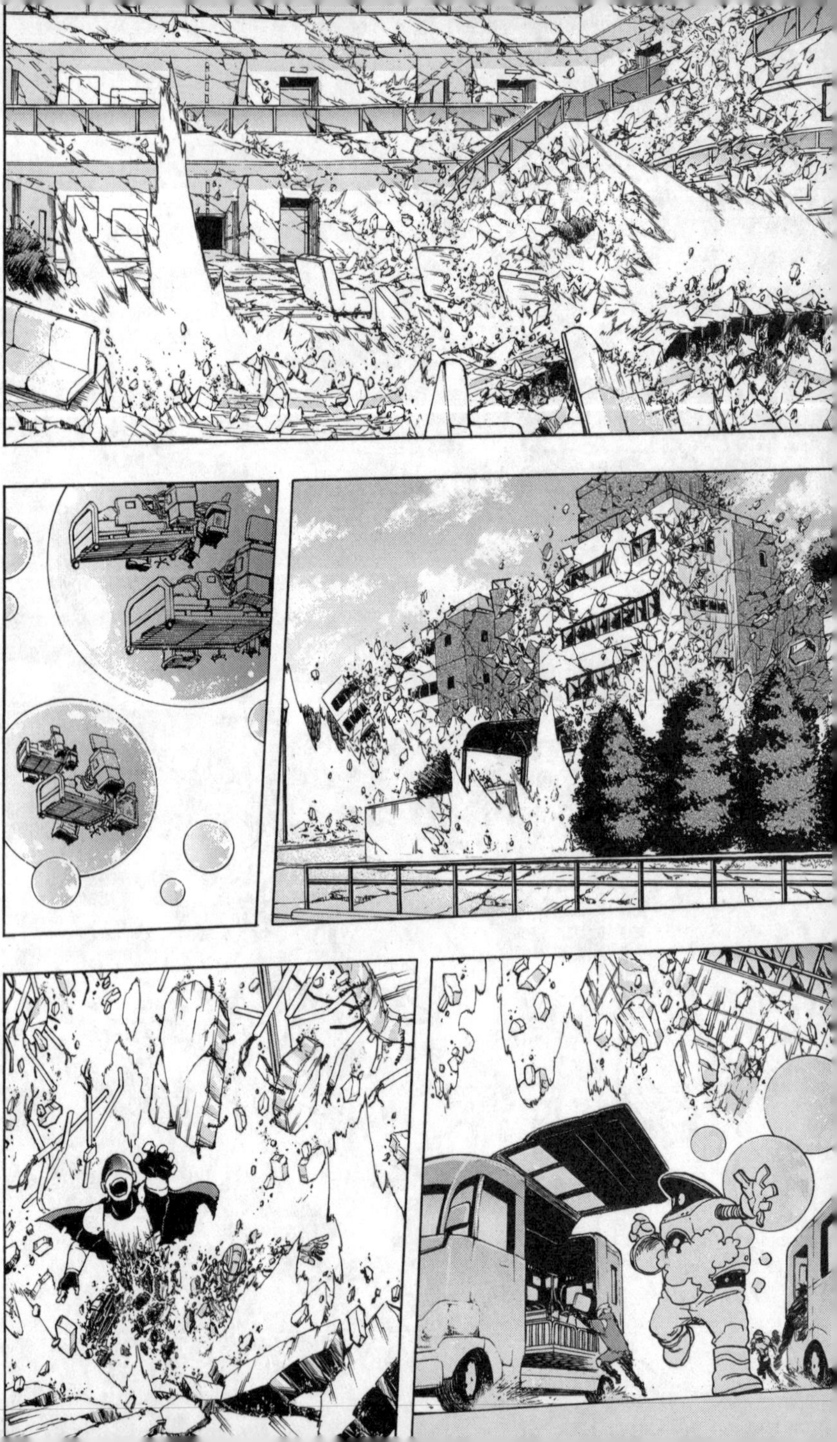

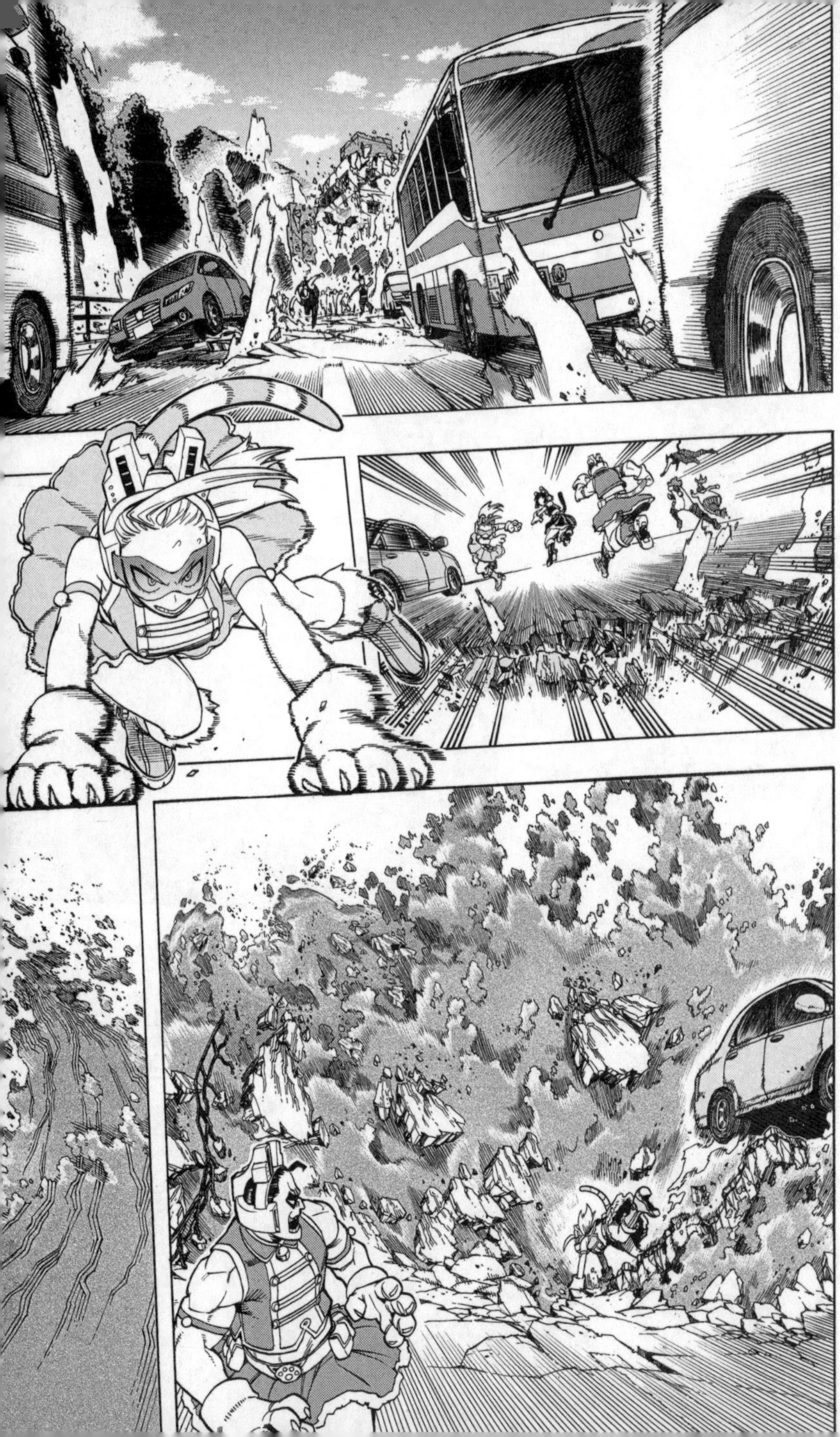

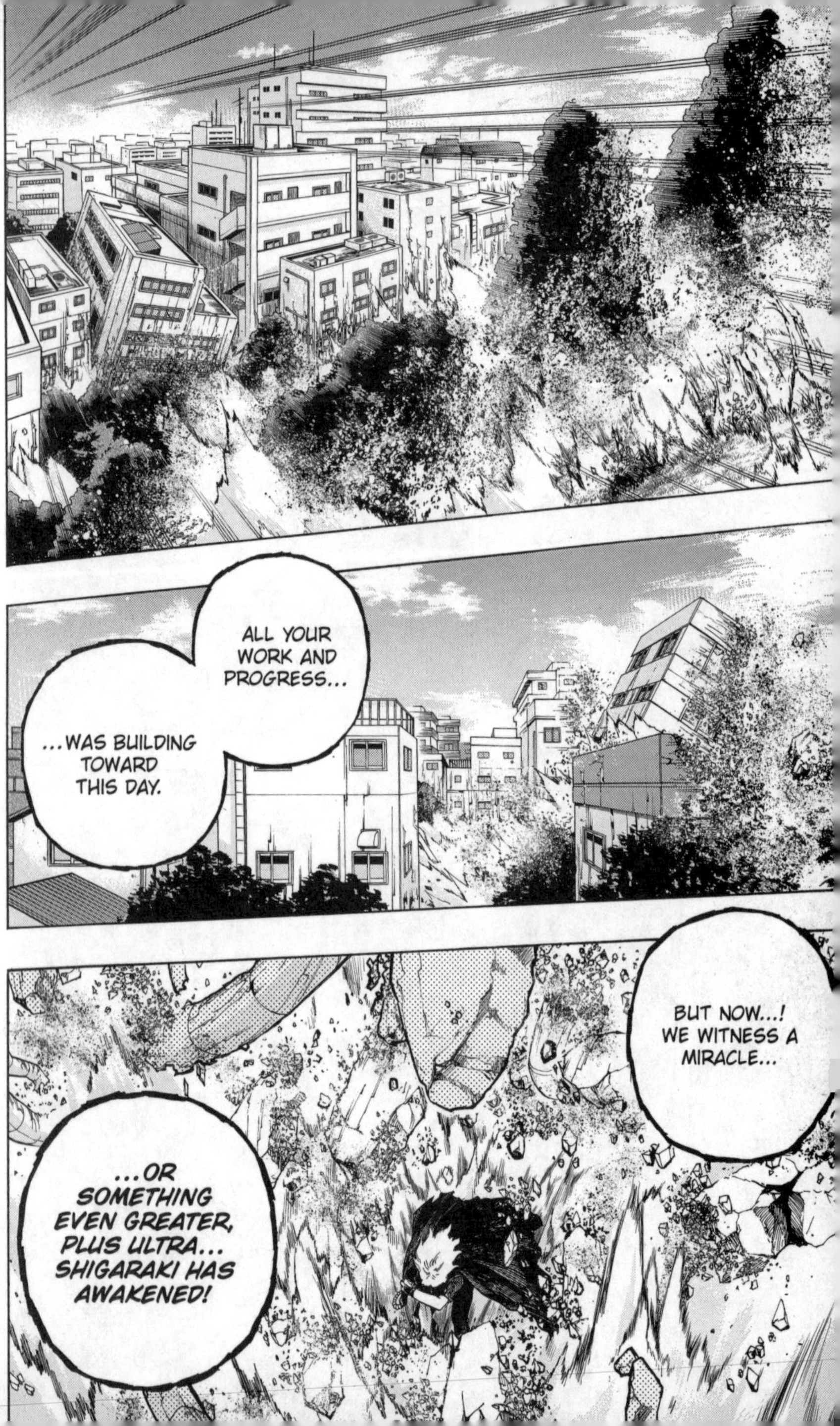
ALL YOUR WORK AND PROGRESS...
...WAS BUILDING TOWARD THIS DAY.
BUT NOW...! WE WITNESS A MIRACLE...
...OR SOMETHING EVEN GREATER, PLUS ULTRA... SHIGARAKI HAS AWAKENED!

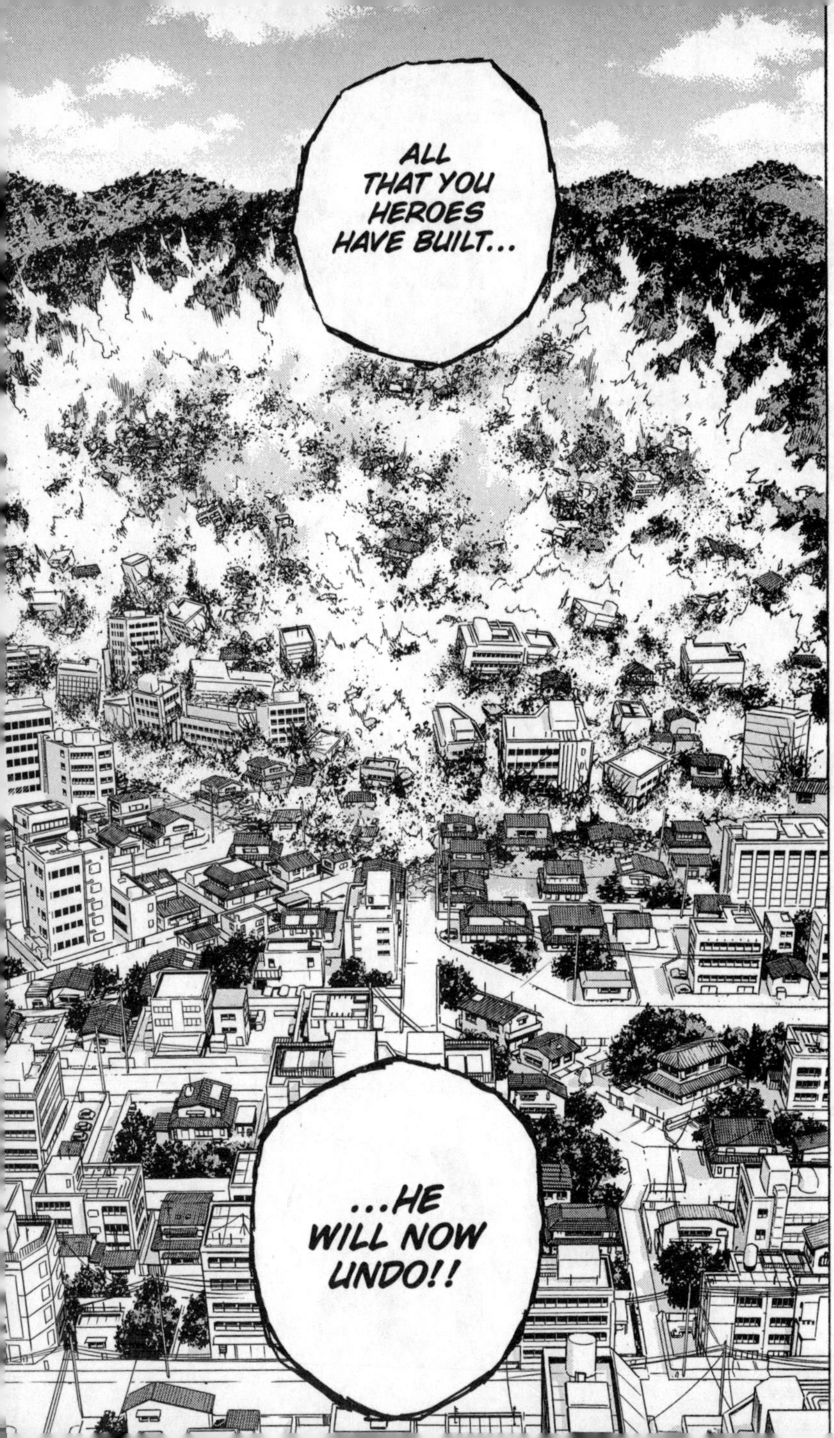
ALL THAT YOU HEROES HAVE BUILT...
...HE WILL NOW UNDO!!

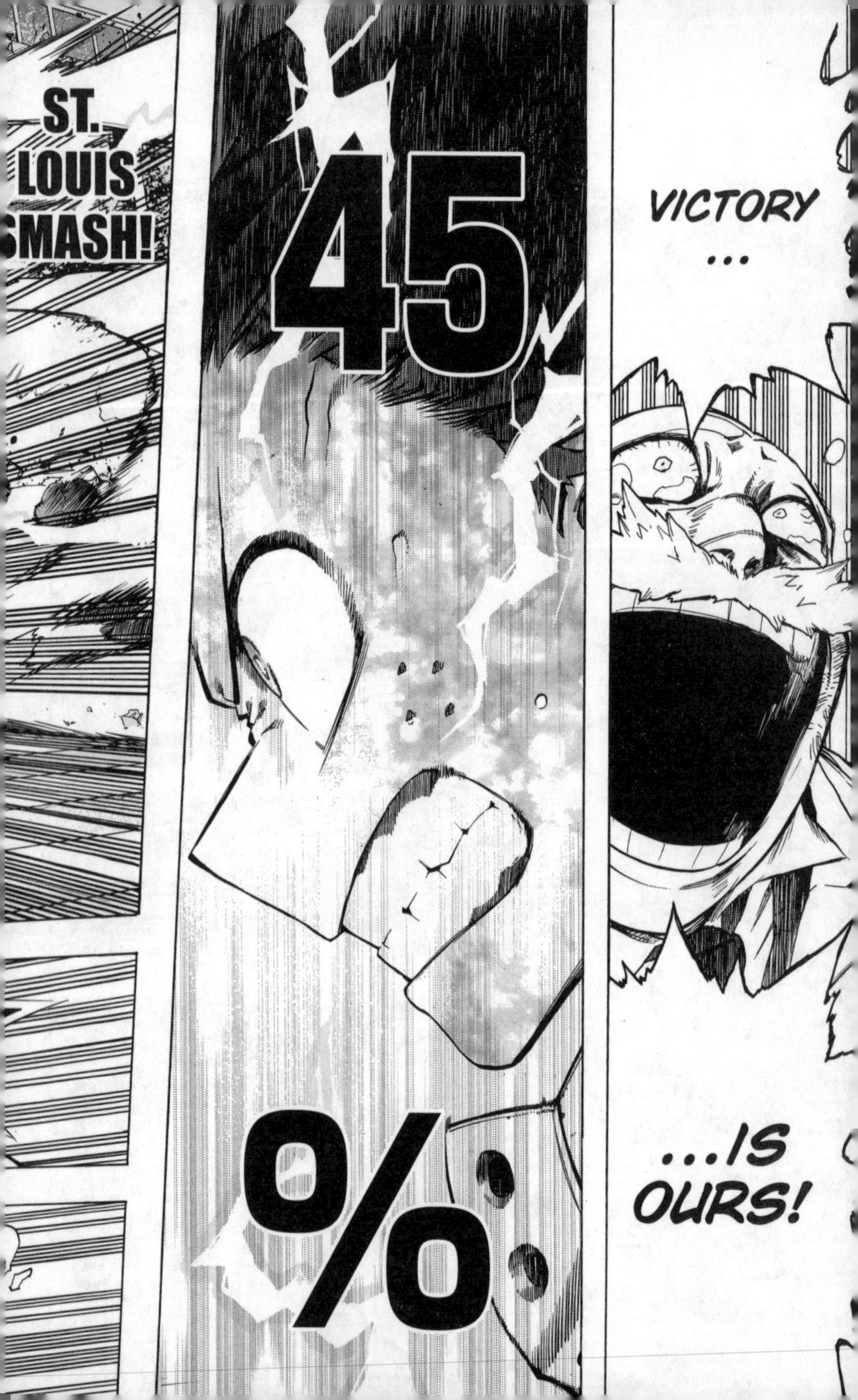
VICTORY ...
...IS OURS!
45 %
ST. LOUIS SMASH!

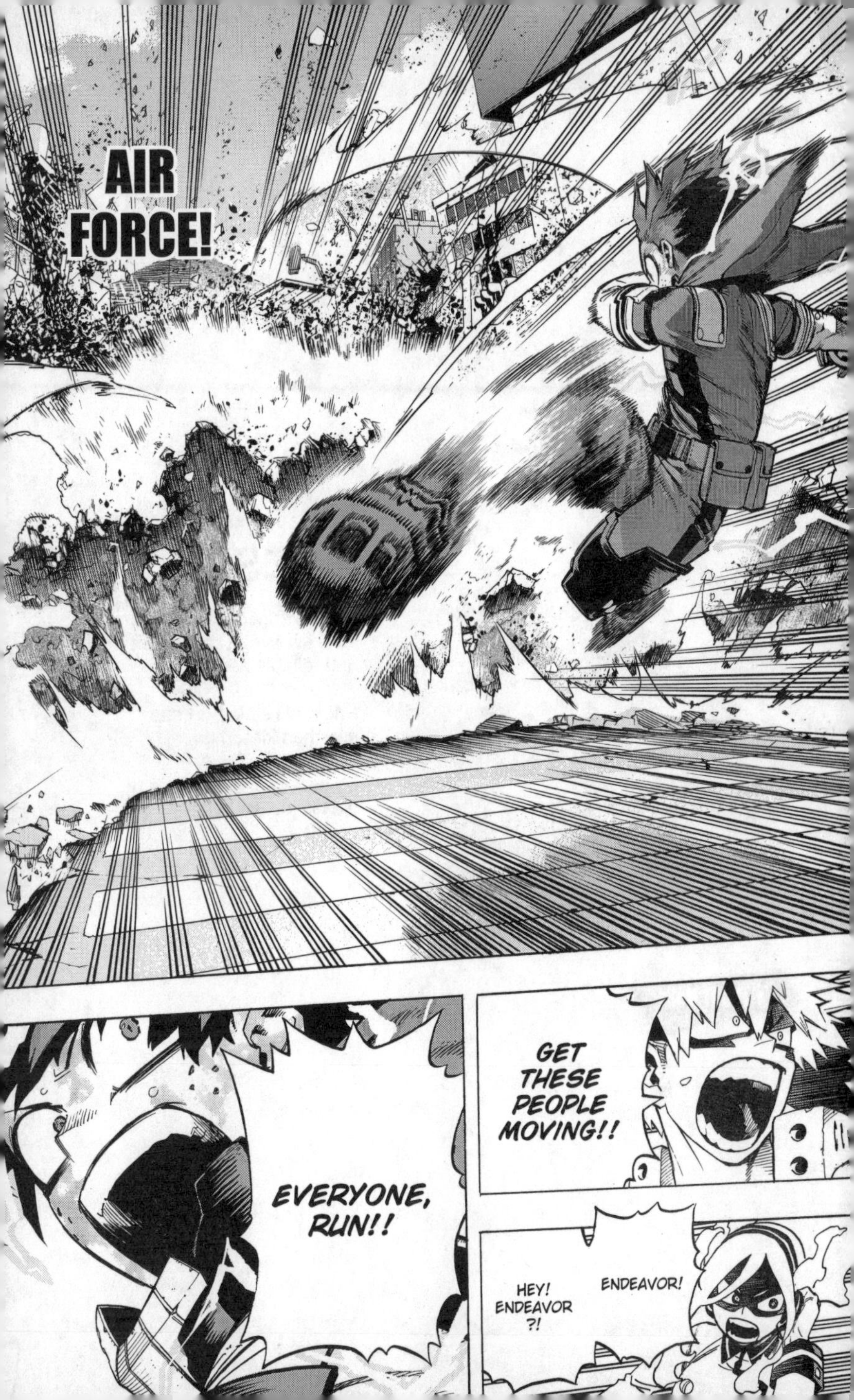
AIR FORCE!
GET THESE PEOPLE MOVING!!
ENDEAVOR!
HEY! ENDEAVOR?!
EVERYONE, RUN!!

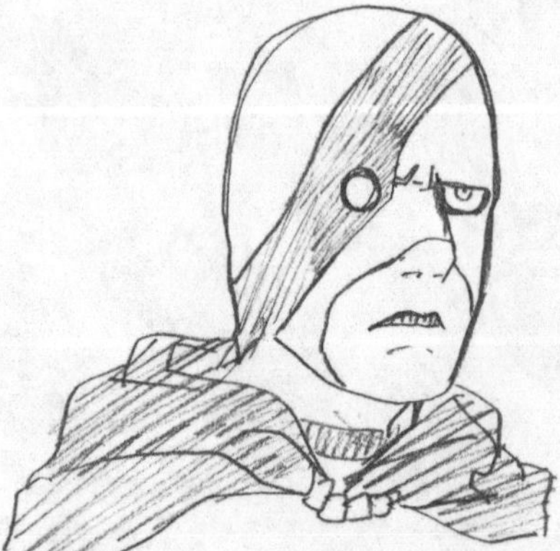

«««X-LESS

He can shoot a laser blast from his eye. A cautious and reliable hero.

Shigaraki stole his cape and then killed him.

It's sad, yes, but X-Less did his job well.

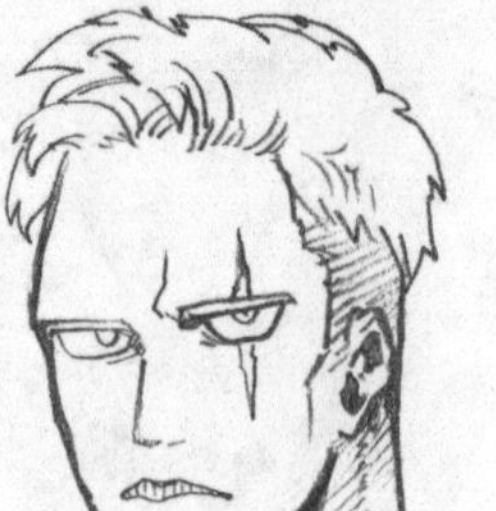

WITHOUT MASK

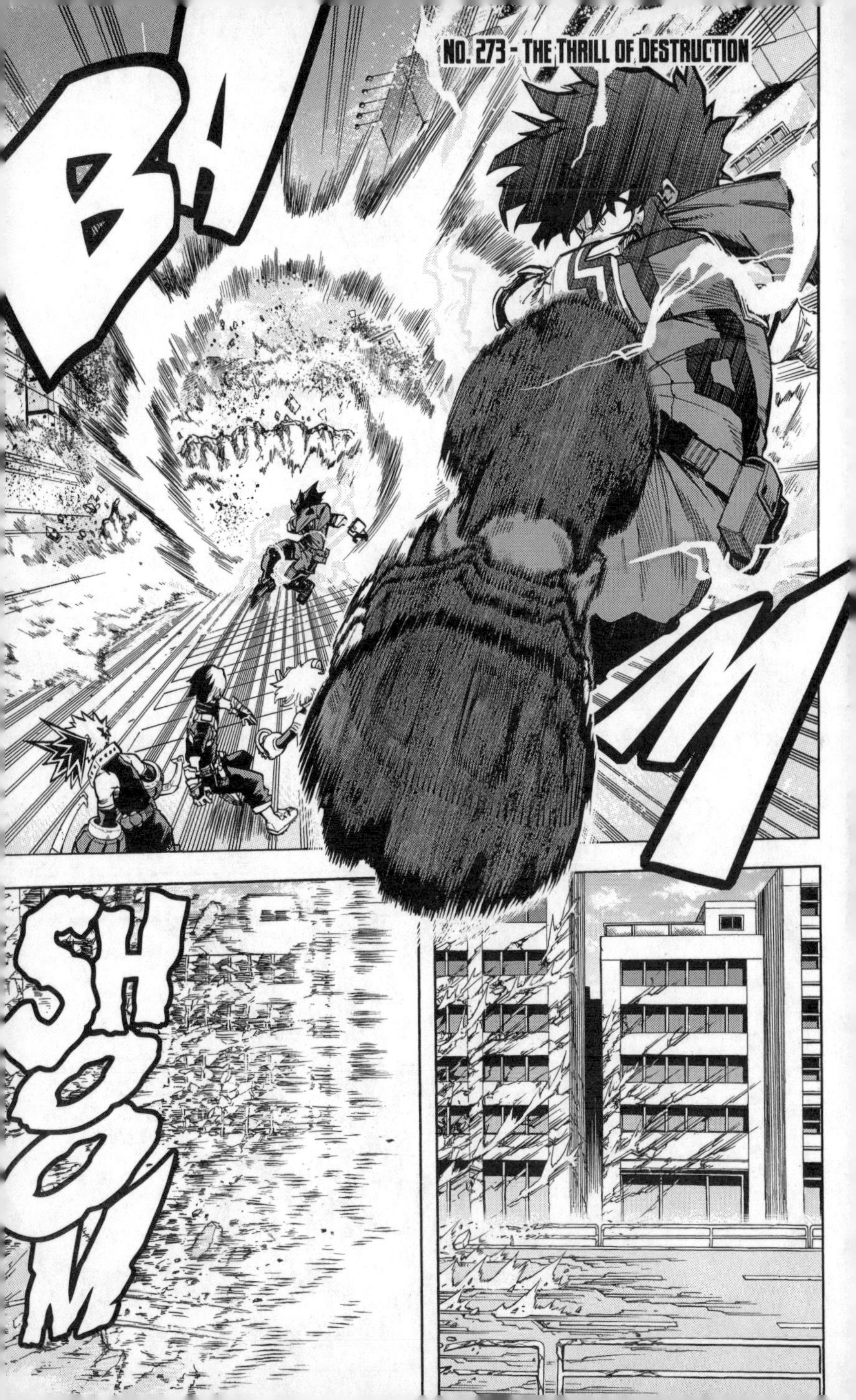
No. 273 - The Thrill of Destruction
SHOOM

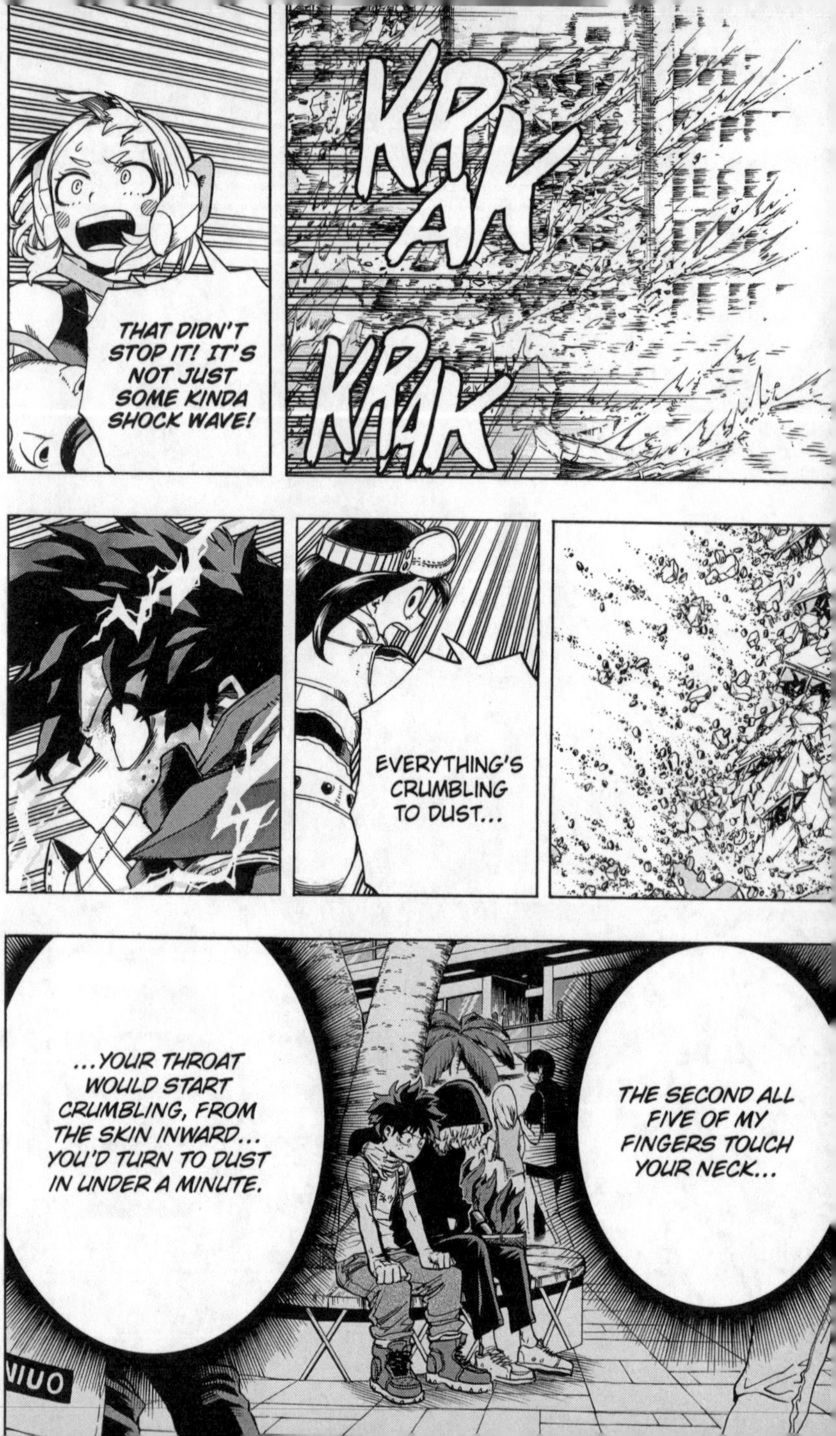
KRAKAK
KRAK
THAT DIDN'T STOP IT! IT'S NOT JUST SOME KINDA SHOCK WAVE!
EVERYTHING'S CRUMBLING TO DUST...
THE SECOND ALL FIVE OF MY FINGERS TOUCH YOUR NECK...
...YOUR THROAT WOULD START CRUMBLING, FROM THE SKIN INWARD... YOU'D TURN TO DUST IN UNDER A MINUTE.

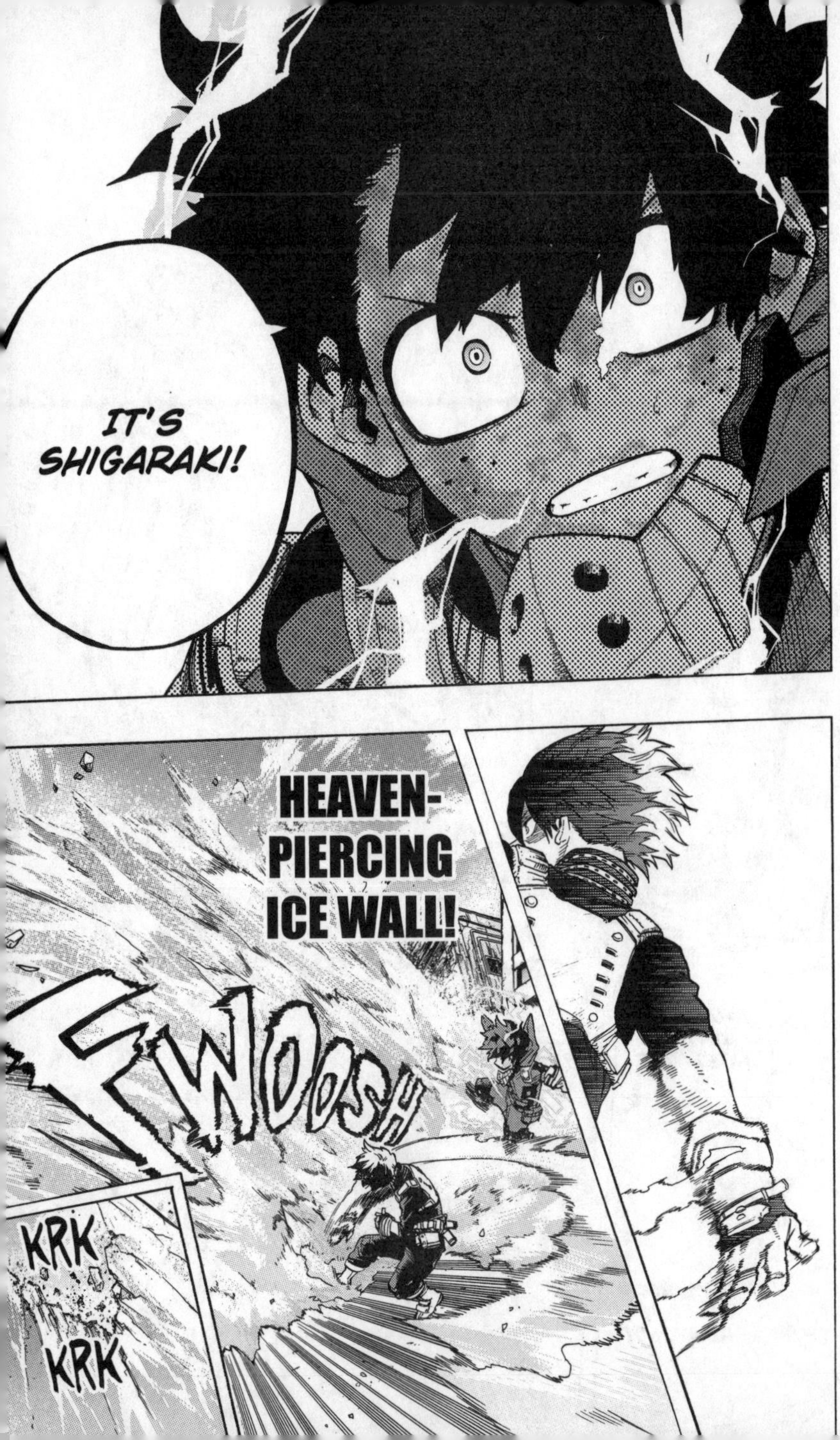
IT'S SHIGARAKI!
HEAVEN-PIERCING ICE WALL!
WOOSH
KRK KRK

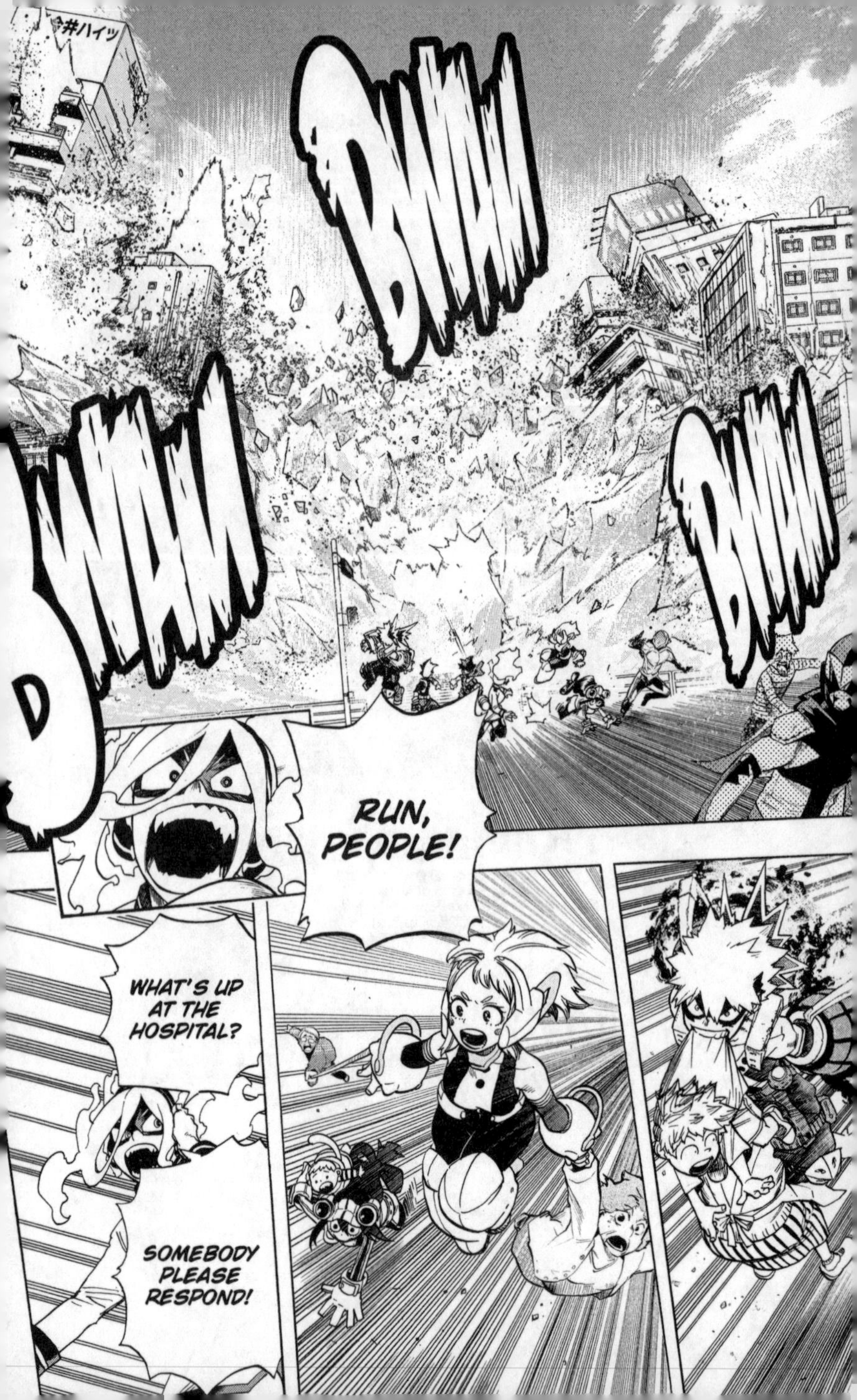
BWAM
BWAM
RUN, PEOPLE!
WHAT'S UP AT THE HOSPITAL?
SOMEBODY PLEASE RESPOND!

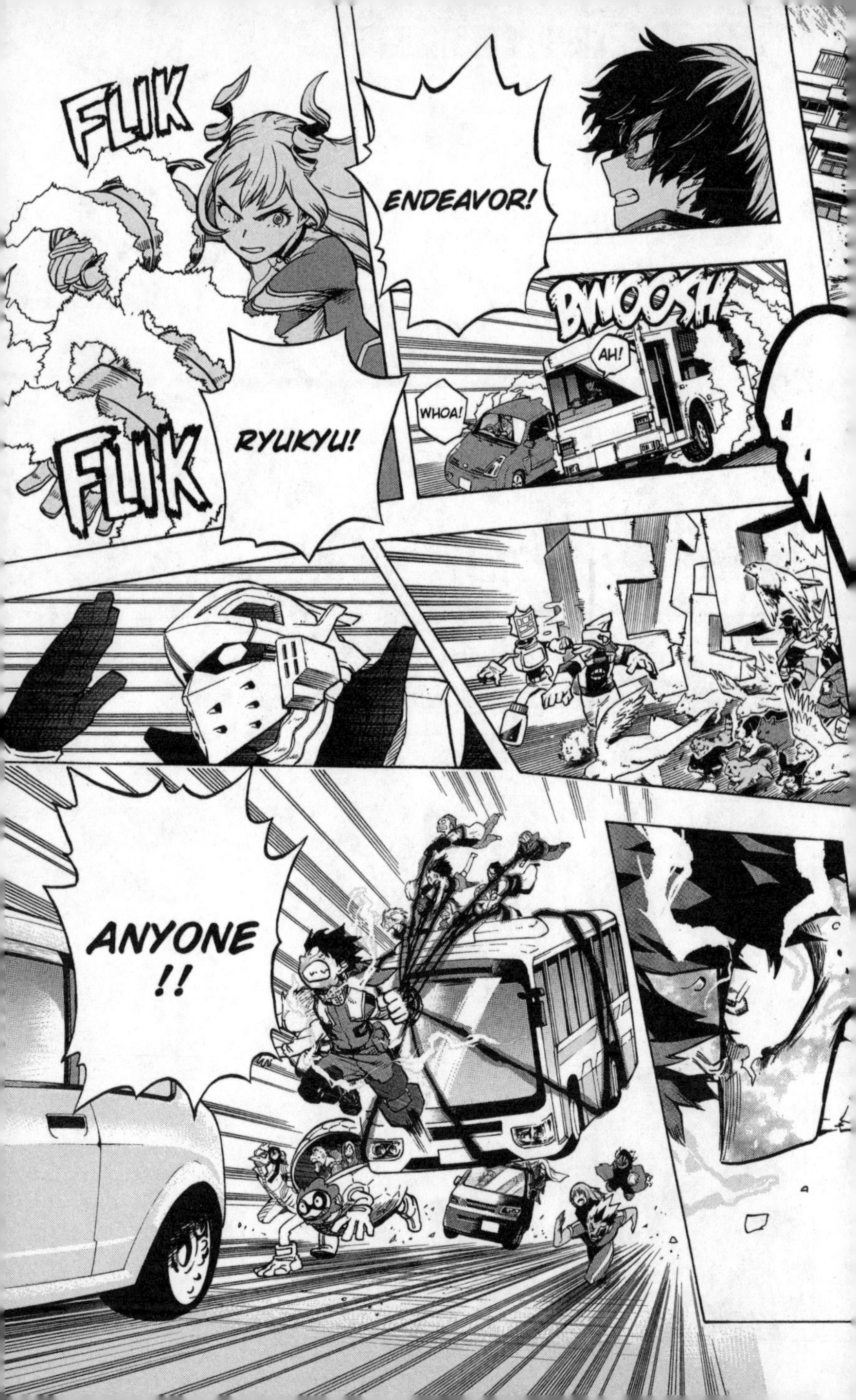
ENDEAVOR!
BWOOSH
AH!
WHOA!
FLIK
FLIK
RYUKYU!
ANYONE !!

NO. 273 - THE THRILL OF DESTRUCTION

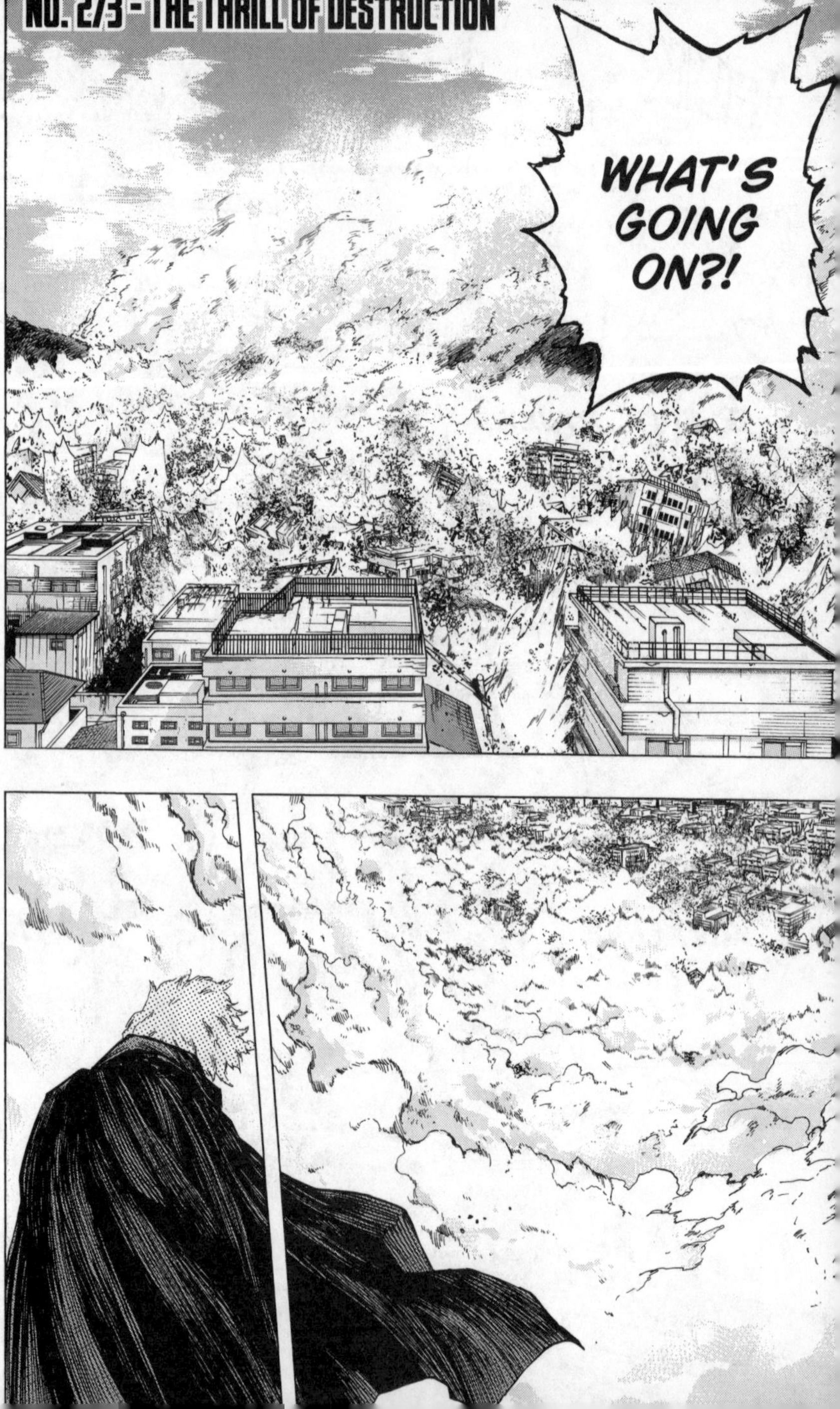
WHAT'S GOING ON?!

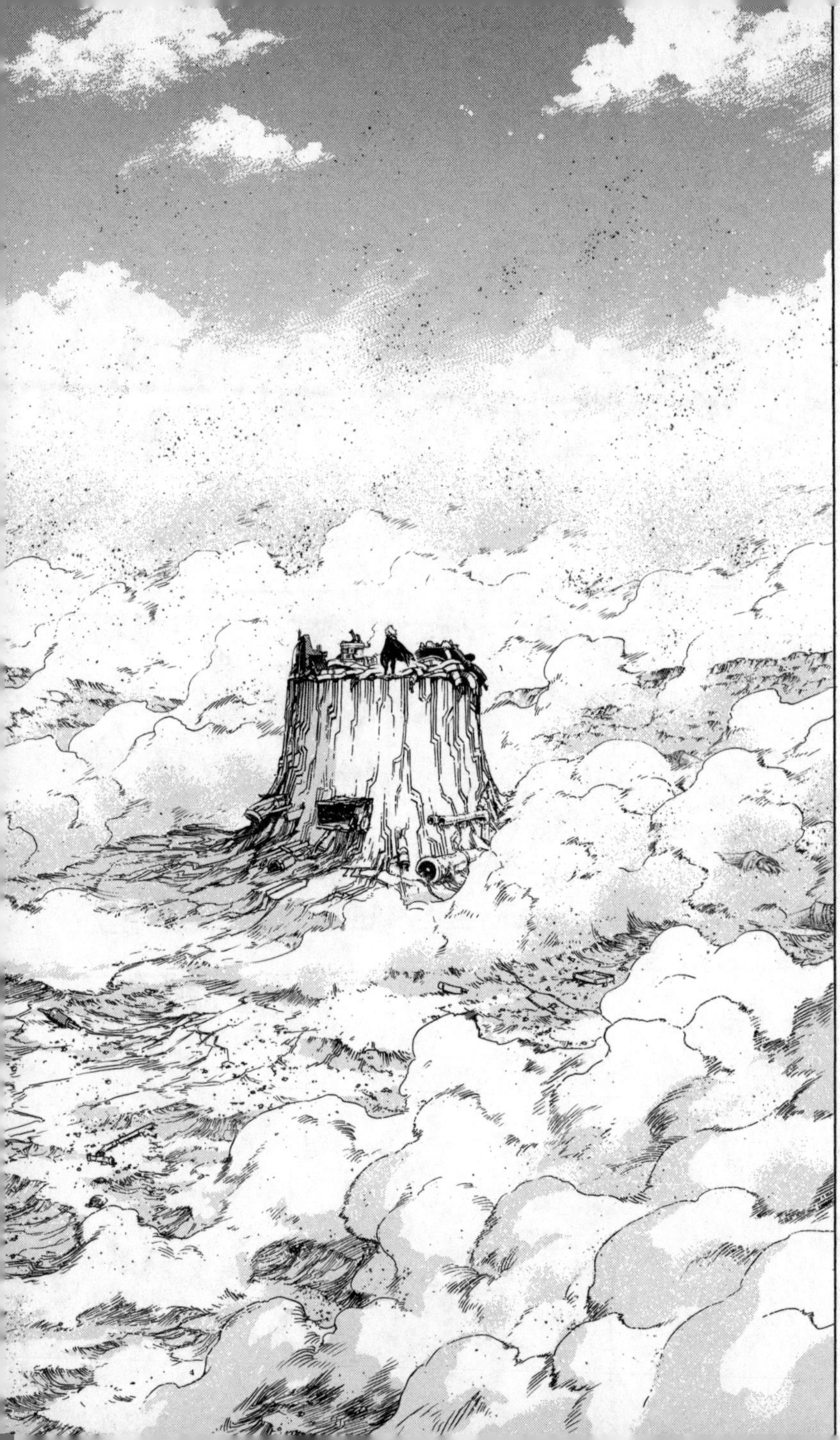

WHOOSH

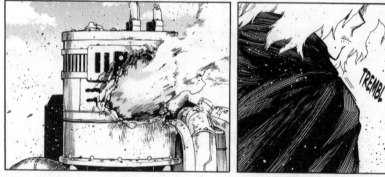

TREMBL

AFTER THE DOC WENT TO ALL THAT TROUBLE TO MAKE MORE, MOST OF 'EM ARE NOW RUINED.

DARN...

OVERHAUL WOULD BE SO DISAPPOINTED.

KAKLANG

KLANG

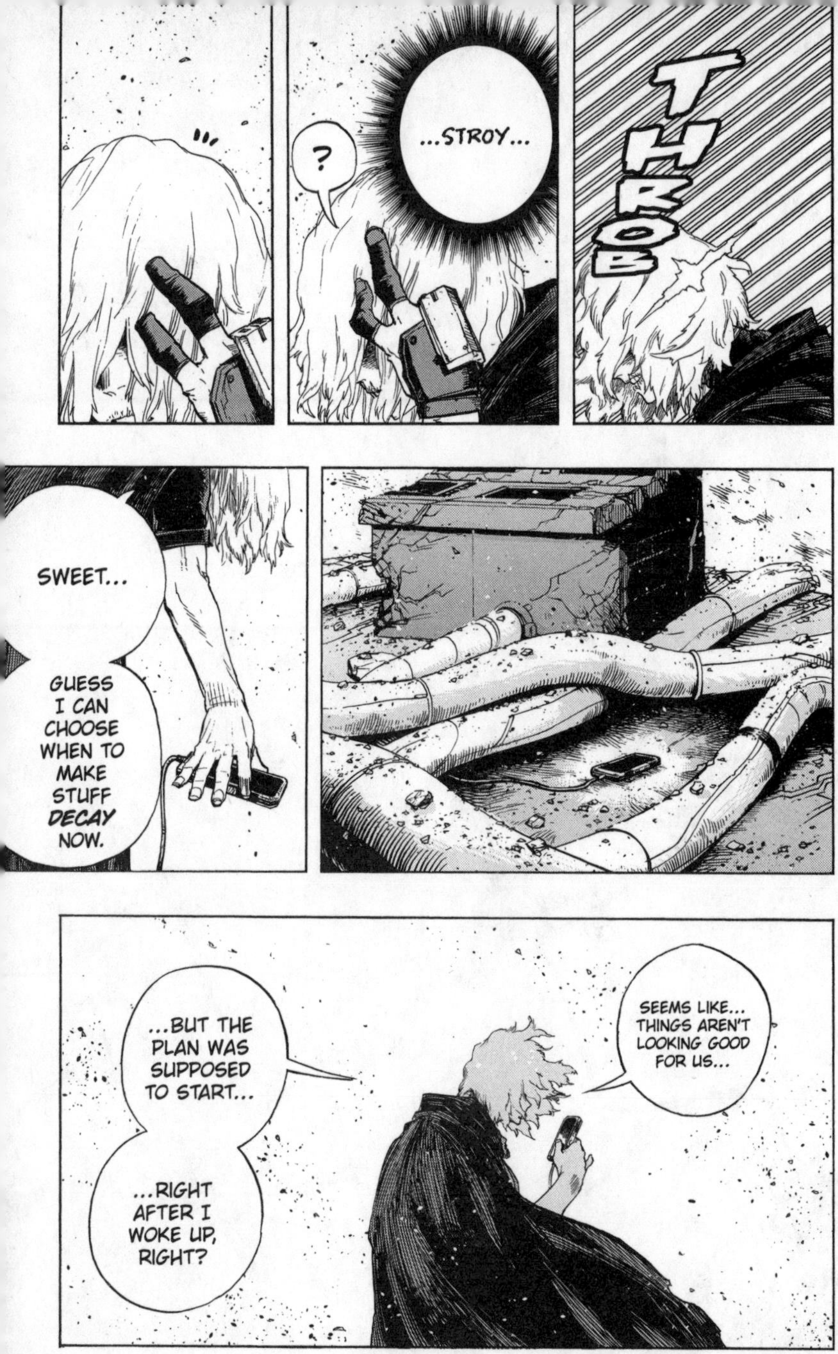
THROB
...STROY...
?
SWEET...
GUESS I CAN CHOOSE WHEN TO MAKE STUFF DECAY NOW.
SEEMS LIKE... THINGS AREN'T LOOKING GOOD FOR US...
...BUT THE PLAN WAS SUPPOSED TO START...
...RIGHT AFTER I WOKE UP, RIGHT?

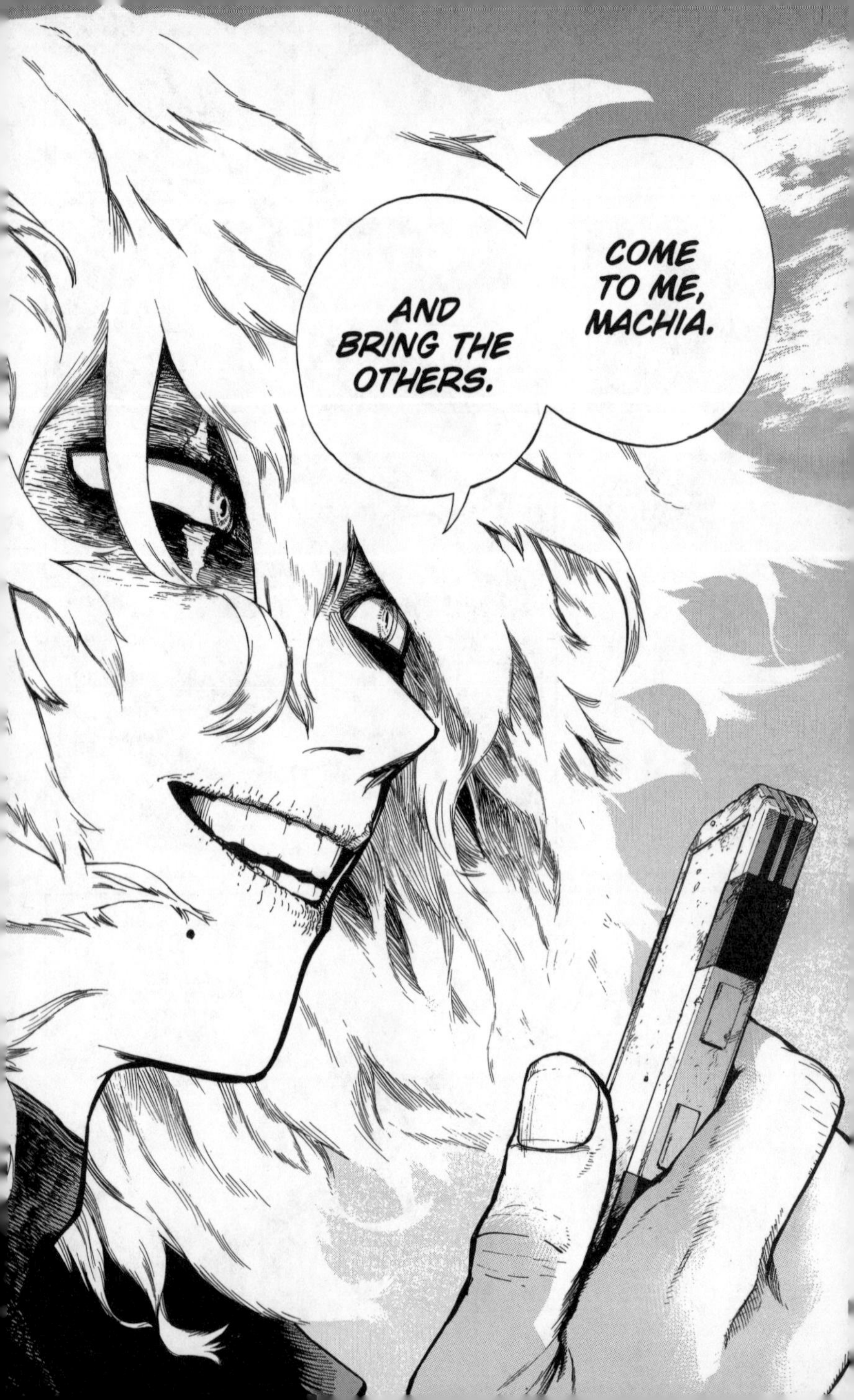
COME TO ME, MACHIA.
AND BRING THE OTHERS.

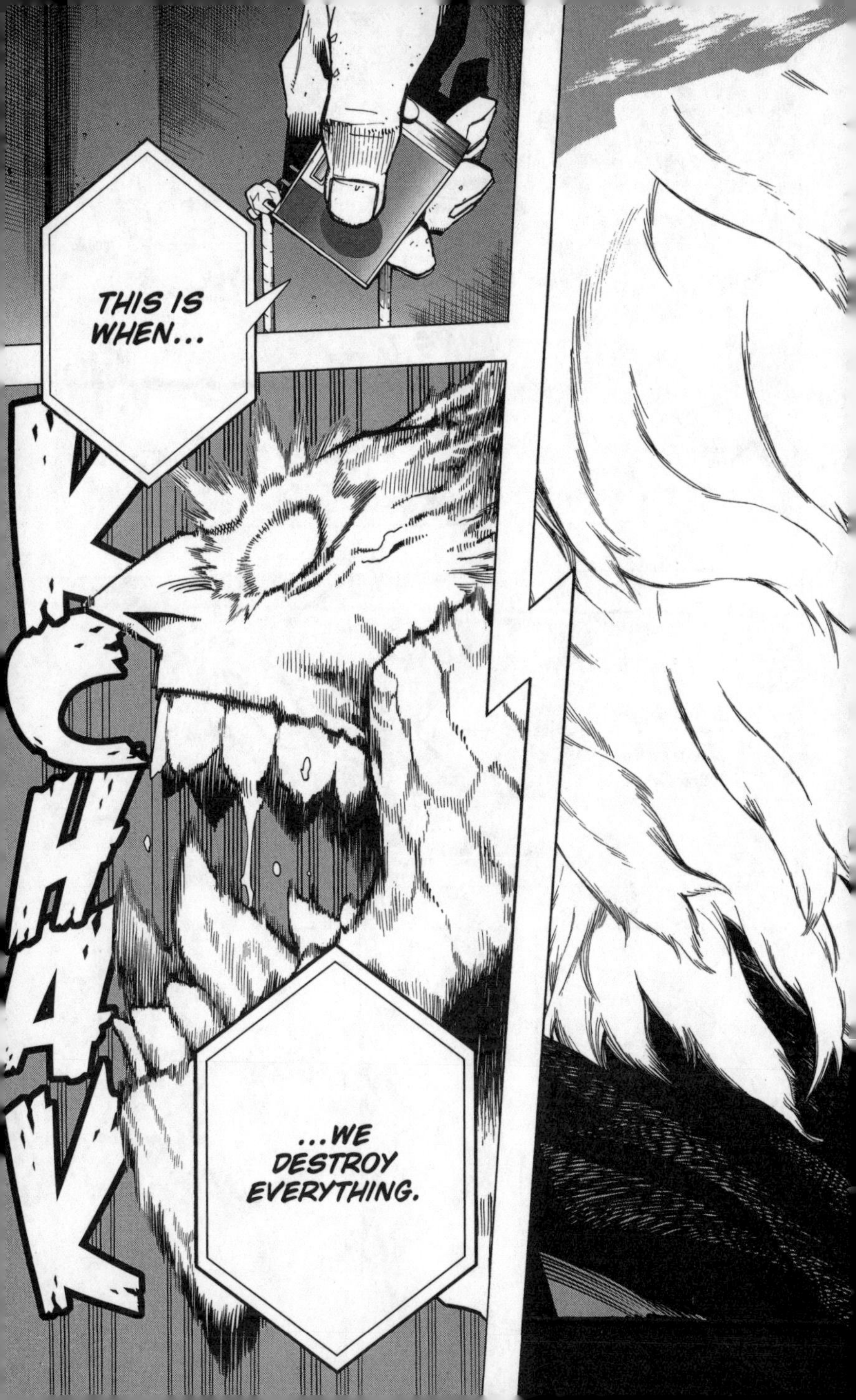
THIS IS WHEN...
KCHAK
...WE DESTROY EVERYTHING.

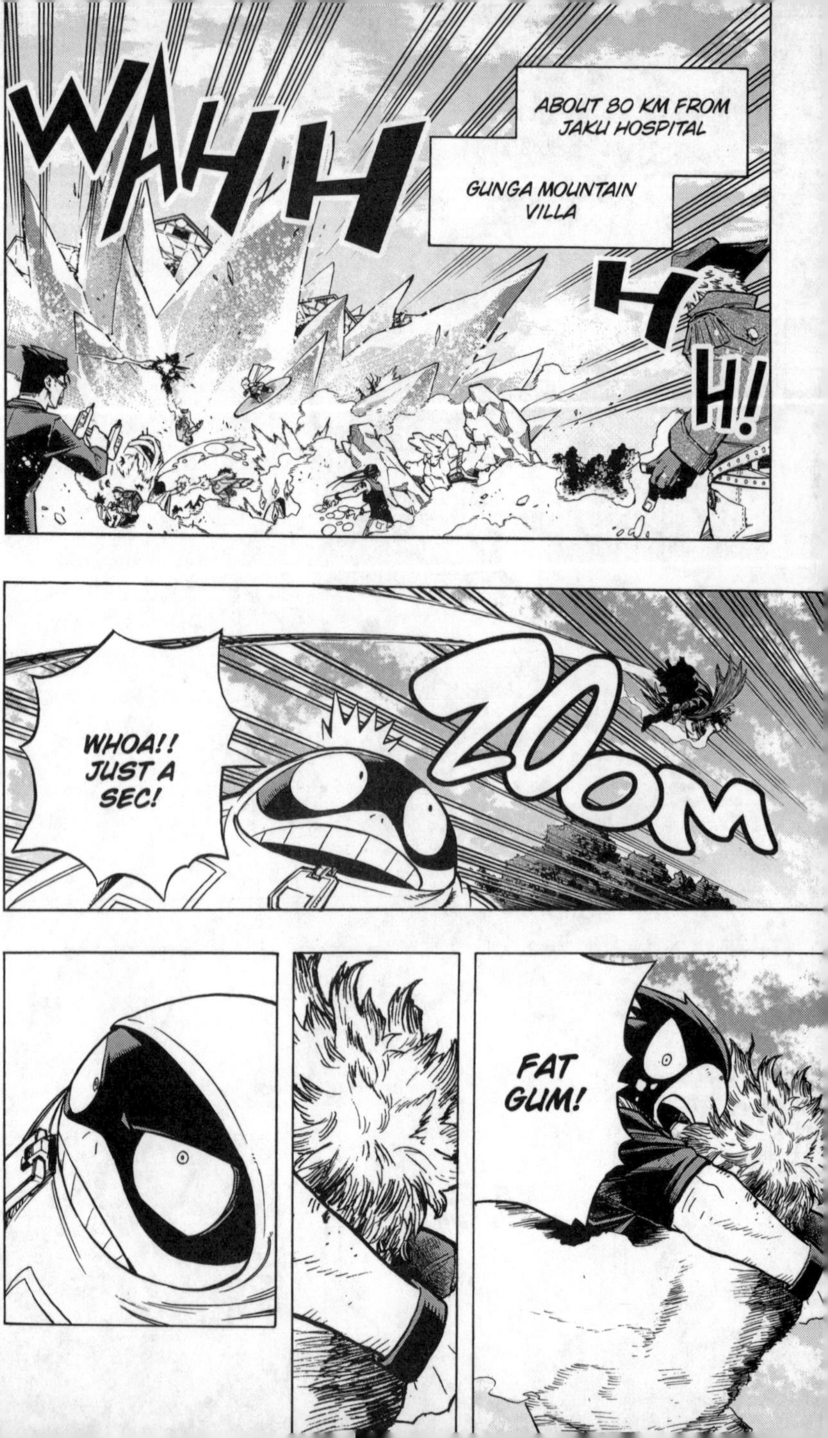
ABOUT 80 KM FROM JAKU HOSPITAL
GUNGA MOUNTAIN VILLA
WAHHHH!
ZOOM
WHOA!! JUST A SEC!
FAT GUM!

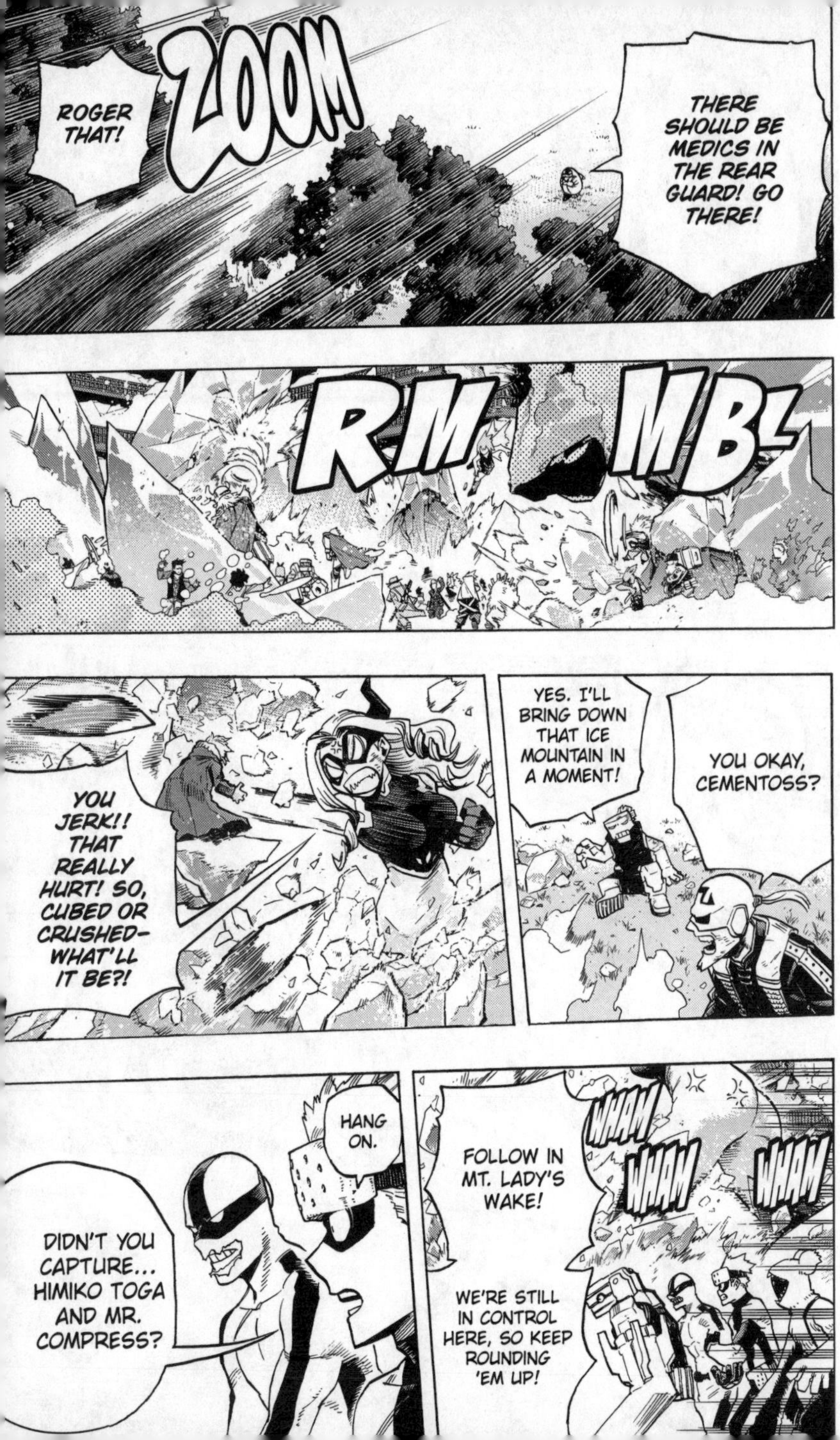
THERE SHOULD BE MEDICS IN THE REAR GUARD! GO THERE!
ZOOM
ROGER THAT!
RM MBL
YOU OKAY, CEMENTOSS?
YES. I'LL BRING DOWN THAT ICE MOUNTAIN IN A MOMENT!
YOU JERK!! THAT REALLY HURT! SO, CUBED OR CRUSHED—WHAT'LL IT BE?!
WHAM
WHAM
WHAM
FOLLOW IN MT. LADY'S WAKE!
WE'RE STILL IN CONTROL HERE, SO KEEP ROUNDING 'EM UP!
HANG ON.
DIDN'T YOU CAPTURE... HIMIKO TOGA AND MR. COMPRESS?

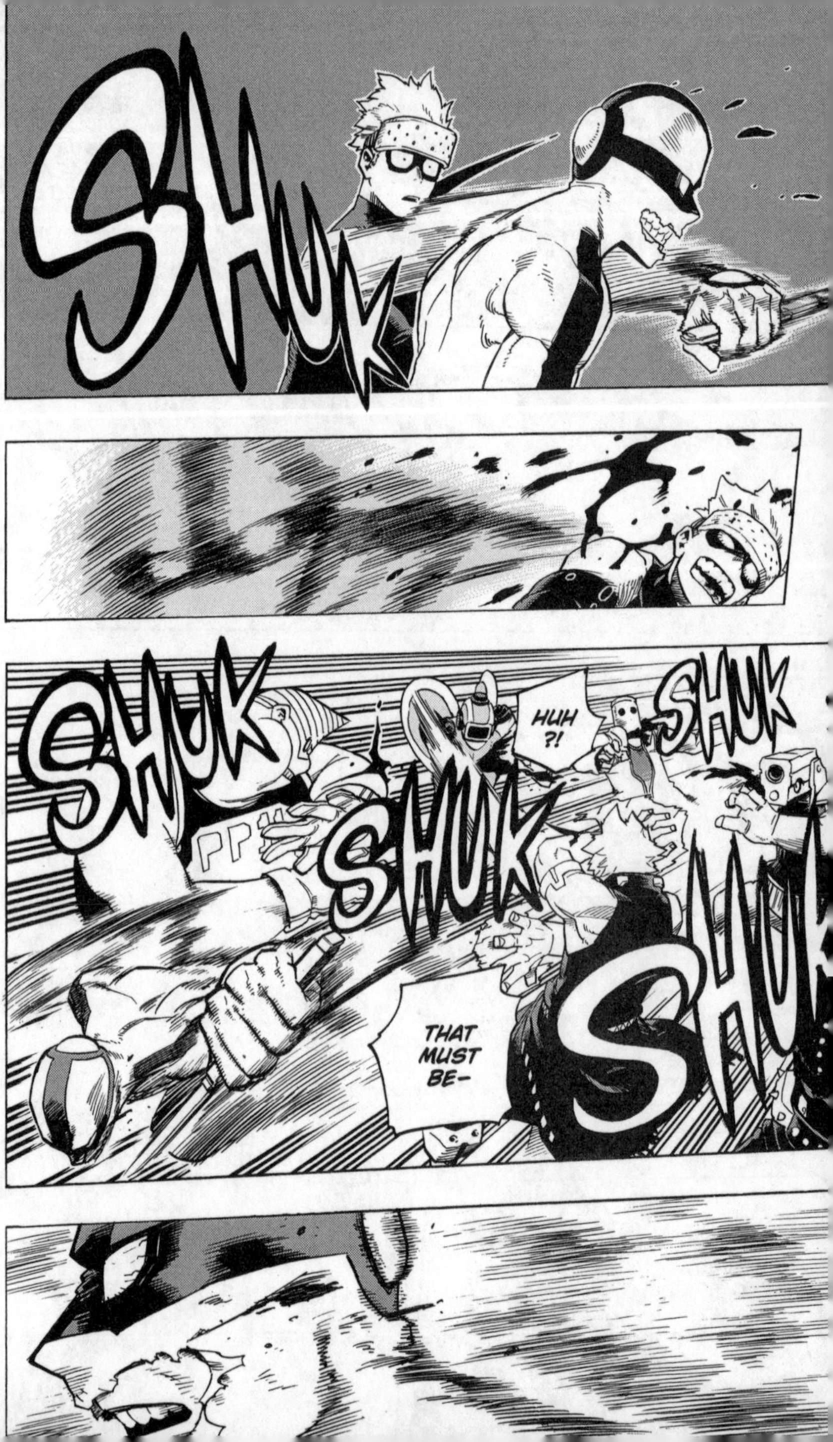
SHUK
SHUK
HUH ?!
SHUK
SHUK
SHU
THAT MUST BE-

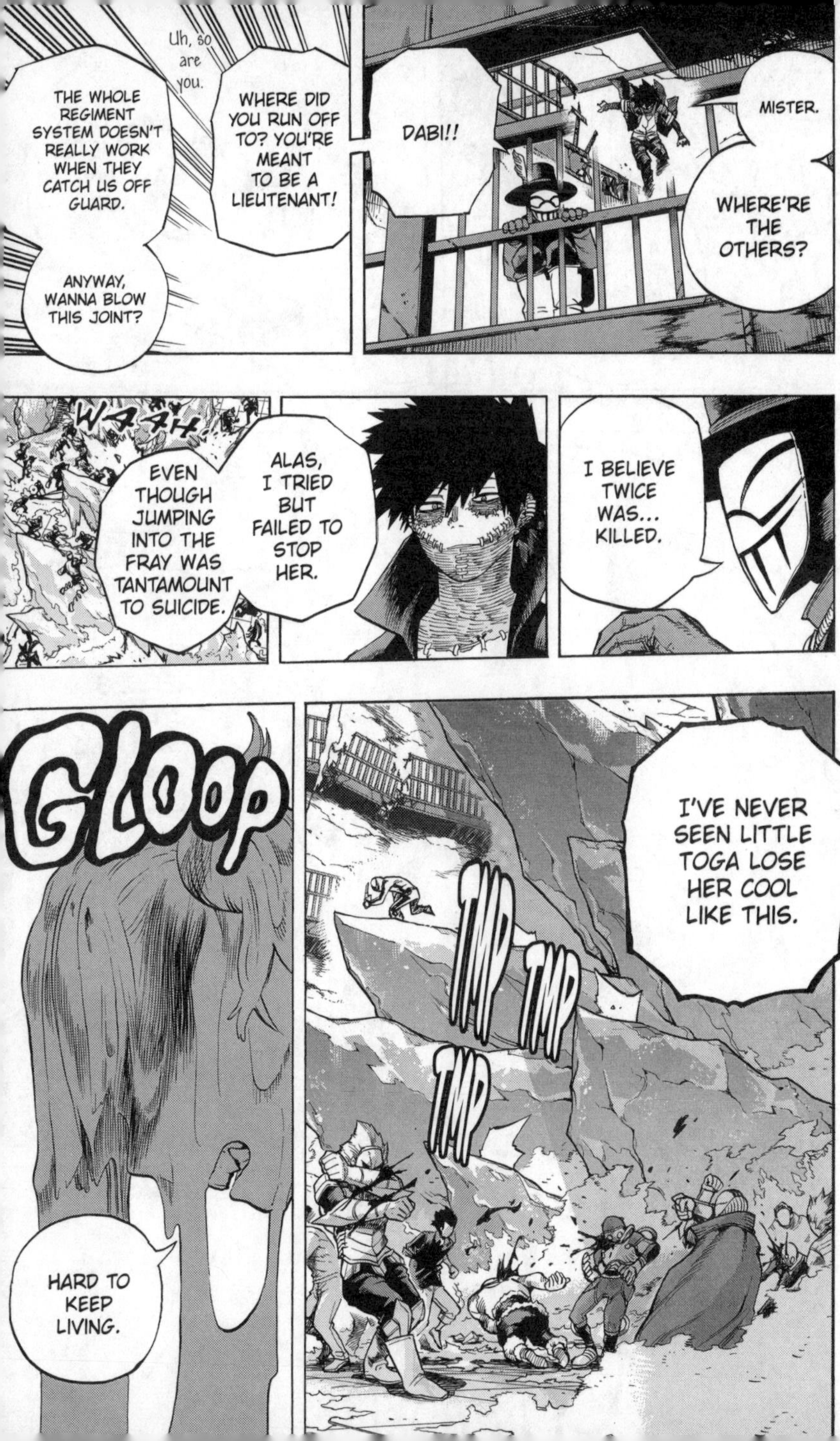
MISTER.
WHERE'RE THE OTHERS?
DABI!!
WHERE DID YOU RUN OFF TO? YOU'RE MEANT TO BE A LIEUTENANT!
Uh, so are you.
THE WHOLE REGIMENT SYSTEM DOESN'T REALLY WORK WHEN THEY CATCH US OFF GUARD.
ANYWAY, WANNA BLOW THIS JOINT?
I BELIEVE TWICE WAS... KILLED.
ALAS, I TRIED BUT FAILED TO STOP HER.
EVEN THOUGH JUMPING INTO THE FRAY WAS TANTAMOUNT TO SUICIDE.
WAAH
I'VE NEVER SEEN LITTLE TOGA LOSE HER COOL LIKE THIS.
TMP
TMP
TMP
GLOOP
HARD TO KEEP LIVING.

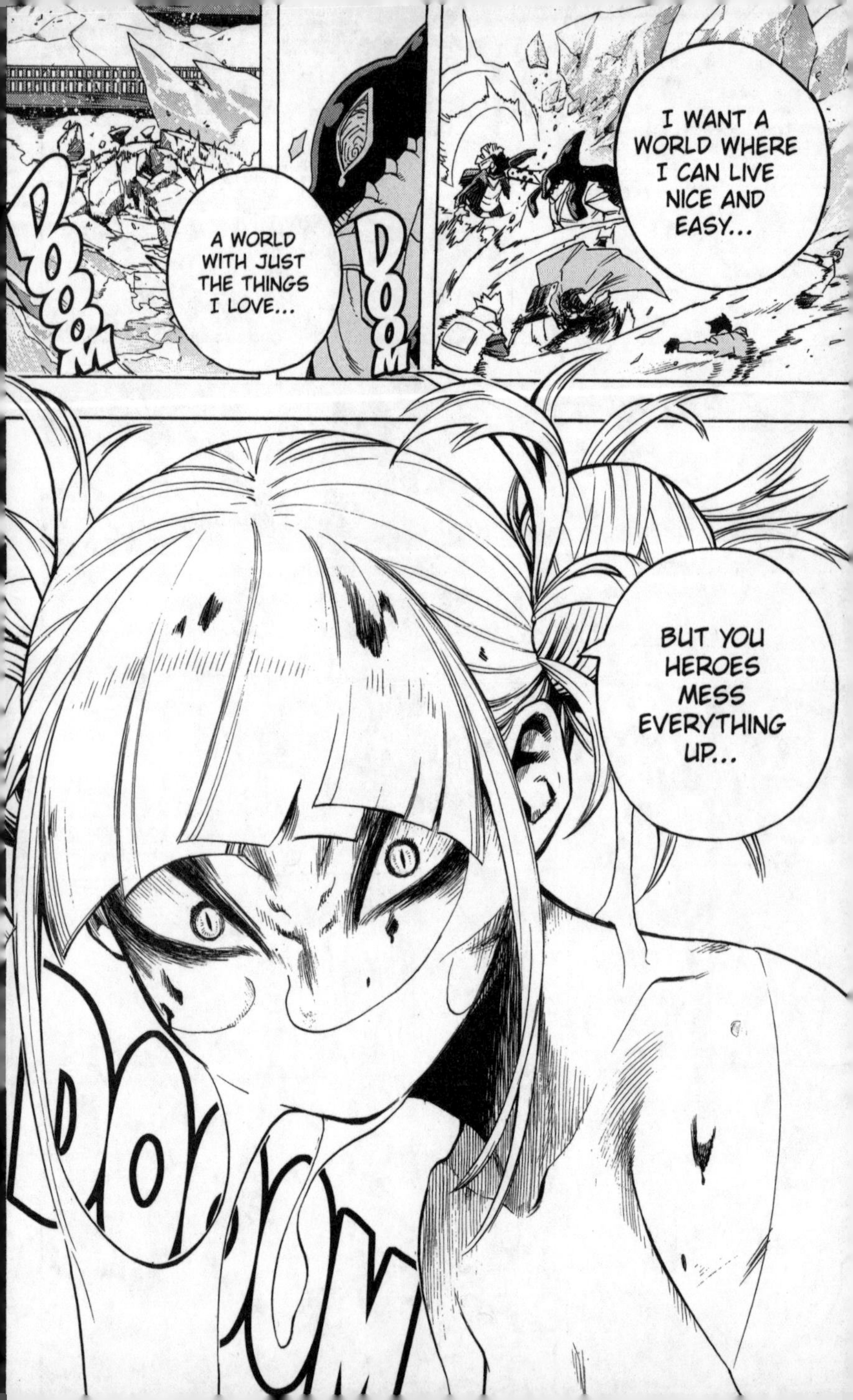
I WANT A WORLD WHERE I CAN LIVE NICE AND EASY...
DOOM
A WORLD WITH JUST THE THINGS I LOVE...
DOOOOM
BUT YOU HEROES MESS EVERYTHING UP...
DOOOM

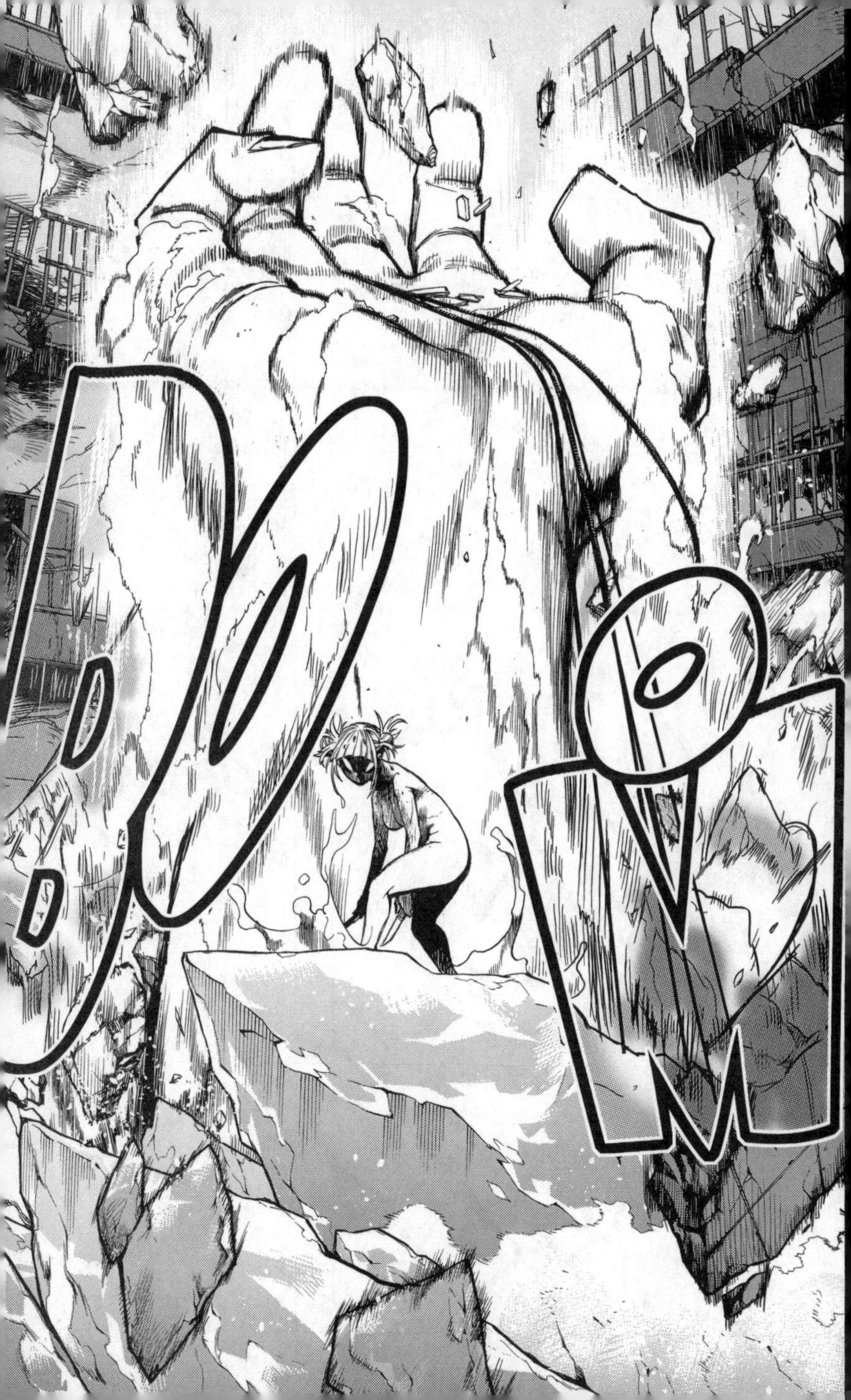
BOOM

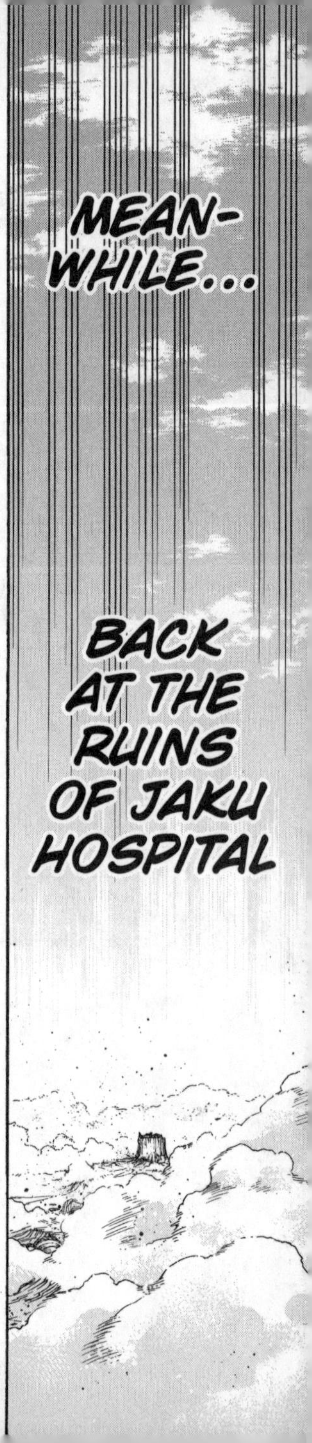
MEAN-
WHILE...
BACK
AT THE
RUINS
OF JAKU
HOSPITAL
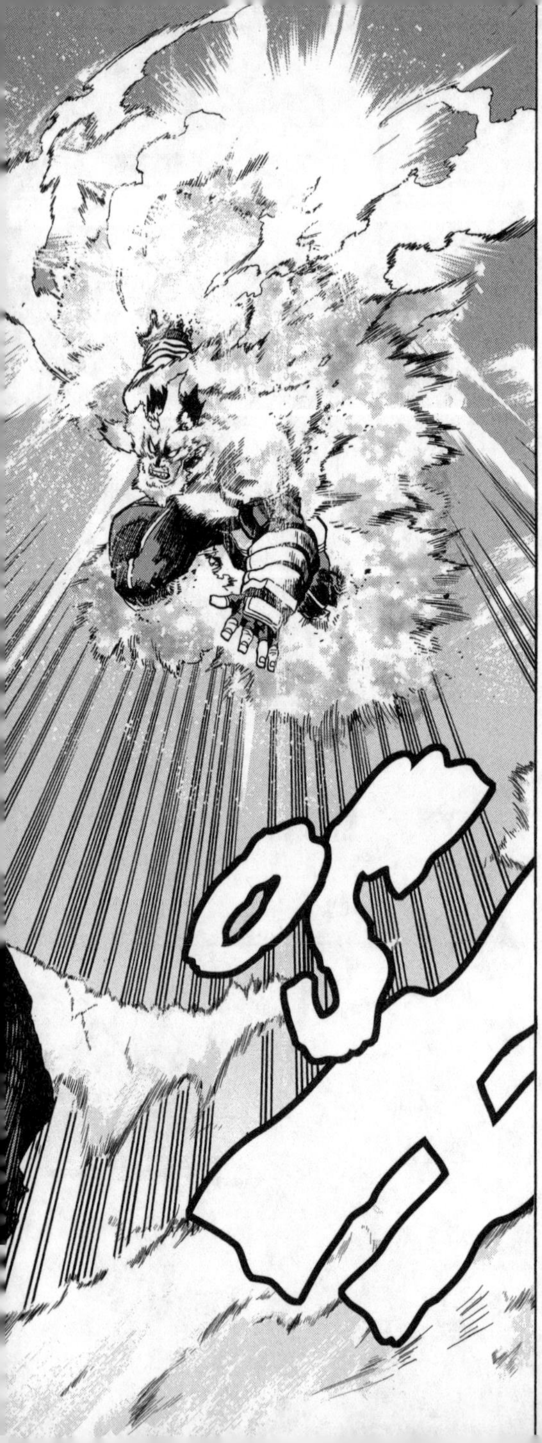

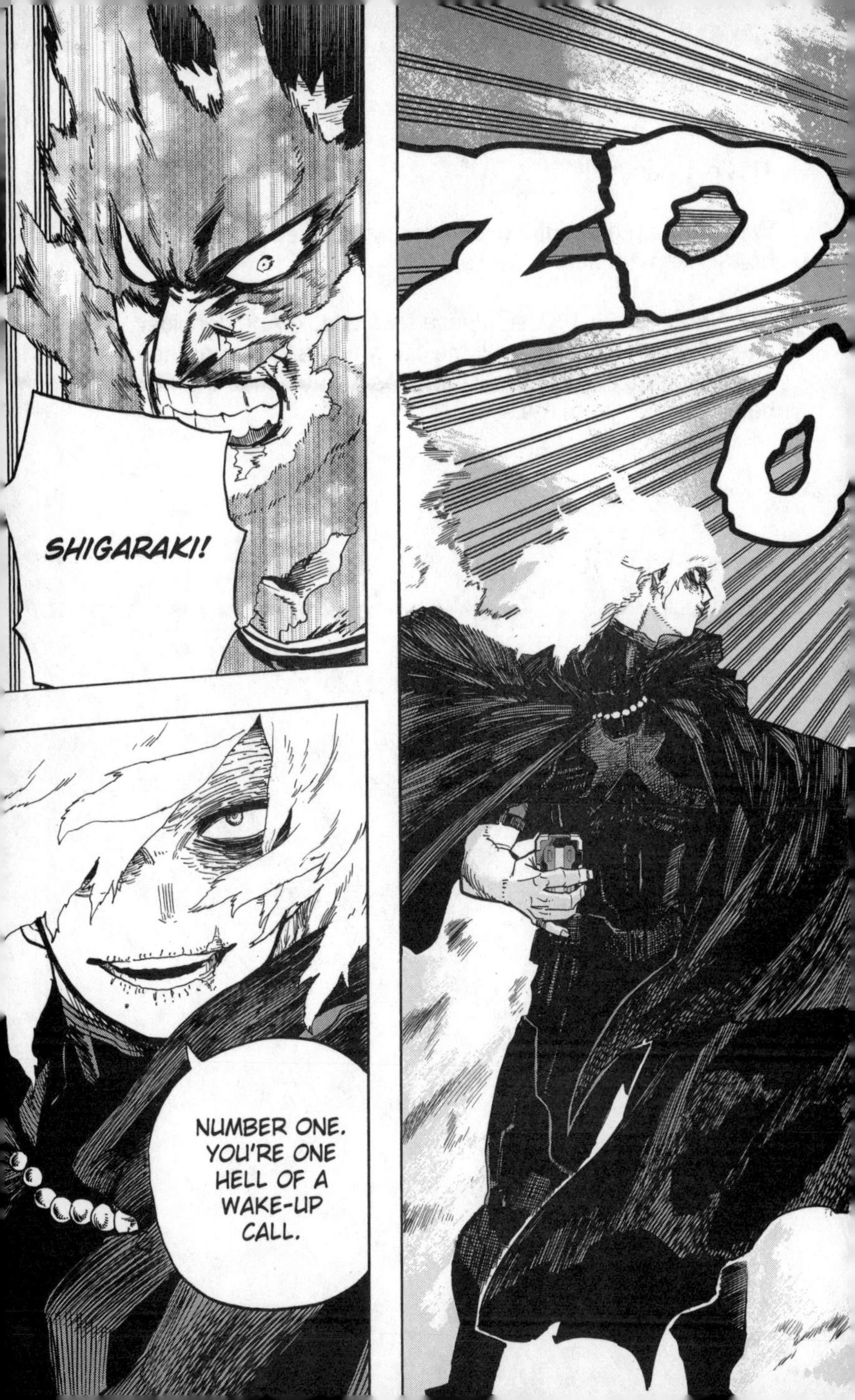

ZOO
SHIGARAKI!
NUMBER ONE. YOU'RE ONE HELL OF A WAKE-UP CALL.

This old standby!!

We've got an art contribution from Betten Sensei, the artist of *My Hero Academia: Vigilantes*!!

It's over on page 140, so please take a look! And consider checking out *Vigilantes* volume 10, which released at the same time as this book in Japan!! As always, that one also has a drawing from me.

Dash over to page 140!!

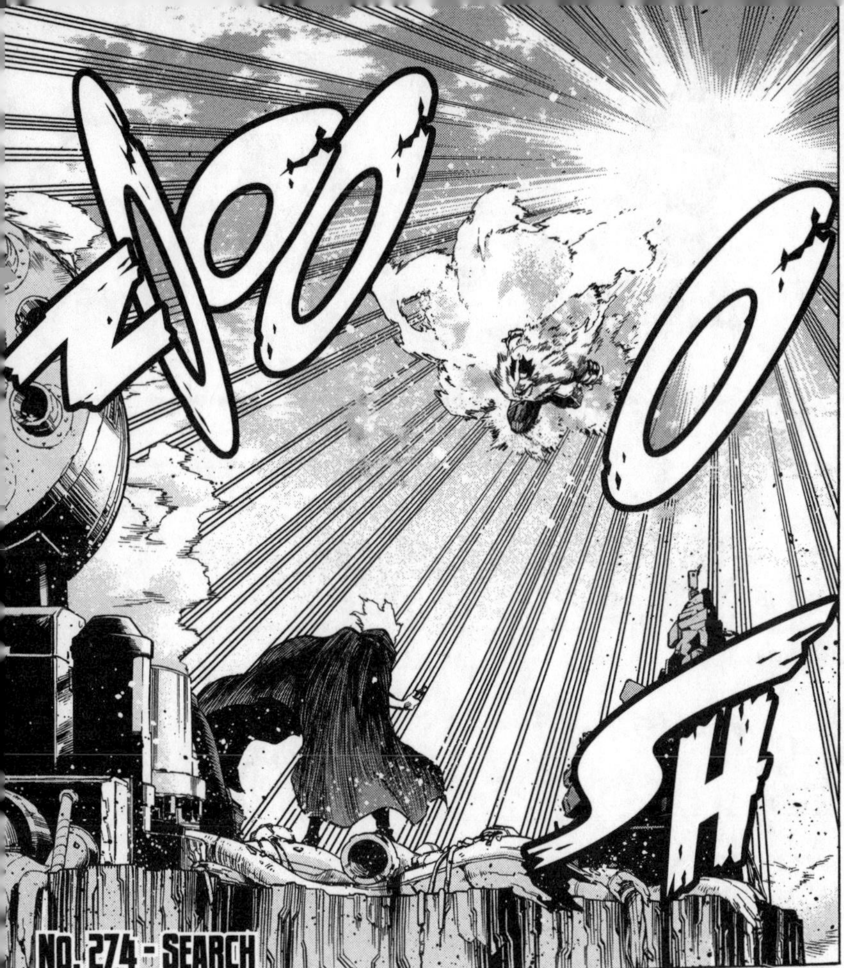
ZOOOSH
NO. 274 - SEARCH

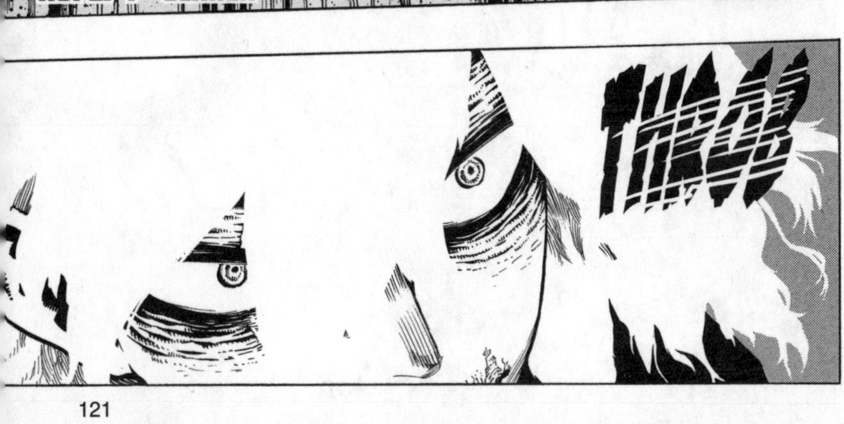
THROB

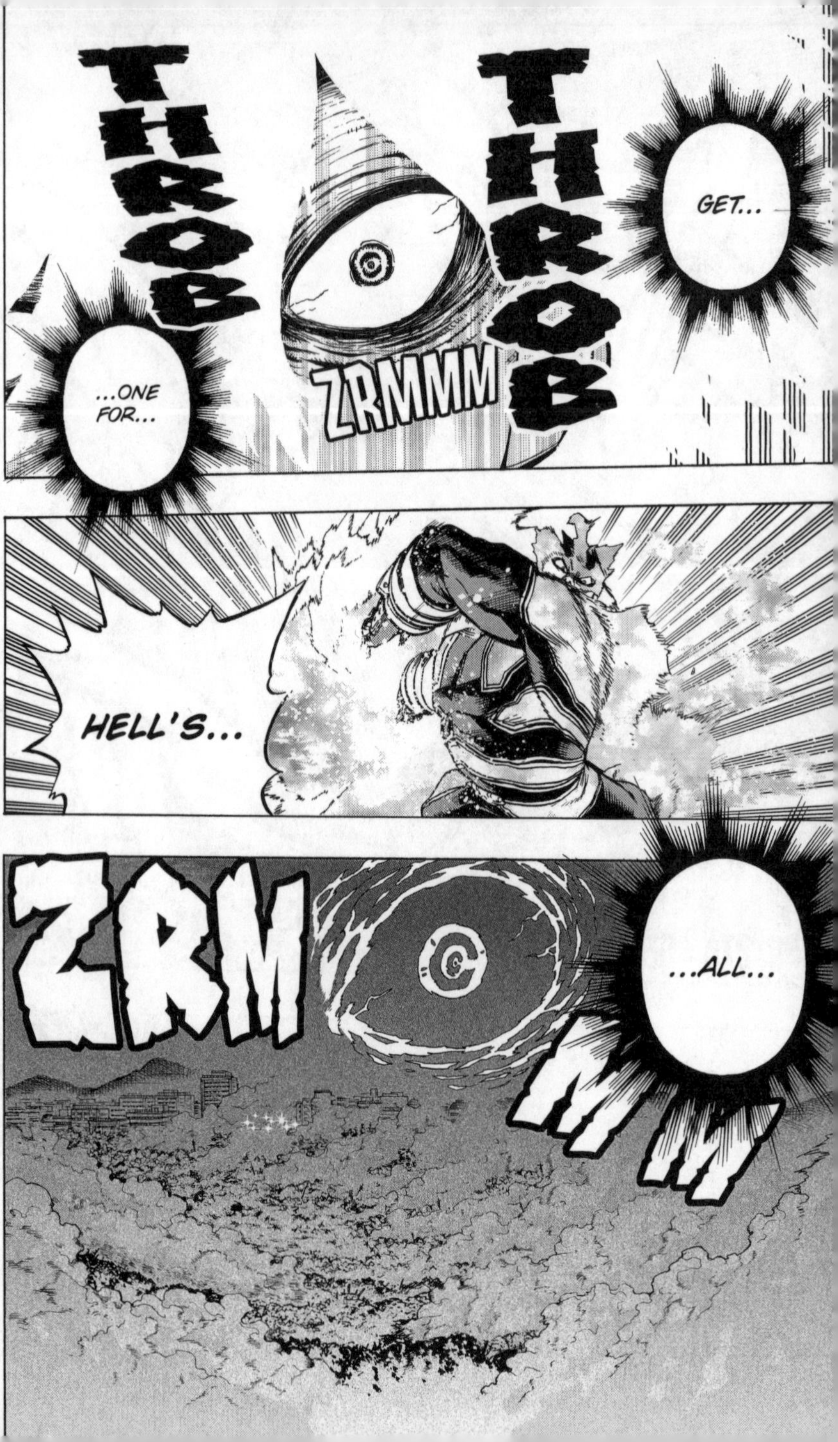
GET...
THROB
THROB
ZRMMMM
...ONE FOR...
HELL'S...
...ALL...
ZRMMM

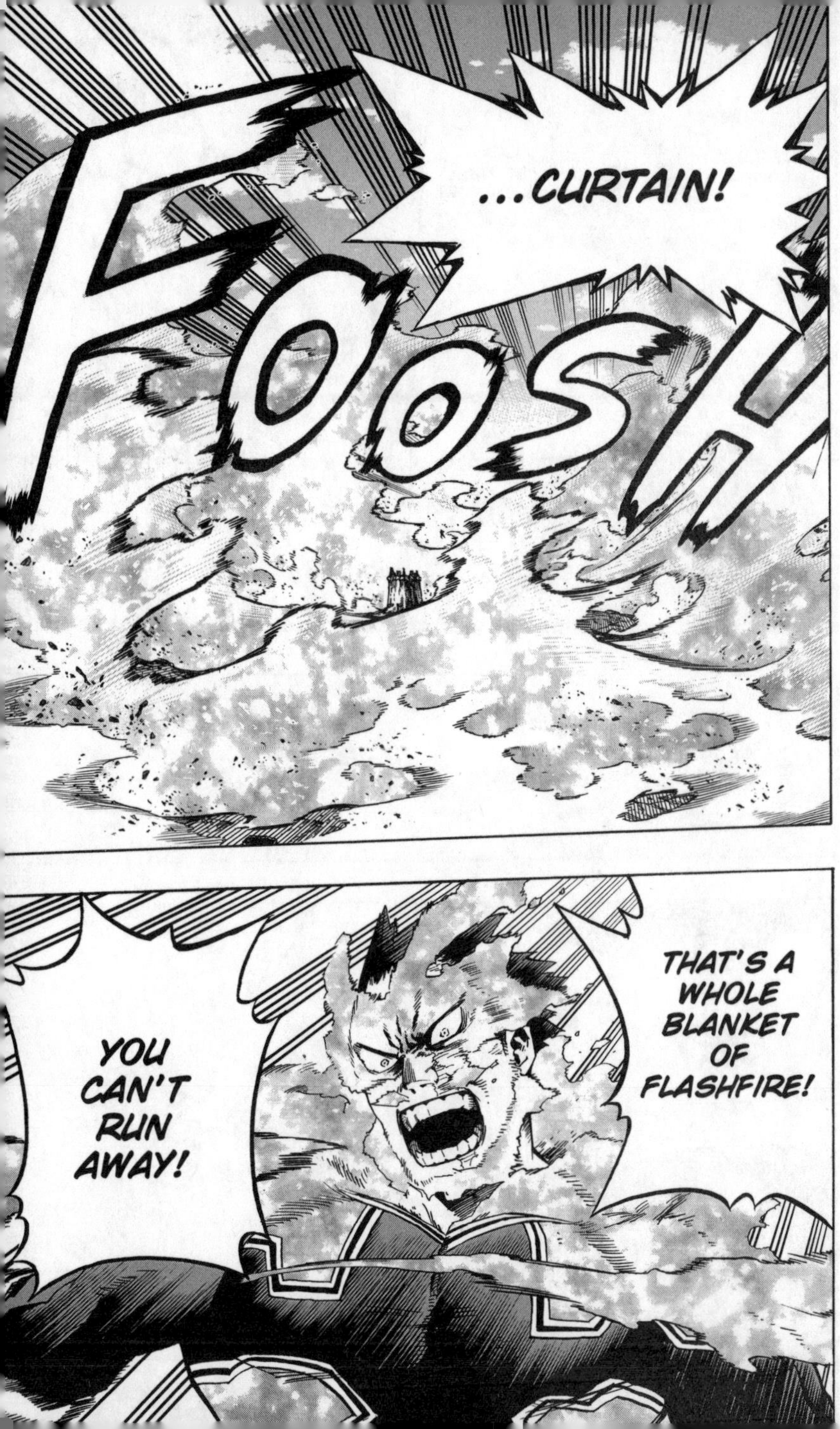
...CURTAIN!
FOOSH
THAT'S A WHOLE BLANKET OF FLASHFIRE!
YOU CAN'T RUN AWAY!

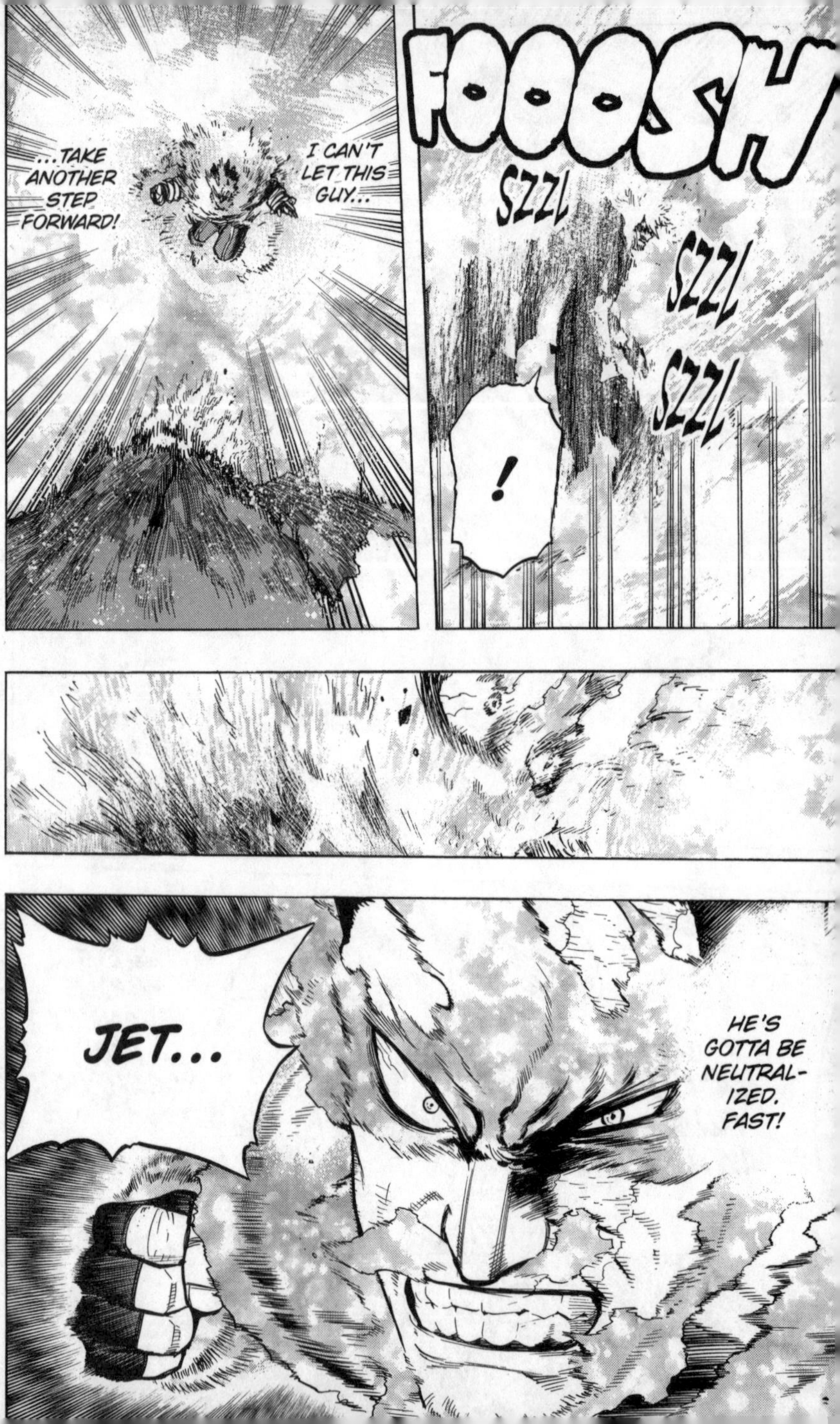
FOOOSH
SZZL
SZZL
SZZL
!
I CAN'T LET THIS GUY...
...TAKE ANOTHER STEP FORWARD!
HE'S GOTTA BE NEUTRAL-IZED. FAST!
JET...

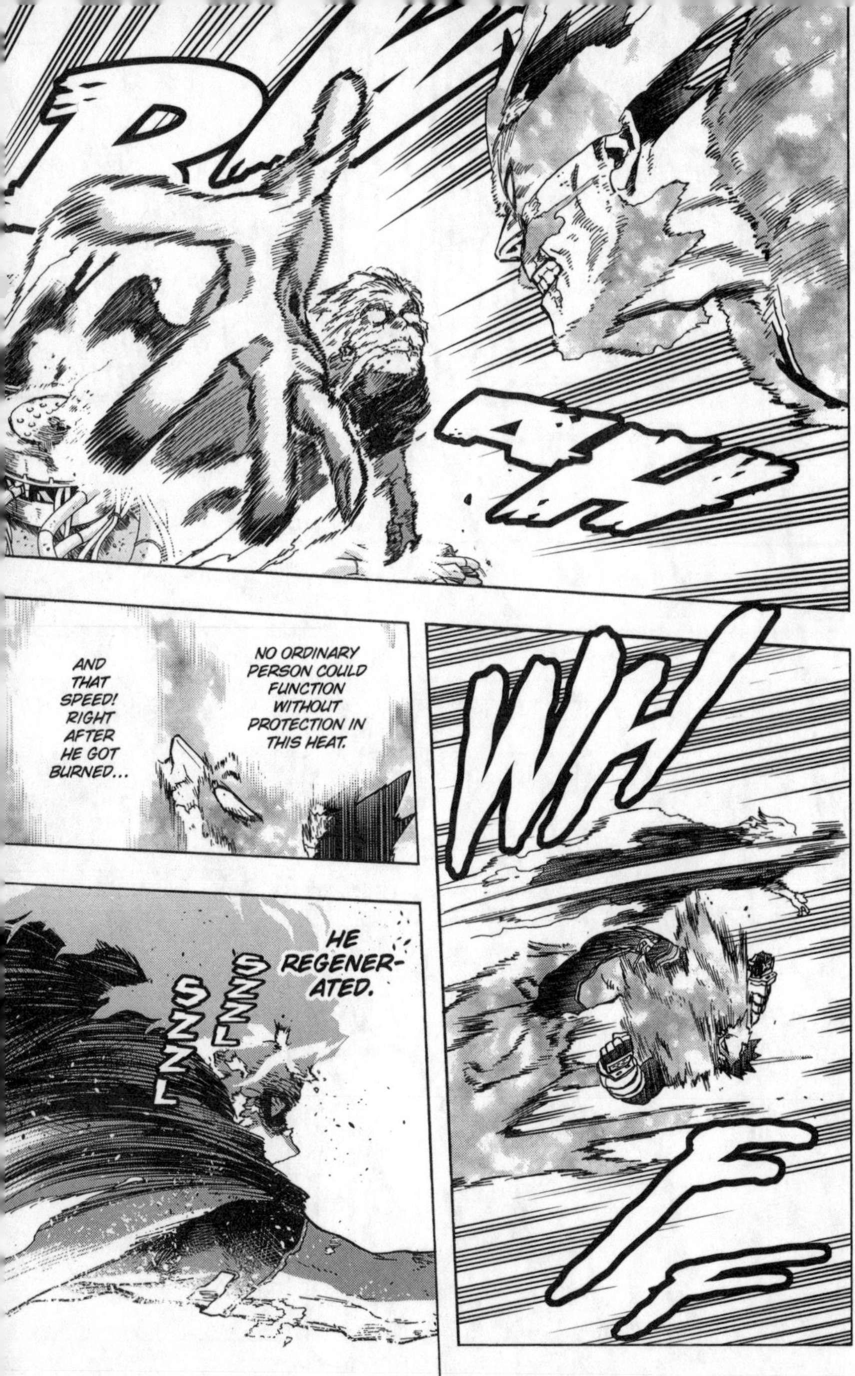

WHFF
NO ORDINARY PERSON COULD FUNCTION WITHOUT PROTECTION IN THIS HEAT.
AND THAT SPEED! RIGHT AFTER HE GOT BURNED...
HE REGENER-ATED.
SZZL
SZZL

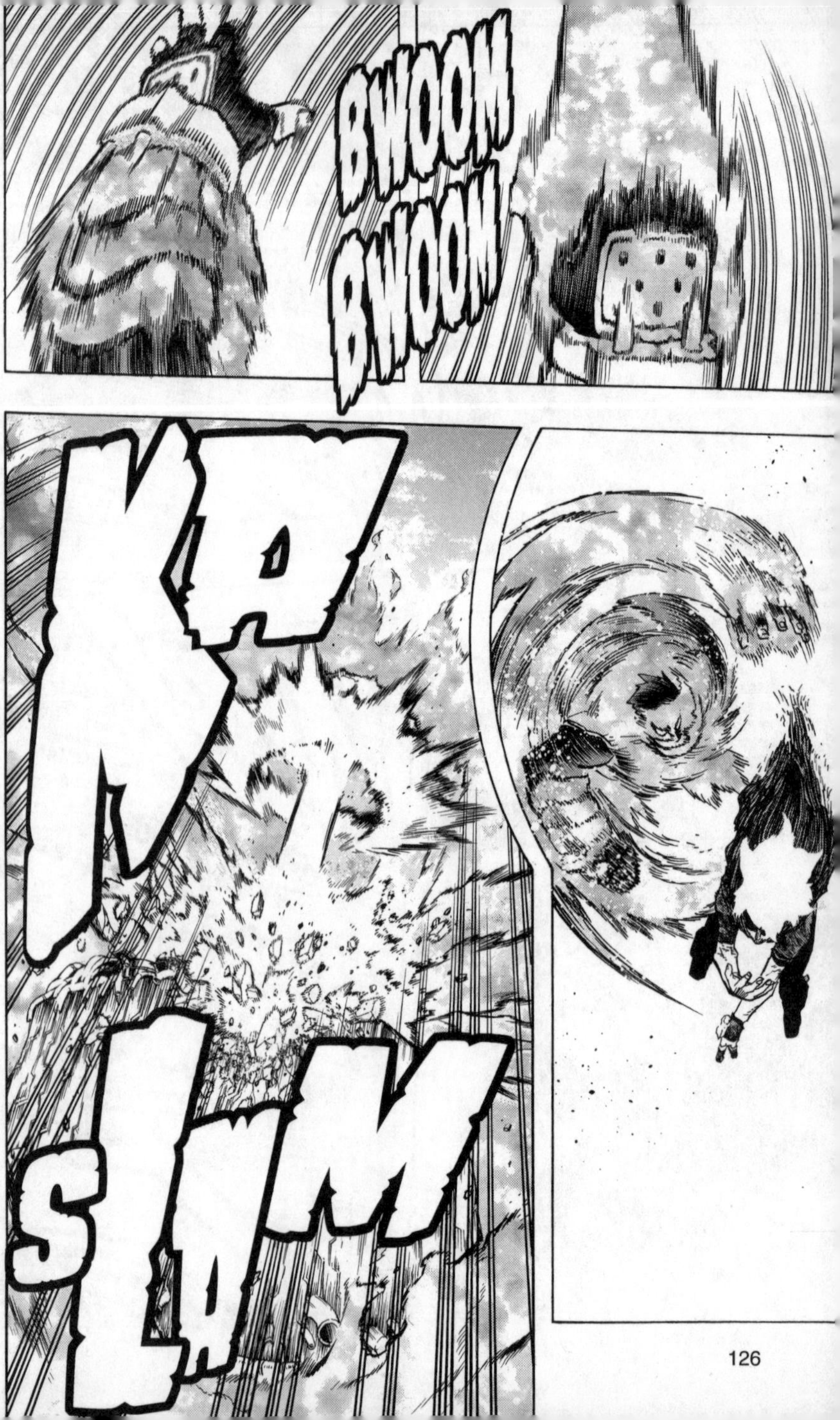
BWOOM
BWOOM
KA
SLAM

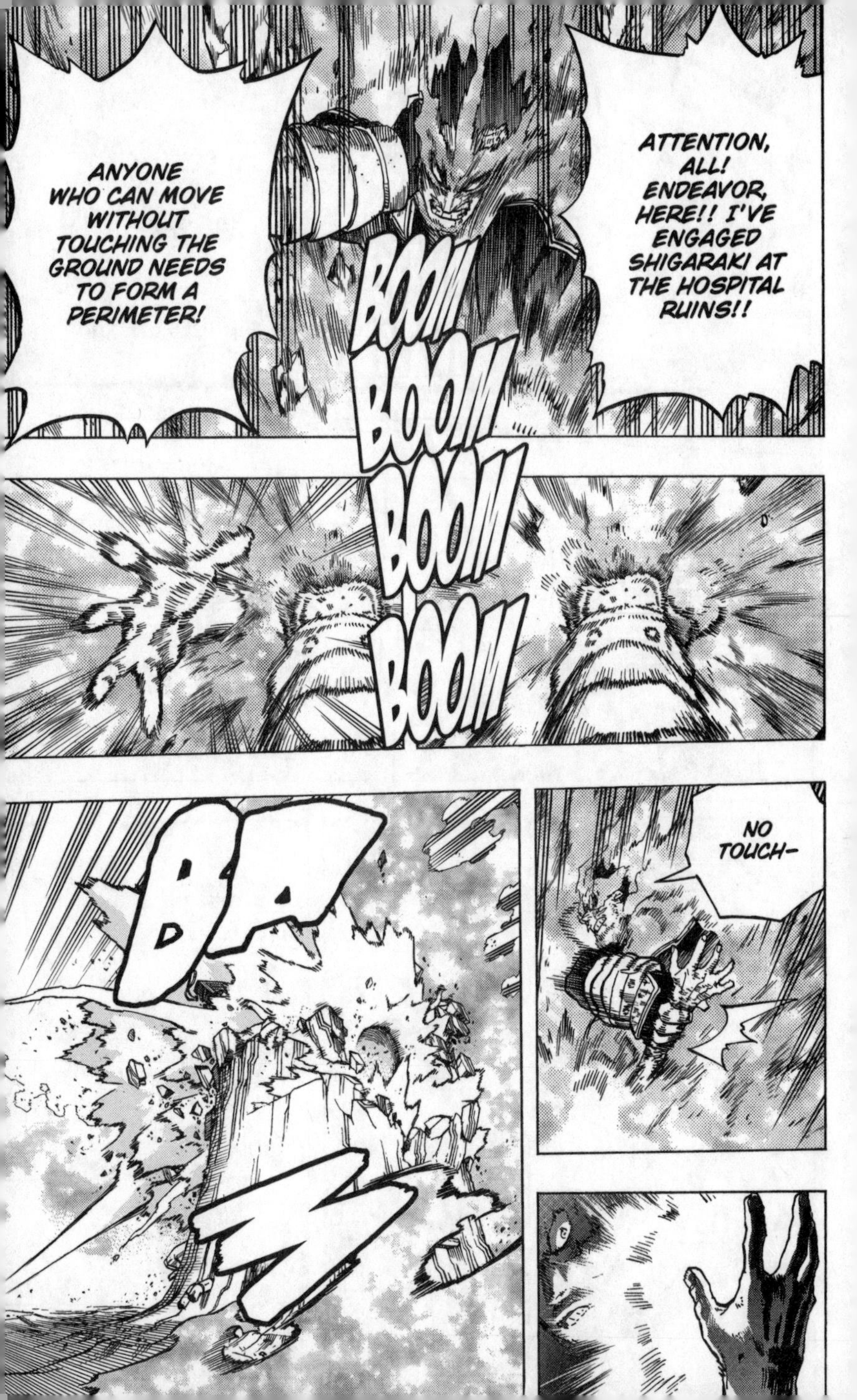
ATTENTION, ALL! ENDEAVOR, HERE!! I'VE ENGAGED SHIGARAKI AT THE HOSPITAL RUINS!!
ANYONE WHO CAN MOVE WITHOUT TOUCHING THE GROUND NEEDS TO FORM A PERIMETER!
BOOM
BOOM
BOOM
BOOM
NO TOUCH-
BA

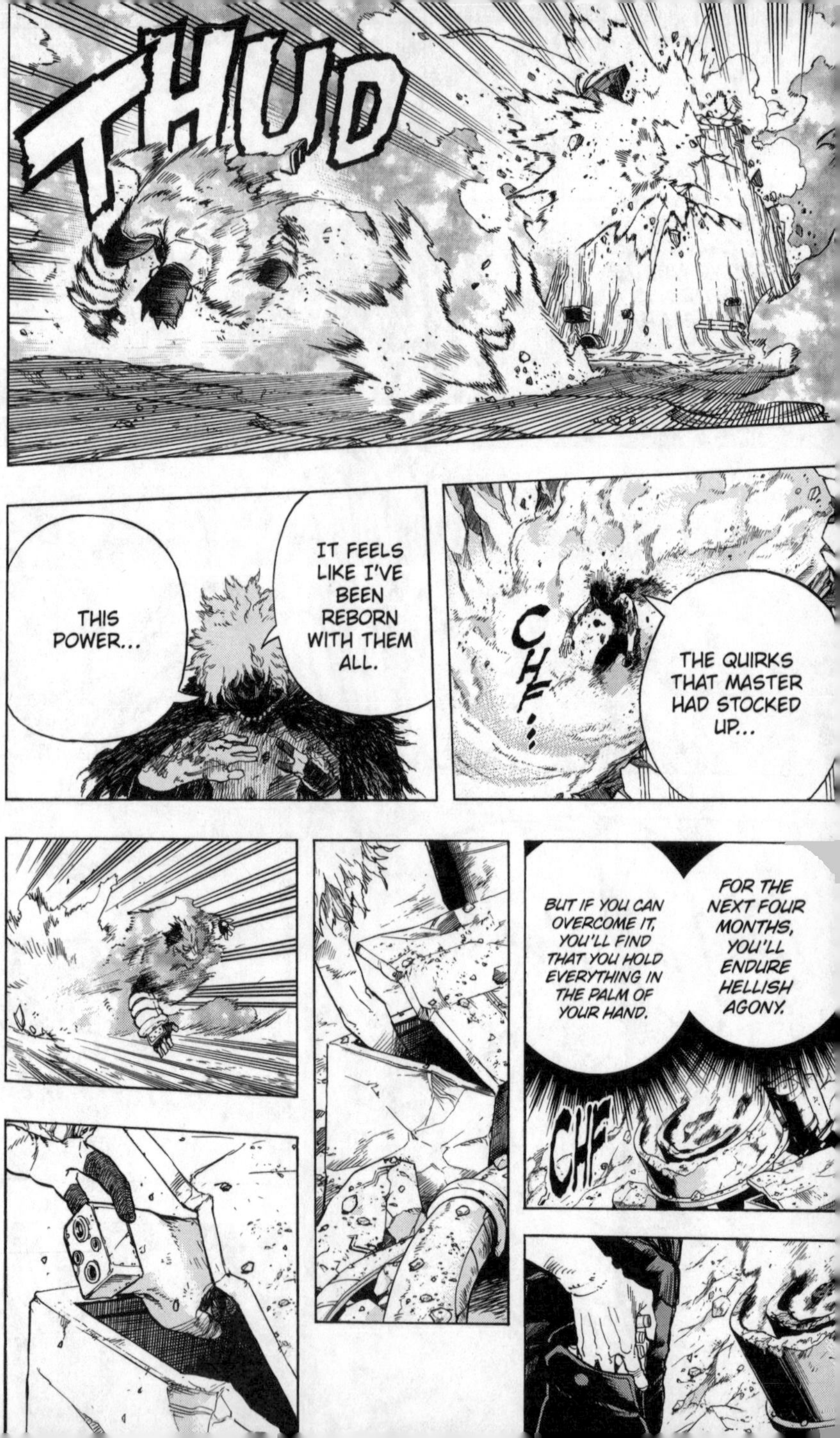
THUD
CHF...
THE QUIRKS THAT MASTER HAD STOCKED UP...
IT FEELS LIKE I'VE BEEN REBORN WITH THEM ALL.
THIS POWER...
FOR THE NEXT FOUR MONTHS, YOU'LL ENDURE HELLISH AGONY.
BUT IF YOU CAN OVERCOME IT, YOU'LL FIND THAT YOU HOLD EVERYTHING IN THE PALM OF YOUR HAND.
CHF

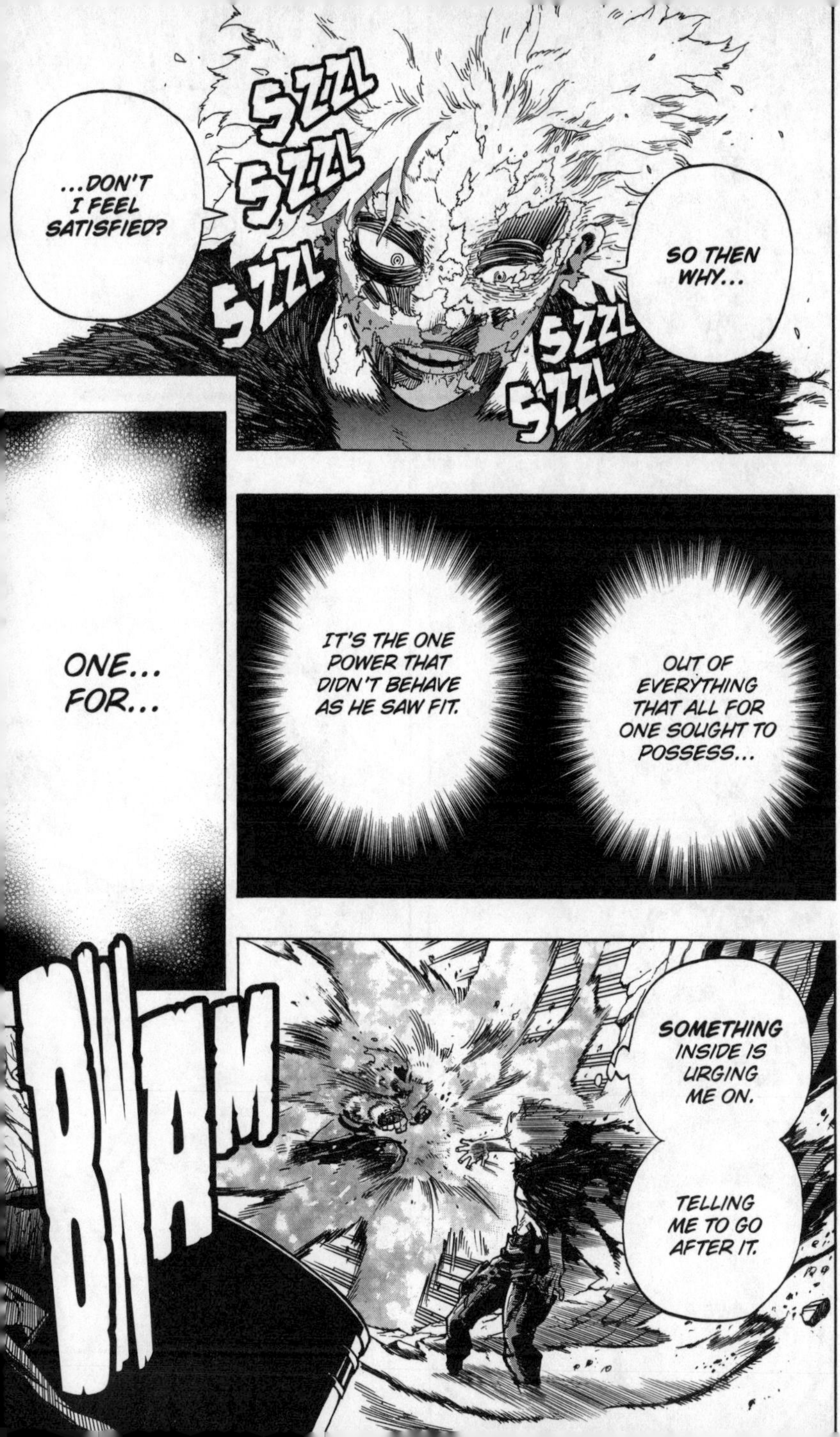
SO THEN WHY...
SZZL SZZL
...DON'T I FEEL SATISFIED?
SZZL SZZL SZZL
OUT OF EVERYTHING THAT ALL FOR ONE SOUGHT TO POSSESS...
IT'S THE ONE POWER THAT DIDN'T BEHAVE AS HE SAW FIT.
SOMETHING INSIDE IS URGING ME ON.
TELLING ME TO GO AFTER IT.
BWAM
ONE... FOR...

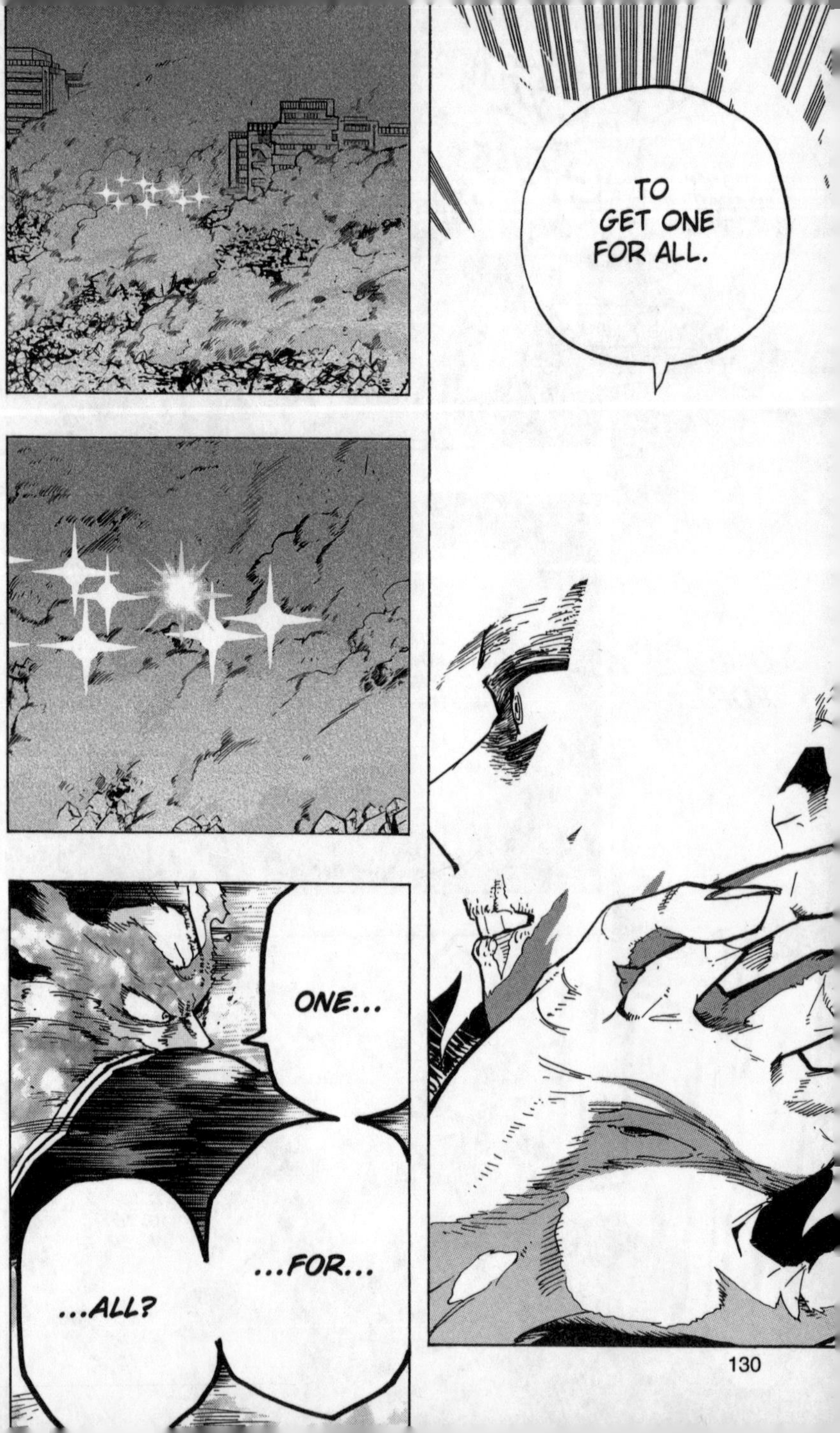
TO GET ONE FOR ALL.
ONE...
...FOR...
...ALL?

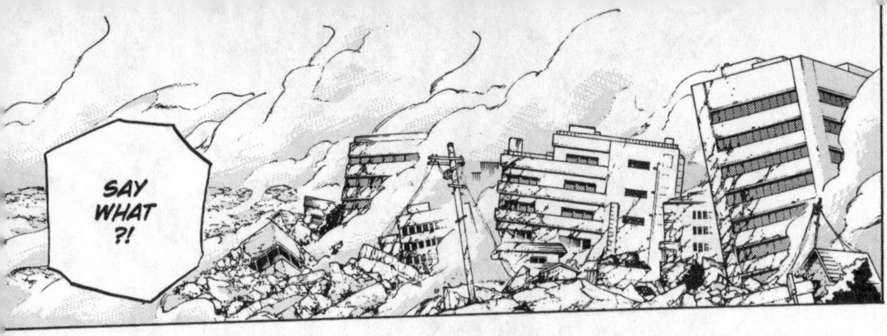
SAY WHAT ?!

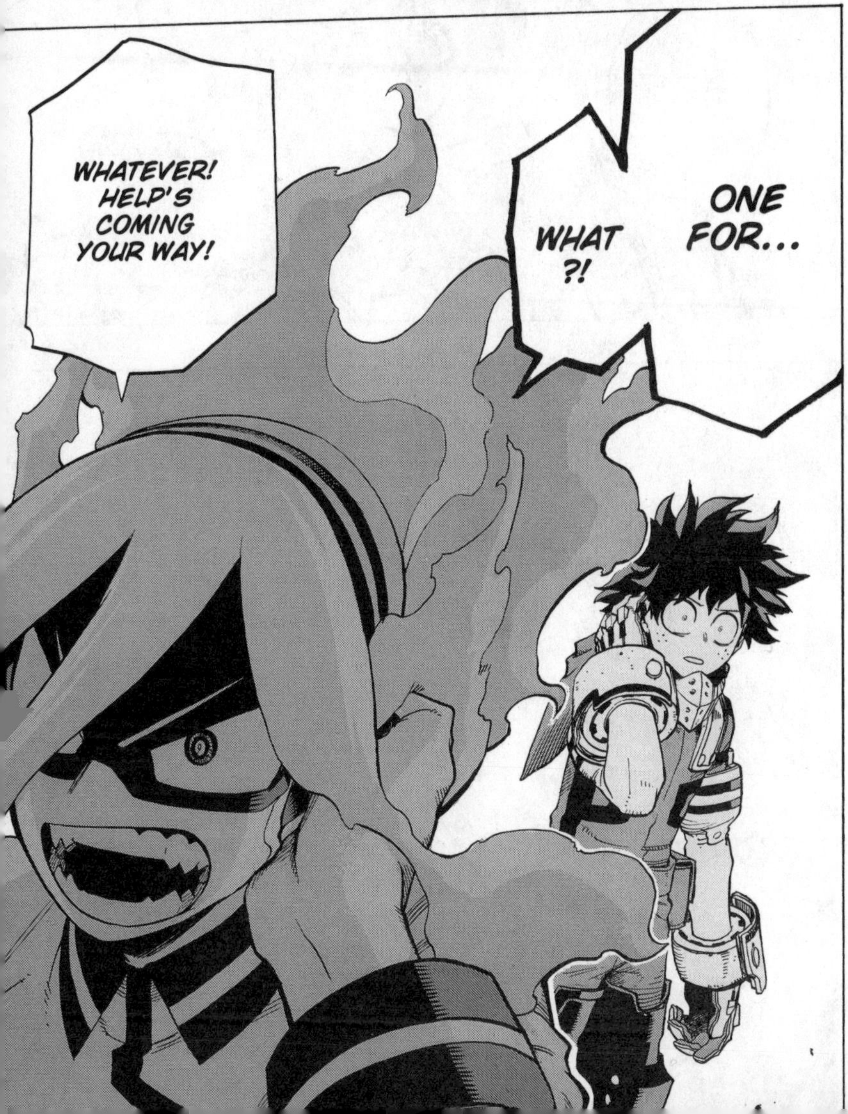
ONE FOR...
WHAT ?!
WHATEVER! HELP'S COMING YOUR WAY!

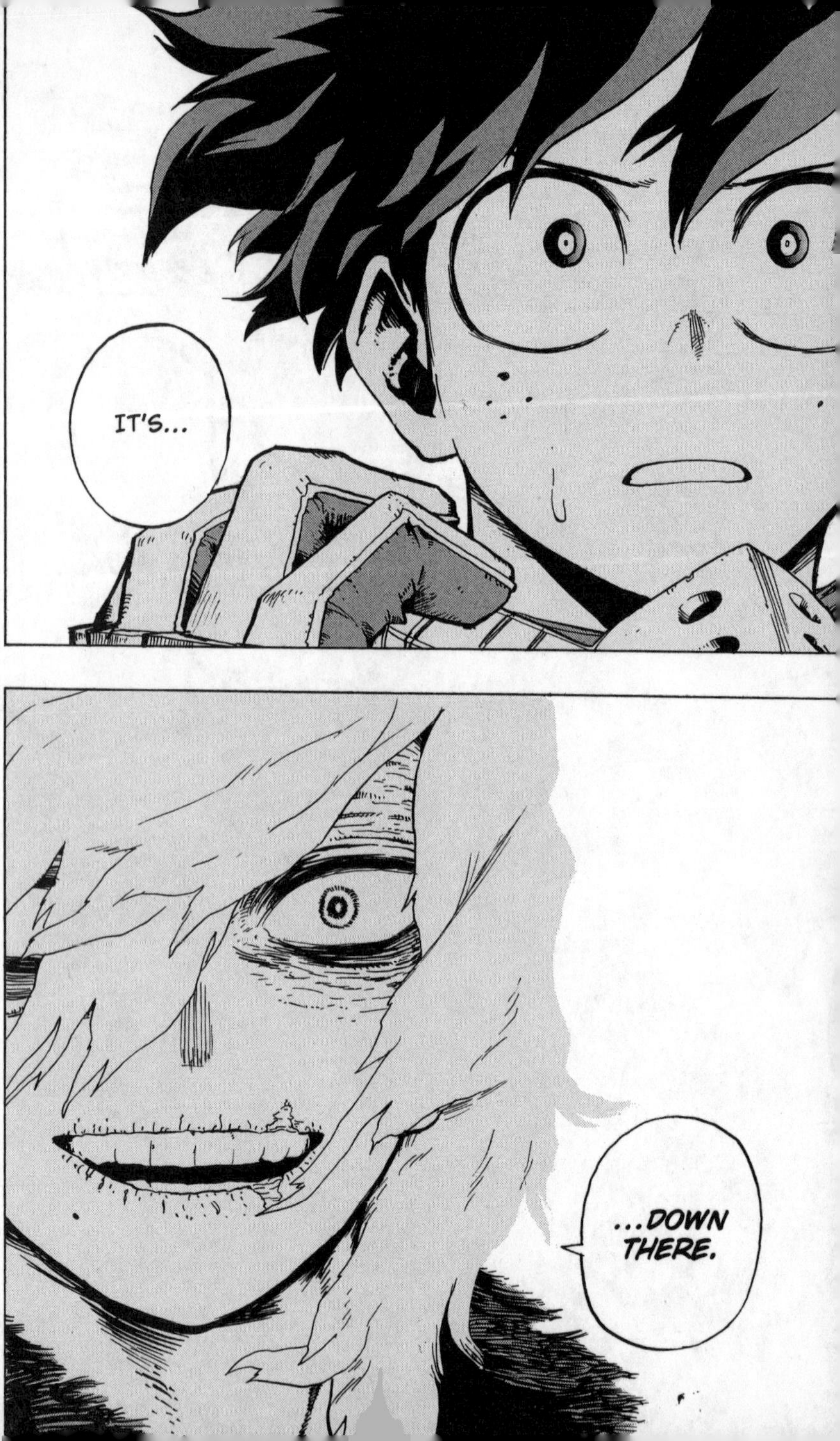
IT'S...
...DOWN THERE.

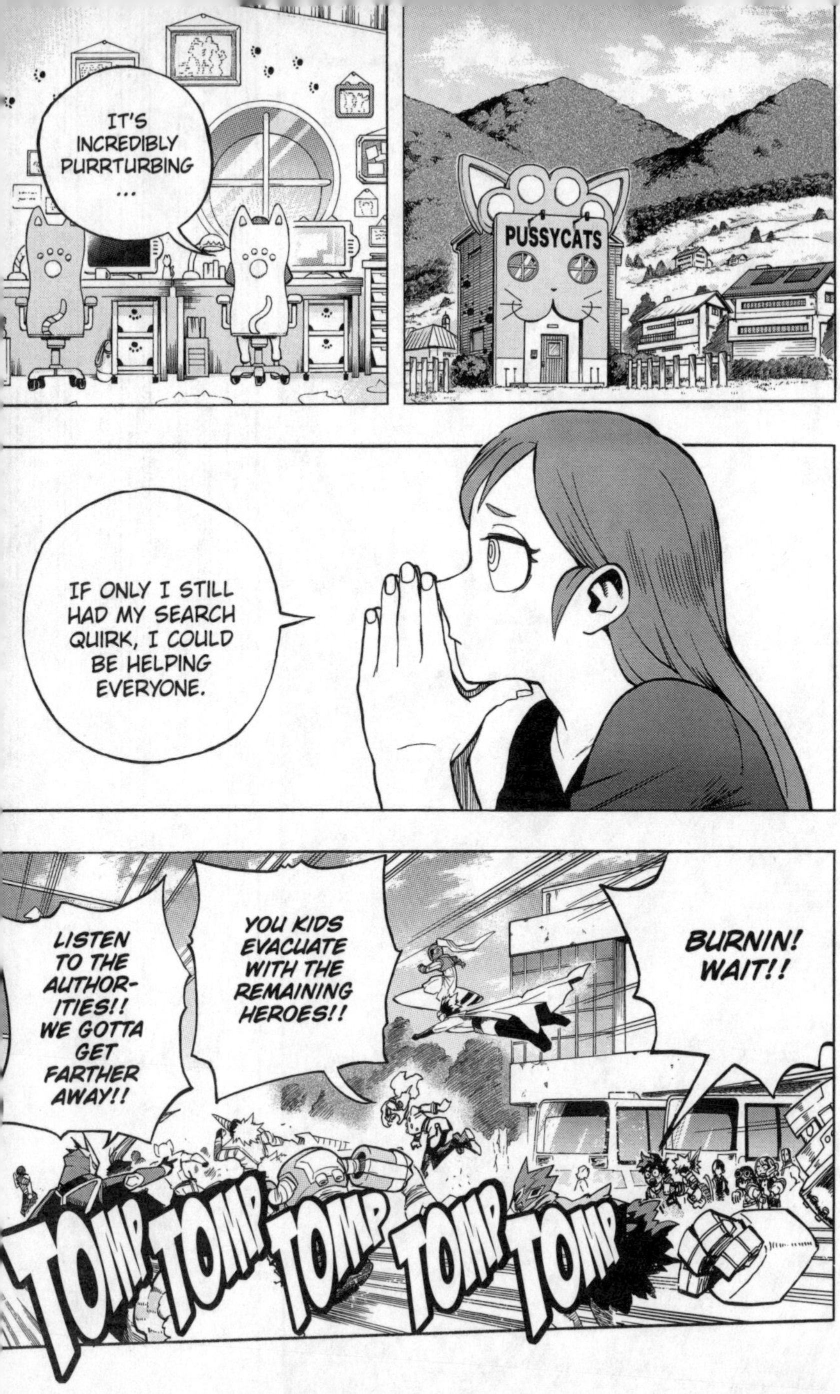
PUSSYCATS
IT'S INCREDIBLY PURRTURBING ...
IF ONLY I STILL HAD MY SEARCH QUIRK, I COULD BE HELPING EVERYONE.
BURNIN! WAIT!!
YOU KIDS EVACUATE WITH THE REMAINING HEROES!!
LISTEN TO THE AUTHOR-ITIES!! WE GOTTA GET FARTHER AWAY!!
TOMP TOMP TOMP TOMP TOMP

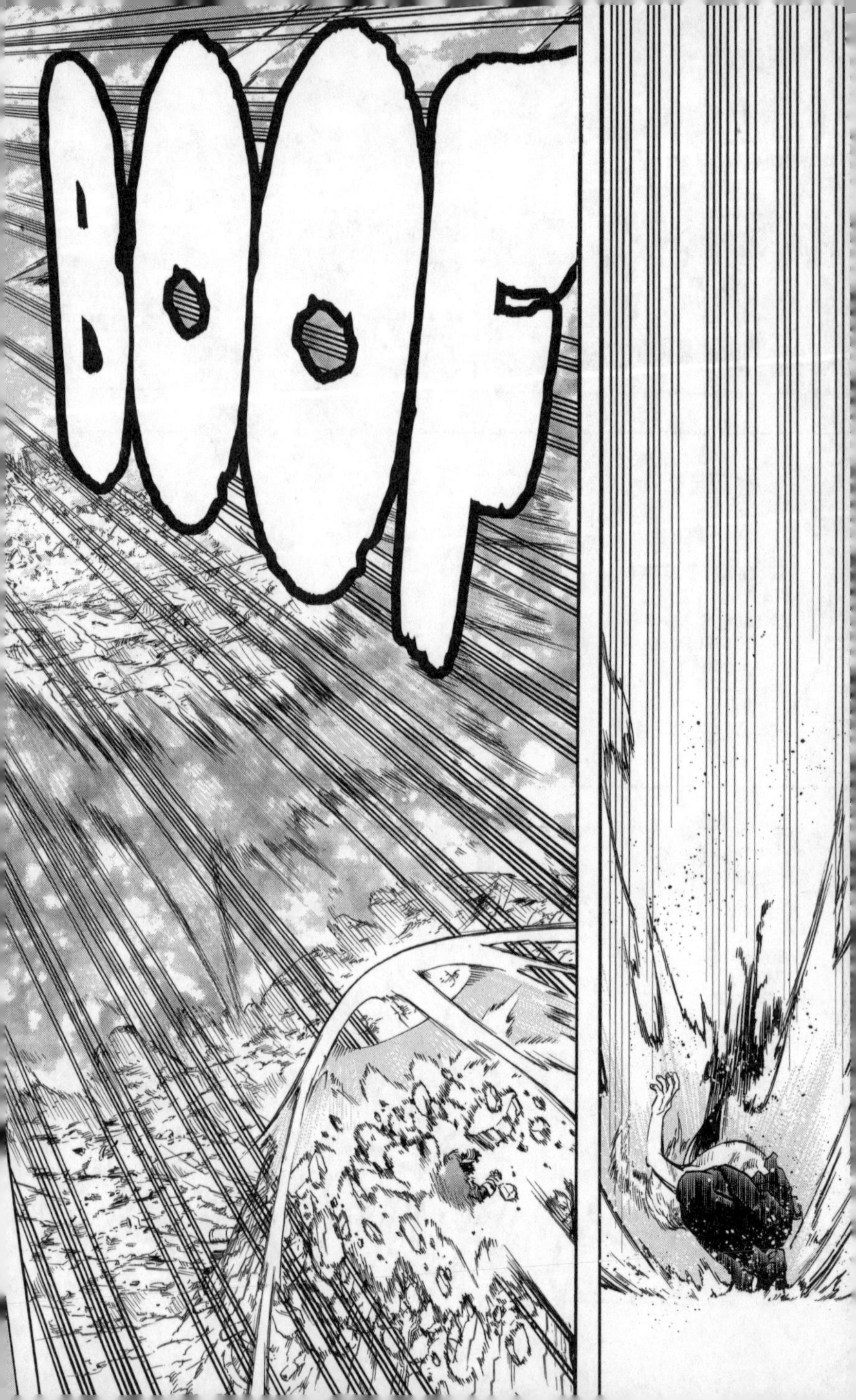

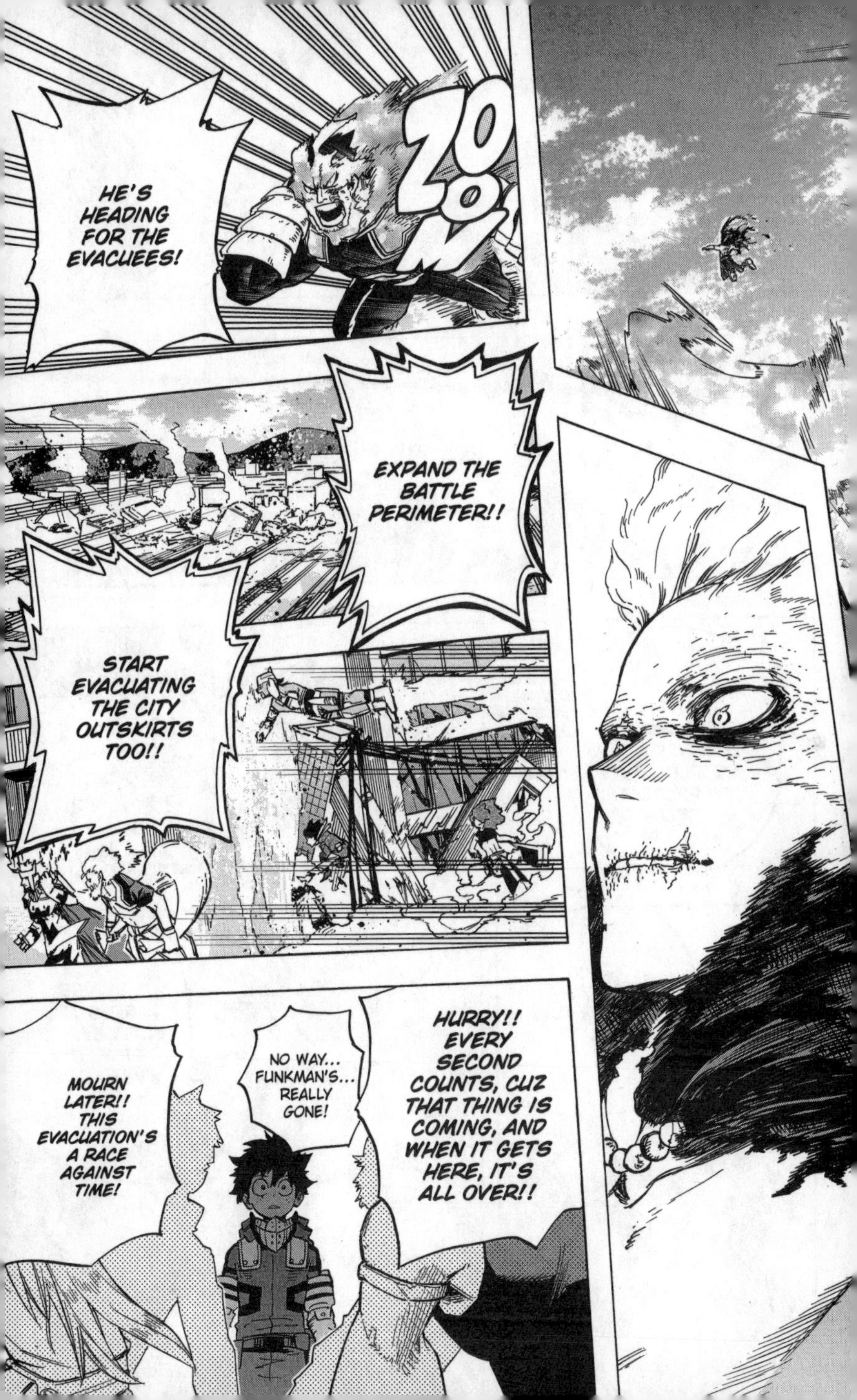
ZOOM
HE'S HEADING FOR THE EVACUEES!
EXPAND THE BATTLE PERIMETER!!
START EVACUATING THE CITY OUTSKIRTS TOO!!
HURRY!! EVERY SECOND COUNTS, CUZ THAT THING IS COMING, AND WHEN IT GETS HERE, IT'S ALL OVER!!
NO WAY... FUNKMAN'S... REALLY GONE!
MOURN LATER!! THIS EVACUATION'S A RACE AGAINST TIME!

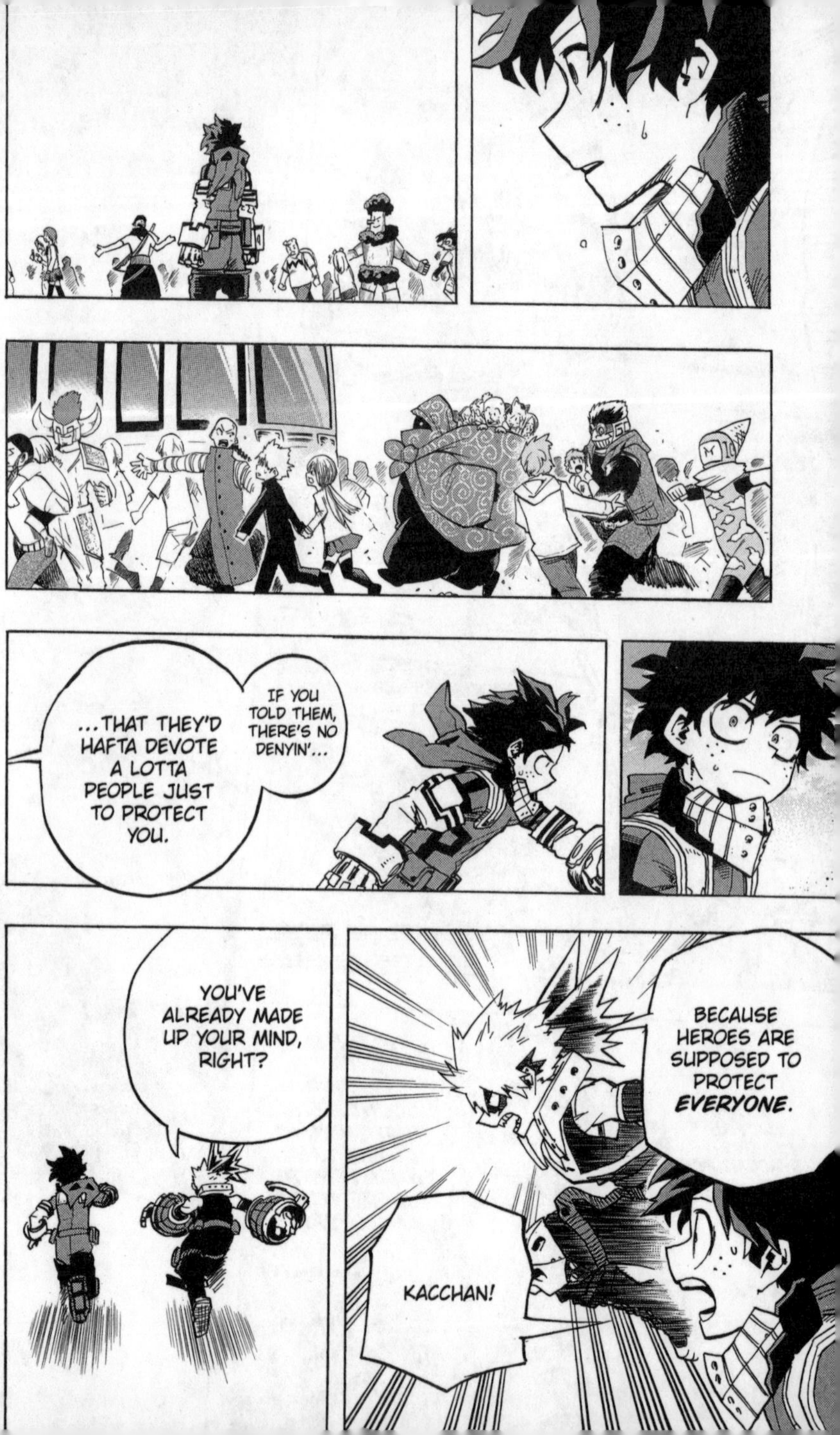
IF YOU TOLD THEM, THERE'S NO DENYIN'...
...THAT THEY'D HAFTA DEVOTE A LOTTA PEOPLE JUST TO PROTECT YOU.
BECAUSE HEROES ARE SUPPOSED TO PROTECT *EVERYONE.*
KACCHAN!
YOU'VE ALREADY MADE UP YOUR MIND, RIGHT?

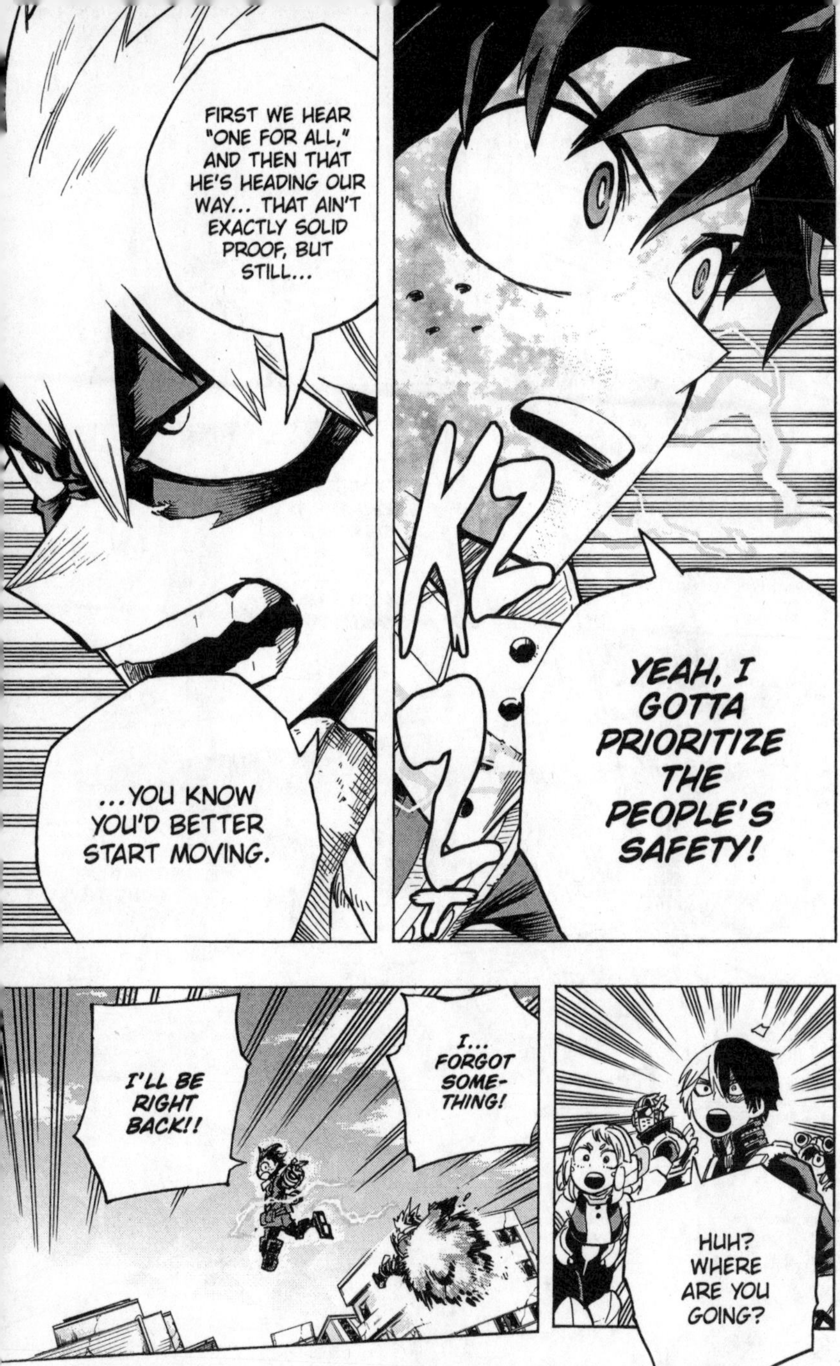
YEAH, I GOTTA PRIORITIZE THE PEOPLE'S SAFETY!
FIRST WE HEAR "ONE FOR ALL," AND THEN THAT HE'S HEADING OUR WAY... THAT AIN'T EXACTLY SOLID PROOF, BUT STILL...
...YOU KNOW YOU'D BETTER START MOVING.
HUH? WHERE ARE YOU GOING?
I... FORGOT SOMETHING!
I'LL BE RIGHT BACK!!

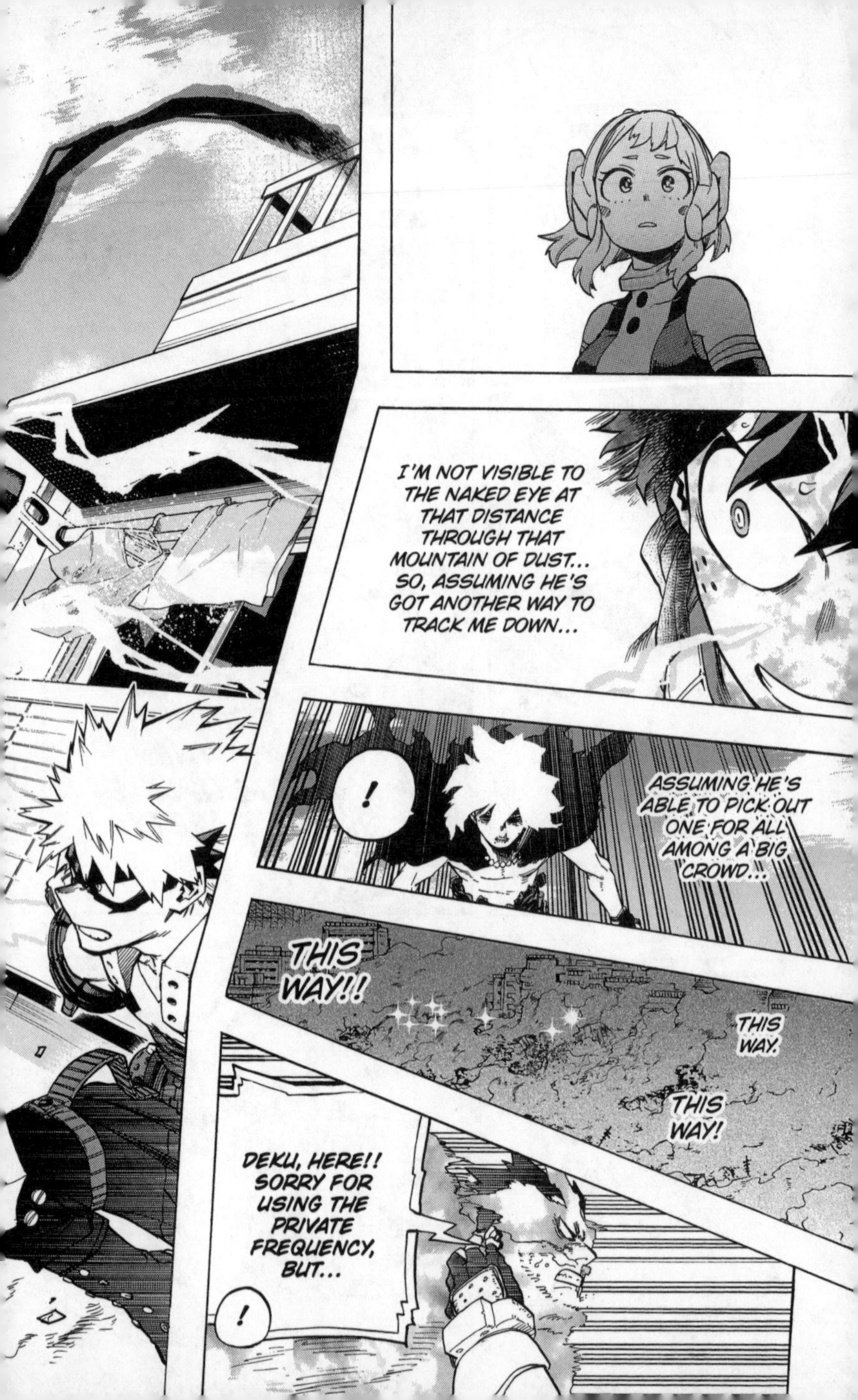

I'M NOT VISIBLE TO THE NAKED EYE AT THAT DISTANCE THROUGH THAT MOUNTAIN OF DUST... SO, ASSUMING HE'S GOT ANOTHER WAY TO TRACK ME DOWN...
ASSUMING HE'S ABLE TO PICK OUT ONE FOR ALL AMONG A BIG CROWD...
!
THIS WAY.
THIS WAY!
THIS WAY!!
DEKU, HERE!! SORRY FOR USING THE PRIVATE FREQUENCY, BUT...
!

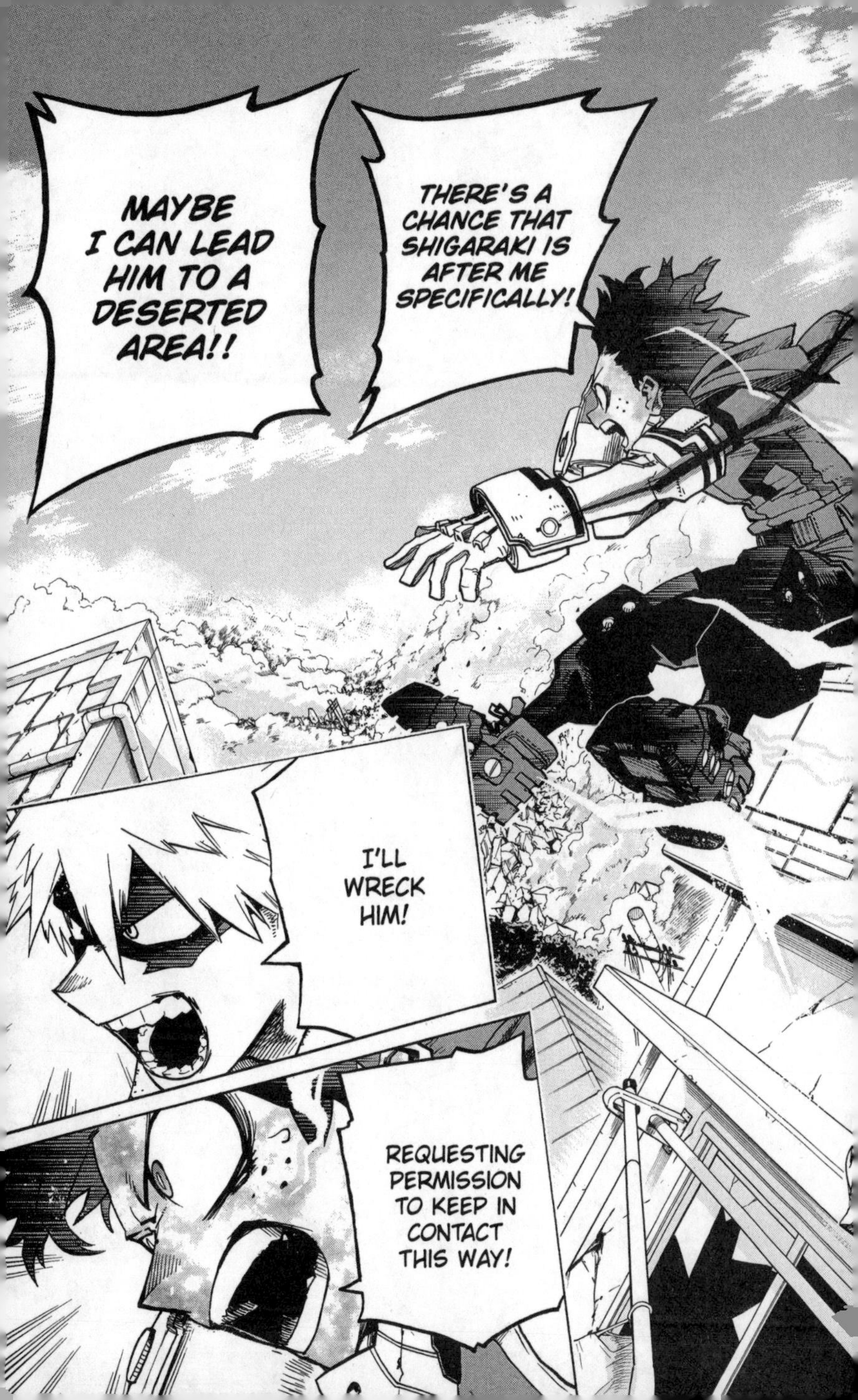
THERE'S A CHANCE THAT SHIGARAKI IS AFTER ME SPECIFICALLY!
MAYBE I CAN LEAD HIM TO A DESERTED AREA!!
I'LL WRECK HIM!
REQUESTING PERMISSION TO KEEP IN CONTACT THIS WAY!

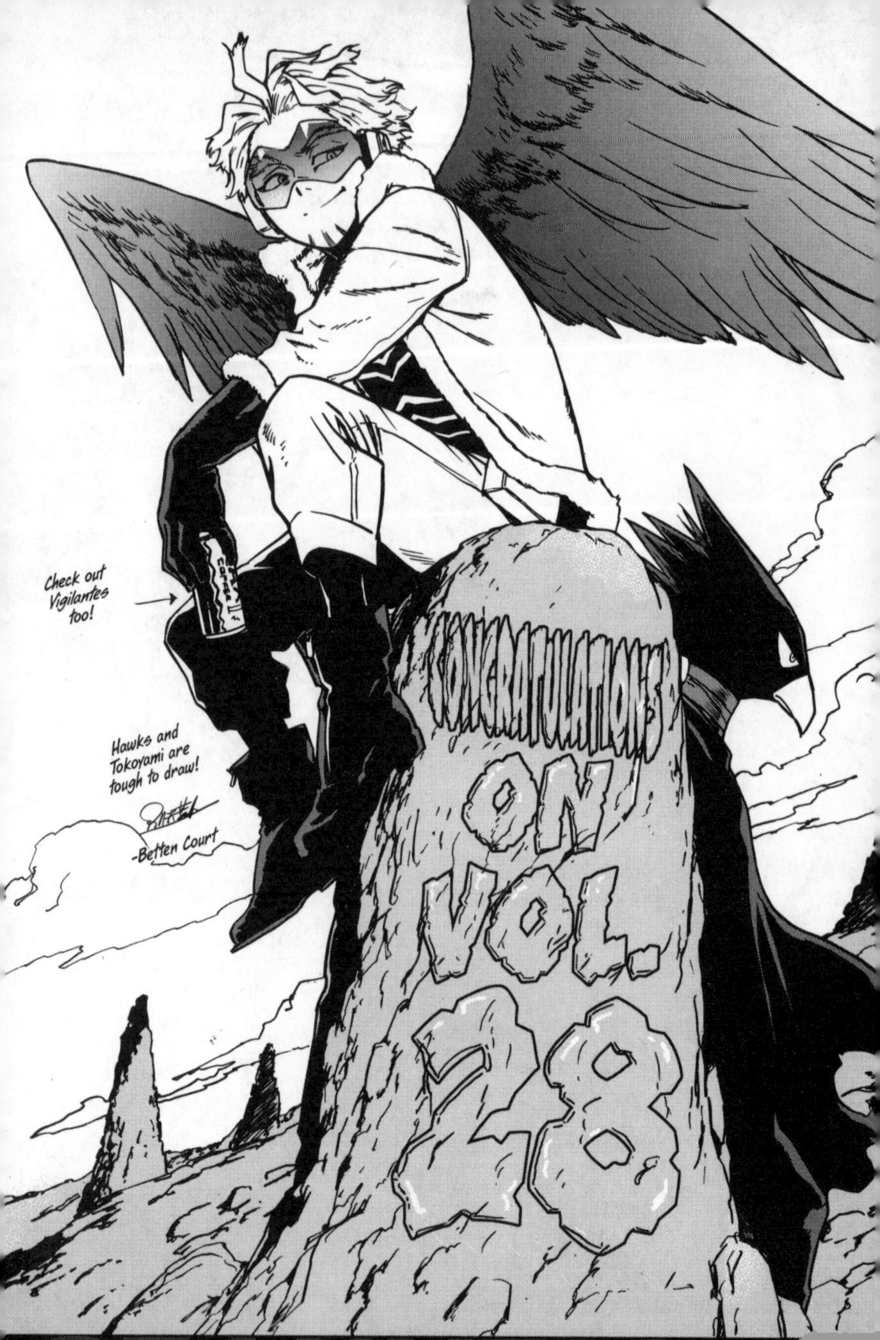
Check out Vigilantes too!
Hawks and Tokoyami are tough to draw!
-Betten Court
CONGRATULATIONS ON VOL. 28

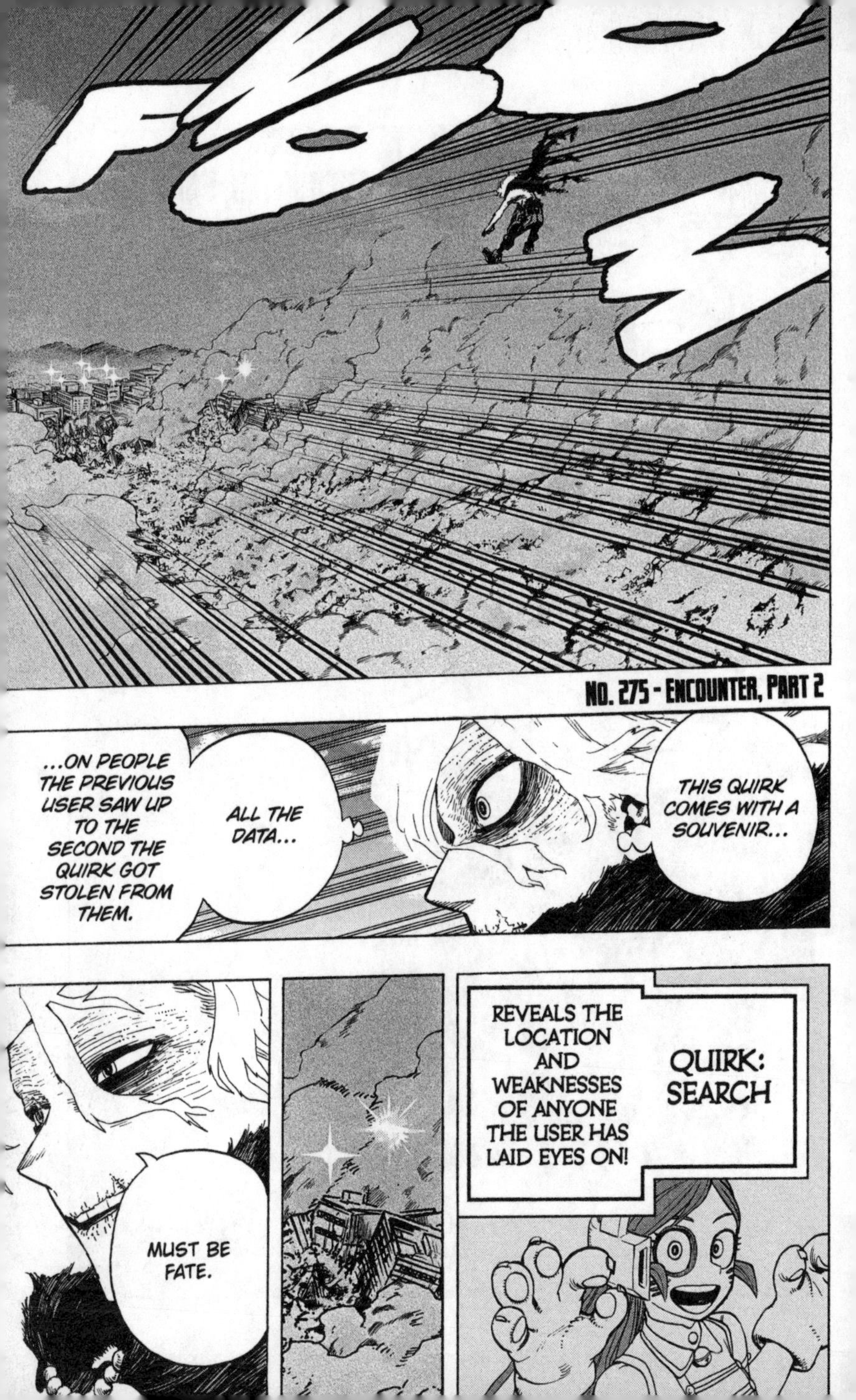
FWOOM
No. 275 - ENCOUNTER, PART 2
THIS QUIRK COMES WITH A SOUVENIR...
ALL THE DATA...
...ON PEOPLE THE PREVIOUS USER SAW UP TO THE SECOND THE QUIRK GOT STOLEN FROM THEM.
QUIRK: SEARCH
REVEALS THE LOCATION AND WEAKNESSES OF ANYONE THE USER HAS LAID EYES ON!
MUST BE FATE.

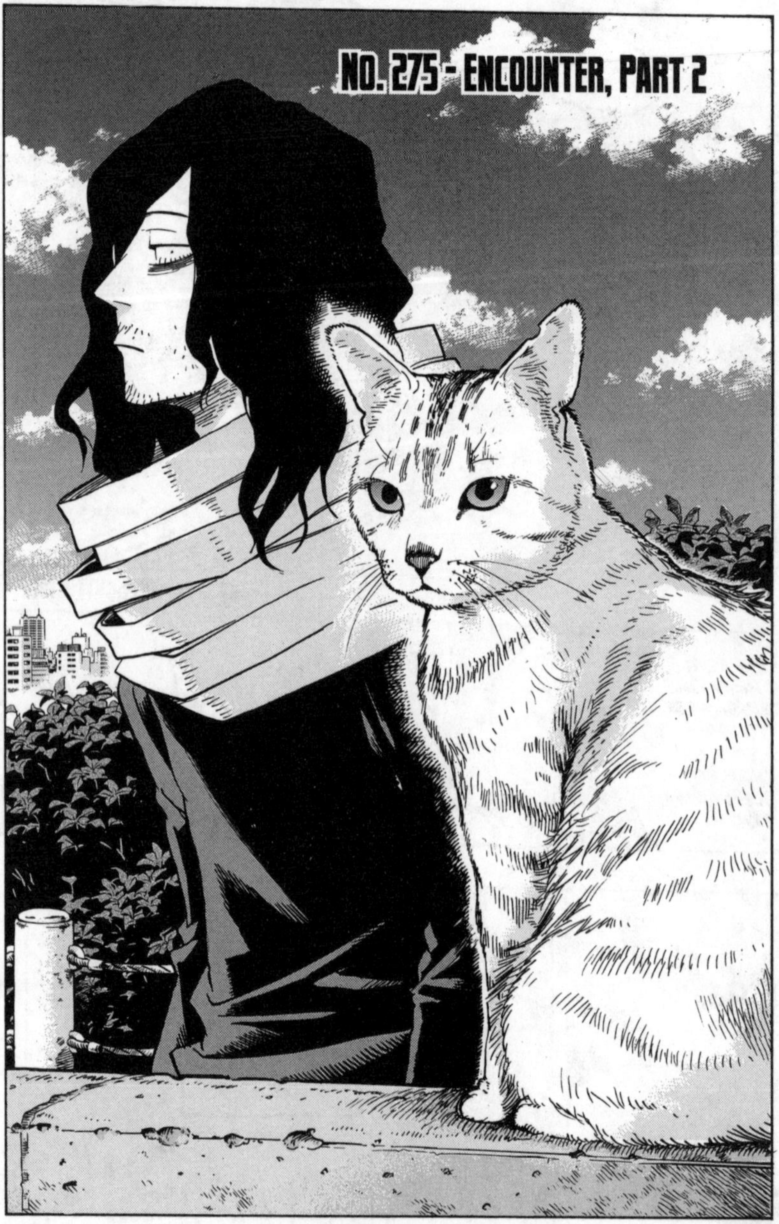
NO. 275 - ENCOUNTER, PART 2

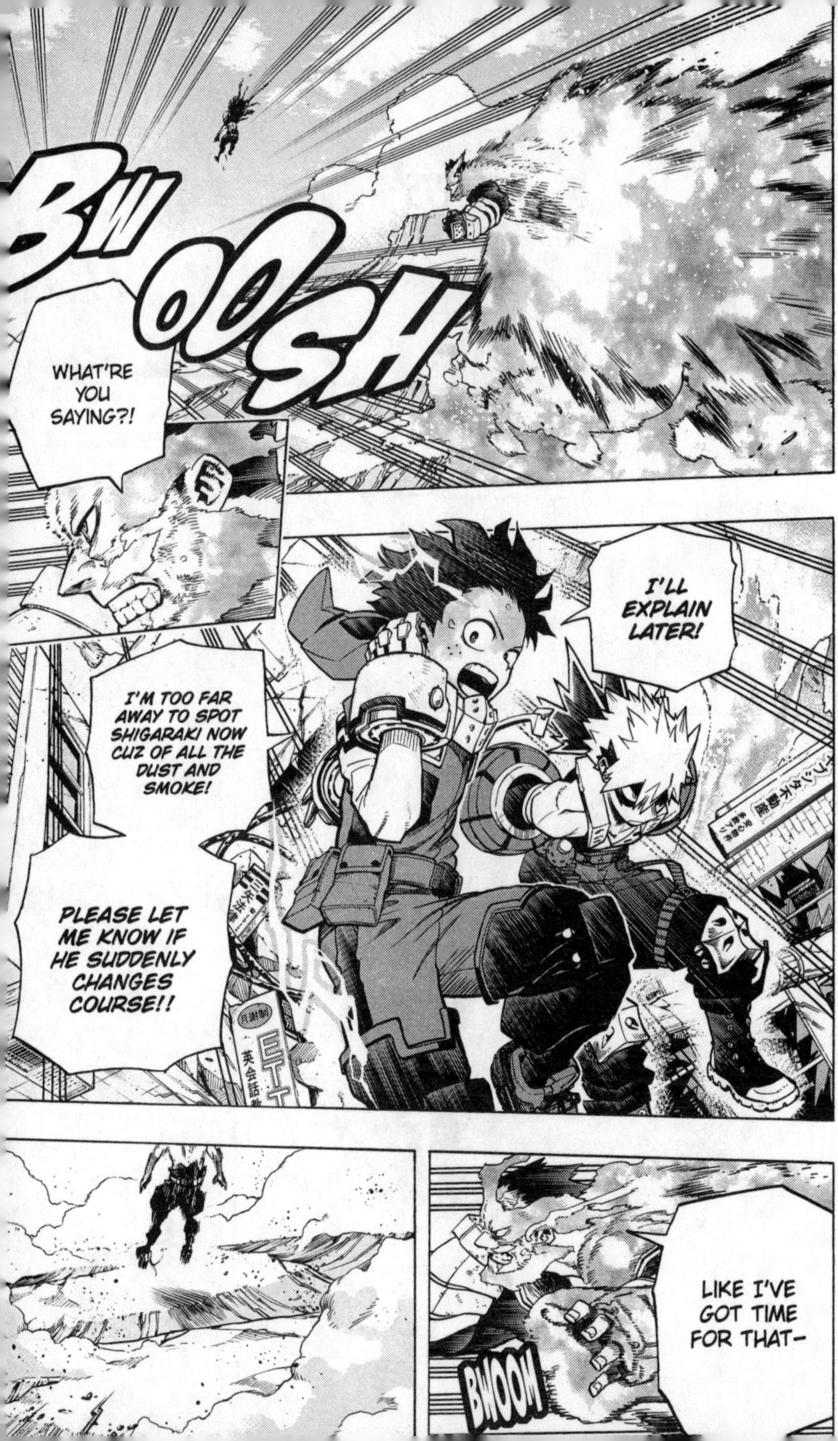
BWOOOSH
WHAT'RE YOU SAYING?!
I'LL EXPLAIN LATER!
I'M TOO FAR AWAY TO SPOT SHIGARAKI NOW CUZ OF ALL THE DUST AND SMOKE!
PLEASE LET ME KNOW IF HE SUDDENLY CHANGES COURSE!!
LIKE I'VE GOT TIME FOR THAT—
BWOOM

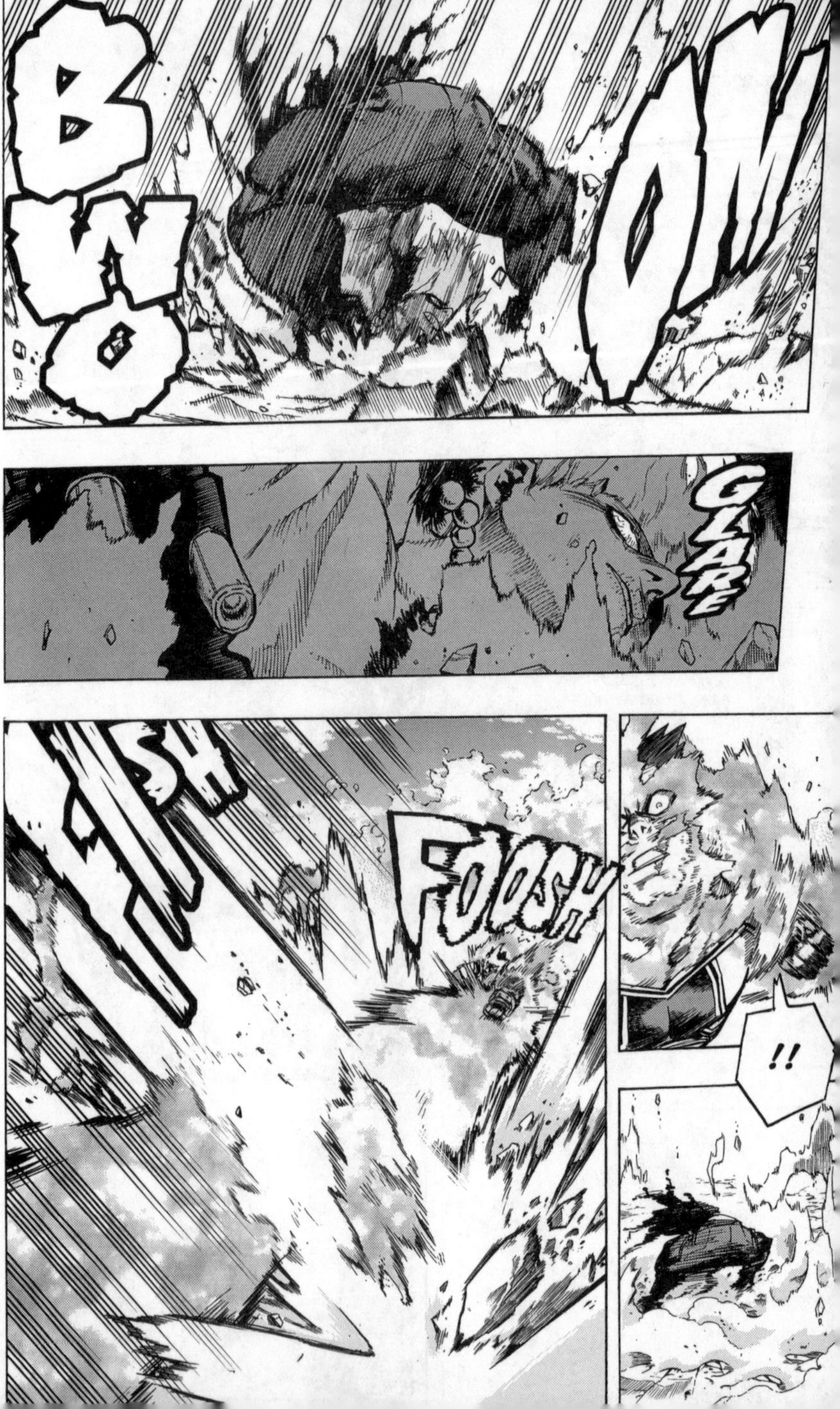
BOOM
GLARE
!!
FOOSH

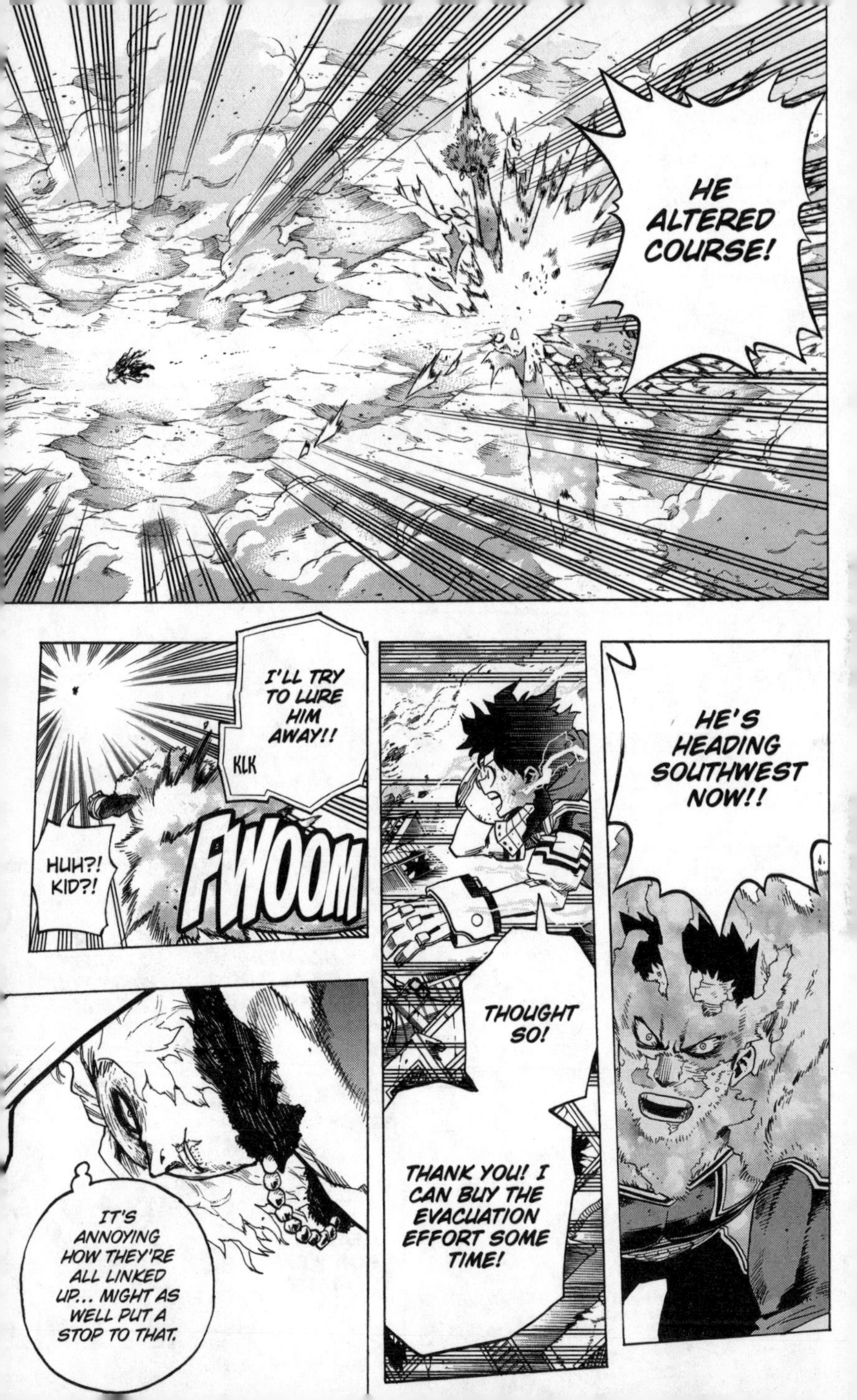
HE ALTERED COURSE!
HE'S HEADING SOUTHWEST NOW!!
THOUGHT SO!
THANK YOU! I CAN BUY THE EVACUATION EFFORT SOME TIME!
I'LL TRY TO LURE HIM AWAY!!
KLK
FWOOM
HUH?! KID?!
IT'S ANNOYING HOW THEY'RE ALL LINKED UP... MIGHT AS WELL PUT A STOP TO THAT.

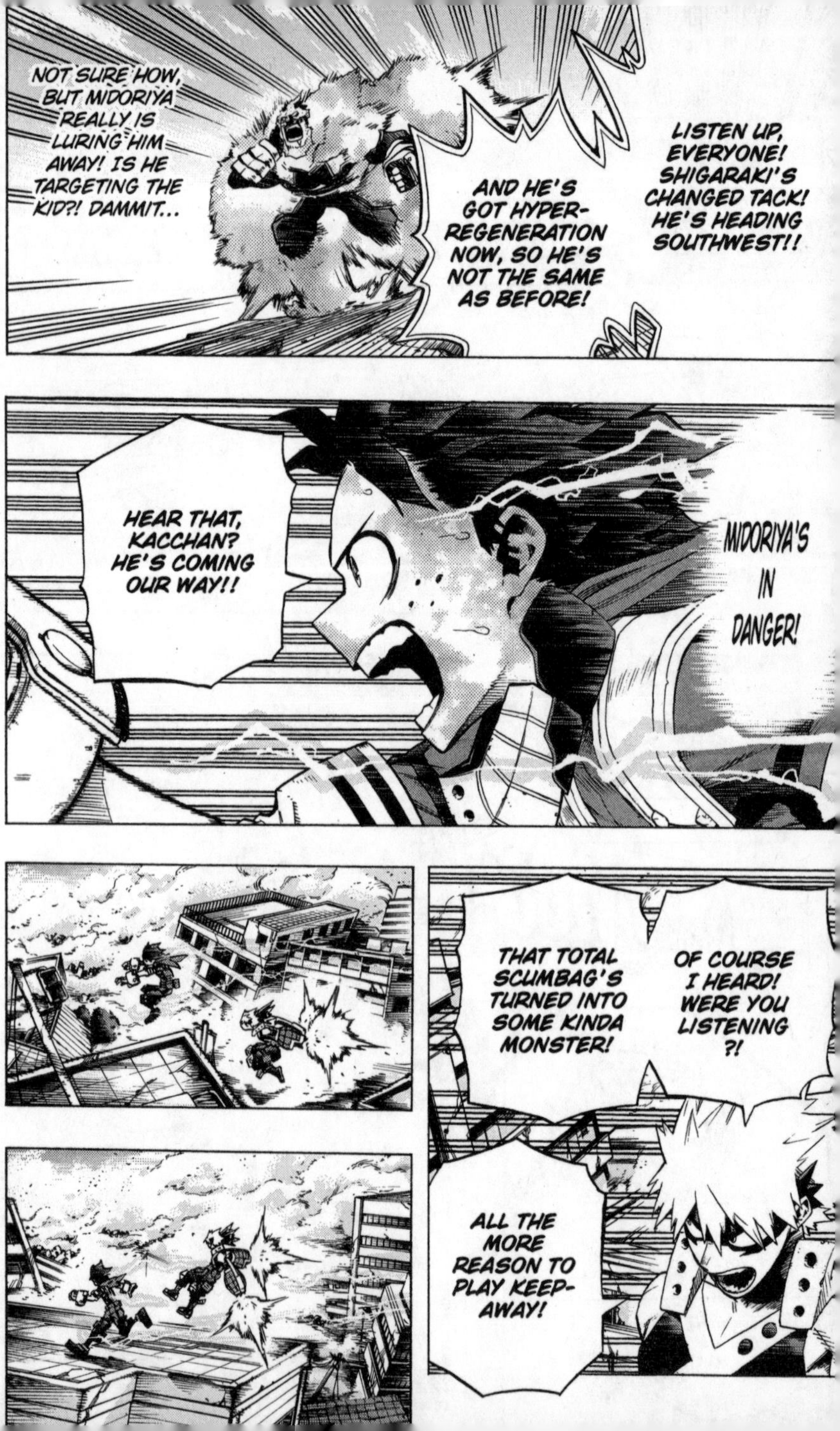
LISTEN UP, EVERYONE! SHIGARAKI'S CHANGED TACK! HE'S HEADING SOUTHWEST!!
AND HE'S GOT HYPER-REGENERATION NOW, SO HE'S NOT THE SAME AS BEFORE!
NOT SURE HOW, BUT MIDORIYA REALLY IS LURING HIM AWAY! IS HE TARGETING THE KID?! DAMMIT...
MIDORIYA'S IN DANGER!
HEAR THAT, KACCHAN? HE'S COMING OUR WAY!!
OF COURSE I HEARD! WERE YOU LISTENING?!
THAT TOTAL SCUMBAG'S TURNED INTO SOME KINDA MONSTER!
ALL THE MORE REASON TO PLAY KEEP-AWAY!

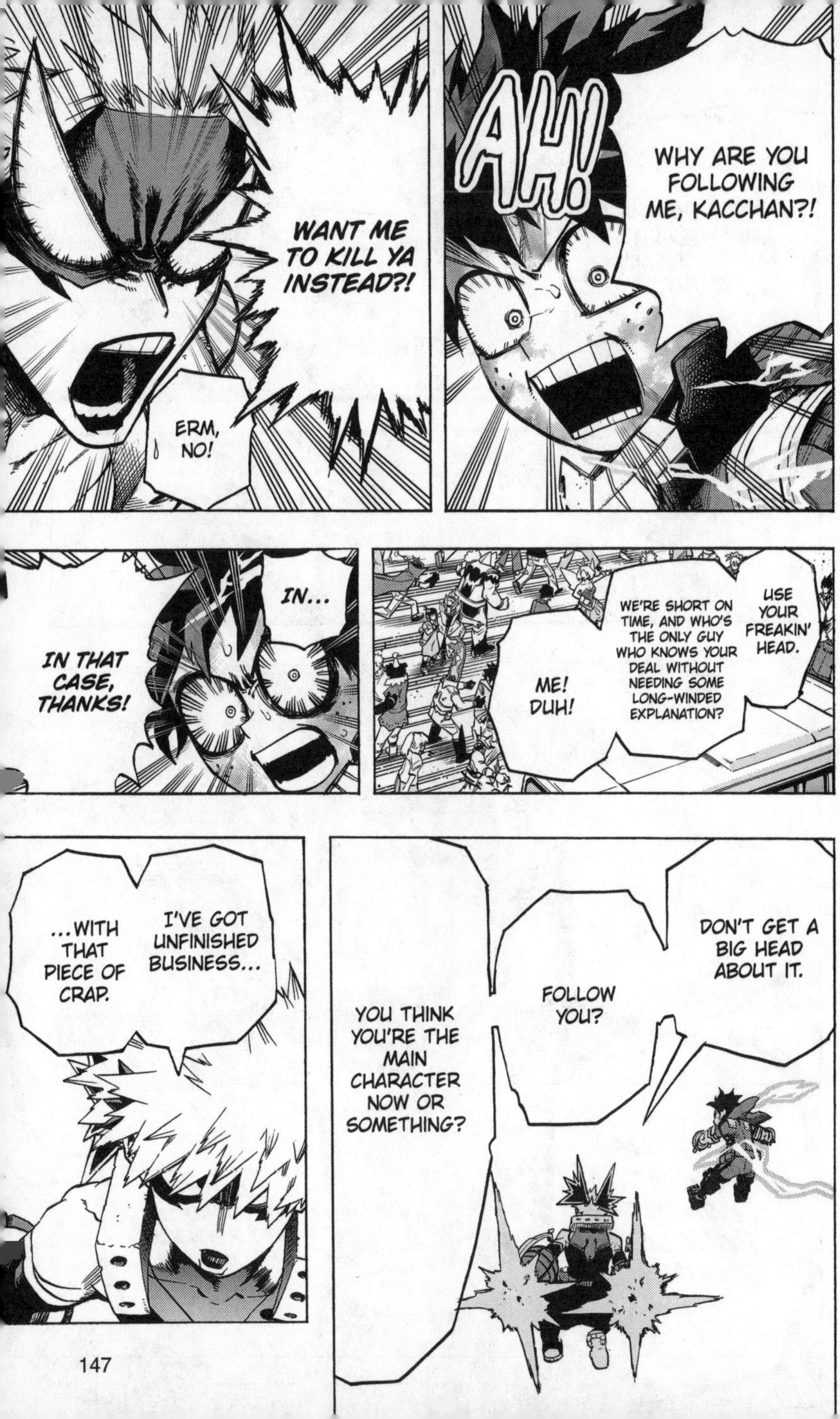
AH!
WHY ARE YOU FOLLOWING ME, KACCHAN?!
WANT ME TO KILL YA INSTEAD?!
ERM, NO!
USE YOUR FREAKIN' HEAD.
WE'RE SHORT ON TIME, AND WHO'S THE ONLY GUY WHO KNOWS YOUR DEAL WITHOUT NEEDING SOME LONG-WINDED EXPLANATION?
ME! DUH!
IN...
IN THAT CASE, THANKS!
DON'T GET A BIG HEAD ABOUT IT.
FOLLOW YOU?
YOU THINK YOU'RE THE MAIN CHARACTER NOW OR SOMETHING?
I'VE GOT UNFINISHED BUSINESS...
...WITH THAT PIECE OF CRAP.

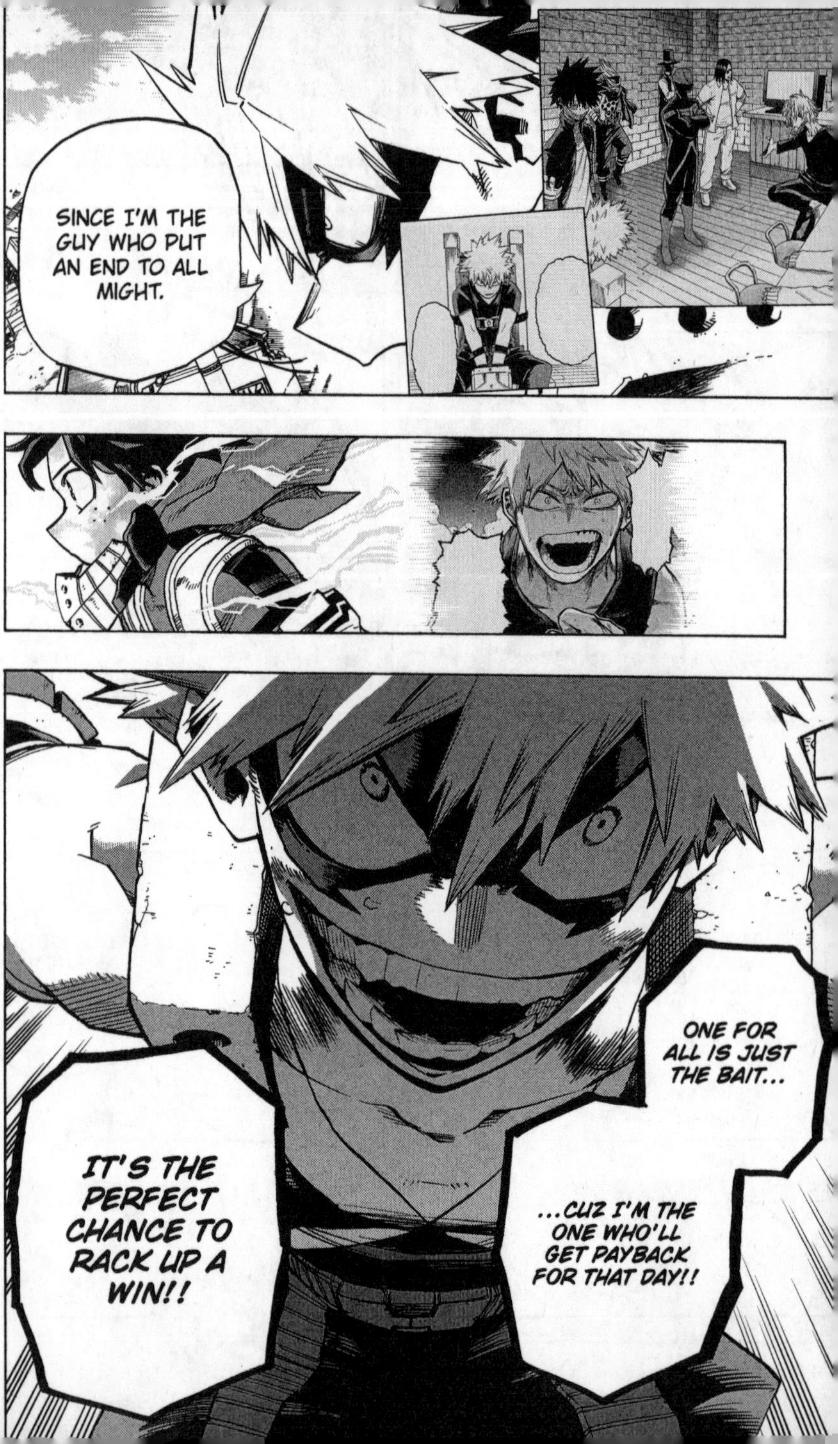
SINCE I'M THE GUY WHO PUT AN END TO ALL MIGHT.
ONE FOR ALL IS JUST THE BAIT...
...CUZ I'M THE ONE WHO'LL GET PAYBACK FOR THAT DAY!!
IT'S THE PERFECT CHANCE TO RACK UP A WIN!!

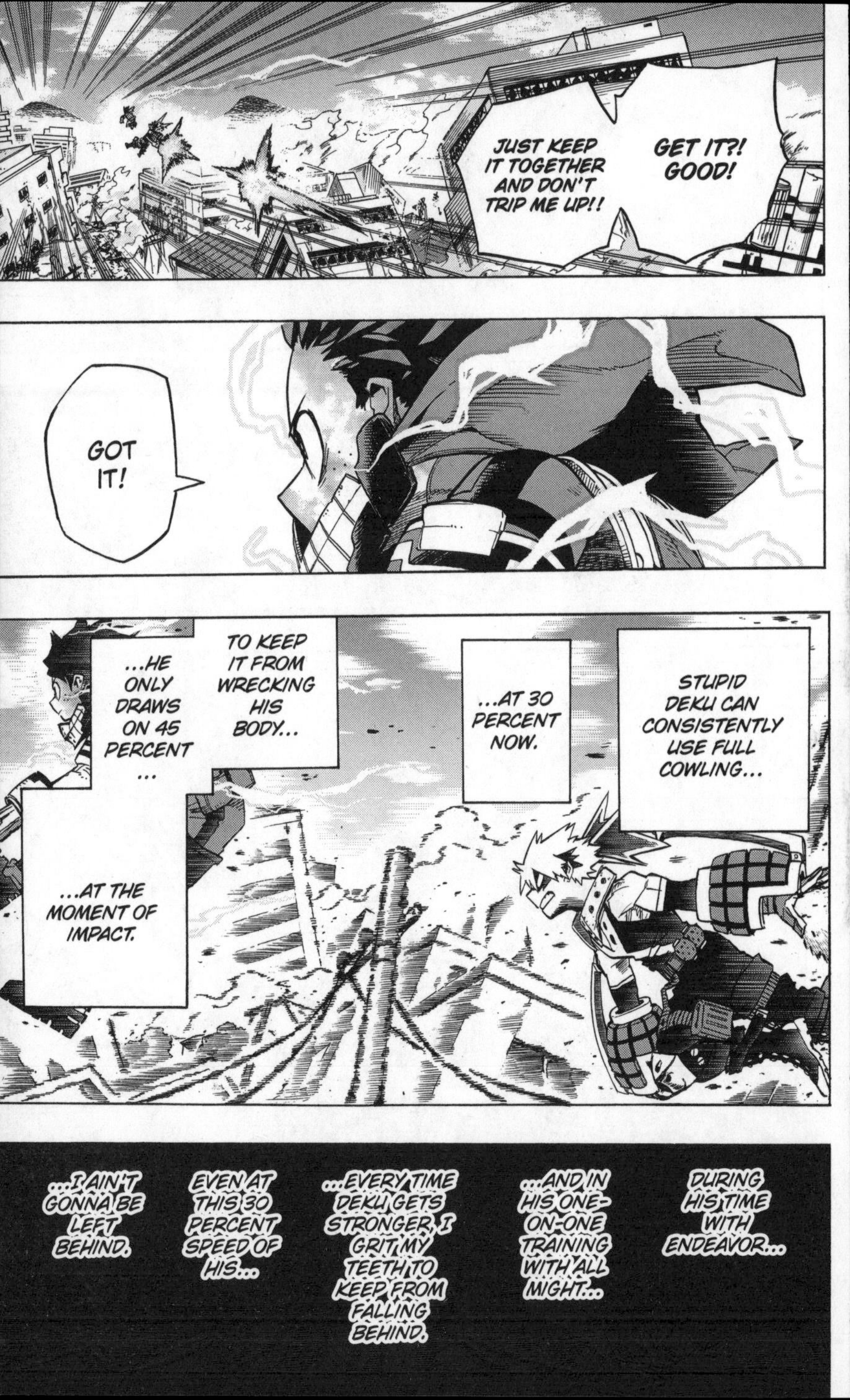

JUST KEEP IT TOGETHER AND DON'T TRIP ME UP!! GET IT?! GOOD!
GOT IT!
STUPID DEKU CAN CONSISTENTLY USE FULL COWLING...
...AT 30 PERCENT NOW.
TO KEEP IT FROM WRECKING HIS BODY...
...HE ONLY DRAWS ON 45 PERCENT...
...AT THE MOMENT OF IMPACT.
DURING HIS TIME WITH ENDEAVOR...
...AND IN HIS ONE-ON-ONE TRAINING WITH ALL MIGHT...
...EVERY TIME DEKU GETS STRONGER, I GRIT MY TEETH TO KEEP FROM FALLING BEHIND.
EVEN AT THIS 30 PERCENT SPEED OF HIS...
...I AIN'T GONNA BE LEFT BEHIND.

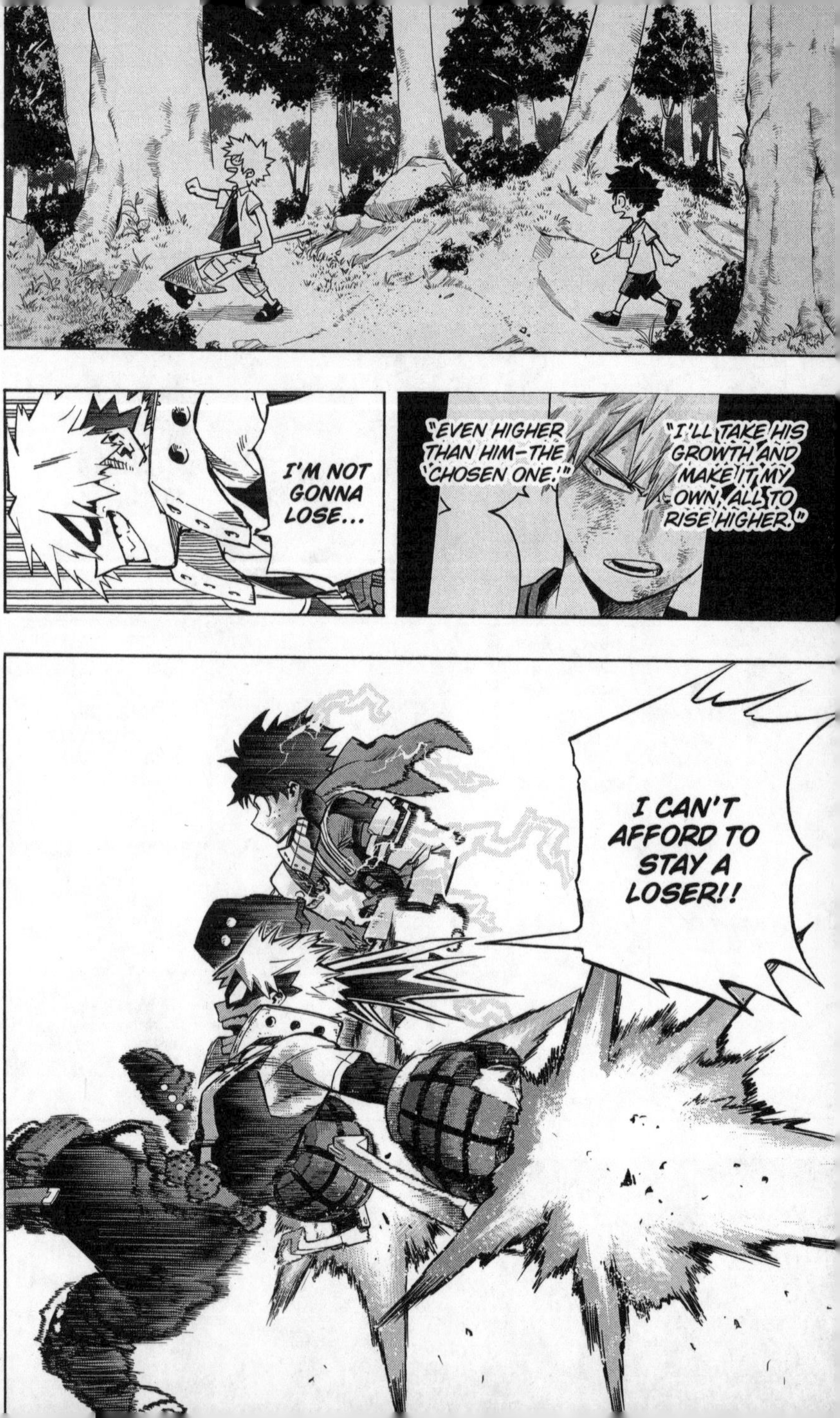
"I'LL TAKE HIS GROWTH AND MAKE IT MY OWN, ALL TO RISE HIGHER."
"EVEN HIGHER THAN HIM—THE 'CHOSEN ONE.'"
I'M NOT GONNA LOSE...
I CAN'T AFFORD TO STAY A LOSER!!

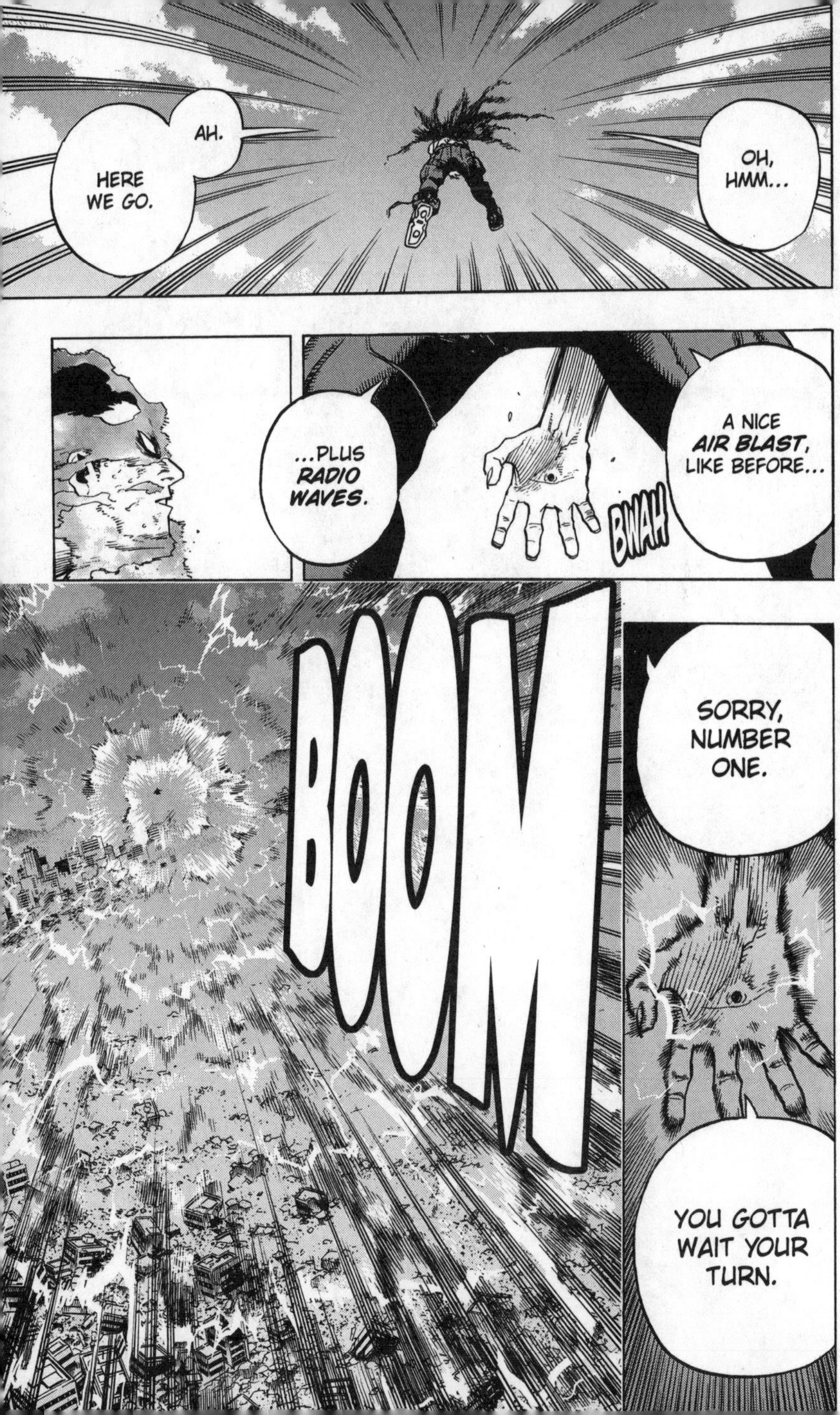
OH, HMM...
AH.
HERE WE GO.
A NICE AIR BLAST, LIKE BEFORE...
BWAH
...PLUS RADIO WAVES.
SORRY, NUMBER ONE.
YOU GOTTA WAIT YOUR TURN.
BOOM

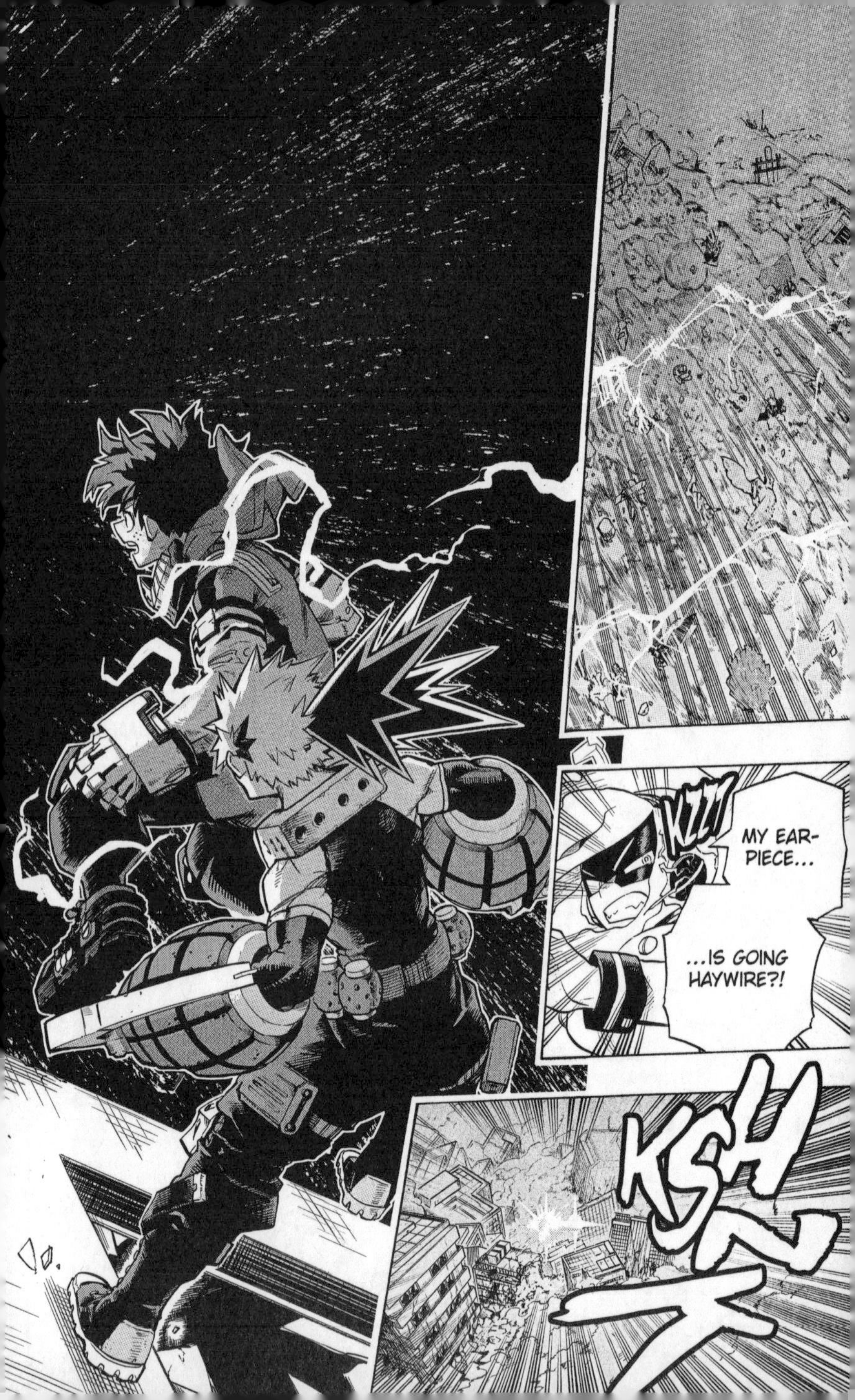
KZZT
MY EAR-PIECE...
...IS GOING HAYWIRE?!
KSH

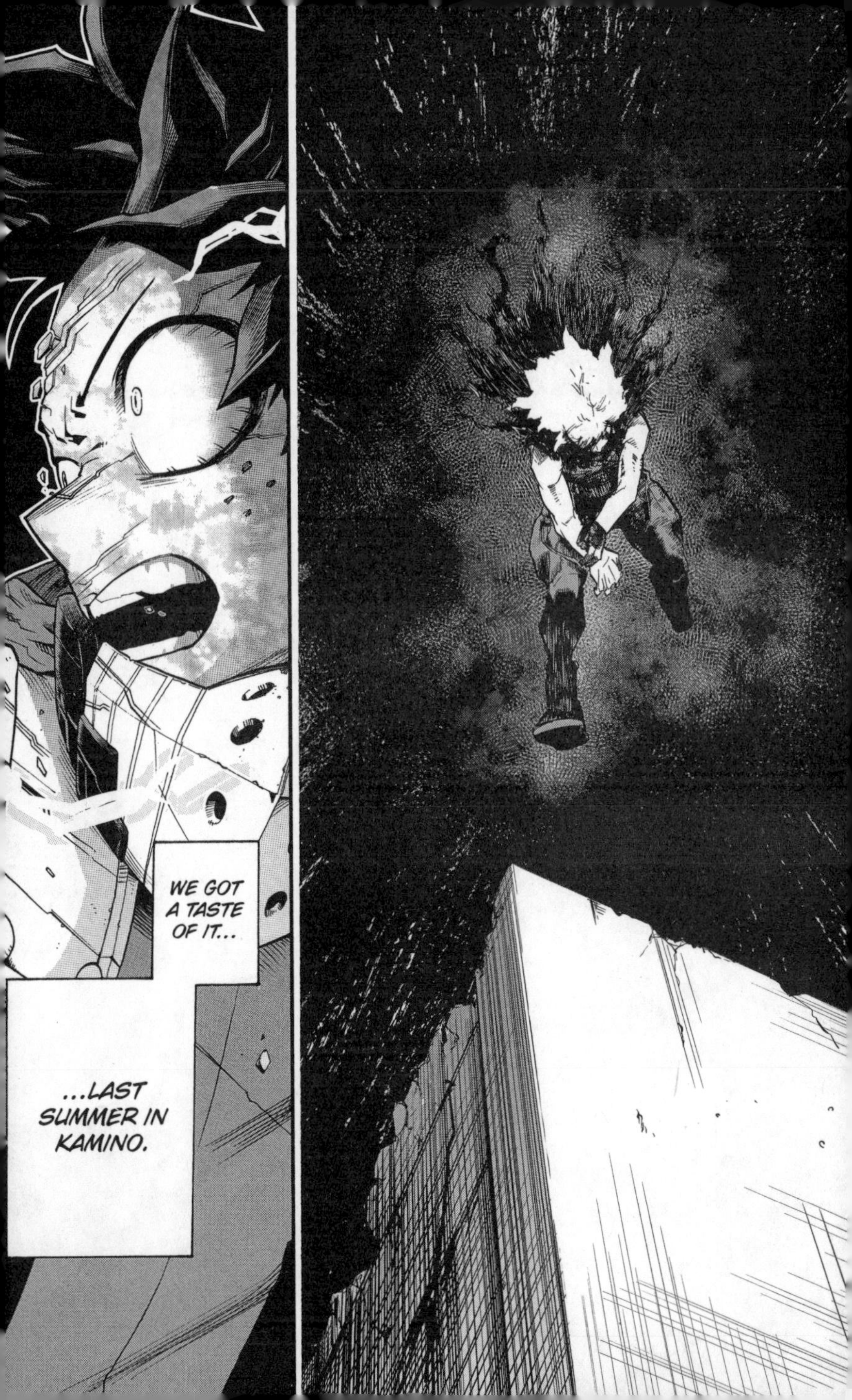
WE GOT A TASTE OF IT...
...LAST SUMMER IN KAMINO.

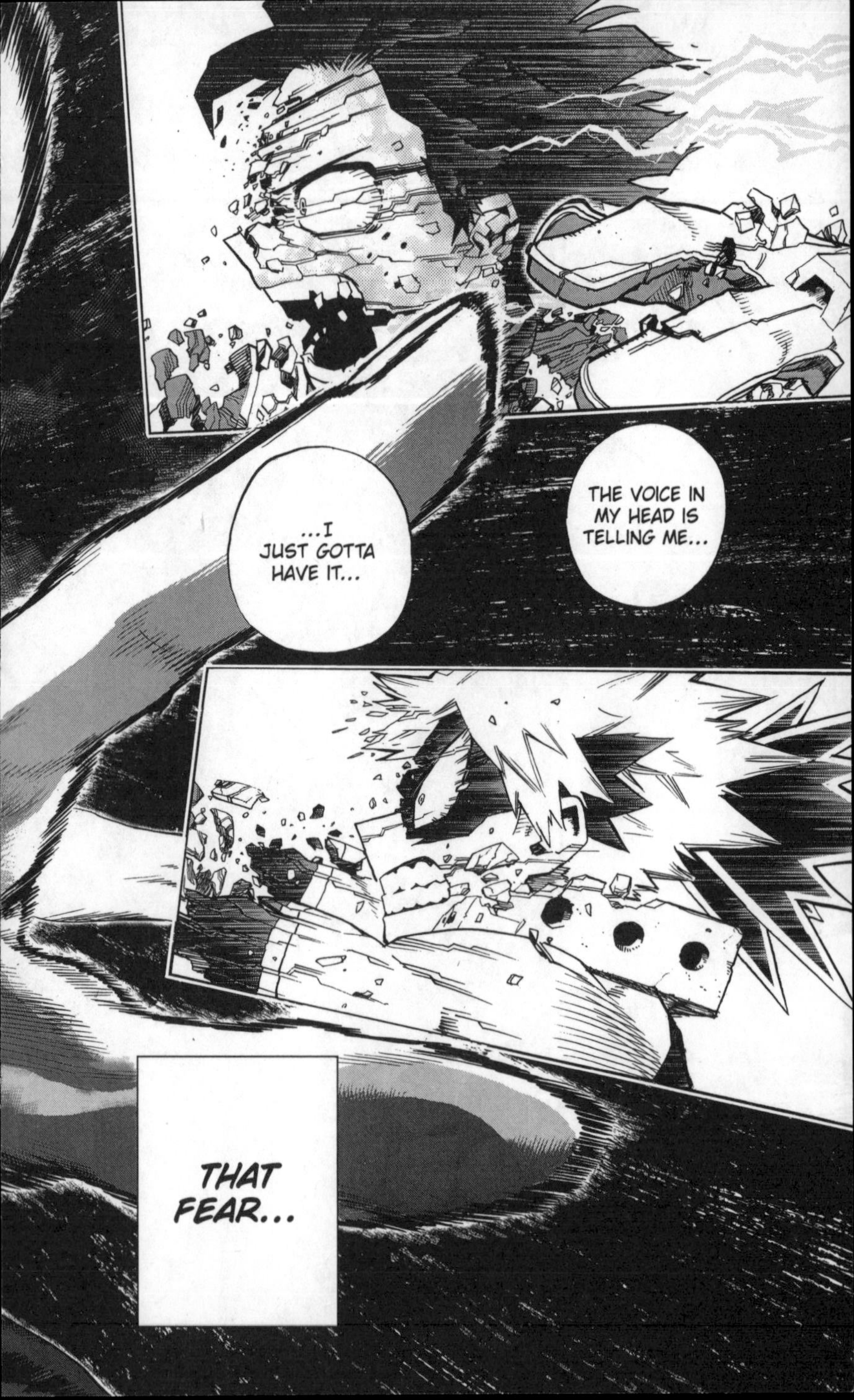
THE VOICE IN MY HEAD IS TELLING ME...
...I JUST GOTTA HAVE IT...
THAT FEAR...

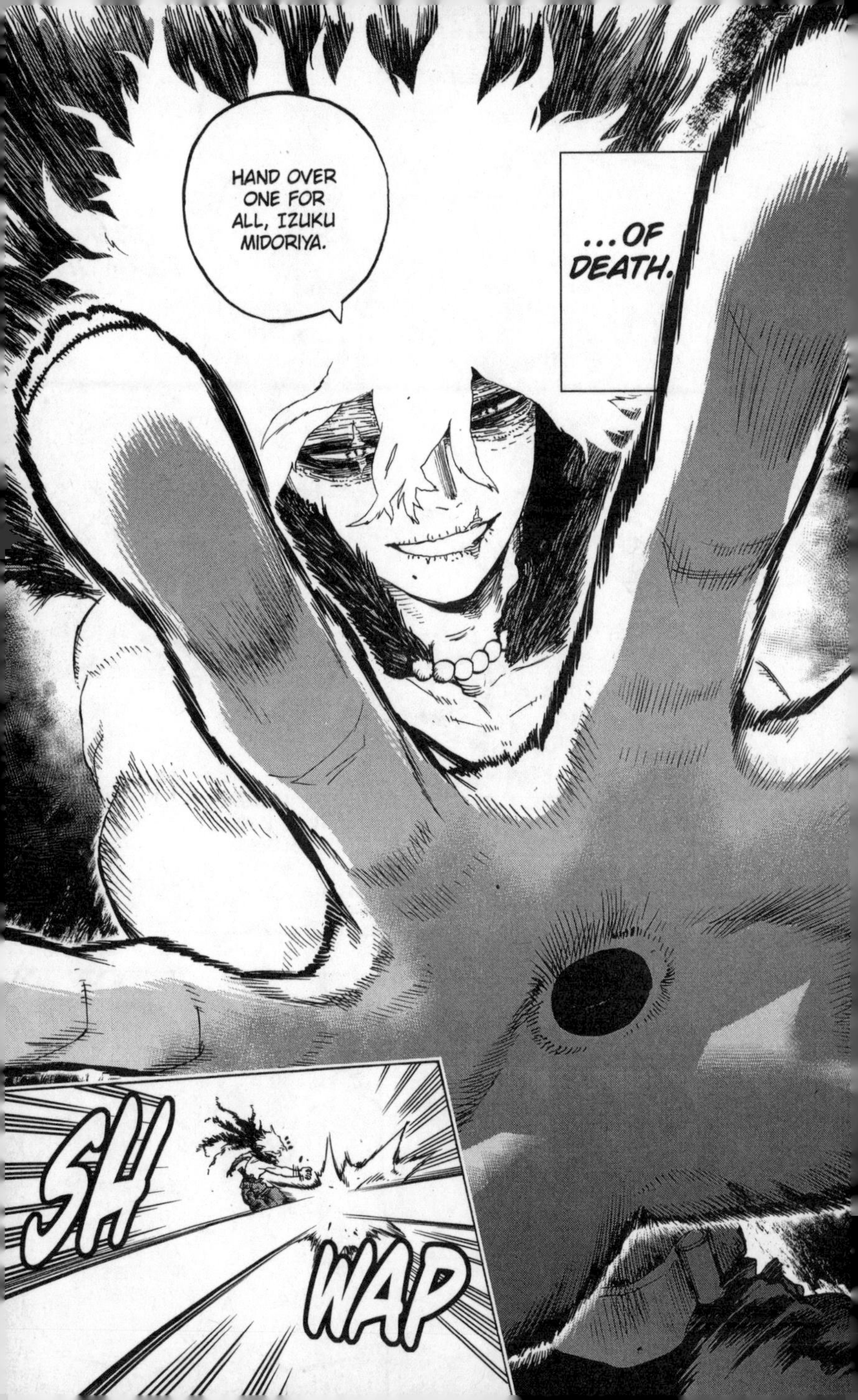
...OF DEATH.
HAND OVER ONE FOR ALL, IZUKU MIDORIYA.
SH WAP

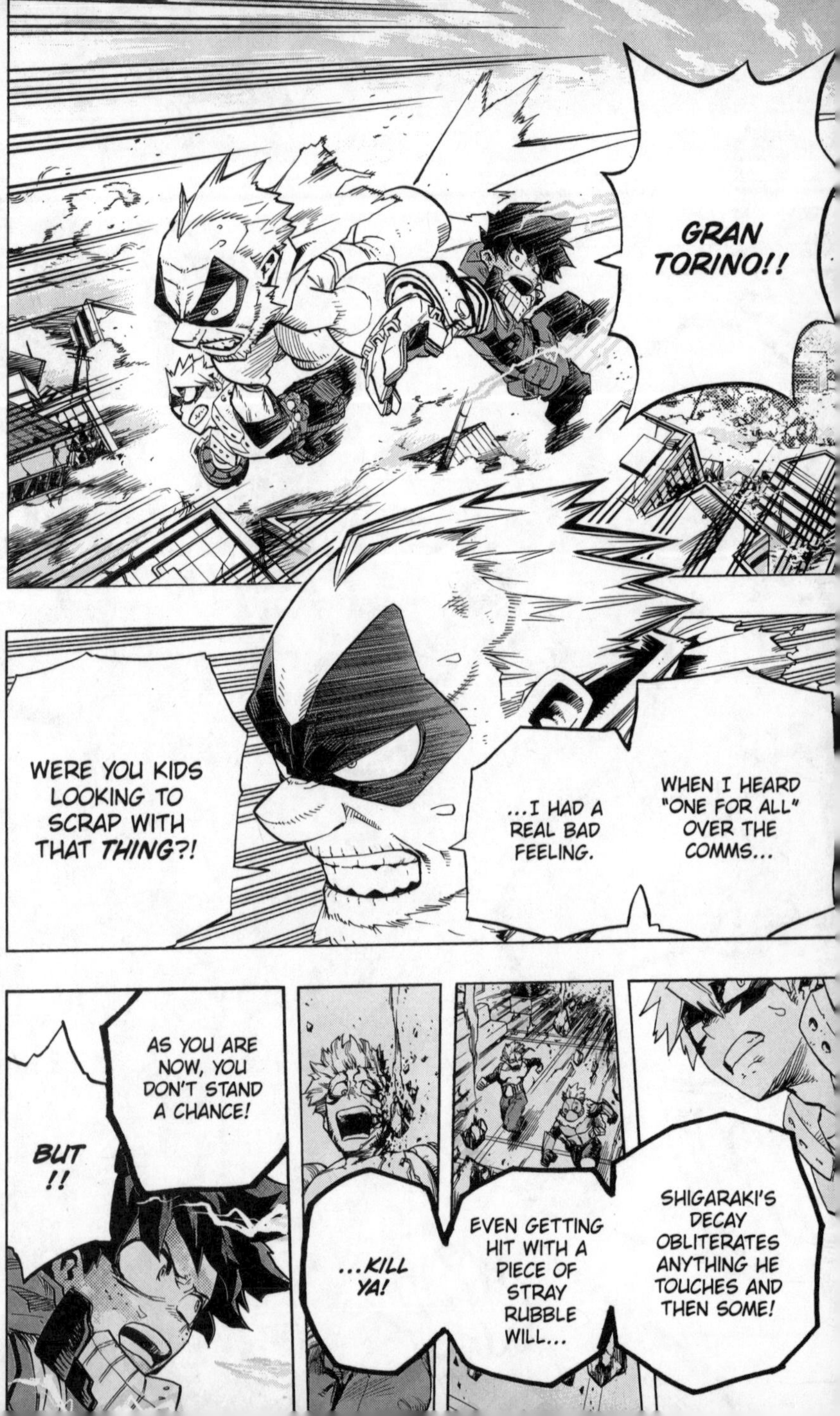
GRAN TORINO!!
WHEN I HEARD "ONE FOR ALL" OVER THE COMMS...
...I HAD A REAL BAD FEELING.
WERE YOU KIDS LOOKING TO SCRAP WITH THAT *THING*?!
SHIGARAKI'S DECAY OBLITERATES ANYTHING HE TOUCHES AND THEN SOME!
EVEN GETTING HIT WITH A PIECE OF STRAY RUBBLE WILL...
...KILL YA!
AS YOU ARE NOW, YOU DON'T STAND A CHANCE!
BUT !!

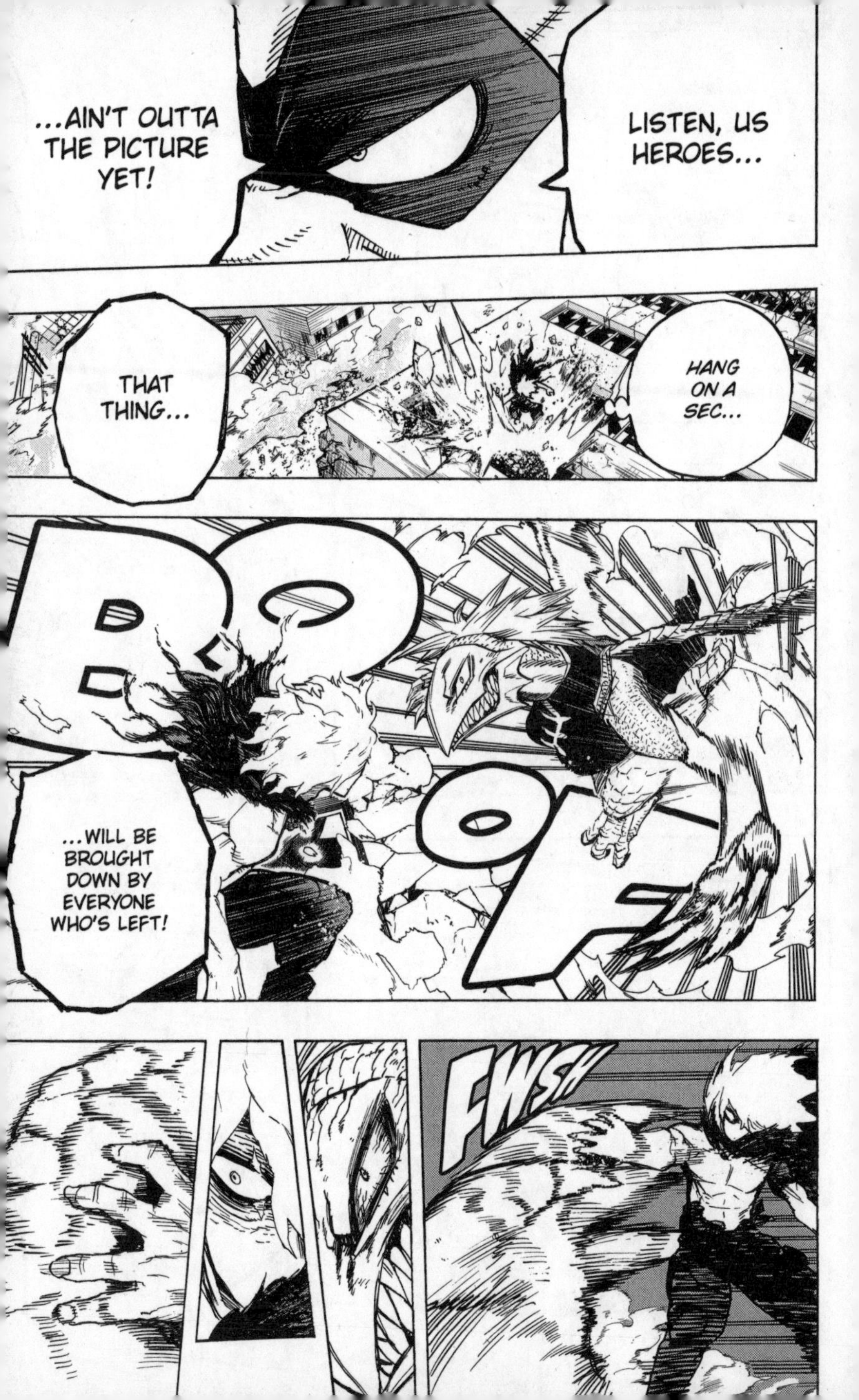
LISTEN, US HEROES...
...AIN'T OUTTA THE PICTURE YET!
HANG ON A SEC...
THAT THING...
BOOM
...WILL BE BROUGHT DOWN BY EVERYONE WHO'S LEFT!
FWSH

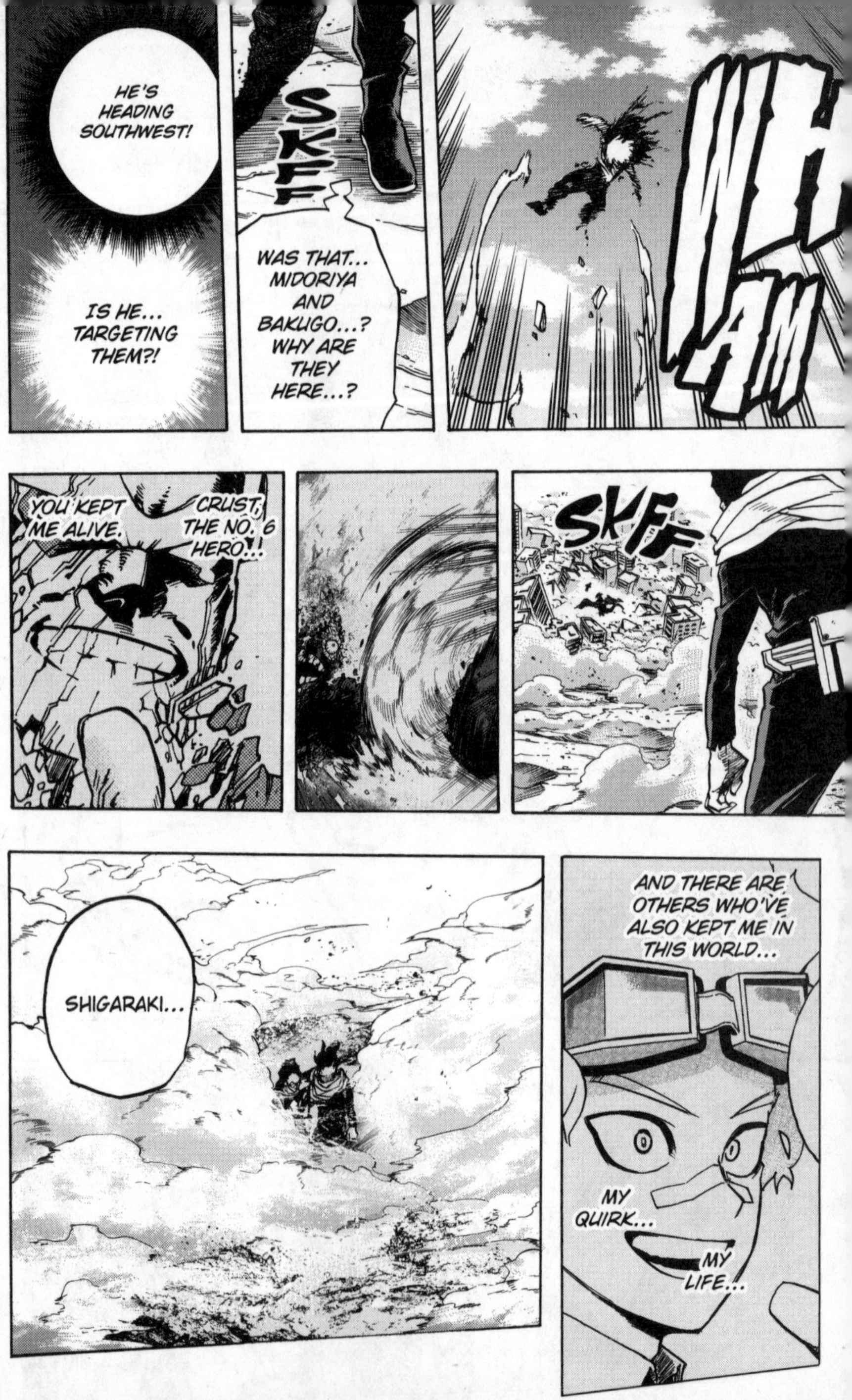
WHAM
SKFF
WAS THAT... MIDORIYA AND BAKUGO...? WHY ARE THEY HERE...?
HE'S HEADING SOUTHWEST!
IS HE... TARGETING THEM?!
SKFF
CRUST, THE NO. 6 HERO...!
YOU KEPT ME ALIVE.
AND THERE ARE OTHERS WHO'VE ALSO KEPT ME IN THIS WORLD...
MY QUIRK...
MY LIFE...
SHIGARAKI...

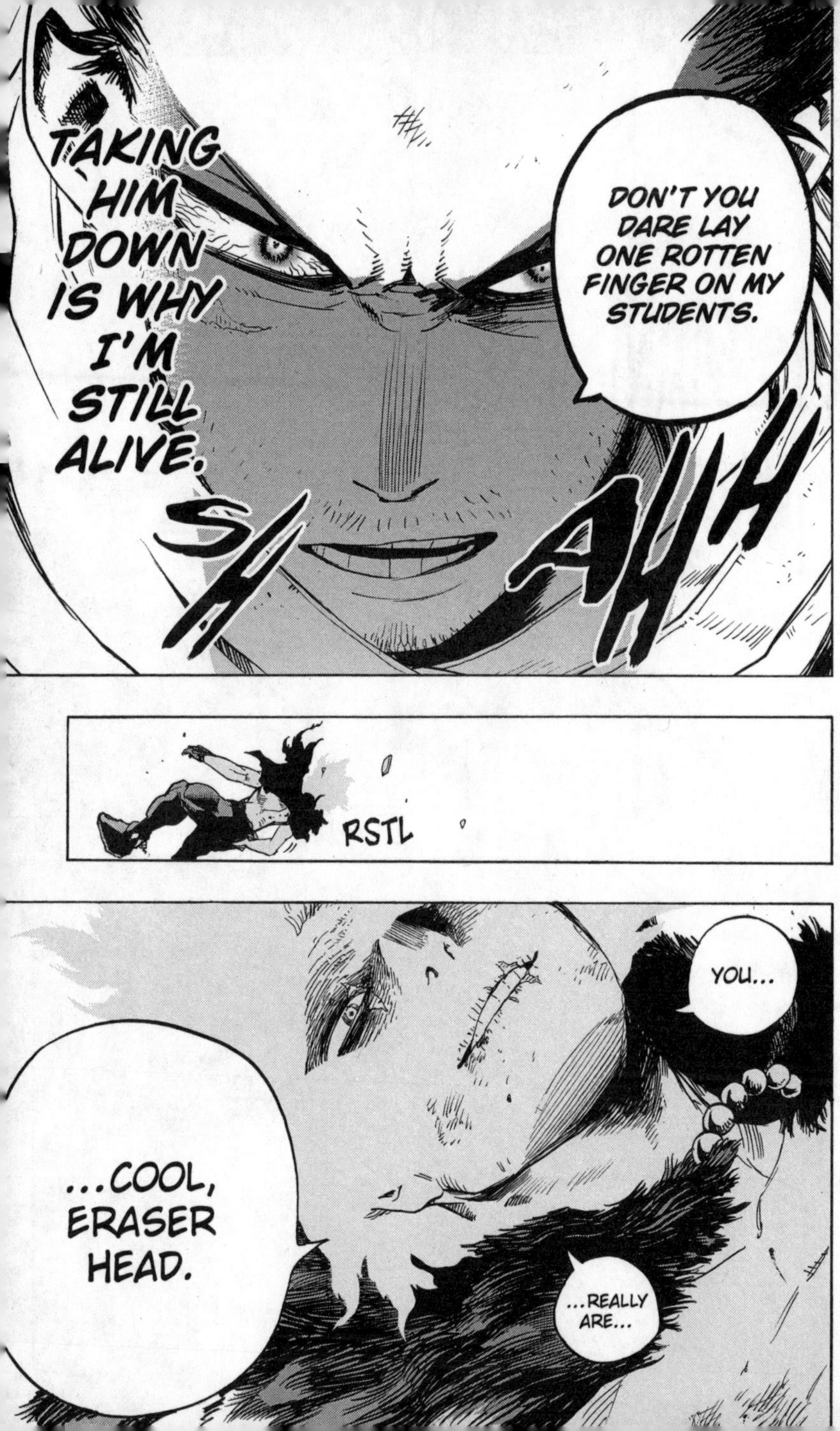
DON'T YOU DARE LAY ONE ROTTEN FINGER ON MY STUDENTS.
TAKING HIM DOWN IS WHY I'M STILL ALIVE.
SHAAH
RSTL
YOU...
...REALLY ARE...
...COOL, ERASER HEAD.

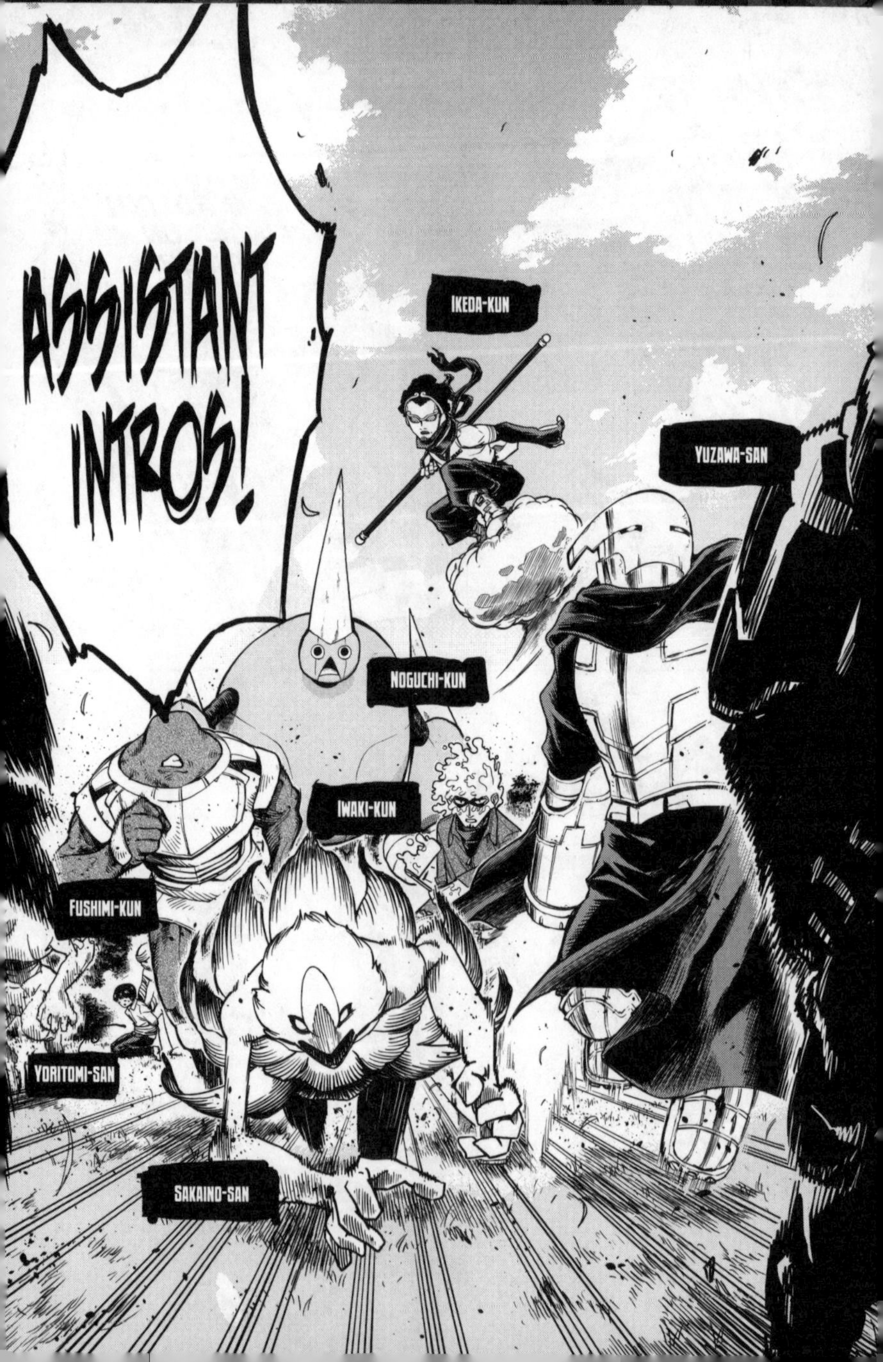
ASSISTANT INTROS!
IKEDA-KUN
YUZAWA-SAN
NOGUCHI-KUN
IWAKI-KUN
FUSHIMI-KUN
YORITOMI-SAN
SAKAINO-SAN

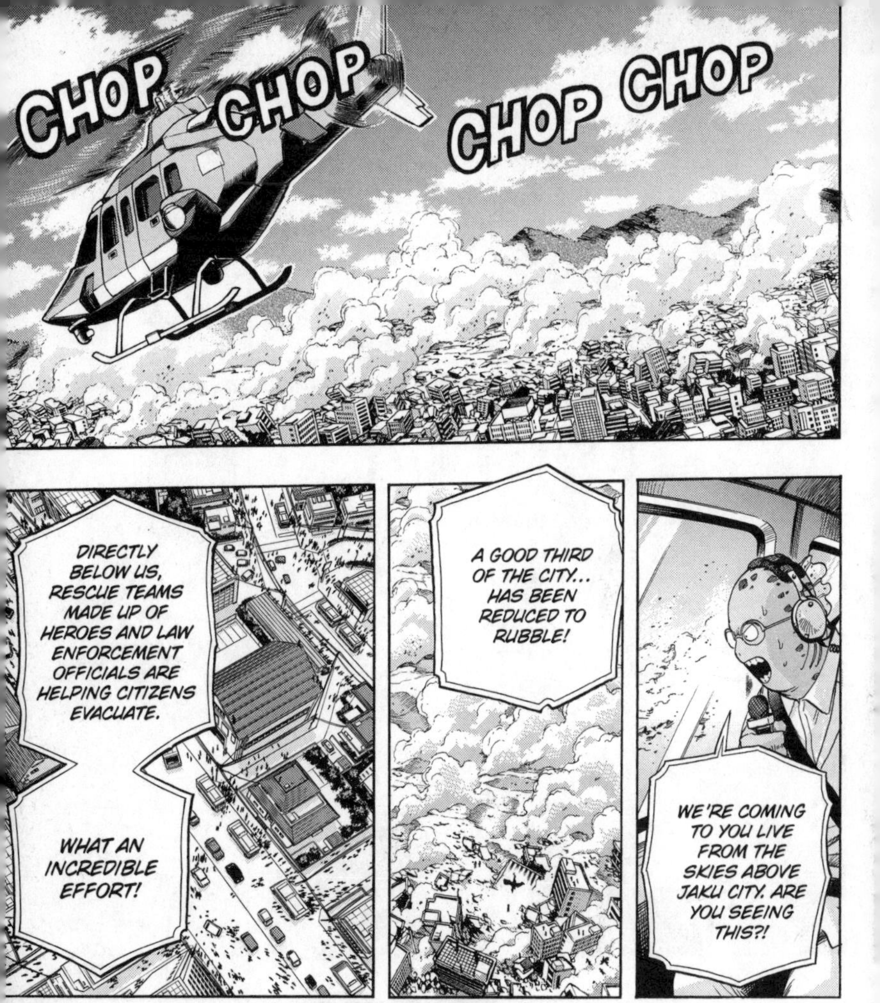
CHOP CHOP
CHOP CHOP
WE'RE COMING TO YOU LIVE FROM THE SKIES ABOVE JAKU CITY. ARE YOU SEEING THIS?!
A GOOD THIRD OF THE CITY... HAS BEEN REDUCED TO RUBBLE!
DIRECTLY BELOW US, RESCUE TEAMS MADE UP OF HEROES AND LAW ENFORCEMENT OFFICIALS ARE HELPING CITIZENS EVACUATE.
WHAT AN INCREDIBLE EFFORT!

NO. 276 - YOU CHEATED...!

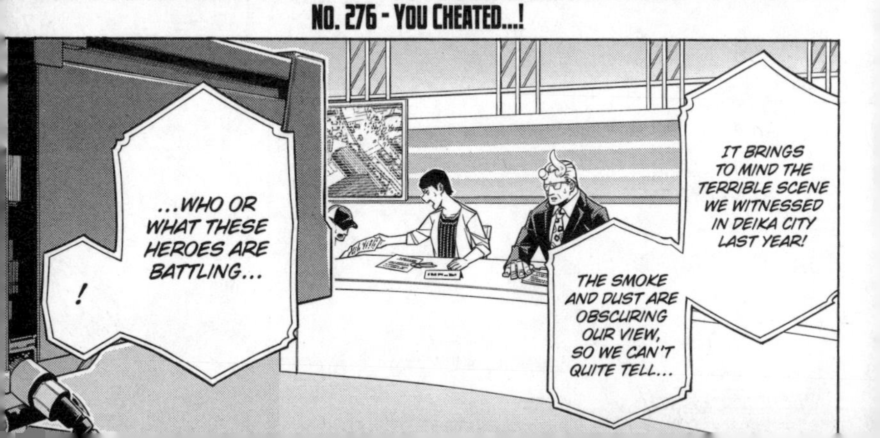
IT BRINGS TO MIND THE TERRIBLE SCENE WE WITNESSED IN DEIKA CITY LAST YEAR!
THE SMOKE AND DUST ARE OBSCURING OUR VIEW, SO WE CAN'T QUITE TELL...
...WHO OR WHAT THESE HEROES ARE BATTLING...
!

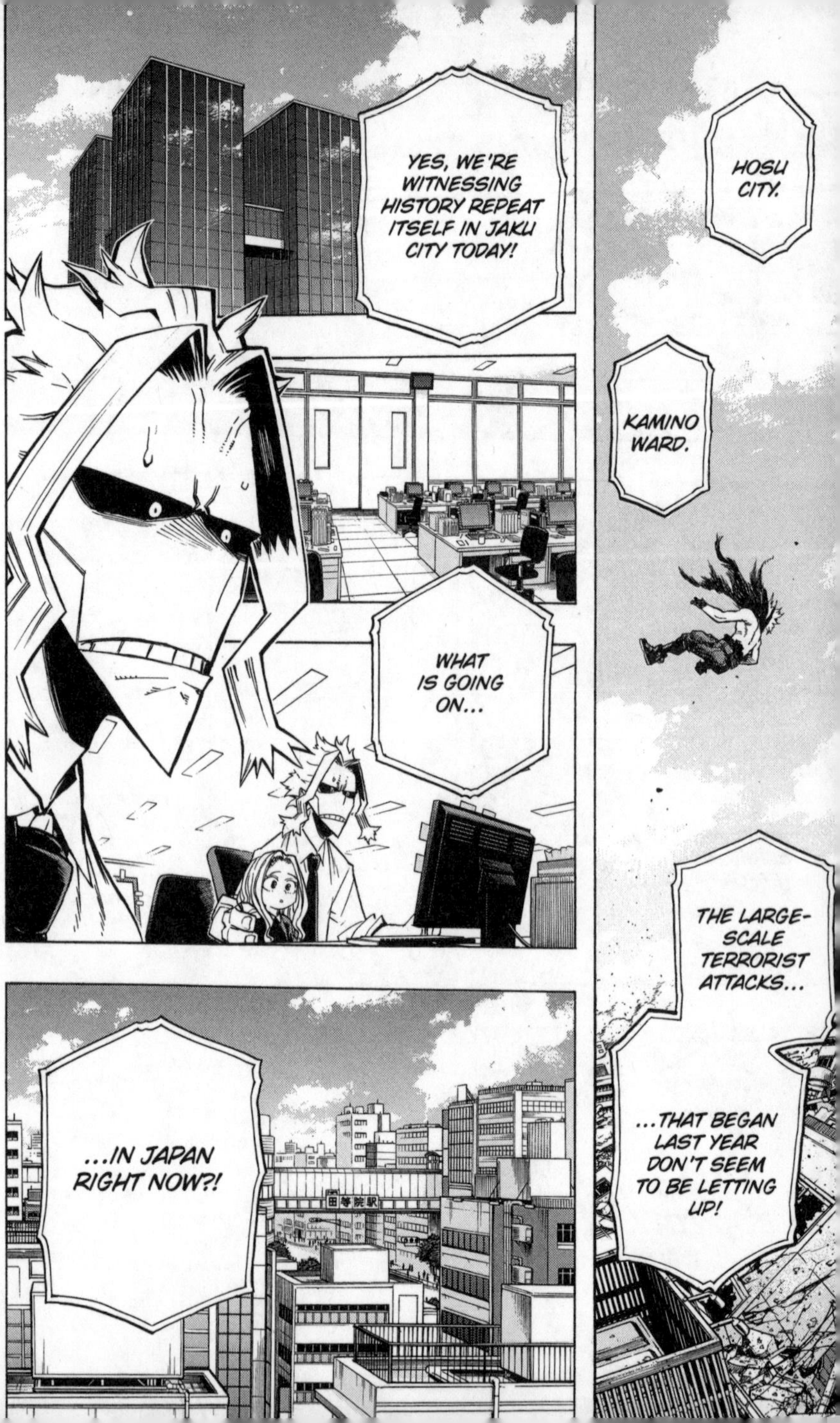
HOSU CITY.
KAMINO WARD.
THE LARGE-SCALE TERRORIST ATTACKS...
...THAT BEGAN LAST YEAR DON'T SEEM TO BE LETTING UP!
YES, WE'RE WITNESSING HISTORY REPEAT ITSELF IN JAKU CITY TODAY!
WHAT IS GOING ON...
...IN JAPAN RIGHT NOW?!
田等院駅

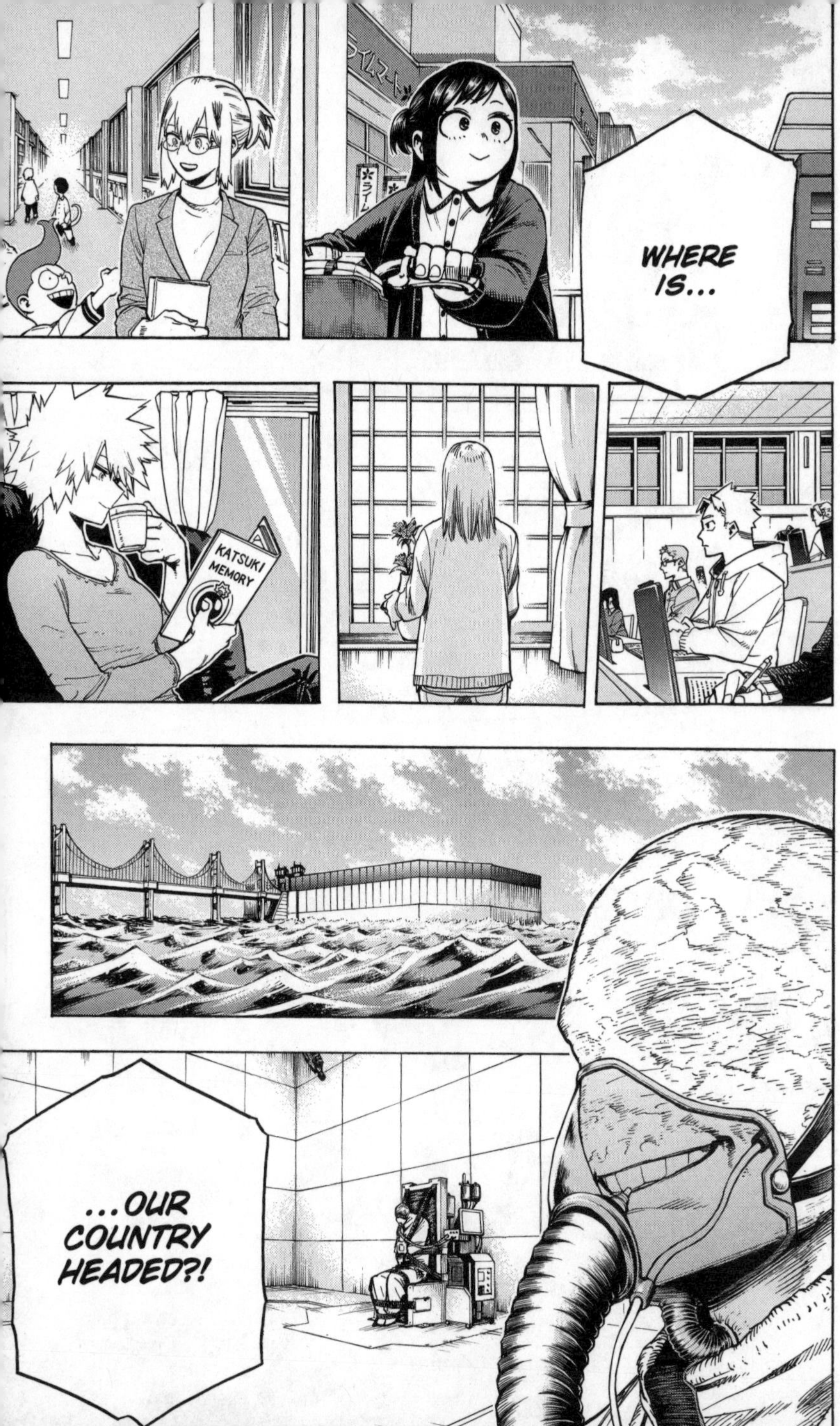
WHERE IS...
KATSUKI MEMORY
...OUR COUNTRY HEADED?!

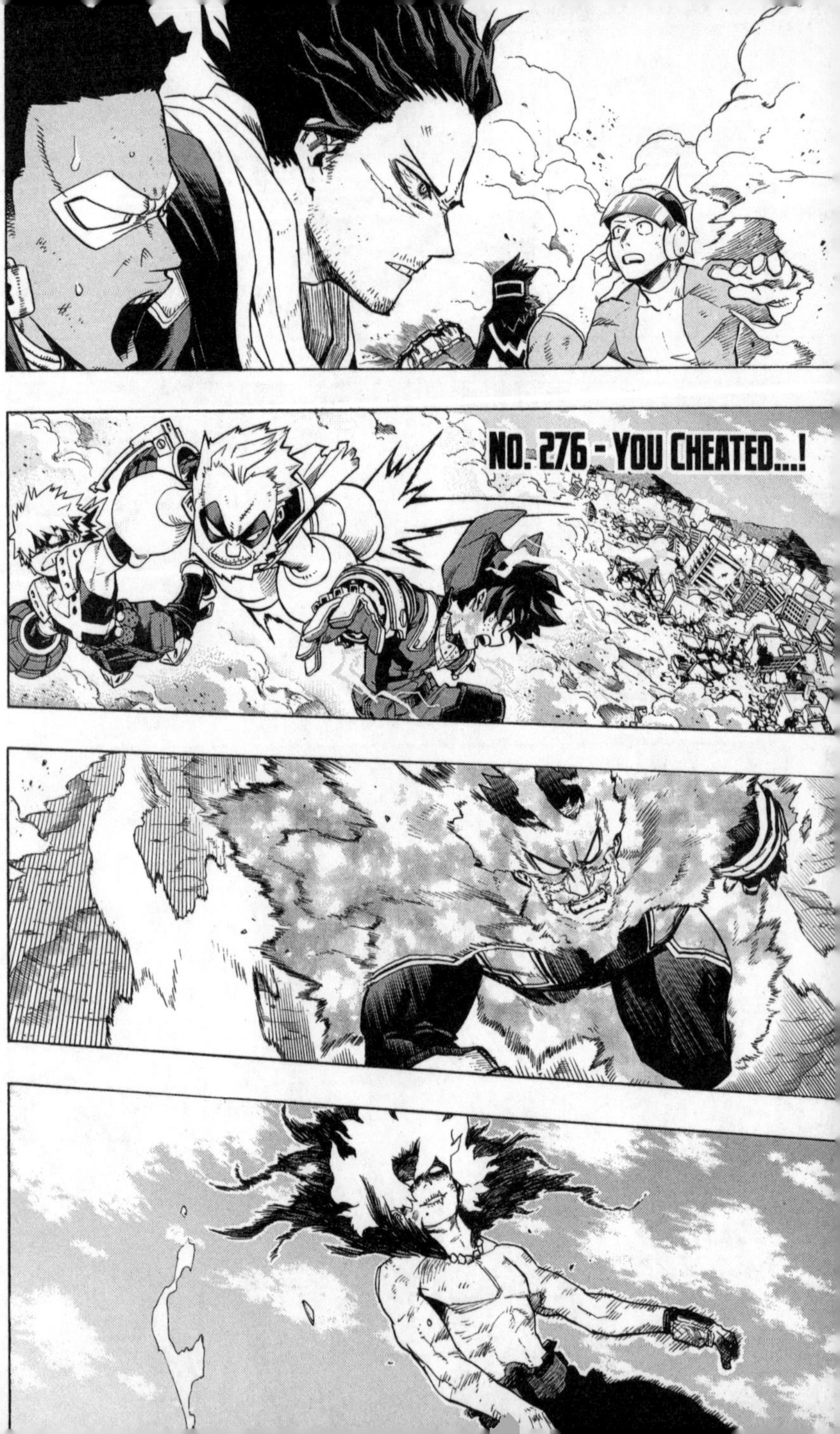
No. 276 - You Cheated...!

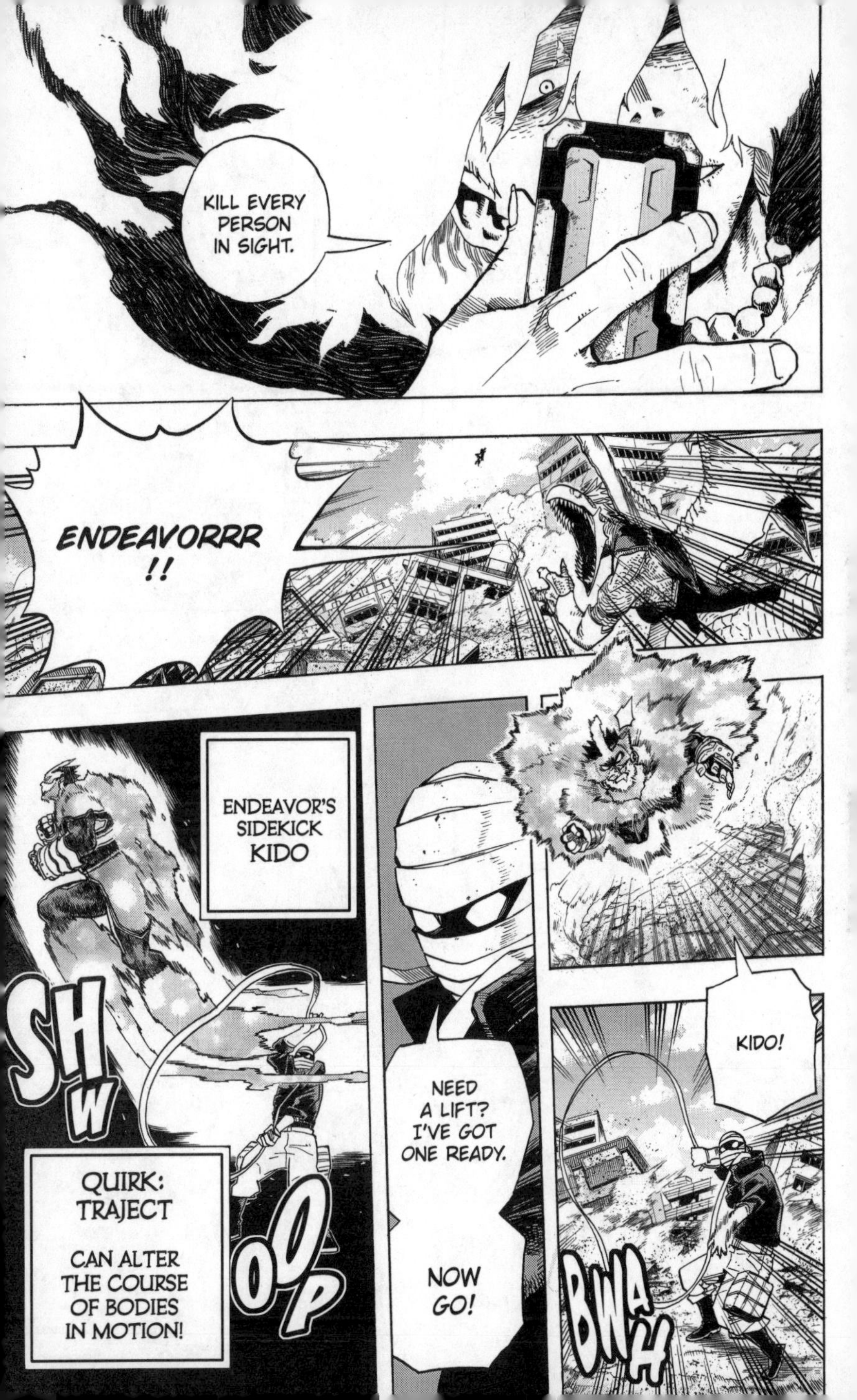
KILL EVERY PERSON IN SIGHT.
ENDEAVORRR !!
KIDO!
BWAH
NEED A LIFT? I'VE GOT ONE READY.
NOW GO!
ENDEAVOR'S SIDEKICK KIDO
SHWOOP
QUIRK: TRAJECT
CAN ALTER THE COURSE OF BODIES IN MOTION!

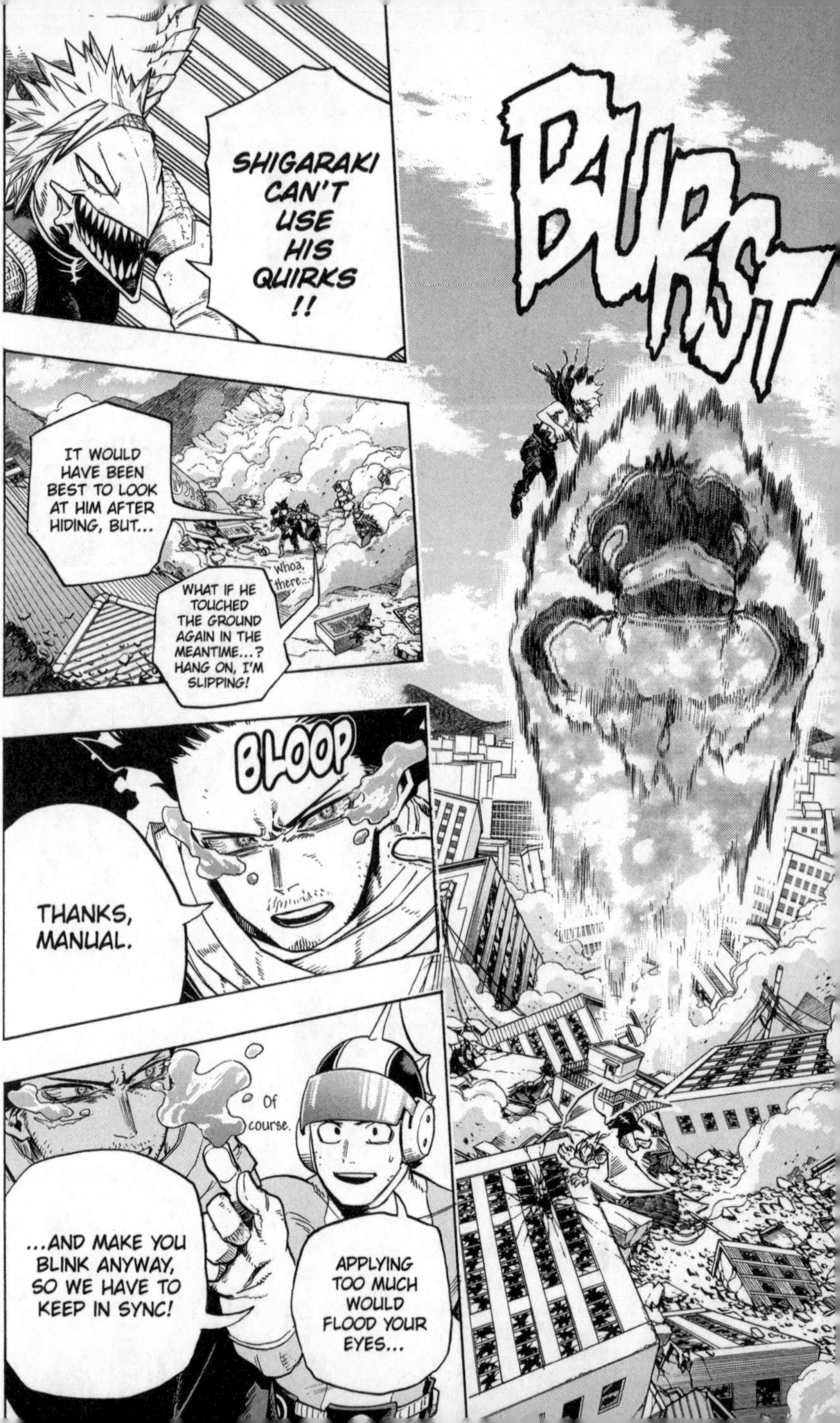
BURST
SHIGARAKI CAN'T USE HIS QUIRKS !!
IT WOULD HAVE BEEN BEST TO LOOK AT HIM AFTER HIDING, BUT...
Whoa, there...
WHAT IF HE TOUCHED THE GROUND AGAIN IN THE MEANTIME...? HANG ON, I'M SLIPPING!
BLOOP
THANKS, MANUAL.
Of course.
APPLYING TOO MUCH WOULD FLOOD YOUR EYES...
...AND MAKE YOU BLINK ANYWAY, SO WE HAVE TO KEEP IN SYNC!

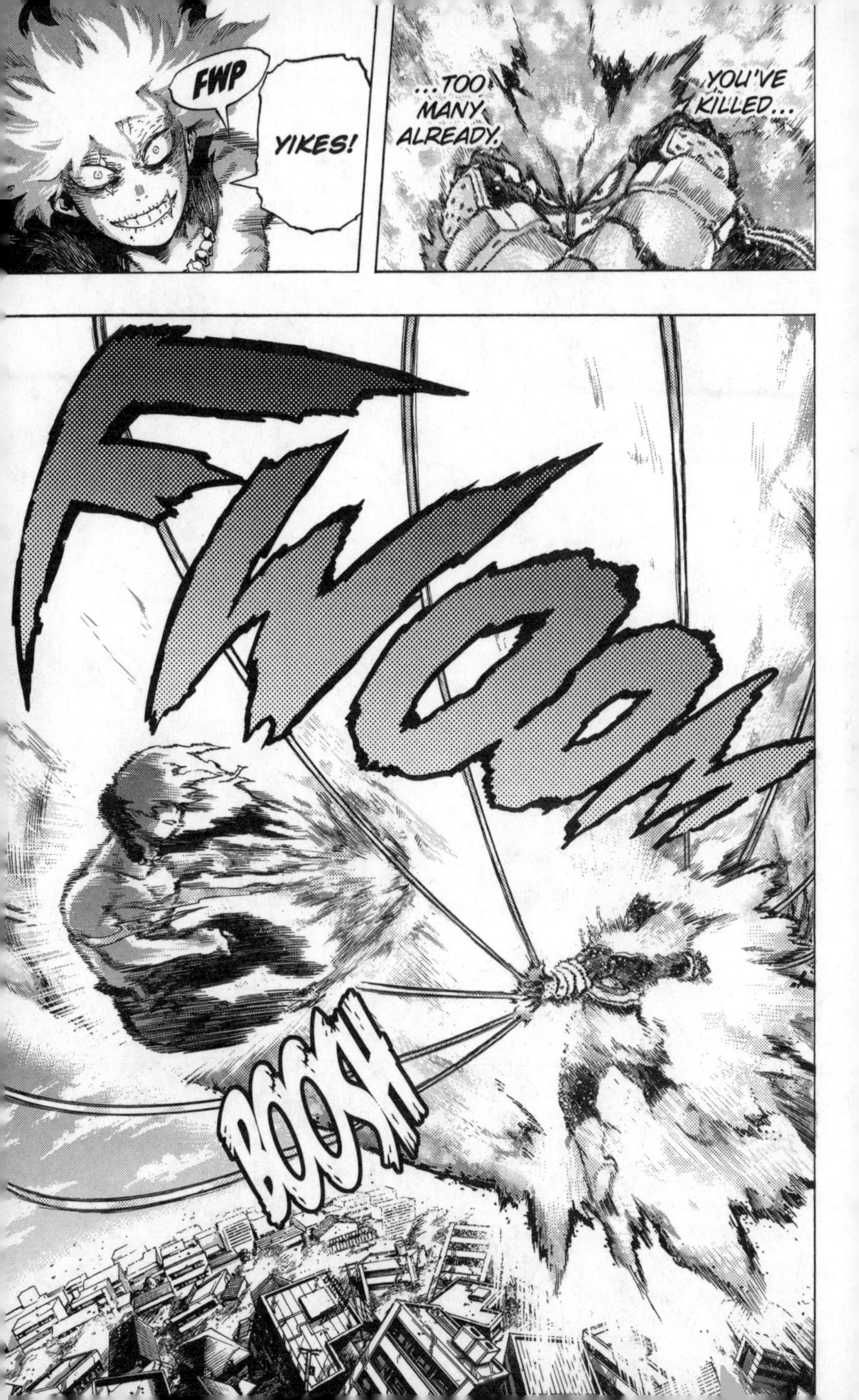
YOU'VE KILLED...
...TOO MANY ALREADY.
FWP
YIKES!
FWOOM
BOOSH

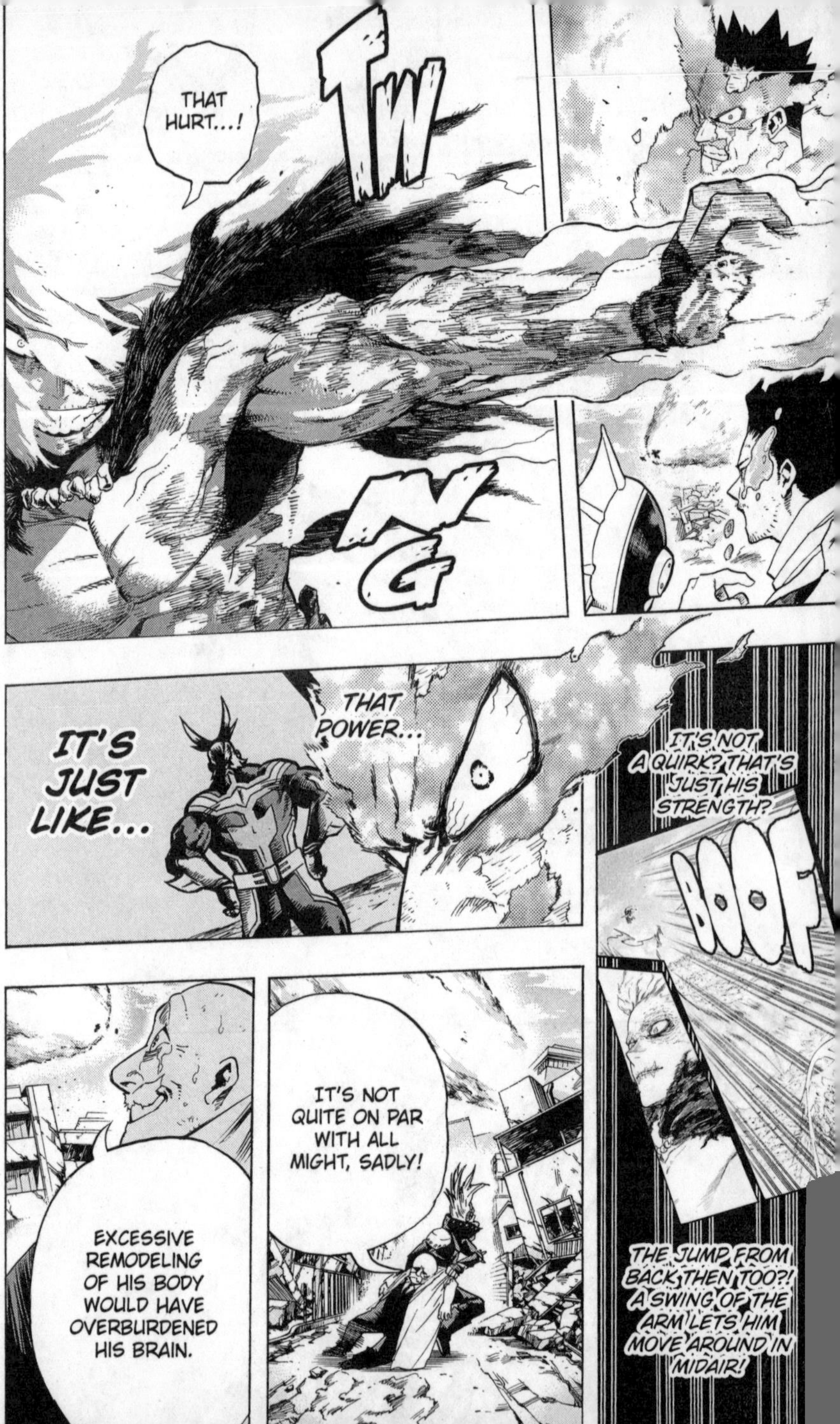
TW
NG
THAT HURT...!
IT'S NOT A QUIRK? THAT'S JUST HIS STRENGTH?
BOOF
THE JUMP FROM BACK THEN TOO?! A SWING OF THE ARM LETS HIM MOVE AROUND IN MIDAIR!
THAT POWER...
IT'S JUST LIKE...
IT'S NOT QUITE ON PAR WITH ALL MIGHT, SADLY!
EXCESSIVE REMODELING OF HIS BODY WOULD HAVE OVERBURDENED HIS BRAIN.

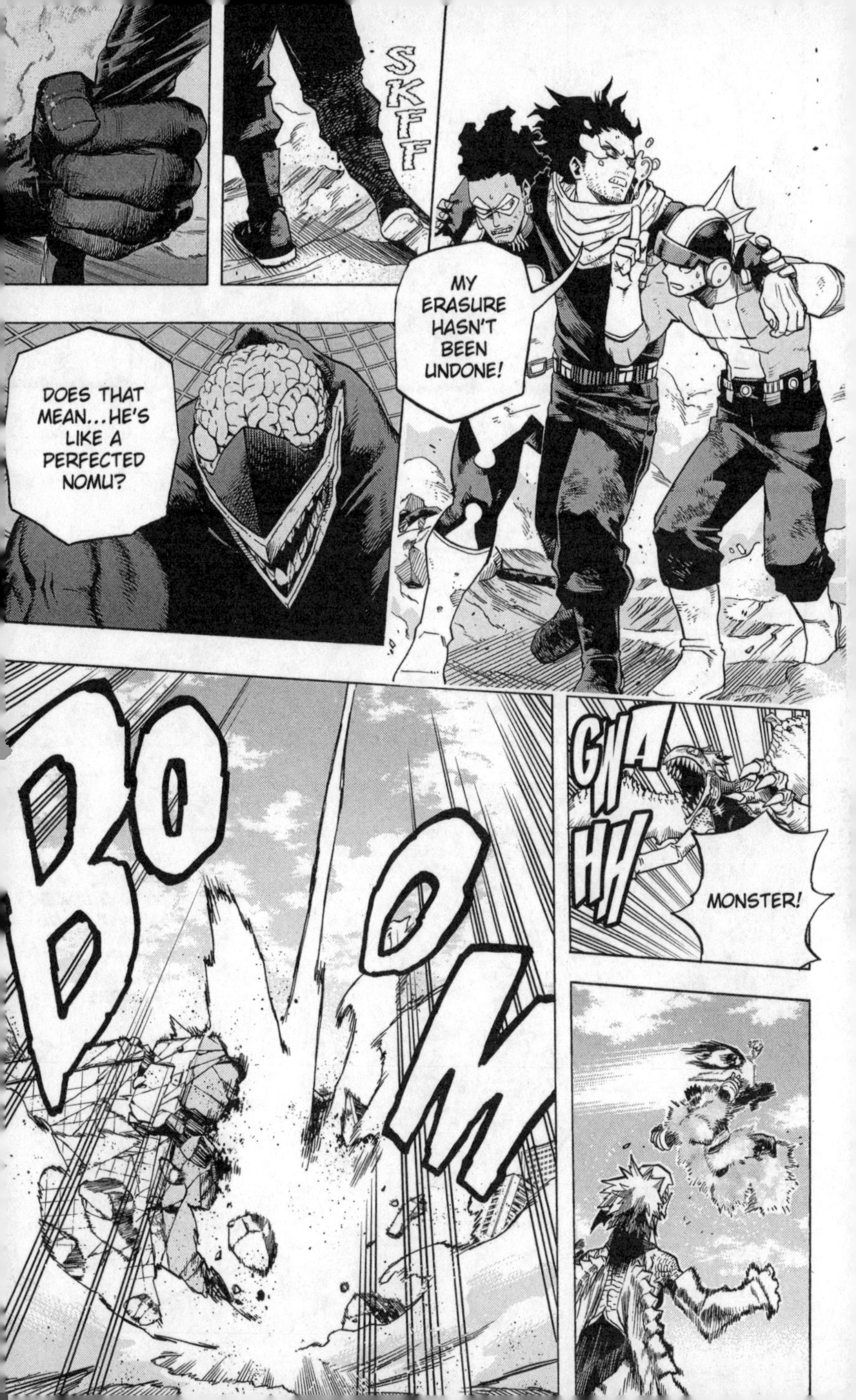
MY ERASURE HASN'T BEEN UNDONE!
SKFF
DOES THAT MEAN...HE'S LIKE A PERFECTED NOMU?
GNAHH
MONSTER!
BOOM

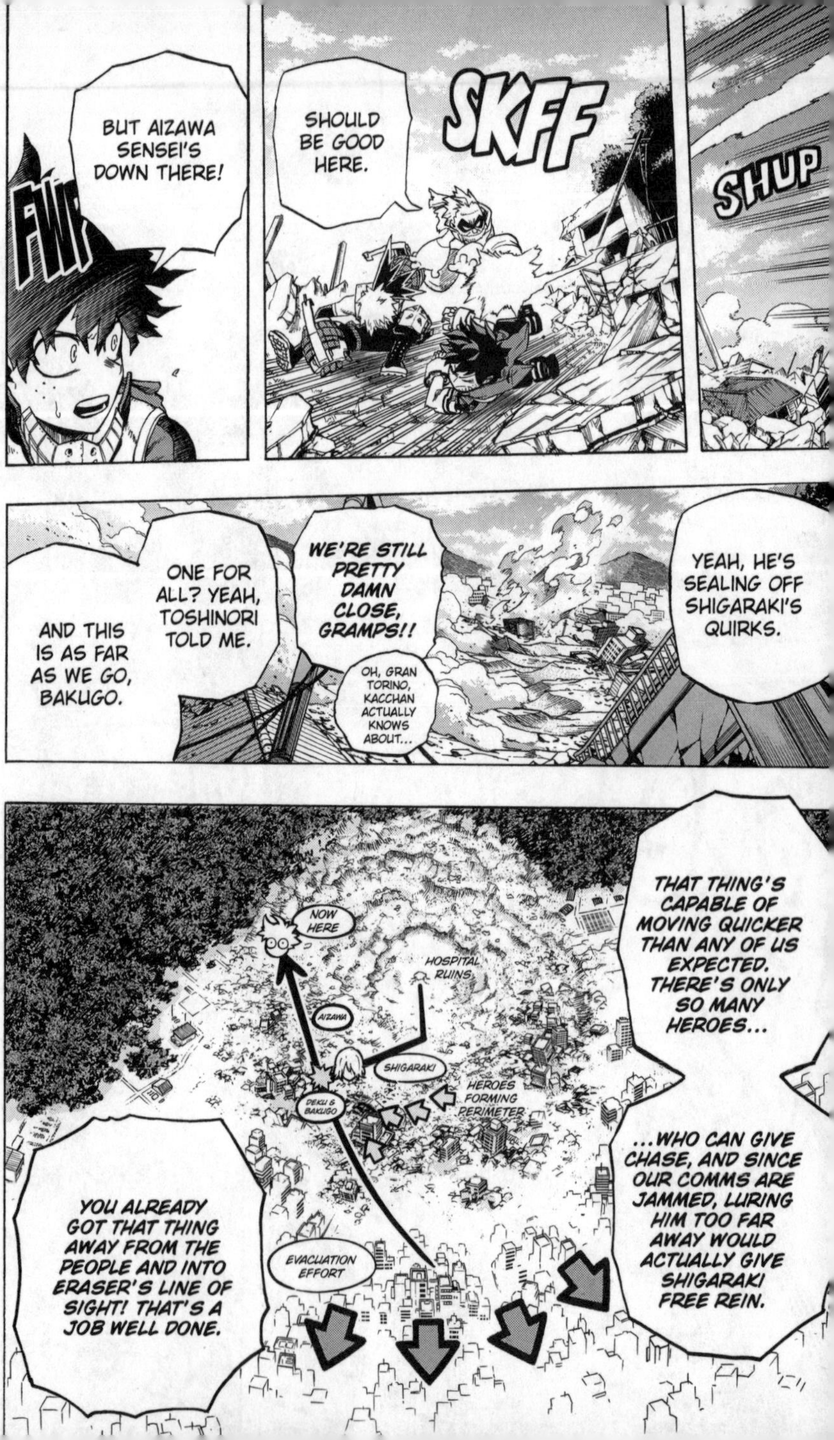
SHUP
SKFF
SHOULD BE GOOD HERE.
FWP
BUT AIZAWA SENSEI'S DOWN THERE!
YEAH, HE'S SEALING OFF SHIGARAKI'S QUIRKS.
OH, GRAN TORINO, KACCHAN ACTUALLY KNOWS ABOUT...
WE'RE STILL PRETTY DAMN CLOSE, GRAMPS!!
ONE FOR ALL? YEAH, TOSHINORI TOLD ME.
AND THIS IS AS FAR AS WE GO, BAKUGO.
THAT THING'S CAPABLE OF MOVING QUICKER THAN ANY OF US EXPECTED. THERE'S ONLY SO MANY HEROES...
...WHO CAN GIVE CHASE, AND SINCE OUR COMMS ARE JAMMED, LURING HIM TOO FAR AWAY WOULD ACTUALLY GIVE SHIGARAKI FREE REIN.
NOW HERE
HOSPITAL RUINS
AIZAWA
SHIGARAKI
HEROES FORMING PERIMETER
DEKU & BAKUGO
EVACUATION EFFORT
YOU ALREADY GOT THAT THING AWAY FROM THE PEOPLE AND INTO ERASER'S LINE OF SIGHT! THAT'S A JOB WELL DONE.

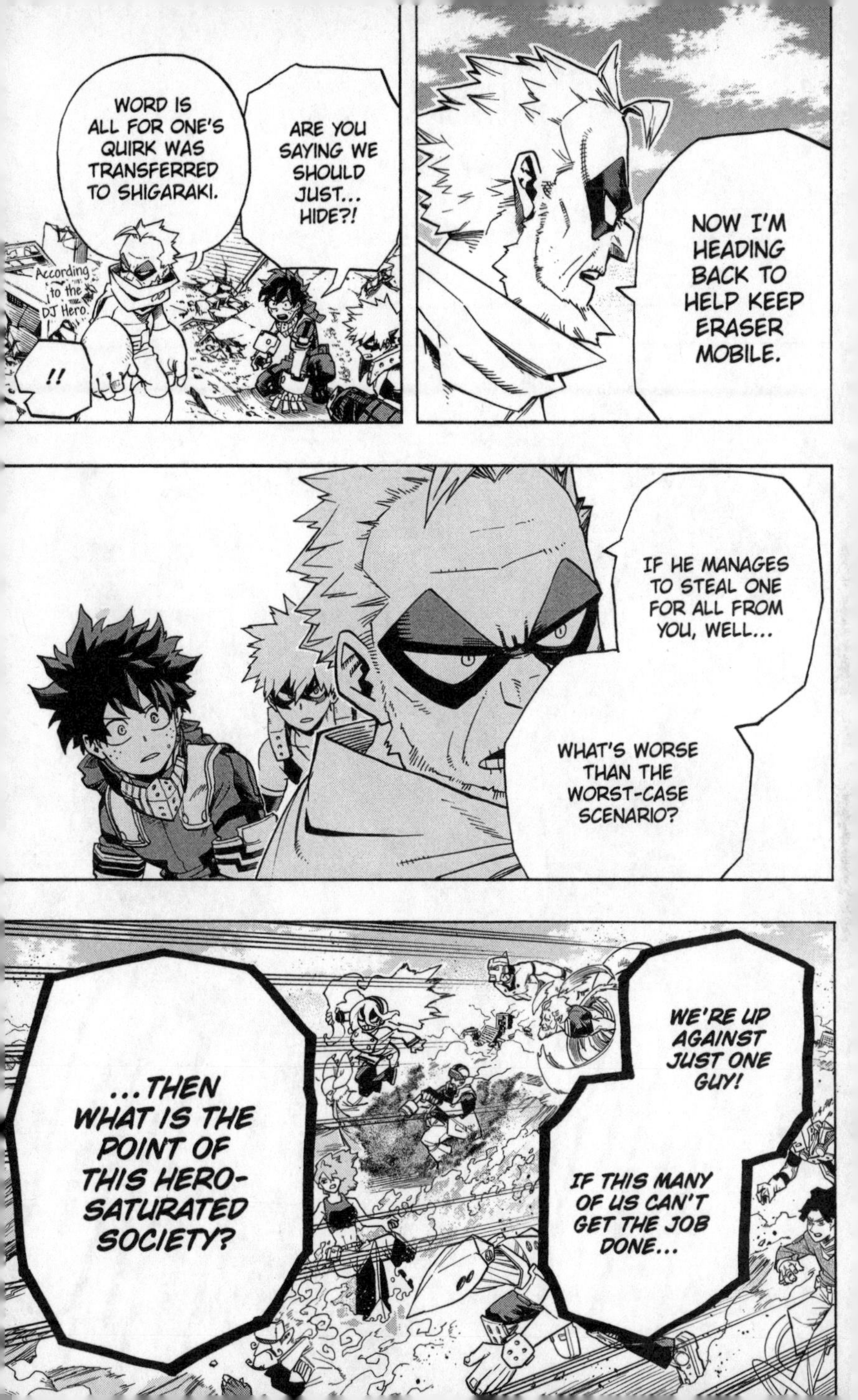
NOW I'M HEADING BACK TO HELP KEEP ERASER MOBILE.
ARE YOU SAYING WE SHOULD JUST... HIDE?!
WORD IS ALL FOR ONE'S QUIRK WAS TRANSFERRED TO SHIGARAKI.
According to the DJ Hero.
!!
IF HE MANAGES TO STEAL ONE FOR ALL FROM YOU, WELL...
WHAT'S WORSE THAN THE WORST-CASE SCENARIO?
WE'RE UP AGAINST JUST ONE GUY!
IF THIS MANY OF US CAN'T GET THE JOB DONE...
...THEN WHAT IS THE POINT OF THIS HERO-SATURATED SOCIETY?

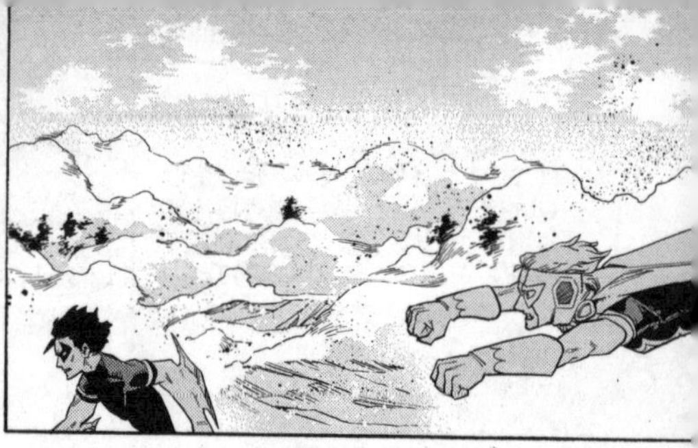

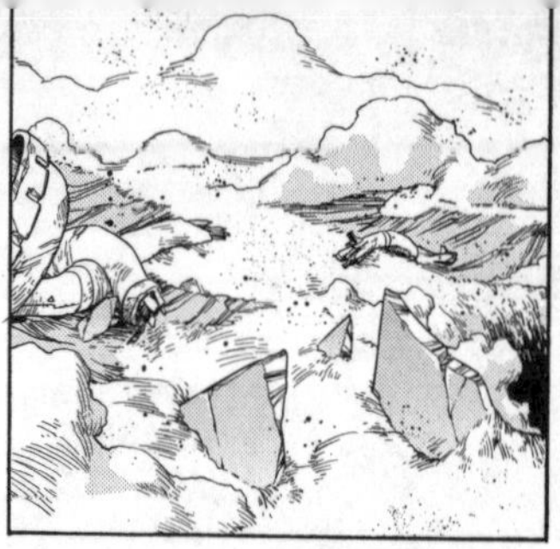

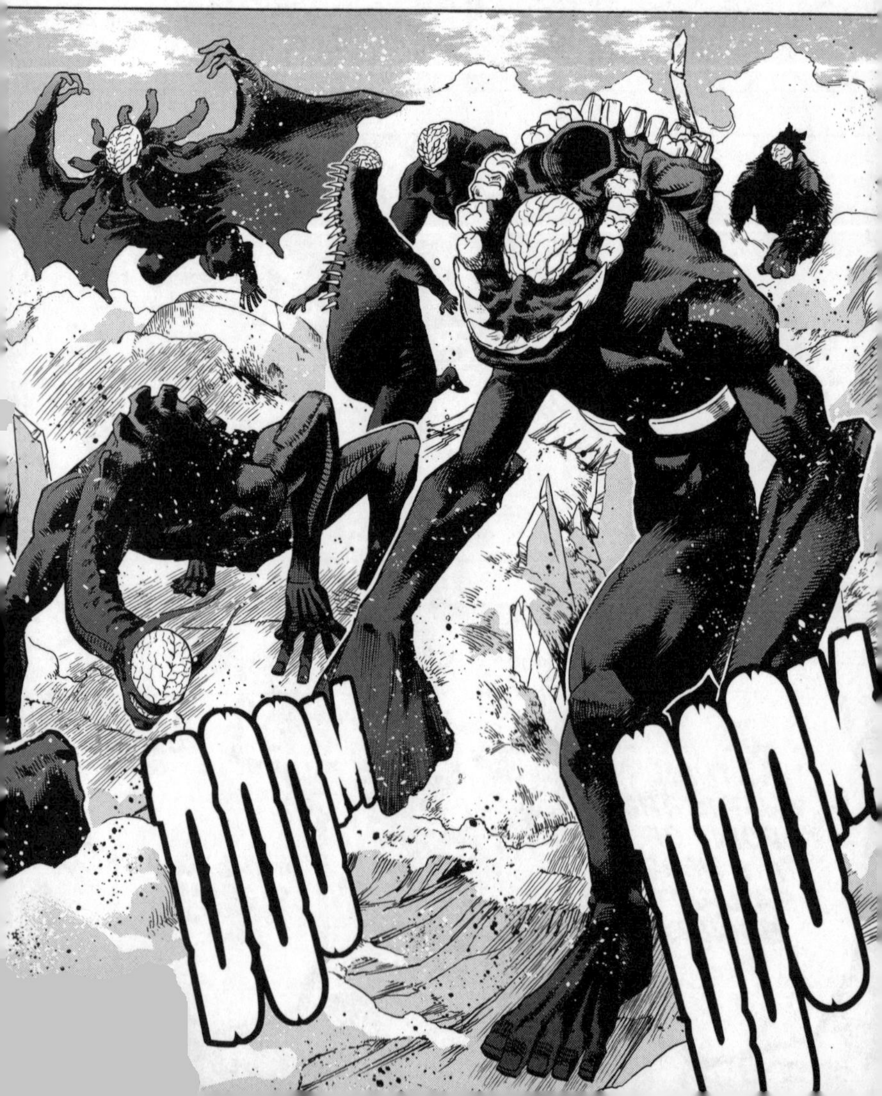
DOOM
DOOM

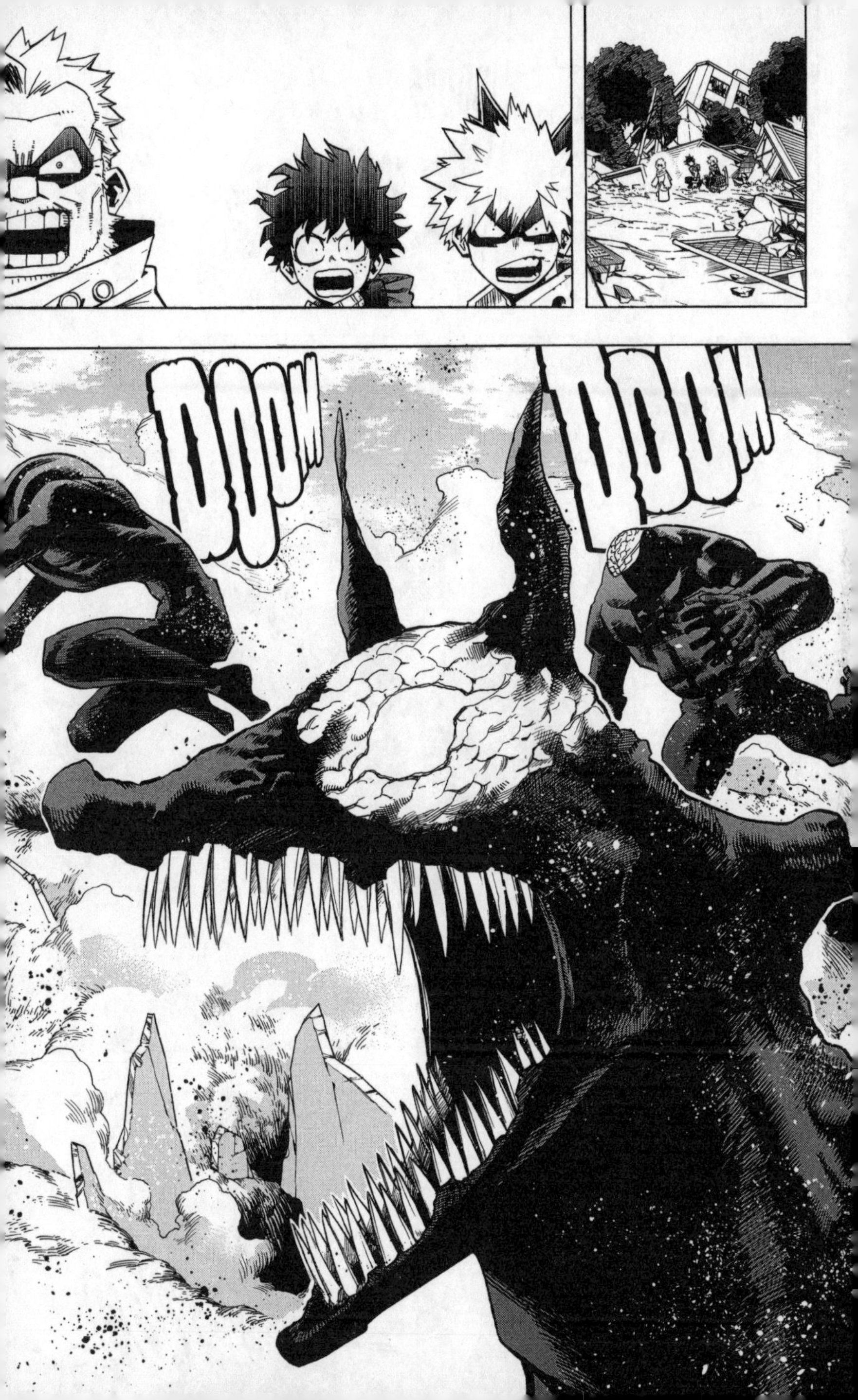
DOOM
DOOM

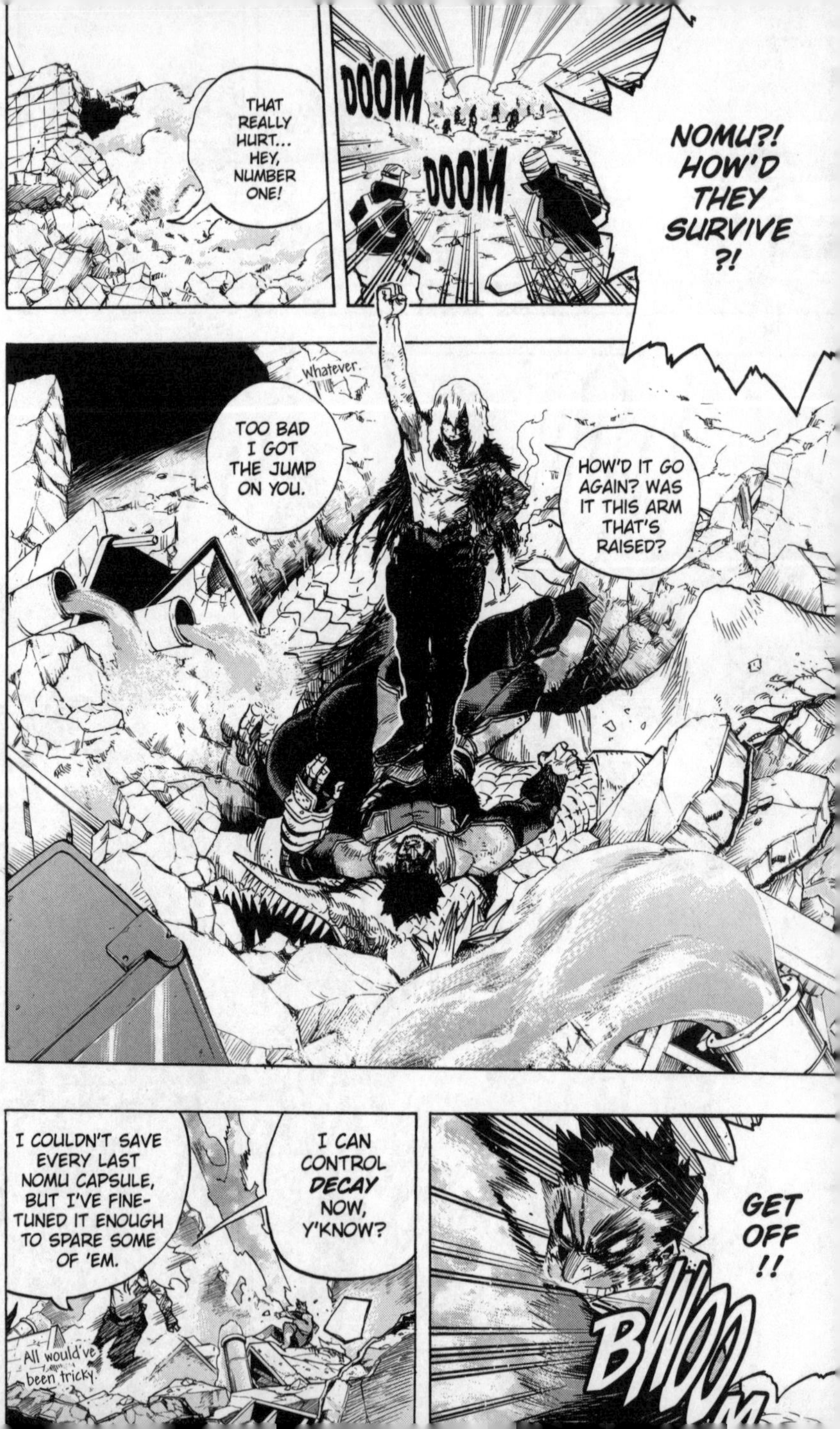
DOOM
DOOM
NOMU?! HOW'D THEY SURVIVE ?!
THAT REALLY HURT... HEY, NUMBER ONE!
HOW'D IT GO AGAIN? WAS IT THIS ARM THAT'S RAISED?
Whatever.
TOO BAD I GOT THE JUMP ON YOU.
GET OFF !!
BWOOM
I CAN CONTROL DECAY NOW, Y'KNOW?
I COULDN'T SAVE EVERY LAST NOMU CAPSULE, BUT I'VE FINE-TUNED IT ENOUGH TO SPARE SOME OF 'EM.
All would've been tricky.

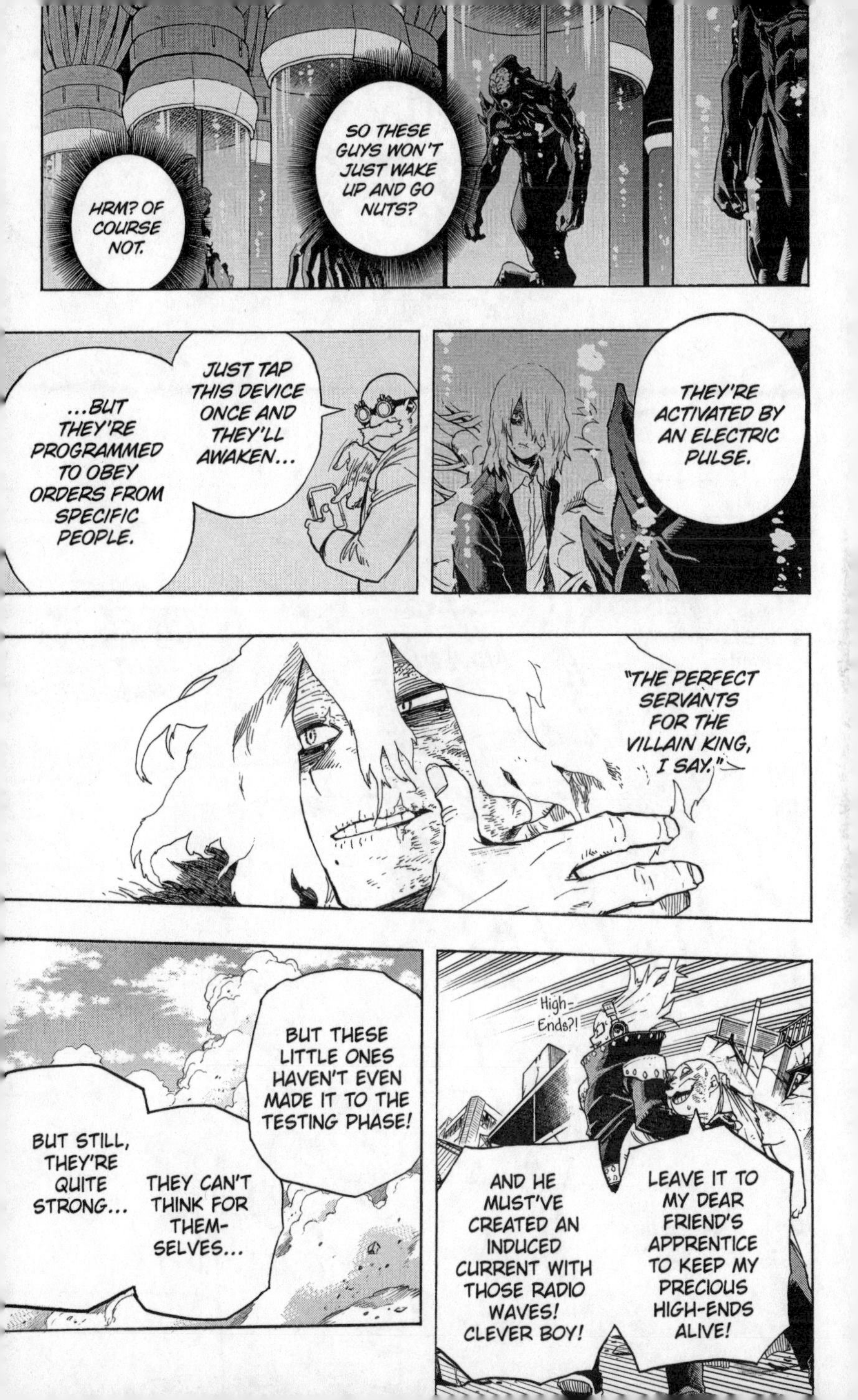
SO THESE GUYS WON'T JUST WAKE UP AND GO NUTS?
HRM? OF COURSE NOT.
THEY'RE ACTIVATED BY AN ELECTRIC PULSE.
JUST TAP THIS DEVICE ONCE AND THEY'LL AWAKEN...
...BUT THEY'RE PROGRAMMED TO OBEY ORDERS FROM SPECIFIC PEOPLE.
"THE PERFECT SERVANTS FOR THE VILLAIN KING, I SAY."
High-Ends?!
LEAVE IT TO MY DEAR FRIEND'S APPRENTICE TO KEEP MY PRECIOUS HIGH-ENDS ALIVE!
AND HE MUST'VE CREATED AN INDUCED CURRENT WITH THOSE RADIO WAVES! CLEVER BOY!
BUT THESE LITTLE ONES HAVEN'T EVEN MADE IT TO THE TESTING PHASE!
THEY CAN'T THINK FOR THEM-SELVES...
BUT STILL, THEY'RE QUITE STRONG...

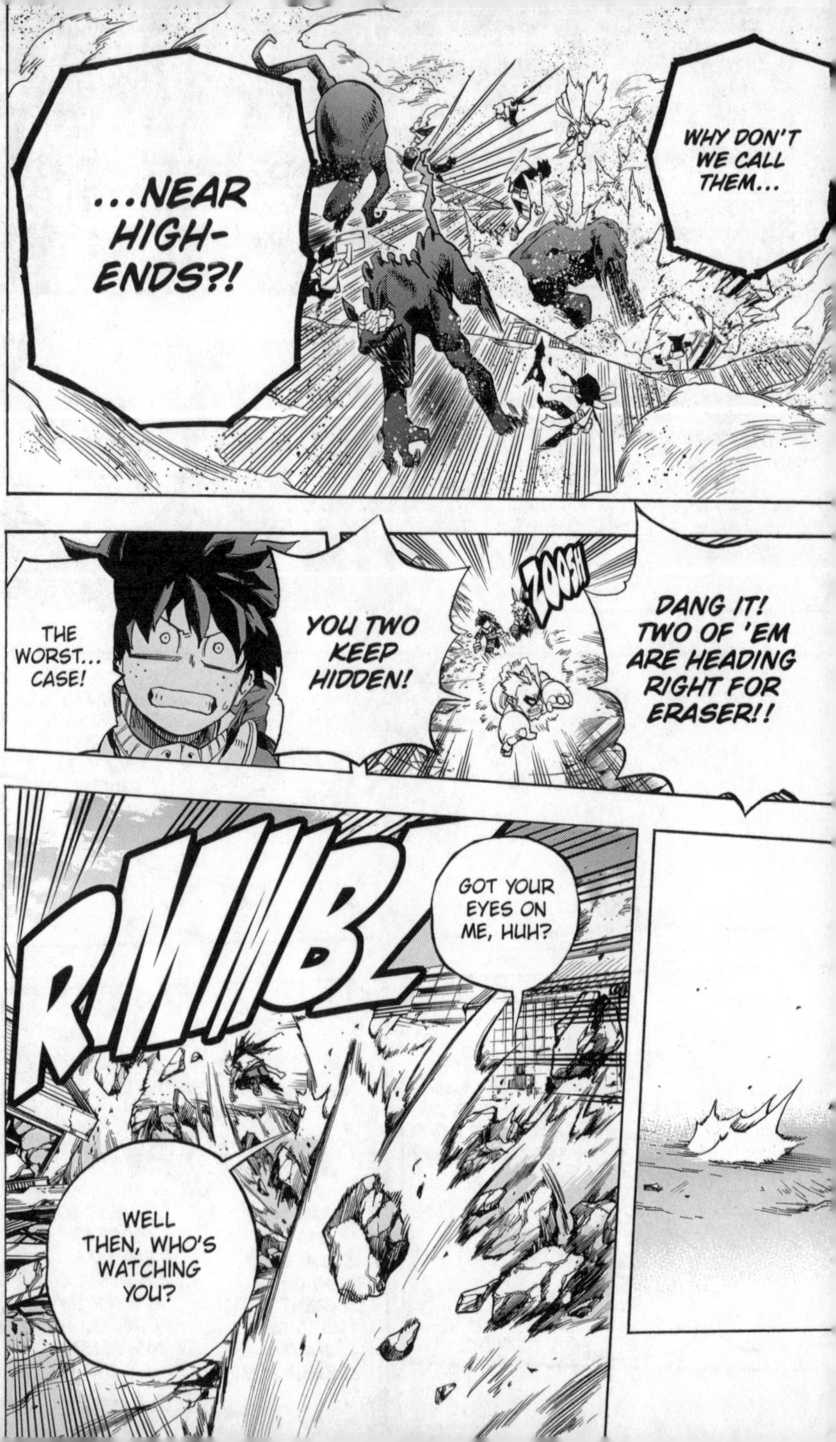
WHY DON'T WE CALL THEM...
...NEAR HIGH-ENDS?!
DANG IT! TWO OF 'EM ARE HEADING RIGHT FOR ERASER!!
ZOOSH
YOU TWO KEEP HIDDEN!
THE WORST... CASE!
GOT YOUR EYES ON ME, HUH?
RMMBL
WELL THEN, WHO'S WATCHING YOU?

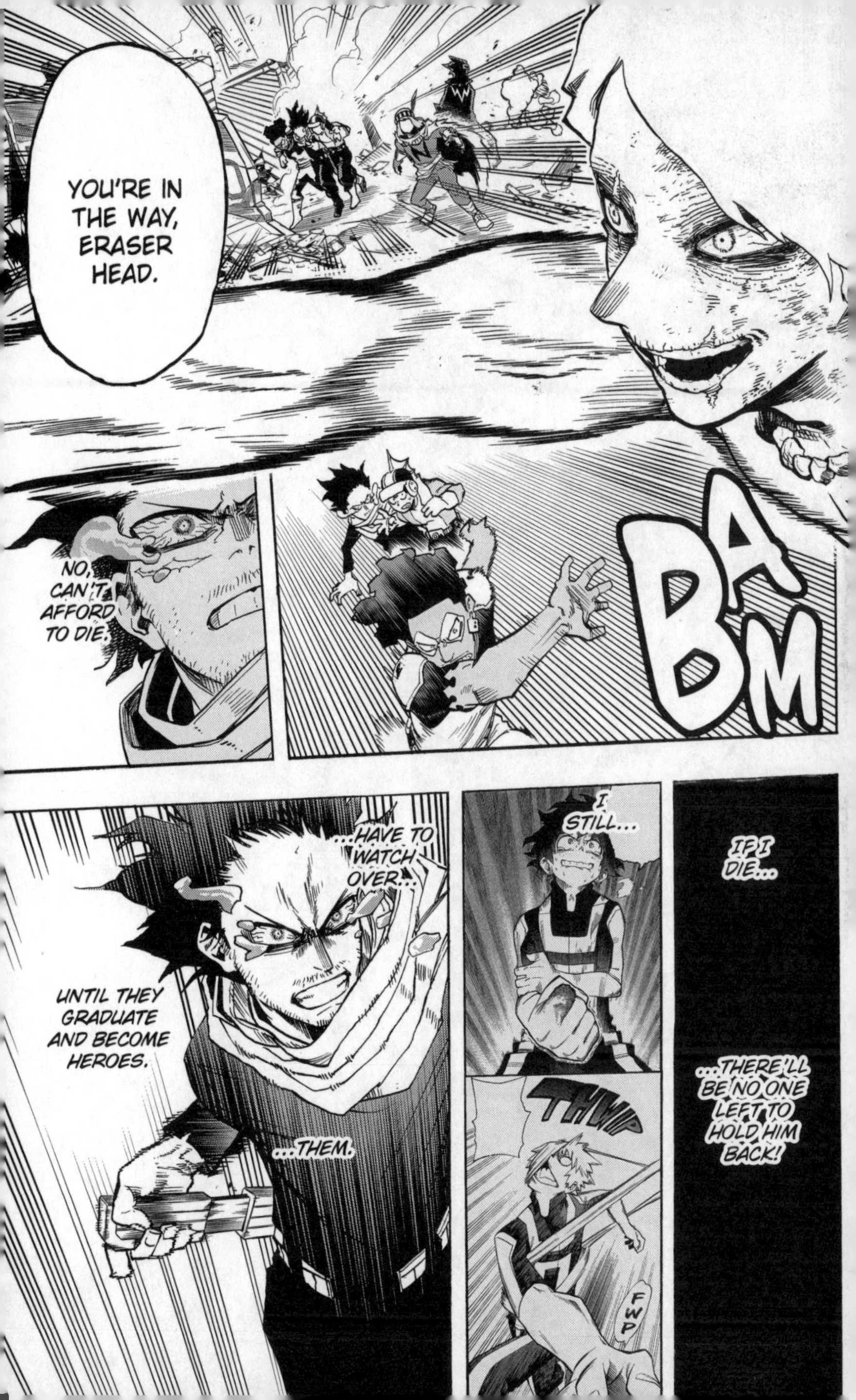

YOU'RE IN THE WAY, ERASER HEAD.
DA BM
NO, CAN'T AFFORD TO DIE.
IF I DIE...
...THERE'LL BE NO ONE LEFT TO HOLD HIM BACK!
I STILL...
THWIP
FWP
...HAVE TO WATCH OVER...
UNTIL THEY GRADUATE AND BECOME HEROES.
...THEM.

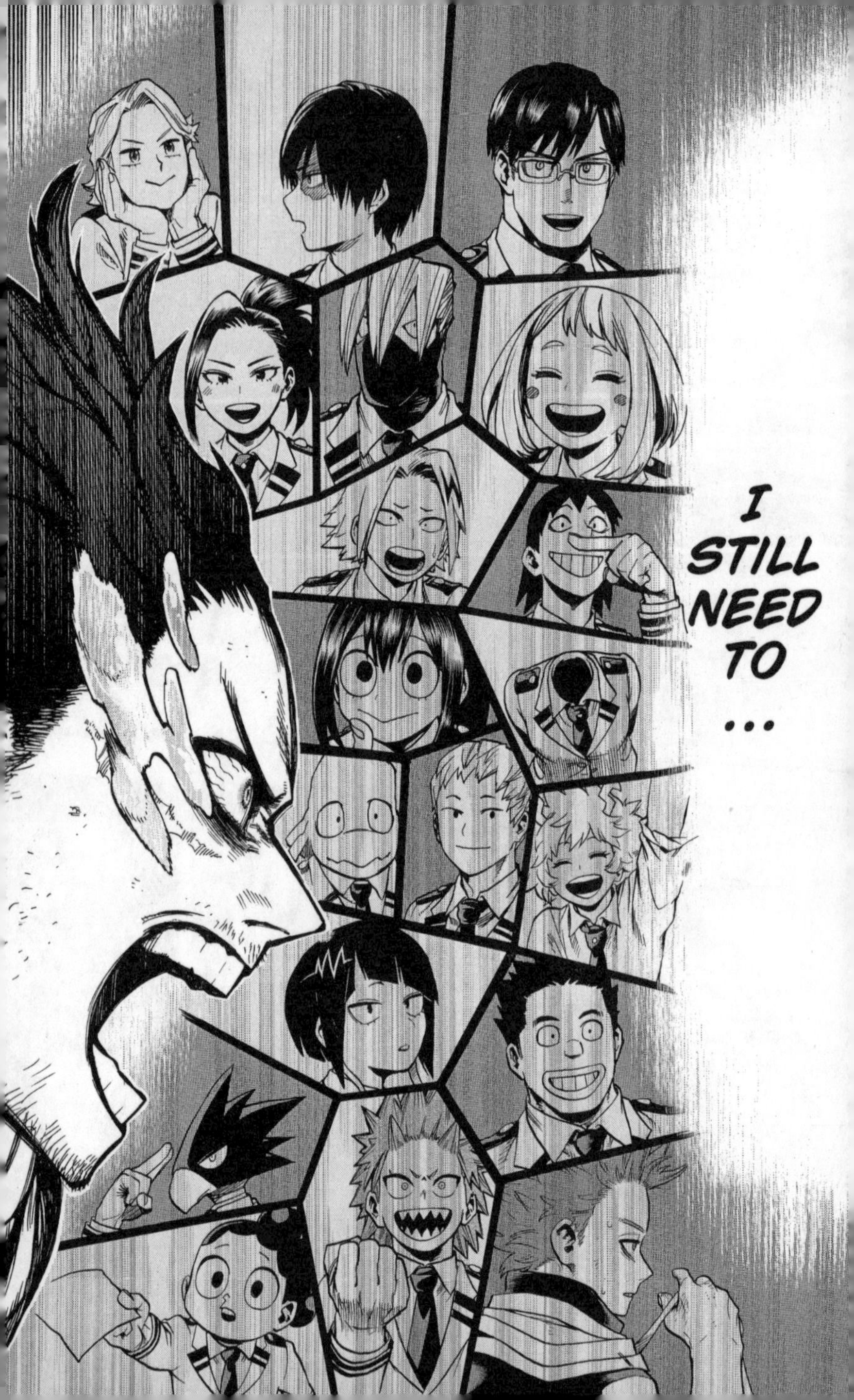
I STILL NEED TO ...

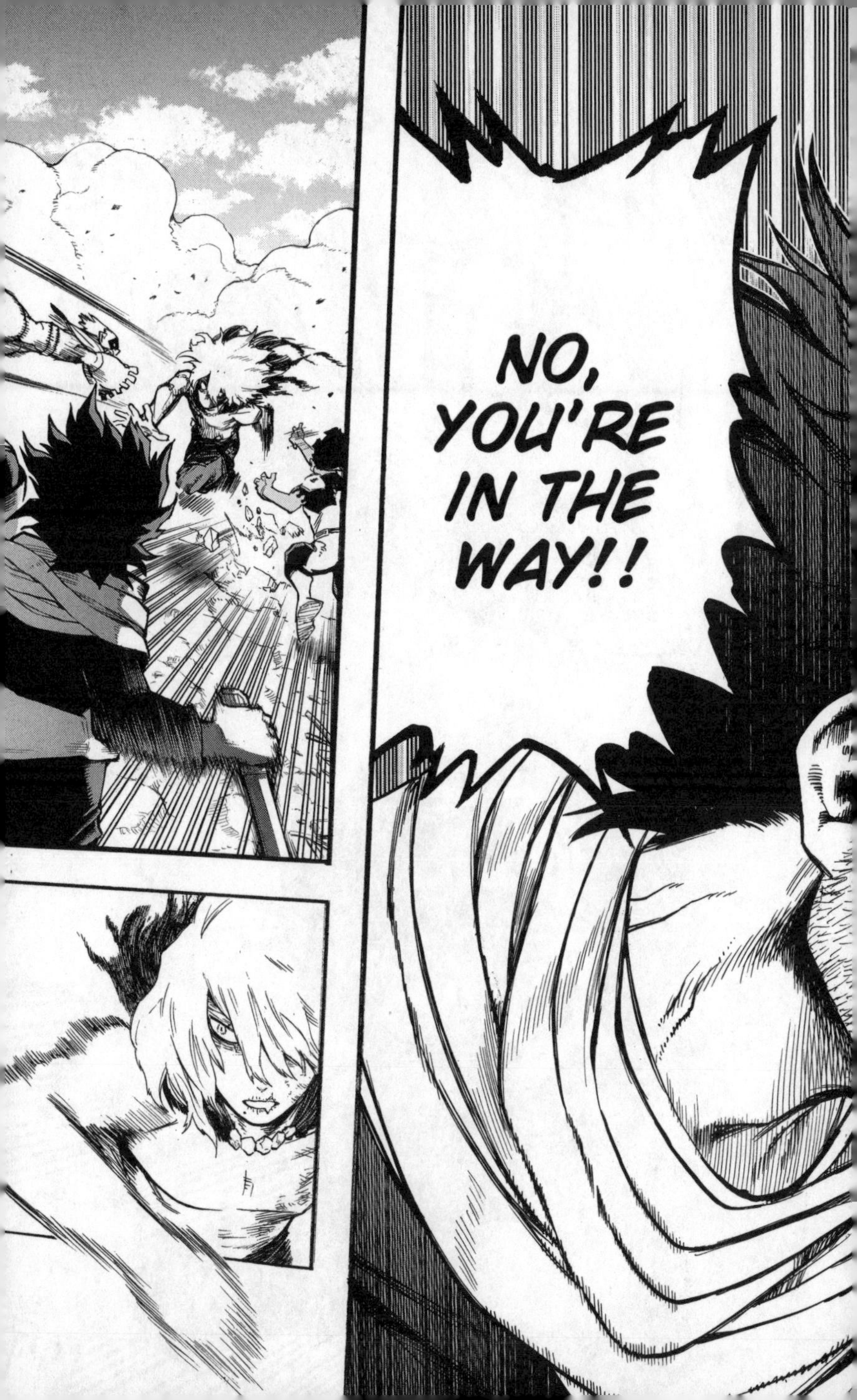
NO, YOU'RE IN THE WAY!!

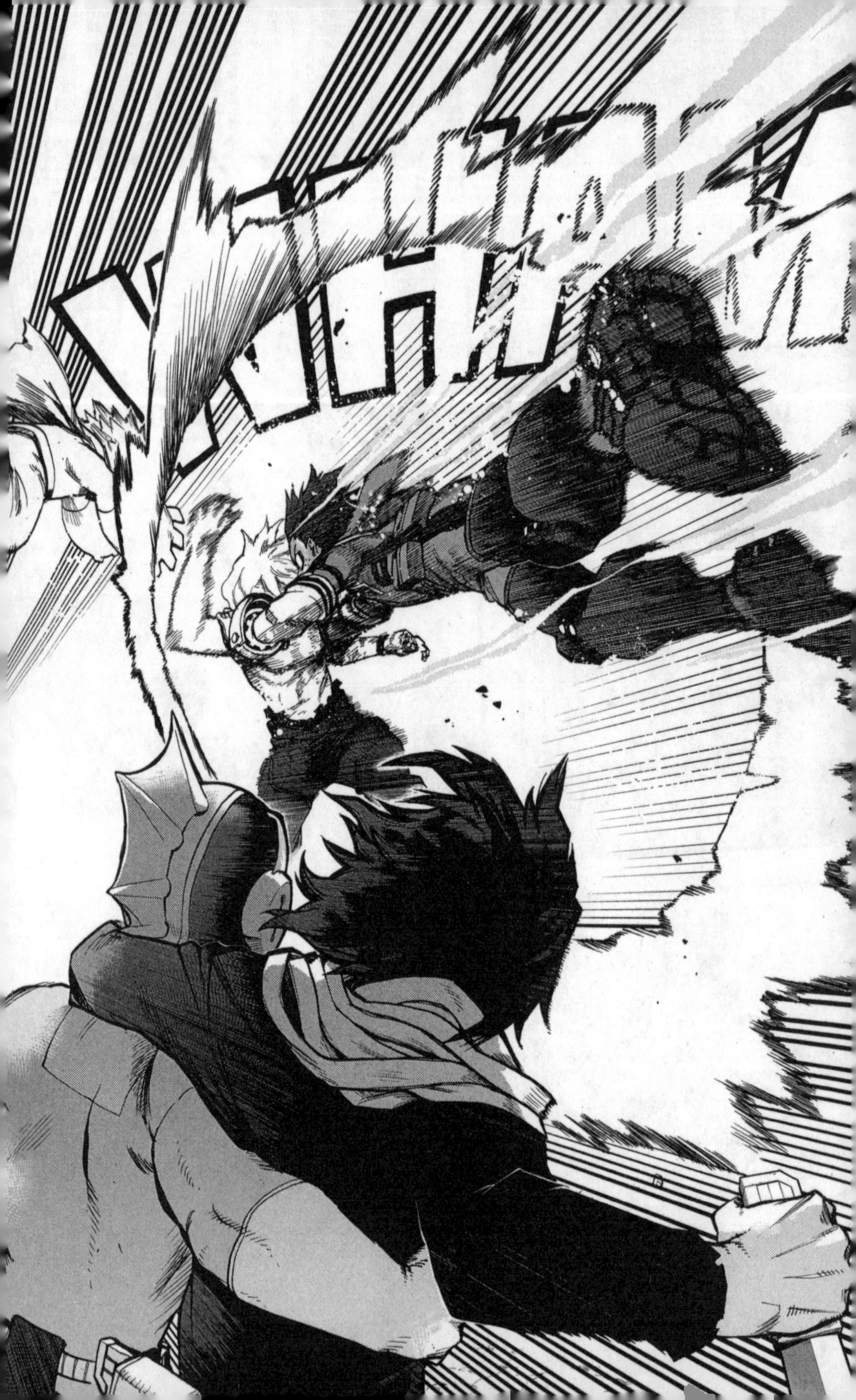

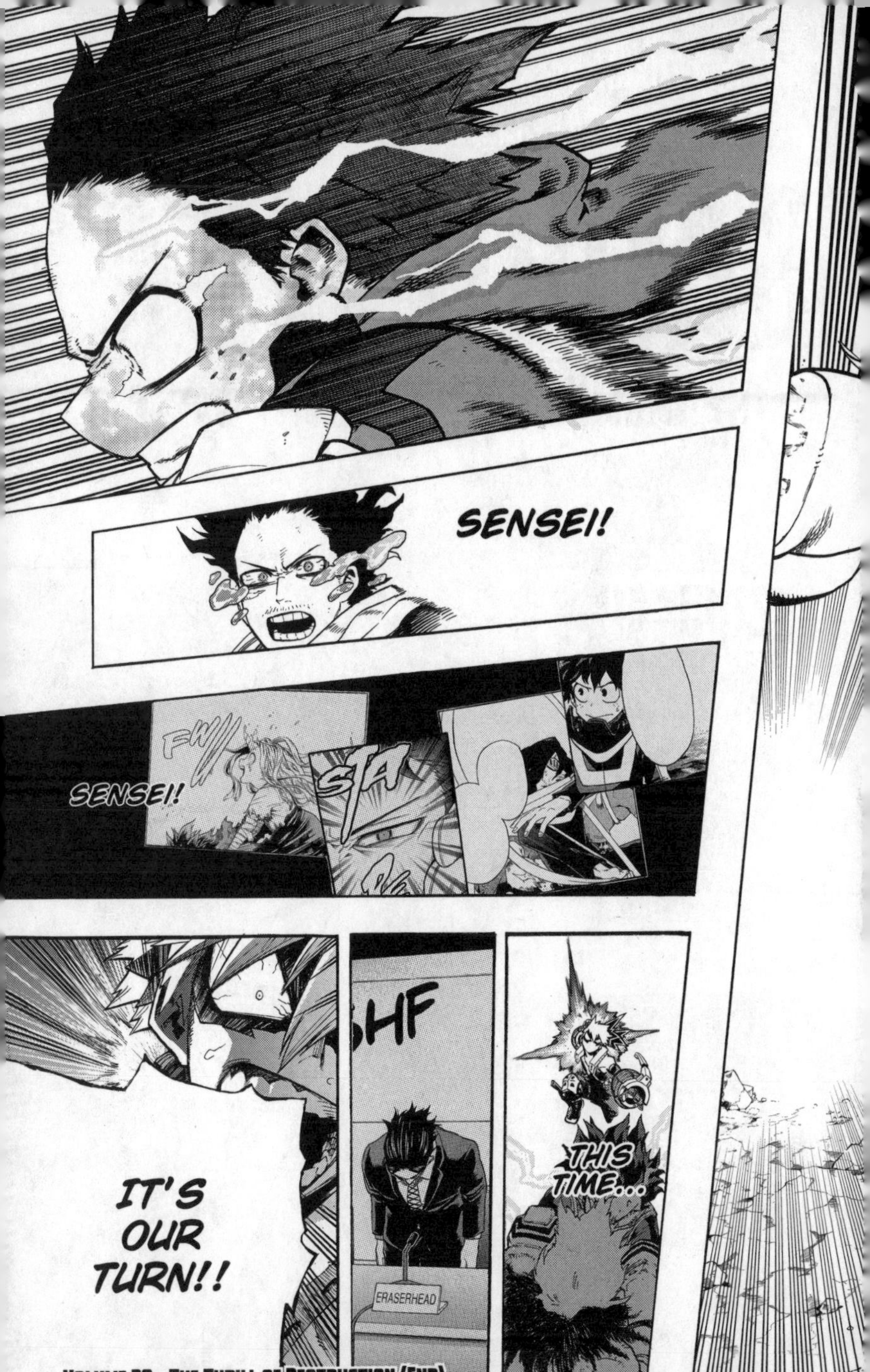
SENSEI!
STA
FW
SENSEI!
THIS TIME...
SHF
ERASERHEAD
IT'S OUR TURN!!

VOLUME 28 - THE THRILL OF DESTRUCTION (END)